Let's End Our Literacy Crisis

The Desperately Needed Idea Whose Time Has Come

Copyright © Bob C. Cleckler, 2005. All rights reserved. No part of this book other than Figure 11-1 may be reproduced or transmitted in any form or by any means, electronic or mechanical, including photocopying, recording, or by any information storage and retrieval system, without permission in writing from the publisher.

Published by
American University & Colleges Press™
An imprint of American Book Publishing
P.O. Box 65624
Salt Lake City, UT 84165
http://www.american-book.com
Printed in the United States of America on acid-free paper.

Let's End Our Literacy Crisis

Designed by Cheryl Klinginsmith, design@american-book.com

Publisher's Note: *This publication is designed to provide accurate and authoritative information in regard to the subject matter covered. It is sold or distributed with the understanding that the publisher and author is not engaged in rendering legal, accounting, or other professional service. If legal advice or other expert assistance is required, the services of a competent professional person in a consultation capacity should be sought.*

ISBN 1-58982-230-7

Library of Congress Cataloging-in-Publication Data

Cleckler, Bob C., 1936-
  Let's end our literacy crisis: the desperately needed idea whose time has come.
  p. cm.
  Includes bibliographical references and index.
  ISBN 1-58982-230-7 (alk. Paper)
  1. Spelling reform. 2. English language—Orthography and spelling—Study and teaching—United States. 3. English language—United States—Orthography and spelling. 4. Literacy—United States. I. Title

PE1150.C57 2005
428.1'3—dc22

2004029540

Special Sales

These books are available at special discounts for bulk purchases. Special editions, including personalized covers, excerpts of existing books, and corporate imprints, can be created in large quantities for special needs. For more information e-mail info@american-book.com.

Let's End Our Literacy Crisis

The Desperately Needed Idea Whose Time Has Come

Bob C. Cleckler, B.S.Ch.E.
Literacy Research Associates, Inc.

A 198-page companion volume, *Let's End Our Literacy Crisis Workbook,* is available for only $9.95. This is a teacher's guide and student's manual which will be helpful for older students and any beginners needing additional teaching materials. It also contains additional details about the English language. See back of book for ordering information.

See About the Author at the end of the book.

Other books by the author:

by Bob C. Cleckler, B.S.Ch.E

Instant Literacy for Everyone
published 1993 by Northwest Publishing Inc.

Material quoted from *The Cambridge Encyclopedia of Language* was reprinted with the permission of Cambridge University Press.

From *Illiteracy: A National Dilemma* by David Harman © 1987 by Cambridge Book Company. Used by permission of Pearson Education, Inc.

Scripture taken from The New King James Bible, New Testament.® Copyright © 1979 by Thomas Nelson, Inc. Used by permission. All rights reserved.

Dedication

This book is dedicated to hundreds of millions of students around the world who tried—and failed—to become proficient readers in English. Now they *can* learn. The problem has been solved, and it was *not* due to any inadequacies in the students.

Every day I became more convinced that nothing could do this world more good than to teach everybody to read and speak English, not because it is English but because it is the world's chief language of communication. Perhaps the research I have been doing...is about to come into its own. **Nothing is so powerful as an idea when its time has arrived** (emphasis added).

Frank C. Laubach
Forty Years With the Silent Billion, p. 386

Foreword

Dr. Robert S. Laubach
Laubach Literacy International

Once in a while one learns of an undaunted person trying to climb the highest mountain, or working towards the impossible dream. Such a person is Bob Cleckler, who is boldly proposing a [solution to our literacy crisis], and laying out a blueprint for its accomplishment.

Cleckler, armed with facts and figures, illustrates the cost to the national economy of the appallingly low rate of literacy in the United States. It's high time, he maintains, that we stop merely treating the symptoms of the disease of illiteracy....Let's get to work, he calls out, on the root causes of the disease....

I have been working for half a century helping organize bands of volunteers to reach out with literacy help to thousands in our nation....

My father, Frank C. Laubach (1884-1970), founder of the worldwide "Each One Teach One" literacy movement, spent almost every spare moment of his last 15 years promoting [a similar solution to our literacy crisis]. He may have been a little ahead of his time...

The "impossibility" of the dream in the first paragraph doesn't refer to the problem of developing a [solution to our literacy crisis]. Others, my father included, have proposed specific new systems. There is great agreement among them, as a common thread runs through them all...

What to do and how to do it are the simplest parts of the problem.

The difficulty comes when the [new system] comes face to face with the vested interests in maintaining "traditional" [systems]....

But as Cleckler points out, only in the past decade has our nation become aware of the vast cost of illiteracy. This continually rising cost may soon deem essential changes in the way we [teach students to read]. So Cleckler sounds the call once again to make order out of chaos. He not only sounds the call. He has developed an orderly [solution to our literacy crisis], and shows how to [implement] it.

Even the skeptic should take heed to his counsel. Those already favoring [similar solutions] should rally around. This is the time for concerted action on the part of all...[His proposed solution] may well become the Reformation of the 21st Century.

Preface

Let's End

Research for this book encompassed areas that few educators involved in beginning reading venture into. As the evidence mounted, it became clear that merely tweaking the existing system will never solve our literacy problems because of dramatically changed conditions in the last seventy years. The writings of numerous linguists and educators over the last two hundred years, however, built an increasingly convincing case that there is a solution to our literacy crisis. The extreme importance of at long last permanently solving our literacy crisis, instead of merely attacking one or more of its symptoms (as virtually 100 percent of all solutions proposed in the last thirty-five years have done), demands an urgent appeal to every reader to honestly and open-mindedly consider all the evidence presented in this book.

Our

Several centuries of history clearly demonstrate that governmental leaders seldom initiate the type of revolutionary changes needed to bring about the "Reformation of the 21st Century" that Dr. Robert Laubach envisions for solving our literacy problems (in the Foreword). Governmental leaders almost never institute revolutionary changes unless pushed into them by the public. We, as concerned citizens, must initiate the changes needed to solve our literacy crisis.

Literacy Crisis

The data presented in chapters 2 through 7 from numerous expert observers of our culture will convince any open-minded reader that our illiteracy rate has now reached crisis proportions. Several linguistic and educational experts say that with the present system of teaching reading in U.S. public schools, some students—even some of our brightest students—will never become good readers. As linguistic expert Sir James Pitman states, "the [reading student] is expected to take on a task that is formidable for all and for some impossible." (See the last section of chapter 7 for the full quote.) No one knows how many people will be unable to learn to read English without extensive one-on-one tutoring, but with more than a billion English-speaking people in the world, it is at least hundreds of thousands too many—especially if it includes one of your loved ones.

How to Get the Most Benefit from This Book

Material in this book will be much more easily understood if it is read in order. Important ideas and concepts are often based upon previously presented material.

Chapter 1 provides an important overview. Understanding later sections will be more difficult without the insights this overview provides. Be sure to read through this chapter before continuing with the rest of the book. Later, you can return to chapter 1 and read through it again as a summary. Solving our literacy crisis is important enough to deserve a diligent effort to gain a complete understanding of both the problem and the solution.

The Book's Purpose and Method—in a Nutshell

The purpose of the book is contained in the title. Yes, it *is* possible to solve our literacy crisis if the method proposed in this book is used—regardless of what the naysayers may claim and regardless of whether or not the method goes against conventional wisdom.

Conventional wisdom may be defined as ideas or beliefs that a large number of people—perhaps the majority—agrees upon. Please note, however, that merely because a large number of people—even everyone—believes something, that does not make it true. At one time almost everyone believed the earth was flat. Conventional wisdom may claim that the method proposed here will not work. You have undoubtedly heard the saying, "We've already tried that. It doesn't work."

There are many responses to that statement as applied to this book. Two will suffice. First, there are those who will be unable to resist the temptation to scan through later sections only long enough to quickly decide what they think is being proposed. Even if what is proposed here were *exactly* what the scanners think (and it will not be unless they know the details), the conditions have changed in the last seventy years or so and the need is *much* greater now. Second, as you may have guessed from the previous sentence, the method proposed has never been tried in English. It has not only been tried, but it has been *successful* in improving literacy *in other languages* in nations both larger and smaller than the U.S. and in both advanced and in Third-World nations.

As chapter 10 explains, English-speaking nations can reduce the money they spend teaching their students to read English by doing so in three or four months instead of the present two or more years, and by replacing students' reading books only when they physically wear out rather than every three to five years when the "reading experts" come up with their latest theories of how to improve the teaching of reading. All that is required is an understanding of the method proposed here. When that is achieved, the readers will want to join others who understand and begin a grass-roots campaign among those most concerned with solving our literacy crisis. Those most concerned are the friends and relatives of the sixty million or more functional illitercatcs and the two million or more functional illiterates who are added to our population each year as schools continue to graduate students who "cannot read well enough to hold a decent job," as was found by the most extensive study of literacy ever undertaken by the U.S. government See chapters 1 and 2 for facts from this study reported in 1993.

Phoneme and Grapheme: Definitions and Terminology

The definitions of these two terms are repeated elsewhere, as needed, for emphasis. Definitions of terms more specific to chapters 8 and 9 are in the glossary at the end of the book. These terminology conventions are not necessarily used in the tables; it depends upon what is highlighted in each individual table.

Phoneme:

Definition: the smallest sound in a given language or dialect which is used to distinguish one word or syllable from another.

Terminology used (using the sound *AE* as an example): /ae/, the sound of *AE*, the *AE* sound, or the *AE* phoneme.

Grapheme:

Definition: the letter or letter combination used to represent a phoneme or the one-letter words *a, I,* or *O* (or in languages other than English: the symbol, letter, or letter combination used for a phoneme, syllable, or word).

Terminology used: graphemes are shown as capitalized and italicized letters (sometimes also in bold).

Contents

1. Illiteracy and Why It Still Exists 1
    The Shocking Problem of Illiteracy 3
    The Exciting Solution to Illiteracy 5
    Do We Really Want to Solve the Literacy Crisis? 7
    Fighting Symptoms versus Curing the Root Cause 12
    Desperately Needed: A Simple Illiteracy Solution 13
    Learning to Read English versus Other Languages 15
    Why Has the Problem Not Already Been Solved? 19
    Why We Must Accept the Challenge to Act 19
    It Couldn't Be Done 20

PART 1: THE PROBLEM 21

2. The U.S. Illiteracy Problem 23
    The Present Extent of Illiteracy in the U.S. 23
        The Number of Adult Functional Illiterates 23
        Elementary School Illiteracy 26
        News Reports and Commentary on Literacy 27
        Comparing U.S. Literacy with That of Other Nations..... 28
        Effect of Illiteracy on U.S. World Trade 29
    Why the Size of the Problem Is Unrecognized 31
        The Hidden Illiterates among Us 31

The Grade-Level Completion Deception	32
The Silent Minority	33
Self-Esteem Teaching in Public Schools	33
The U.S. Census Reports	34
Sensory Overload	35
Present Adult Literacy Teaching in the U.S.	35
The Four National Literacy Programs	36
State and Local Literacy Programs	37
Corporate Literacy Programs	38
Adult Literacy Recruiting and Dropout Problems	39
Successful Adult Literacy Students	40
The Future of Literacy in the U.S.	40

3. Worldwide Literacy 43
   Advantages Illiterates Gain by Becoming Literate 43
   Why Worldwide Literacy Is Desperately Needed 44
   English as a Worldwide Language 46
      Easy Grammar and Syntax 47
      Widespread Use 48
      Easy Adoption of New Words 50

4. The Monetary Costs of Illiteracy 51
   Workplace Illiteracy: True Horror Stories 57
   The Cost of Crime 58
   What Is the Total Cost of Illiteracy? 59

5. The Human-Suffering Costs of Illiteracy 61
   Employment 61
   Crime 62
   Standard of Living 63
   Consumer Rights 63
   Citizens' Rights 64
   Education 65
   Basic Lifestyle Choices 66
   Dangers and Health Risks 67

6. The Causes of Illiteracy 71

The Foundational Cause of English Illiteracy	72
Why Learning to Read English Is So Difficult	73
Sounds per Symbol: Effect upon Reading	75
Comparing English to Chinese Picture Writing	76
To Read English: Only Learn 294 Graphemes?	76
Symbols per Sound: Effect upon Spelling	80
How Can Anyone Defend English Spelling?	80
What Is the Logic Behind Our Problems?	87
How Bad Is the Cause of Our Problems?	88
How We Must Learn English Spelling	88
Comparative Difficulty of English versus Other Alphabets	90
The Complex Logic Our Spelling System Requires	90
What Does All This Mean to Us, Today	92
Summary	93

PART 2: THE SOLUTION 99

7. The Only Proven Solution to Illiteracy 101

Seeing with an Unprejudiced View	101
Unrealistic Views of Illiteracy	102
A Proposed Solution in Other Nations	104
Effects on the Teaching Method	105
Difficulties Imposed on Specific Subjects	105
Remedial Reading Classes	106
Beginning Reader Teaching Methods	107
The Subject Matter of Textbooks	108
General Effects of the Present System	109
English versus Other Languages	109
How Can We Improve the Educational System?	110
Grade Inflation	113
Can Fluent English Readers Read Unfamiliar English Words?	113
Final Effects of the Present System	114
Delinquency and Backwardness in Reading	114
Delinquency, Crime, and Self-Destructive Violence	114
Difficult for All, Impossible for Some	115

Developing Problem-Solving Skills 115
Teaching English Reading... 116
The Need for Logic in Learning 117
Why It Is Difficult for *All*, Impossible for Some........... 119

Special Note to Language Scholars 121

8. The Proposed Solution 123
The Logic behind the Proposed Solution.............................. 123
    Vowels.. 124
    Consonants 124
Details of the Proposed Solution 125
Understanding Pronunciation 129
    Differences in Pronunciation We Will Hear................. 133
    Accents and Assimilations 134
    Understanding Those Who Pronounce Differently 136
Characteristics of the Proposed Solution 137
This Proposal versus Previous Proposals 138

9. Effective Literacy Training... 143
Requirements for an Effective Teacher 145
The Latest Scientific Studies on Dyslexia 145
Teaching Principles and Overview.. 148
The Correct Order for Teaching Reading Skills 151
Letter Names (Optional) 155
Teenage and Adult Teaching Guidelines............................... 157
The Psychology of Learning.. 158

10. Advantages and Supposed Disadvantages of This
                  Proposal for Worldwide Use 161
Advantages of Implementing This Proposal......................... 161
Supposed Disadvantages That Really Aren't 166
    Will Existing Writings Become Inaccessible? 166
    Is a Standard Pronunciation Required? 167
    Will Linguistic History Be Lost? 168
    Must We Standardize Plural and
        Past-Tense Spelling? 168

  Philosophical Overtones of Frozen Spelling 169
  Why Do Some Scholars Oppose Our
    Proposed Solution? 170
  Real Disadvantages for Worldwide Usage 171

11. How to Implement This Proposal 177
  The Method 179
    Step One 180
    Step Two 180
    Step Three 181
  A Clarification of the Method 181
  Reading Textbooks 183
    Reading Books for Four Months—Then School Books ... 184
  Implementing This Proposal 185
    Governmental Considerations 185
    Private Sector Considerations 186
    The Interim Period 186
    Dictionaries 187
    School Considerations 187
    International Considerations 190
  Why Implementing This Method Is Critical 190

12. Summary and Challenge 193
  Is More Research Needed? 193
  Is a Quick Fix Possible? 194
    Impossibility of a Quick Fix Using…
      Traditional Methods 195
  Understanding the Problem 195
  The Cost of Solving Literacy Problems 197
  Adult Illiteracy 198
  Human-Suffering Costs 199
  A Nation at Risk 201
  Summary 204
  Fighting the Disease 207
  Challenge 208
  The Final, *Irrefutable* Arguments 209

Appendixes 213
   1: Relative Frequency of the English Phonemes
      and Example Words for Table 6-1 219
   2: Usage Frequency of Letters for English
      Phonemes and Choices of Graphemes 227
   3: Why English Spelling Is So "Bad" 229
   4: Thu Good Nuez uv John 231
   5: Creative Problem Solving 267
   6: Comparing Our Proposal with Other Proposals 273
   7. Is There Really a Literacy Crisis? 285

Notes 291
Glossary 313
Bibliography 317
Index 327
Acknowledgments 335
Ordering Information 337
About the Author 339

List of Tables

4-1	The Monetary Costs of Illiteracy, Type 1	53
4-2	The Monetary Costs of Illiteracy, Type 2	54
6-1	The Number of Phonemes That Each of the. 294 Graphemes Used in English Represents	79
6-2	Spelling of the Vowel Sounds	82
6-3	Spelling of the Consonant Sounds	84
6-4	The Dirty Dozen: The Twelve Sounds of OUGH	94
6-5	Using Logic to Spell English Will Confuse	95
8-1	The System in a Nutshell	126
8-2	How the English Phonemes Are Formed	132
9-1	The Pronunciation Used in Reciting the Alphabet	156
9-2	The One Hundred Most Used English Words	160
A1-1	Relative Frequency of the English Phonemes	219

A1-2	All of the Single Letters in English	220
A1-3	Partial Listing of *Two-Letter* Blends with a. Single Vowel Sound	221
A1-4	Partial Listing of *Three-or-More-Letter* Blends with a Single Vowel Sound	224
A1-5	Partial Listing of *Two-or-More-Letter* Blends with a Single Consonant Sound	225
A1-6	Partial Listing of Blends with Only One Common Pronunciation	226
A2-1	Usage Frequency of Letters for English Phonemes	227
A2-2	Choice of Graphemes to Represent Each Phoneme	228
A6-1	Letters with More than One Pronunciation	275
A6-2	Eight Pre-1970 Diagraphic Proposals	277
A6-3	Four Diagraphic Proposals on the Internet	279

List of Figures

	Employers and College Professors' Ranking of High School Graduates	33
	Homeless Family	63
	Industrial Accident	68
6-1	A Dreadful Language?	70
	Phoneme and Grapheme Usage Summary	94
6-2	Why English is So Hard	97
6-3	Homophones	98
8-1	Frequency of Occurrence of Two or More Adjacent Consonants	139
11-1	Format for Use on Magazine and Book Title Pages and Newspaper Mastheads	189
	John Corcoran *The* [High School] *Teacher Who Couldn't Read*	200
	Creative Problem Solving Problem Solutions	272
	Summary of Table A6-2 Vowels	275

Chapter 1
Illiteracy and Why It Still Exists

You are invited to begin a journey of discovery in this book that *can be* both shocking and exciting. You may be shocked as you discover the extent to which illiteracy adversely affects almost everyone, as well as the monetary costs and human suffering involved. You may become excited as you realize that at long last there *is* a simple solution to illiteracy. It is a proven solution that will take only a few minutes of your time and will save rather than cost money, as it does now.

By far the most exciting news for parents and friends of people who are having trouble learning to read is the recently proven fact that all children and adults—except the most mentally disabled—can be taught to read. Some parents who are embarrassed by their child's inability as well as teachers who have not yet learned the revolutionary teaching concepts presented here, may initially cling to the belief that their child or student has some type of brain disfunction. Samuel Blumenfeld and other researchers have been disputing the validity of these diagnoses for years. *Why Our Children Can't Read* by Diane McGuinness, Ph.D., published in 1997, correlates the findings of dozens of reading studies—most of them in the last ten years. The studies prove that when the methods Dr. McGuinness and other researchers have perfected are used, all but the most mentally disabled can learn to read. This is true whether or not the diagnoses of dyslexia, attention deficit disorder, learning disabilities, brain anomalies, and similar labels applied to non-readers and poor readers are correct. In fact, many of those diagnoses are not correct. Many students who have been given one of these labels *have* learned to read using methods described in Dr. McGuinness's book.

The reason the words *can be* are emphasized earlier is that we live in an age of skepticism. Almost everyone has heard the statement, "If it sounds too good to be true, it probably isn't true." Although what is presented in this book as the solution to illiteracy may sound too good to be true, it is in fact quite true. It has been proven in practically every nation on earth with an alphabetic language other than English. The reason the first paragraph says *can be* instead of *will be*, however, is that many of us believe that it's probably not true if it sounds too good. As a result, we may be tempted to skip ahead, scanning here and there to find something that—without knowing the details—seems to be untrue. Without realizing we are doing so, we often look for a catch—an error or misrepresentation that makes an argument false. We want to quickly decide if we should spend more time on something that seems too good to be true. There is a danger in the procedure of scanning here and there in this book, however. Although we can easily understand the details of the illiteracy problem, we must consider many relevant facts before we can reach an accurate conclusion.

In other words:

ideas in this book aren't just those of the author. The recommendations have been made by many scholars for well over two centuries.

This book contains more than 175 quotes from dozens of authorities, all carefully referenced (246 total reference notes). Most of the quotes included are short ones summarizing a much longer explanation in which the details are given. A bibliography—with a few references other than those used in this book—is included so that the more serious skeptics can examine the sources and verify that the author has not quoted out of context, misunderstood, or misrepresented the authorities quoted. An expanded bibliography, containing dozens of similar but unused references, can be made available to genuine researchers.

This book is divided into two logical parts, the problem and the solution. The first part explains the seriousness of the illiteracy problem. Among other things, it explains how many people in the U.S. are illiterate, why the size of the problem is generally unrecognized, why we desperately need U.S. and worldwide literacy, how much illiteracy costs each taxpayer and each consumer of U.S. products, how illiteracy causes severe hardship and suffering to the illiterates, and the causes of illiteracy. The second part explains why the proposal set forth in this book and shared by many scholars over the past two centuries is the only proven and permanent solution to illiteracy—both for schoolchildren and adults. The second part also describes the proposed solution and the way it easily can be adopted throughout the U.S. and other English-speaking areas.

The Shocking Problem of Illiteracy

For several reasons, functional literacy declined in the U.S. throughout most of the twentieth century and is now considered a serious problem by those who have examined the literacy rate most closely. The problem is beginning to get the attention of the U.S. public. Parents are becoming increasingly upset with their children's education. A survey in *PARADE* magazine on May 16, 1993, showed that "63% of Americans rate the quality of public education as poor or fair."[1] In 1996, and even earlier in some areas, education came to be considered one of our most serious problems.

A September 3-15, 1996, Knight-Ridder Washington Bureau poll asked registered voters to rank sixteen current U.S. problems. The top seven problems the voters listed were: crime and drugs—81 percent; public education—77 percent; attention to children—72 percent; government spending, deficit—72 percent; poverty, homelessness—62 percent; welfare system—61 percent; and low moral, ethical standards—59 percent.[2] This book will demonstrate that these problems are related.

A January 1998 news report stated that "urban schools appear to have hit bottom: More than half of the urban first- and eighth-graders fail to meet even minimum national standards in reading, math and science, according to the *Education Week* student assessment released earlier this month."[3] An October 28-31, 1998, poll by Pew Research Center showed that 88 percent of those questioned cited education as "very important," the highest of any of the national issues. Based upon these and other facts reported here and in chapter 2, it is understandable that a 1996 article in *The Salt Lake Tribune* reported that parents seemed "desperate," sometimes standing in line all night to get their children enrolled in what they believed would be a better elementary school.[4]

As you may know, illiteracy and crime are closely related. U.S. Department of Education figures for 1995 show that "75% of prison inmates and 85% of juveniles in correctional facilities are functionally illiterate."[5] This compares to illiteracy rates of 26 to 48 percent of all U.S. adults reported between 1985 and 1993. Discussing the illiteracy problem and its effect on crime, former first lady Barbara Bush stated, "All this tells us that some people can't make a living in the legitimate world, and they turn to crime and sometimes even to drugs out of frustration. I'm not making excuses for them. I'm just telling you a fact of life."[6]

Not only do those with a poor education have difficulty getting a job, which often leads to crime, but the frustration of being unable to read causes a significant portion of the discipline problems in school. Students who cannot read develop coping strategies. They become class clowns, they become "tough guys," or they adopt some other role. Most of these coping strategies are disruptive in some way, making learning almost impossible for these students as well as more difficult for their classmates.

If students cannot read, they have difficulty learning any subjects that require reading for classwork, homework, or testing. In a sense, reading ability is the primary foundational stone of education, and lack of reading ability is a primary cause of all educational problems.

Most of the discipline problems in school, and much of the crime, both in the school and elsewhere, are blamed on drugs. It is indisputable, however, that those who have good self-images because of success in school are less likely to begin using drugs. Those who are failing in school have much less to lose than those who are succeeding. They are also more likely to seek a chemical way of feeling better about themselves and escaping, for a time, the pain of their failures.

Many in these polls thought education should be our top priority based upon educational experiences of their children or the children of relatives and friends. Many may have ranked education highest because of statistics they have seen in news reports. Chapter 2 shows statistics on illiteracy in the 1980s and afterward from several different sources. Front page articles in *The Salt Lake Tribune* on September 9 and 10, 1993, stated, "Nearly half of all adult Americans read and write so poorly that it is difficult for them to hold a decent job, according to the most comprehensive literacy study ever done by the U.S. government" and "47 percent of adults have such poor reading, writing and computing skills they cannot perform tasks any more difficult than filling out a bank deposit slip."[7] It is probably difficult for many readers to believe the problem is as severe as it is. We read, and we believe most of the people we know read, but chapter 2 presents seven reasons why the illiteracy problem is much worse than we realize.

Illiteracy adversely affects you—and all of us—in ways you probably do not realize. It definitely affects your family finances. Illiteracy costs each taxpayer an average of $2,550 each year in higher taxes and higher costs of U.S. consumer products. An April 23, 1996, report in *The Salt Lake Tribune* showed that U.S. crime costs $450 billion per year. Assuming that 30 percent of that amount can be directly linked to illiteracy (it may be twice that; see chapter 4), it costs each taxpayer another $1,150 a year. It costs businesses millions of dollars each year in additional employee training costs, labor costs, and workmen's compensation.

Illiteracy probably affects a relative, friend, or acquaintance who is—perhaps unknown to you—a nonreader or a very poor reader. Although illiteracy affects everyone's pocketbook, the effect of illiteracy upon those who cannot read well enough to hold an above-poverty-level job is far more severe. Chapter 5 briefly lists ways in which illiteracy causes real emotional and physical suffering among illiterates. Jonathan Kozol's book *Illiterate America* explains this suffering more thoroughly. He describes people he knows and loves, rather than abstractly discussing nameless, faceless persons who are easier to ignore. No compassionate person can learn the size of the U.S. illiteracy problem without some degree of outrage that we make so little corrective effort.

The Exciting Solution to Illiteracy

Although the solution proposed for illiteracy in this book has been recommended by many scholars, it has not received widespread notice. The scholars' recommendations are in academic works with limited distribution. There have been few, if any, books published in the last thirty-five years that even mention the solution proposed here. Other than informing you of the enormous need for solving our illiteracy problem, the heart of this book is the solution itself.

Your first question might be, "If the solution proposed here is so simple and so well established in every alphabetic language other than English, why is the solution so little known?" We often believe that if a problem is serious enough, scholars and governmental leaders will research thoroughly enough to consider all practical solutions to the problem, and books will be written discussing the findings. This is not always true, however. *Books in Print,* which lists all the books presently available in U.S. bookstores, lists more than a hundred thousand different books in print. Only two books are listed under the subject of the previously mentioned scholars' proposals. Neither proposes the solution mentioned earlier. As a result, answering the question of why the solution to illiteracy is so little known before helping you understand how complicated problems are solved could call forth some of the skepticism mentioned earlier. Many examples throughout history have disproved the belief that if a problem is serious enough, scholars will consider all the possibilities. In fact, there is truth to the adage, "The only thing that we learn from history is that we don't learn from history."

Psychologists and others who study human nature find that when we attempt to solve problems, we usually do not consider all the possibilities. More often than not, as soon as we find what we consider a workable solution to an urgent problem, we implement it. In attempting to solve problems, we often try to do so within assumed but nonexistent limits. Many published reports on creative thinking and problem solving have documented this. Books of mental puzzles and games contain problems many readers cannot solve—not because of a lack of intelligence but because the solution lies in an approach never considered. The reader incorrectly assumes that such an approach is outside of the allowable limits. The bibliography lists a magazine article (see a brief excerpt in appendix 5) and a book by Eugene Raudsepp on creative thinking that demonstrates this by having the readers exercise their abilities on games and mental problems.

Trying to solve problems only within well-established—but often nonexistent—limits is especially true within a profession such as education or the sciences, where, as a result of teacher training, certain methods and beliefs are accepted by almost all members of the profession and others are not. Those who disagree with the currently accepted teaching methods or beliefs often do not remain in the profession. They fail to advance in their profession because they disagree with their superiors and are fired or choose to leave. The longer we try to solve problems within assumed but nonexistent limits, the more likely we are to think the limits cannot be exceeded.

We are not solving our illiteracy problems, and the resulting monetary and human-suffering costs are increasing. It is bad enough that we tolerate these costs for ourselves. It is much less excusable that we tolerate these increasing costs for those most affected—the illiterates who cannot act effectively on their behalf to solve the illiteracy problem. There have been many proposed solutions to our very serious illiteracy problems in the last few years, but our illiteracy problems cannot be completely solved within the assumed limits. Extensive quotes from several authorities in chapter 7 give conclusive evidence that, because of changed conditions within the last seventy-five years, we cannot completely and permanently solve our illiteracy crisis without spelling reform.

Spelling reform is seldom mentioned in books and reports concerning illiteracy and, presumably, is not even considered as a solution to illiteracy by most people. This is true even though scholars have been recommending it for more than two centuries. In other words, spelling reform is outside assumed but nonexistent limits on the solutions we can consider. Our spelling is considered unchangeable. As Edward Rondthaler and Edward Lias explain in their book *Dictionary of Simplified American Spelling,* "we refuse to challenge our spelling. We accept it as a 'given.' We struggle along blindly, desperately using what is no more than remedial measures; never attacking the underlying source of the trouble."[8] This book will show why spelling reform is the only complete, permanent, and proven solution to illiteracy.

Do We *Really* Want to *Solve* the Literacy Crisis?

Chances are, when you first saw the words *spelling reform,* you thought, (1) "I learned to read without 'tampering with our mother tongue,' and I'm no genius, so other people can, too!" (2) "I think there will be difficulties involved in implementing spelling reform;" or (3) "I dread the difficulty of learning to read again." Let's carefully, honestly examine these three concerns, remembering that this is just an introduction—the remainder of this book provides details constituting the proof.

1. Can everyone learn to read using the system that we did?

The belief that others can learn to read without spelling reform because we did misses the point for two important reasons. First, *our* reading ability is irrelevant to the abilities of millions who did not or cannot learn to read. Students of human nature know that as we grow older we have a strong tendency to forget unpleasant events from our past and remember only good events—that's why the phrase "the good old days" is so common. If you learned to read several years ago, you have undoubtedly forgotten how difficult it was. Perhaps you were above average and had little difficulty in learning to read. That is certainly no proof that the average student today should be able to do what you did. In either case, the second reason is even more important: conditions have changed in the last thirty-five years.

In our increasingly complex technological and competitive world, learning to read is not only more necessary, but it is also more difficult. In our faster-paced nation (where televised problems are solved in thirty to sixty minutes) few students or teachers will accept the rote memorization and dull drill needed to learn to read used in the nineteenth century. As a result, teachers use inferior methods, which not only fail to teach nearly half of their students to read, but also requires two or more years to teach those who *do* learn to read, as opposed to about four months for most students of other alphabetic languages.

2. Will there be serious difficulties in implementing a new system?

When spelling reform was mentioned, you may have thought of one or more difficulties of implementing spelling reform. Every reasonable objection will be answered to your satisfaction. Chapters 6 through 12 will quite adequately demonstrate that not only can all objections be answered, but implementing spelling reform will save money rather than costing it, as all presently attempted solutions do. As you read this book, make notes to yourself of any questions or objections you have. Then systematically find and record the answers to each of your questions. If you fail to do this, you may reach the end of the book remembering your questions or objections but not remembering if you found answers to them. The problem of illiteracy is a serious one. It warrants diligent investigation and intellectual honesty with yourself in your discoveries.

Almost everyone occasionally complains about English spelling but

Illiteracy and Why It Still Exists

then assumes nothing can be done. Paradoxically, some who complain most bitterly about our ridiculous spelling and schools that cannot teach our children to read or to spell correctly will object to spelling reform.

Some will object by saying that English is a beautiful language. You will note, however, that most of the people making such claims are those who have mastered English spelling. This has come as a result of hundreds of hours of study, which they have forgotten or proudly downplay the difficulty of. Can we honestly believe that ninety million functional illiterates in the U.S. and hundreds of millions of those who speak English as a second language would call English "a beautiful language?"

In a few short years, millions of English-speaking people will call N'wenglish (=N'w English = New English), the spelling system proposed in this book, a beautiful language—not because it has an interesting variety of ways of spelling the sounds in our language, but because of its invariability and simplicity. More importantly, it will be called a beautiful language because at long last it will enable easy communication among English-speaking people throughout the world. Enabling communication—rather than admiring the beauty of the words—is and should be the real purpose of a language. No one will prevent those who so greatly admire the "beauty" of English spelling from continuing to read it in the books they own and from using it in their writings. N'wenglish, however, will enable hundreds of millions of people who cannot now read or write English—among the 1.2 billion or more who speak English—to communicate by mail, e-mail, and all types of published material, which is less expensive, less intrusive, and more convenient than voice communication.

People often become defensive because "someone is trying to tamper with our mother tongue." Since you or I did not invent our spelling, we need not defend it. People would far too often rather continue to endure the disadvantages of the known than to implement changes that would bring the advantages of the unknown. Almost anyone can think of reasons why spelling reform won't work, but if they were to thoroughly investigate the validity of the objections in today's conditions, they would find that every objection can be answered. Few have carefully compared the illogical and inconsistent spelling of English words with the spelling of words in other alphabetic languages. Even fewer have researched the ease of learning, reduced educational costs, and reduction of all the disadvantages of illiteracy that would come from reforming our spelling as other nations have done.

3. Will learning a new spelling system be too difficult for me?

In truth, there is only one significant objection to spelling reform: "I don't want to expend the effort to learn it." Fortunately, this is the easiest of all objections to meet. The spelling system proposed here is so simple, logical, and easy to learn that anyone who can presently read English can learn the new spelling system in five minutes. Briefly, the proposed spelling system is to spell every word exactly as it sounds, always using the same letter(s) to represent each sound. Most of what you need to know is contained in two simple memory aid sentences. The first includes all fourteen vowel sounds: "Kae Greenwood fried Joe Paul Bluepoint's bug in our red-hot pan." The second includes the six consonant phonemes represented by two letters and the WH consonant cluster. These seven two-letter blends are underlined here for highlighting only (it is not a rule of spelling). "Which yuett mezhurz this shelving?" In English spelling it is "youth measures." *TT* represents the *TH* sound as in *thin*. This is the only phoneme not spelled in one of the ways it appears in English. This is because English spelling does not distinguish between the two *TH* sounds, as in *thin* and *then*. Together, the two memory aid sentences combined show the spelling of each of the phonemes represented by a single consonant.

N'wenglish is so simple that everyone who has tried could read material written in the new spelling system knowing *nothing* about the spelling system. This is because 81.6 percent of the spellings of the phonemes are the most used spelling of those phonemes in English spelling. This figure would be 92 percent if it were not for the pronunciation of the sounds of *F* and *OE* in the very common words *of* and *does*; the /z/ of the common words *is*, *was*, and plurals such as *bags*; and the /ee/ of words ending in Y. (The problem with English spelling, of course, is that there is not only a most used spelling but a next-most used, next-most used…and so on. See chapter 6.) Persons knowing no more about the spelling system than you do now will stumble over words occasionally, but after one or two hours spent reading chapters 8 and 9, a person can read the new spelling system with few, if any, stumbles. Skipping ahead to these chapters and reading a few short passages and then deciding "it won't work" is equivalent to demanding to know the price of an item without first being convinced you need it and without knowing the details that explain how it can work. Part 2 of this book explains why this system is needed. Part one will convince you of the desperate need of solving our literacy problems if you carefully examine the evidence presented. For the benefit of more than a billion people around the world who speak English and of hundreds of millions of people who want to read and write English but are hindered by the spelling, you are challenged to carefully, honestly examine both part 1 and part 2.

There are many ways a book can be read, of course, but for the purposes of this section there are two primary ways:

1. you can read a book superficially, not paying much attention to detail, because the book espouses ideas you do not want to deal with, or,

2. you can read a book in an honest effort to determine if the facts support the book's conclusions.

When presented with the details of an issue, it becomes increasingly difficult to criticize but stay involved in the issue. Critics often fear they would need to get involved; instead they prefer to criticize from a distance.

Almost everyone, when asked, will say, "Yes, we should simplify our spelling," or "I wish we would simplify our spelling—it is so bad!" But when someone seriously suggests doing so, people often dismiss the idea with the same tedious rhetoric, "…but (sigh) it will probably never happen," because they do not want to expend the effort to study the details proving how it can happen. Depending upon how resistant one is to change, it may take two complete evaluations of all the details presented in this book before realizing the truth of what is presented.

Although they may vehemently claim they want to reduce the monetary and human-suffering costs of illiteracy, two groups may be most resistant to the changes proposed in this book. The first group is educators. Like people in most other professions, educators often want to maintain the status quo in their profession. The second group is parents who are embarrassed by and seeking an easy explanation for their child's apparent inability to learn to read. These parents often accept without question the explanation of the "experts" that their child is dyslexic or has attention deficit disorder or some type of minimal brain disfunction.

Those who are interested in solving our literacy crisis (as opposed to those who merely claim to be) will take action. They will honestly examine Dr. McGuinness's, Sir James Pitman's, and others' claims—as chapters 6 and 7 show—that learning to read the present English spelling is so difficult that a different solution than the one governmental and educational authorities are now advocating is drastically needed. They will honestly examine the claims of this book—that only spelling reform will at long last permanently solve the foundational, root cause of literacy for children *and adults*. As a result, they will seriously consider the ideas presented in the remainder of this book—even if they have scanned (or read) portions of the remainder of the book enough to know the broad outlines of what the book proposes, and even if they have some initial reservations about what is proposed.

Fighting Symptoms versus Curing the Root Cause

Any proposed solution to illiteracy other than spelling reform attacks one or more of the symptoms of illiteracy rather than the root, foundational cause. It is equivalent to taking cough medicine for a cough rather than taking penicillin to cure the disease causing the cough. As long as a disease is left uncured, new—and often more dangerous—symptoms will continue to appear.

Changing the spelling of our words will obviously not solve all the problems that prevent students from learning. There is, however, one indisputable, overriding fact which is true for all but the most mentally disabled. Using a perfectly phonemic spelling system—spelling every word as it sounds—will make learning to read so easy that children will learn to read in the first half of first grade (or in kindergarten), and adults will learn in two to four months—as they do in other nations! They will learn to read long before the frustration of failing in the spotlight of their reading class causes the discipline problems and damaged self-esteem that stop the students from believing they *can* learn to read.

The educational history of practically every alphabetic language nation on earth—especially when compared to our own educational history—has proven that a perfectly phonemic spelling will greatly improve our literacy rate. This is because, unlike any other improvement we can make to our educational system—which would merely combat some symptoms of the problem—phonemic spelling will cure the root cause of the problem: the inconsistent, illogical, and confusing spelling system.

Although we may not learn as much as we should from history, we usually learn even less from educational history—especially that of language groups other than English. How many people would even think to compare our educational history with that of non-English-speaking nations? It is largely a matter of national pride. Some people may equate the situation with that of converting to the metric system. Only the U.S., Liberia, and Myanmar (formerly Burma) still use the English measuring system—they have not yet made the use of the metric system mandatory. It is not equivalent, however. Although some of the changes to metric would be inexpensive, others would not. For example, the cost of converting hundreds of huge metal-cutting machines—costing hundreds of thousands of dollars each—to metric would be financially devastating to many companies. On the other hand, converting to the spelling system proposed here would save rather than cost money.

Desperately Needed: A Simple Illiteracy Solution

As our nation becomes more technologically advanced and more communication oriented, fewer and fewer jobs are available that do not require reading skills. And, of course, world trade is becoming increasingly competitive. Instead of improving, however, our national functional literacy (the ability to read well enough to get by in an increasingly complex society) has been dropping. As one of many possible indicators, Scholastic Aptitude Test (SAT) scores dropped for more than thirty years at the end of the twentieth century. Furthermore, absolutely nothing done within the school system—other than spelling reform—will affect the tens of millions of adult illiterates who have left school. Adult illiterates are increasing in number by more than two million per year, and it is currently estimated that less than 1 percent of them ever become good readers after leaving school. As later chapters will show, it is more difficult to solve the problem of adult illiteracy than of students' not learning to read before they leave school. Unfortunately, adult illiteracy receives only a small fraction of the attention the schools receive.

Today's schoolchildren have many distractions and detriments to learning to read that students did not have before the 1920s. Among other things, today's students have a multitude of time-consuming and pleasurable activities. These activities can easily distract them from devoting long hours to what for many is an unpleasant process: learning to read.

Charles Leadbeater, in his book *The Weightless Society,* says what many students, teachers, and parents know by experience, "too much schooling kills off the desire to learn." He is referring to schooling that is boring and confusing rather than enlightening and exciting. He is referring, more than anything else, to learning to read and spell English, which is so difficult and time-consuming that our nation actually offers prizes to the very few who manage to get the spelling right—a program known as the National Spelling Bee, a program virtually unknown in other languages.

We often learn best by analogy. Two instructive analogies to our spelling system are sports and the traffic system on our roads. Would anyone really be interested in watching a basketball game in which a basket sometimes was worth two points and other times was worth 200 points and there were over 300 rules for how much the basket was worth and almost every rule had exceptions—and some of the exceptions had exceptions? Furthermore, imagine the chaos if traffic signs were illogical and inconsistent. If the stop sign only *sometimes* meant stop or if the yield sign did not always mean that you must yield, disaster could result. If you were doomed to a life of near-poverty because of your poor reading ability, would it be a disaster to *you*?

Unfortunately, our students have no choice but to follow the rules of "the game of spelling." They have no choice but to learn to adapt to the chaos caused by our spelling. Although tone-deaf students are not forced to become musicians, every student *must* learn to read and to spell if they wish to live significantly above the poverty level—even those who have great difficulty memorizing the spellings of tens of thousands of words because they have an ingrained aversion to something as illogical and inconsistent as English spelling. Even the most brilliant engineers, medical doctors and scientists will have difficulty getting a good job if their resume includes a spelling error or two. One cannot help but wonder how many very talented workers have been lost to society because we believe only good spellers are competent to be our leaders in the workplace.

Rather than simplifying our spelling, we blame the student for not adapting to an illogical and inconsistent spelling system; we often believe poor spellers and poor readers are lazy or just not trying hard enough. In other words, rather than placing the blame where it belongs—on the spelling—we place the blame on the people who are *victims* of the spelling. We try to locate those who cannot read and spell and do whatever it takes to get them to read and "spell correctly"—and we have believed for centuries that there is only one correct way to spell most of our words. That one "correct" way for many words is totally unrelated to the pronunciation of the words.

Some educational researchers and teachers try to defend our indefensible spelling system and place the blame on the students by claiming that if only the students would learn all the spelling rules they could be good spellers. As the "How Bad *Is* the Cause of Our Problems" section of chapter 6 explains, even a computer programmed to use a set of over 200 rules to spell 17,000 common words was wrong 51 percent of the time.[9]

It will become apparent to the truly inquiring mind that the solution to our illiteracy problem must be to make the process of learning to read much easier and faster. In other words, spelling must be so simple, logical, and consistent that the student—whether schoolchild or adult—can learn in three or four months, as do students in most of the other alphabetic languages of the world. At present, the 52 percent or so of American students who do become good readers require an average of two to two and one-half years. After about two and one-half years, students who learn to read English can read second-grade or third-grade reading books, then throughout elementary school, students can achieve higher levels of reading ability as they learn more words—either through rote memory or through repetition.

Learning to Read English versus Other Languages

Those who have not studied the differences between English spelling and the spelling of other alphabetic languages may have difficulty understanding why learning to read English takes so much longer than learning other languages. Most of us had several years of spelling classes in elementary school. If we are familiar only with English, we may be surprised to learn that students of most other alphabetic languages do not have separate classes for spelling, as we do.

We may also be surprised to find that students who learn to read a phonemic language do not have the artificial "grade level" reading classification present in U.S. schools. In U.S. schools, a teacher may say, for example, "This student knows twelve hundred words by sight and reads at a third-grade level. Next year, he should know sixteen hundred words and read at a fourth-grade level." Students of most other alphabetic languages learn the sounds of the letters in their language in the first few days of school. After three or four months, they can pronounce any word in their language. They can even correctly and unfailingly pronounce unusual words they have never seen before—something impossible with our present English spelling. When they pronounce or sound out in their minds a word in their vocabulary, they recognize (read) it.

Practically every English-speaking adult has experienced a situation in reading or in listening to someone speak that most other language groups do not: forgetting the pronunciation or spelling of a word we have not used for years. This is because other language groups only have to remember the spelling of the sounds instead of having to remember spellings and pronunciations of every word.

Those familiar only with English may be even more surprised to learn that English spelling is more confusing than Chinese picture writing. "The most unusual effort of this medium centered approach was probably 'American children with reading problems can easily learn to read English represented by Chinese characters.' (Rozin, 1971)"[10]

Chapter 8 shows that all English words can be spelled with only thirty-eight phonemes. A cursory study of the 736 or more ways of spelling these thirty-eight phonemes (see Tables 6-2 and 6-3) and an understanding of how we learn will reveal why this is true. As you know, different people have different abilities. Some people—especially young children and girls—are good at memorizing. Others like to learn by logic. Adults and many young boys prefer to learn new things by comparing them with previous knowledge. Some people—even some very intelligent people—are confused and completely turned off by things that are needlessly inconsistent and illogical. In fact, the above-average intelligence of some students is one factor causing them to *search* for logical connections between related facts and information. When learning English words using Chinese picture writing, students have no choice but to learn strictly by memorization. On the other hand, students learning English spelling may see, for example, two words spelled the same except the first letter. These words would rhyme in almost any other language. In English they may sound completely different. As you will see in chapter 6 there is not even *one* invariable rule of English spelling. Students have no choice but to learn by memorization or repetition.

Reference is made in this book to "boring reading textbooks." These references are based upon quotes concerning the so-called "Dick and Jane" readers used in previous years but seldom used today. Today's reading textbooks may be less boring, but they are still just as frustrating to new readers. If the method used in Dr. McGuinness's book, *Why*

Illiteracy and Why It Still Exists

Our Children Can't Read, and in this book is not used, students will have difficulty learning to read. Before the age of eleven or twelve, children must be taught spelling by rote memory or repetition because they cannot yet understand two of the types of logic needed in relating sounds to letters as used in English words. The logic needed in learning to read English is explained near the end of chapter 6. After age twelve, students can learn to spell some words by grouping words spelled similarly, but remembering which specific words are in each group is little if any easier than simply doing the hard work of rote memorization. Regardless of the teaching method, however, roughly 80 percent of present English spellings are not phonemic and many months of memorization or learning by repetition are required. Some authorities will claim as little as 20 percent of English words are not phonemic, but this is only because they recognize more than one spelling of several of the sounds as phonemic.

Learning to read is difficult for some students, either because they are not good at memorizing or because they have a strong conscious or subconscious objection to expending so much effort on something so confusing. Even more important, less than 1 percent of the forty to ninety million adult functional illiterates in the U.S. today will ever get enough help to achieve the equivalent of an eighth-grade education. These schoolchildren and adult illiterates will never become good readers without intensive one-on-one tutoring or unless we, as a compassionate and patriotic American public, insist upon solving our literacy crisis using the only proven, logical, and economically feasible solution—the one proposed in this book.

Some reading authorities have concluded that our present spelling is so inconsistent, illogical, and confusing that some students—even some very intelligent students—will never become proficient in reading English until it is simplified. Research has not shown how many students fit into this category, but as stated in the preface, even if it is only 0.1 percent, that is still hundreds of thousands too many—especially if one of them is your friend or loved one!

Alphabetic languages vary widely in difficulty. As far as grammar and syntax are concerned, English is neither the easiest nor the most difficult—it is easier than many European languages, for example. But in one way—the spelling—English is by far the most difficult alphabetic language in the world. Frank C. Laubach wrote, "Ninety-five percent of the languages of the world are almost perfect phonetically."[11] Frank C. Laubach has found that students in many of these languages can learn to read using Laubach Literacy methods in one to twenty days! In some simpler languages, such as some dialects in the Philippines, adults can learn to read in as little as one hour![12]

Students in no other nation on earth have the difficulty that our students have in learning to read. Although we like to take pride in our literacy level, the truth is that in our nation—where by law every child must attend school throughout childhood (and almost all do)—we have more adults who cannot read than in some nations with far less than universal schooling. News reports from 1982 and 1983 stated, "The United States ranks forty-ninth among 158 member nations of the U.N. in its literacy levels."[13]

What does all this mean? Rather than risk overstating the obvious, perhaps the best approach is to ask two questions with obvious answers:

1. Which is easier, learning the letters that represent the thirty-eight phonemes in English or learning the specific letter sequence required to represent each of the twenty to seventy thousand words in our reading vocabulary by memorization or by repeated use?

2. Does it tell you anything about our spelling to find that students having trouble learning can more easily learn to read English using Chinese characters?

Chapter 6 will convincingly show how confusing, inconsistent, and illogical our spelling is to new readers.

There are obviously many reasons for our illiteracy problems, but no other reason affects everyone, as our spelling does. It is true that there are many reasons why schoolchildren devote their energy to tasks other than learning to read, but if our spelling were as logical and dependable as that of other alphabetic languages, students would have learned to read in first grade. They would also be much more likely to enjoy reading and to see themselves as successful in their schoolwork. They would therefore be more likely to see themselves as able to be successful in any worthwhile task they choose to undertake. The frustration of considering themselves failures causes many of their behavior problems and many of their failures. Many of their attitudes and failures carry over into adult life.

Why Has the Problem Not Already Been Solved?

Our illiteracy problem remains unsolved because most of us do not understand or believe the following:

1. The vast extent of illiteracy in the U.S. Warning reports have appeared periodically over the last twenty years, but the public has treated illiteracy as it does many other problems—by ignoring it until it reaches crisis proportions. Most of the public has paid little attention to the education problem until the last few years.

2. The vast cost of illiteracy, in economic loss and in human misery.

3. The great difficulty of learning English reading and spelling, especially as compared to other alphabetic languages.

4. The great effect that the difficulty of learning written English has upon illiteracy.

5. The near impossibility—due to human nature and economic realities—of solving illiteracy through the standard means (improved teaching methods, better textbooks, better teacher training, student motivation, etc.)

6. The vast increase in the need for literacy. Manual-labor jobs are rapidly being replaced by jobs requiring more reading skills, and world trade is rapidly becoming more competitive.

7. How easy and how helpful the changeover to a logical spelling system would be.

Why We Must Accept the Challenge to Act

Although this book is written to benefit those who did not or cannot learn to read, it is written *to* those who are readers—not only for the obvious reason that nonreaders cannot read it but also because those who cannot read do not have the knowledge, ability, or political power to implement the proposals in this book. The desperate hope is that you, the reader, will have the compassion to act in their behalf.

If we, who do not personally need a simplified spelling system to function, do not show compassion for the millions of present and potential illiterates among us and act for them, their pain and suffering will increase, as will all the problems and expense that we and our nation must endure as a result. A 1990 report showed that, "[i]f this situation goes unremedied for another decade, this nation is doomed to decline. We simply cannot survive as a first-class economic power in the information age with 'minimal' capacity to acquire and communicate facts, information, concepts or ideas."[14] Without understanding the details of the proposals made in this book, it would be easy to feel overwhelmed by the size of the task. It would be easy to say that it cannot be done, but almost anything can be done if enough people insist on it. Just a few minutes, used properly, can perform wonders. This book shows how. Spelling reform has occurred in several nations larger and smaller than the U.S. and in both advanced and unsophisticated nations. Amazingly, it almost occurred in English—in England in 1949 and again in 1952! So it is possible, as Edgar Guest so eloquently states:

It Couldn't Be Done

> Somebody said that it couldn't be done,
> But he with a chuckle replied
> That "maybe it couldn't," but he would be one
> Who wouldn't say so till he'd tried.
> So he buckled right in with the trace of a grin
> On his face. If he worried he hid it.
> He started to sing as he tackled the thing
> That couldn't be done, and he did it.
>
> Somebody scoffed: "Oh, you'll never do that;
> At least no one ever has done it";
> But he took off his coat and he took off his hat,
> And the first thing we knew he'd begun it.
> With a lift of his chin and a bit of a grin,
> Without any doubting or quiddit,
> He started to sing as he tackled the thing
> That couldn't be done, and he did it.
>
> There are thousands to tell you it cannot be done,
> There are thousands to prophesy failure;
> There are thousands to point out to you one by one,
> The dangers that wait to assail you.
> But just buckle in with a bit of a grin,
> Just take off your coat and go to it;
> Just start in to sing as you tackle the thing
> That "cannot be done," and you'll do it.[15]

PART 1
THE PROBLEM

At this point, I would beg the reader to forget the numbers game. Whatever the precise calibrations, it is obvious that these statistics represent an enormous, an unconscionable amount of human suffering....They should be read with a sense of outrage.[1]

Michael Harrington
The Other America

Chapter 2
The U.S. Illiteracy Problem

The Present Extent of Illiteracy in the U.S.

Most people who have not studied illiteracy in the U.S. do not realize how serious the problem is. It is almost certain to be worse than you think. Before people are willing to change, they must see the need, so the obvious first step is to understand the facts regarding the size of the problem. The second section of this chapter will explain why the extent of the problem is so often underestimated. Although data will be presented only for the United States, other English-speaking countries have similar problems.

The Number of Adult Functional Illiterates

The most significant statistics on illiteracy are those that measure a person's ability to respond properly to what they read. This is "functional literacy." Discussions of illiteracy in this book usually refer to functional illiteracy. In the mid-1980s, various studies of the extent of illiteracy showed that there were from forty-six to eighty-four million functional illiterates in the U.S.[2] This amounted to 26 to 48 percent of the population.

On September 9, 1993, a writer for the *Washington Post* explained that the study entitled Adult Literacy in America initiated by

Congress in 1988 was "the most comprehensive literacy study ever done by the U.S. government." This was a five-year, $14 million study by the National Assessment Governing Board, in conjunction with the National Center for Educational Statistics, "based on lengthy interviews with [26,700] adults [sixteen years old or more] in a dozen states."[3] The survey was in three parts: 13,600 people surveyed nationally, 1,000 people in each of a dozen states, and 1,100 prisoners in eighty state and federal prisons.[4]

Dr. Diane McGuinness, in her book *Why Our Children Can't Read*, lists some of the characteristics of the study:

- It used a careful statistical sampling to achieve a true representation of the population regarding gender, racial and ethnic groups, and geographical location (including inner city, suburban, and rural areas).
- It included development of an accurate *objective* means of judging reading ability based upon predetermined absolute standards. These standards measured "functional literacy," the test subjects' ability to read and correctly act upon what they read by finding information and performing certain operations upon that information.
- Educational Testing Service (ETS) personnel used an accurate means of ensuring that test information was (1) gathered under strict guidelines prepared for evaluating test responses, (2) verified by independent outside testers, and (3) protected from being changed by anyone who might have any reason to want the data to show different results than they appeared to show (for example, no school was given access to the data until the study was complete).[5]

There were five levels of proficiency in the test. As examples, the most difficult task those with Level 2 or less proficiency could perform "include...filling out a Social Security form." Those with Level 1 proficiency "could locate the expiration date on a driver license, but not an intersection on a simple city map."[6] Understanding "a fact sheet sent to potential jurors outlining jury selection procedures." required a Level 5 proficiency. Results, extended percentagewise to all of the U.S., show the following:

Proficiency Level	% of Adults	No. of Adults
0 to 1 (functionally illiterate)	22	42.0 million
2 (barely literate)	26	49.6 million
3-4	49	93.6 million
5 (advanced)	3	5.7 million
	Total:	190.9 million[7]

This means that 48 percent "of all adult Americans [92 million] read and write so poorly that it is difficult for them to hold a decent job."[8] Amazingly, most of those with Level 1 skills and nearly all of those with Level 2 skills said they could read "well" or "very well." Twenty-five percent of those with Level 1 skills were immigrants, and 62 percent of them had not completed high school. Thirty-three percent of them were 65 years old or older, 26 percent had health problems—either physical or mental and 19 percent had visual problems.

Those with Level 1 skills earned an average of $240 per week, and 44 percent of them were living below the poverty line; those with Level 5 skills earned $650 per week. The Level 1 respondents reported working eighteen to nineteen weeks the previous year; the top three levels reported working thirty-four to forty-four weeks the previous year. Less than 58 percent of the Level 1 respondents said they had voted in recent state or national elections; 80 percent of Level 4 and 90 percent of Level 5 respondents had voted.[9]

Statistics Canada, which carried out the same kind of testing in the United States, Canada, and five non-English-speaking European countries, replicated these findings for the United States in 1994. The study also showed that U.S. high school students and young adults (16 to 25 years old) were six times more likely to be functionally illiterate (Level 1) than those in Sweden Only 13 percent of today's sixteen- to twenty-five-year-olds scored at Levels 4 and 5.

There is little evidence that the number of years of schooling plays any major causal role in improving literacy.

The study also showed the following:

approx. % of total population, high school grads:	80
approx. % of total population entering college:	40
approx. % of total population graduating college (with a four-year degree):	20
percentage of college grads with adequate literacy:	85
percentage of all adults with college degree and adequate literacy (33 million): (.85 times .20)	17

Dr. Diane McGuinness believes the figures in this table show we are condemning the majority of Americans to second-class citizenship.[10] The figures in this table show an alarming apparent college dropout rate of roughly 50 percent (40% enter college, 20% graduate). A 1998 news report shows that this may have improved somewhat: "the United States, at 37 percent, has one of the world's highest college dropout rates."[11]

Elementary School Illiteracy

At the same time as the Adult Literacy in America study, the National Assessment Governing Board and the National Center for Education Statistics tested almost 140,000 students in grades four, eight, and twelve. Dr. McGuinness claims that prior to this time, school district testing had become a national disgrace. Not only were some of the schools blatantly teaching to the test, but they were reusing also the tests for several years. According to many parents, their children were asked by the teachers to stay home if they could not read well.

The National Assessment Governing Board and the National Center for Education Statistics used the same rigorous testing methods for children as described for the Adult Literacy in America study. The students were classified as advanced, proficient, basic, or below basic. Below basic students were functionally illiterate for their grade because they could not understand what they read.

In an apparent attempt to raise test scores, the schools claimed an amazing *12 percent* of the students were untestable. Dr. McGuinness's explanation of what is involved in this 12 percent figure essentially verifies such a conclusion—regardless of the reasons given by the schools for excluding the students.

- Four percent of the students were disallowed by ETS personnel as being untestable, leaving only 8 percent as being untestable.
- Three percent were considered untestable because of a poor understanding of the English language.
- The remaining 5 percent were in special education classes, most of them because they were diagnosed as having a learning disability that prevented them from being able to read.
- About half of this 5 percent of students *could have been tested* because, according to national statistics, only 2 to 3 percent of students are mentally retarded, deaf, or blind.[12]

Students from forty-one states and the District of Columbia were tested. State test scores ranged from 75 percent below basic (Washington, D.C.) to 27 percent below basic (New Hampshire) for fourth graders. An average of 29 percent of students was rated as below basic in the five states with the best rankings. Nationally, 43 percent of the students in the fourth grade were rated below basic.[13] As Jonathan Kozol has convincingly argued in *Illiterate America*, very few students who cannot read in fourth grade ever become fluent readers.[14]

Why Our Children Can't Read includes research proving the statistical impossibility that such huge numbers of students reading below basic levels could be due to any type of minimal brain disfunction. This is also confirmed as true since these students can be taught to read using the effective teaching methods covered in Dr. McGuinness's book.

As Dr. McGuinness points out, when the vast majority of teachers are using the same teaching method (as was the case, by law, in California in 1992) and yet 57 percent of the students are reading "below basic" (as were students in California in the 1992 test reported earlier), the only logical conclusion is that the method is failing. Furthermore, when the best result is 27 percent of fourth grade students' reading "below basic," it is almost certain that there is more trouble to come.

News Reports and Commentary on Literacy

Despite the need to improve it, scholastic performance has been falling for the last few decades. A September 4, 1991, report of a

Let's End Our Literacy Crisis

Washington Post writer in *The Salt Lake Tribune* states,

> The College Board announced that the reading and writing skills of the high school class of 1991 are the poorest in the history of the SAT examinations. The million or so kids who took the test tend to be the cream of the crop—A and B students. It is a fair presumption that their untested classmates (about 1.5 million) are even less bookish.
>
> This is rotten news for the country. It comes after eight years of so-called "education reforms," large increases in educational spending (30 percent on top of inflation adjustments) and what was supposed to have been tougher school curricula.
>
> …The implications for our economy are frightening. "Even our best educated students," Secretary of Education Lamar Alexander observed the other day, "don't know enough and can't do enough to assure success in tomorrow's world."[15]

Chester Finn in his book, *We Must Take Charge,* stated that many of our public school students—perhaps even a majority—cannot show competency in challenging subjects including math, science, English, history, or geography, and that an even smaller number seem to be able to adequately use their minds.[16] Furthermore, Albert Shanker, president of the American Federation of Teachers, stated that 95 percent of American college students would not be able to gain admission to any college outside the United States.[17]

As the performance gap between students in the U.S. and other nations continues to widen, the trade advantage between nations will continue to widen. Now is definitely *not* the time to require our students to enter the international scholastic arena with the disadvantage of having the most confusing alphabetic spelling system in the world. Our spelling delays the education of our students who do learn to read well by one and one-half to two years. It takes that much longer than in most non-English-speaking nations.

Comparing U.S. Literacy with That of Other Nations

The earlier facts bring up two very important questions. First, how does U.S. literacy compare to other nations?

*"The United States ranks forty-ninth among 158 member
nations of the U.N. in its literacy levels."*[18]

Effect of Illiteracy on U.S. World Trade

Second, how does our low literacy rate affect our internal national welfare and our national economic welfare in world markets? Perhaps the most definitive statement of the nation's state of education appeared in the editorial of the October 1989 *Air Force Magazine*:

> "The education system has failed the nation. It has not produced enough well-educated, technically qualified graduates who can enter the work force and become productive members of society. This is true at every tier from entry-level technician to research scientist. And the future doesn't look any better."
>
> That is the somber conclusion of "America's Next Crisis: The Shortfall in Technical Manpower," a report published in September by AFA's Aerospace Education Foundation. "The United States," it says, "spends more than any other nation for education while simultaneously ranking at the bottom of the industrialized world in terms of educational achievement.
>
> The Commerce Department says one company in three is already forced to provide basic or remedial instruction for new employees."[19]

> [T]here is a large body of evidence that America's level of literacy is far from what is necessary for this country to effectively compete, even survive, economically and politically in a highly sophisticated industrialized world.
>
> The unhappy truth is that although many people go through school, they don't come out literate enough to "make it" in today's society.[20]

Rick Gladstone, an Associated Press writer, quotes federal officials as saying that seventy-two million adults—33 percent of the 1988 U.S.

population—may lack the literacy skills needed to find work, and that this number is increasing by more than two million each year. This illiteracy rate is occurring at a time when

- the need is increasing not only for literate workers but also for workers who can understand the technology and who can think independently,
- the nation is changing from manufacturing to services and information technology, and
- our nation's European and Asian competition is gaining in their percentage of an educated workforce.

The competition may come to dominate the twenty-first century technology business. Gladstone quotes government policy makers as saying that illiteracy is threatening our ability to compete in world markets and is "an economic time bomb." [21]

A report from the front page of *The Salt Lake Tribune* on June 22, 1992, entitled "Competitively Speaking, U.S. Sinking" shows the outcome of not correcting the literacy problems.

> Japan remains the world's most competitive country, while the United States has dropped from second place to fifth, according to a report published today by two Swiss-based economic consulting firms....
>
> The assessment is based on a nation's domestic economic strength, internationalization, government, infrastructure, finance, management, science and technology, and work force. It covers 37 countries and is based on surveys from international organizations and questionnaires to 18,000 executives....
>
> "Most alarming for long-term competitiveness is the U.S. drop in the quality of its people—from second position to seventh this year," [the report] said. "This is partly due to the current inability of the educational system to meet the needs of a competitive economy."
>
> The report rated the U.S. education system 21st overall, trailed only by Greece among industrial nations.[22]

Although there are several books in print defending present methods of teaching students to read, appendix 7 is a point-by-point refutation of the only known book published since the 1993 "Adult Literacy in

America" report which claims there is no literacy crisis. Appendix 7 is included for those who may have encountered and believed information claiming there is not a literacy crisis.

Why the Size of the Problem Is Unrecognized

Many readers may have difficulty believing the extent of the problem of illiteracy. Although these readers may not be able directly to dispute the figures, they can quote the clichés, "There are lies, damned lies, and statistics" and "Figures don't lie, but liars figure." More charitably they may simply say, "You can prove almost anything if you quote only part of the figures and quote them in a certain way. There is probably some sort of trick to the figures."

There is one "trick" to the figures, if you can call it that, that has already been mentioned: the figures refer to functional illiteracy. If, however, people read so poorly that they cannot get by in life as well as they should, their reading ability is of little value. Besides this explanation of functional literacy, there are six more major reasons why the extent of illiteracy is not widely known.

The Hidden Illiterates among Us

Today there are many who pass as literate, although they aren't. These people are known as "passers." We might be surprised, for example, at how many businessmen and others carry a newspaper only to make people believe they can read. Illiterates seldom look any different. Also, you can't identify an illiterate person by talking with one. Many illiterates are knowledgeable and eloquent speakers. They just didn't gain their knowledge or eloquence through reading.

Passers are significantly helped by real estate zoning laws which essentially keep lower income illiterates separated from higher paid literate workers and by the natural economic and cultural separation that occurs in any group of people. Those who can read are more likely to be close associates with others who can read and vice versa.

Passing can even occur within closely knit families. Many parents can conceal their inability to read from their children, especially if their spouse can read and will cover for them. Spouses often help their non-reading mates with reading tasks necessary for employment, beginning with the employment application form. If something occurs in the workplace which threatens to expose them as nonreaders, they often simply disappear. They dread the embarrassment of being "found out."

Anyone who doubts these conclusions should read John Corcoran's book, *The Teacher Who Couldn't Read*. Mr. Corcoran graduated from Texas Western College in 1961 with a degree in education. He admits that he cheated on tests in college—although he states in his book, "I am not advocating cheating." He had gotten into college without taking entrance exams because he had an athletic scholarship. Amazingly, he became a teacher of tenth, eleventh, and twelfth grades in California, where he taught for eighteen years, without being able to read! He taught social studies, typing, history, physical education, and one year he even taught English. Although his wife thought for twenty-five years that he could read, even if he couldn't read well, she didn't know that he could hardly read at all until she overheard him trying to read a simple child's story to their three-year-old. It was not until then that she came to understand the emotional pain he had been living with all those years. He suffered emotional pain caused by feeling there was something wrong with him which prevented him from learning, by having to develop so many coping methods to hide his illiteracy, and by feeling alienated from his associates who could read.

The Grade-Level Completion Deception

Many people assume that if someone has completed high school or even grade school, they must have learned to read and learned other things they were taught. Teachers and education experts know that this is not always true. Having sat it out for twelve years of school does not guarantee that students learn even a small portion of what they are exposed to. A January 9, 1998 report in *The Salt Lake Tribune* verifies this:

> Grammar and spelling problems top the list of complaints that employers and college professors have about recent high school graduates.
>
> Next on the gripe list, according to a poll released Thursday by Public Agenda, is the grads' inability to write clearly....
>
> Seventy-six percent of professors and 63 percent of employers say a diploma is no guarantee a student has learned the basics....
>
> Said Deborah Wadsworth of Public Agenda: "...If parents,

teachers, and students don't grasp what the outside world expects of them, we are witnessing a communications gap of enormous and potentially devastating consequences."

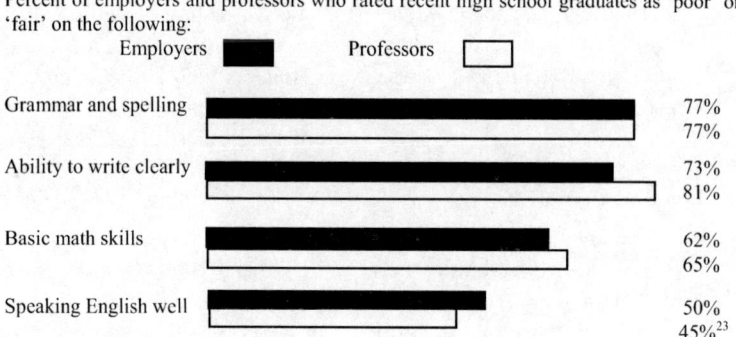

Percent of employers and professors who rated recent high school graduates as 'poor' or 'fair' on the following:

	Employers	Professors
Grammar and spelling	77%	77%
Ability to write clearly	73%	81%
Basic math skills	62%	65%
Speaking English well	50%	45%[23]

The Silent Minority

Illiterates are a silent minority. They do not write to their legislators. They can't. Out of embarrassment they do not lobby in their behalf. They don't want to be known as a part of the illiterate minority. Community and cultural leaders of groups with large proportions of nonreaders do not like to call attention to these members' illiteracy. They fear this will give their "enemies" (racists, the "elitist" wealthy, or other class-conscious persons) ammunition to use against them. Since they are silent, they (like the reading majority) do not realize that millions of others are in the same condition. If they knew, they might be less embarrassed to stand up for what is best for them.

Self-Esteem Teaching in Public Schools

Perhaps the most successful teaching imparted to present-day students concerns self-esteem. Despite the true performance, U.S. adults and children tend to overestimate their scholastic abilities. The 1993 U.S. Department of Education Adult Literacy in America report stated that among the forty to forty-four million adults with the most limited skills, roughly fourteen million admitted they could not read or write well, and only about six million admitted to needing help with any tasks requiring literacy. In short, they felt good about what is actually very poor performance.[24]

An earlier report by the U.S. Department of Education quoted students who were asked to rate their abilities in math and science; 68 percent said they were "good at math."[25] These were students who had just ranked near the bottom in international scholastic testing in science and math.

The U.S. Census Reports

Many believe that the U.S. is a highly literate society because of the official U.S. Census Bureau reports. The 1970 and 1980 census reports showed America to be 99 percent and 99.5 percent literate, respectively. In the interest of national pride, our governmental leaders like to present us as highly literate. Also, it is in the short-term interest of teachers and education officials to believe and promote belief in these figures. Conscious deception may not be taking place, but let's look at exactly how the Census Bureau obtained these figures.

The Census Bureau included questions about literacy in each census from 1840 to 1930. Many of those most knowledgeable about U.S. literacy believe that literacy began to drop in 1963 and has been declining ever since. The Census Bureau reintroduced questions about literacy in 1970 at the insistence of the military.

In the 1970 census the only question asked about literacy was on grade completion. The Census Bureau considered those with fifth-grade completion or higher to be literate. A little more than 5 percent reported less than a fifth-grade education. For some reason, the Census Bureau decided that 80 percent of these could read, so they reported 99 percent literacy.

In 1980 the Census Bureau mailed out forms and based most of their calculations upon written responses to questions about grade completion. In addition they used a small sample of home visits and telephone interviews. They asked people what grade they had completed. If the answer was "Less than fifth grade," they asked if the person could read and write. This technique of determining literacy is quite certain to underestimate illiteracy for the following reasons:

1. Illiterates would not respond to written forms, and their family members—likely also to be illiterate—would not either.

2. Because of unemployment or low-paying jobs, fewer illiterates have telephones.

3. The underprivileged poor, and especially illiterates, may feel they are being singled out like criminals They therefore have cause to distrust salespersons, bill collectors, or strangers knocking on their door seeking information—especially if the answers to the questions would be embarrassing. Home visits by Census Bureau officials who are not known by the person answering the door cannot be expected to yield accurate information under such circumstances.

4. Grade-level completion does not equal grade-level competence.

5. Those who have no permanent address, no phone number, no post office box, or no regular job—a condition shared by almost six million people, most of whom are illiterate—often are not counted. They can't be found by the Census Bureau in time for the census.[26]

Sensory Overload

Finally, this is an age in which we see one kind of crisis or another on TV nearly every day. As a result, we have a tendency to suffer from sensory overload. We learn to ignore or disbelieve much of the bad news because the world goes on with little visible effect. Also, far too often a radio or TV report we hear will dispute the seriousness or the truth of the previous day's report.

However, the extreme seriousness of our illiteracy problem should prevent us from letting other crises dull our senses to this one. We can't afford to ignore the facts. We need to ask ourselves, "Can we, as a nation, keep ignoring a problem affecting our competitiveness in world markets and the health and well-being of over one-third of our people?"

Present Adult Literacy Teaching in the U.S.

A brief examination of the number of adult illiterates who are learning to read may be somewhat encouraging. A careful examination of the details behind these figures, however, robs us of any encouragement we may think we've found.

The Four National Literacy Programs

There are now four major national literacy programs:
1. Adult Basic Education (ABE), the government's official program
2. U.S. military services' programs for their recruits
3. Laubach Literacy programs
4. Literacy Volunteers of America (LVA)

According to information published in 1985, the government programs (items 1 and 2) together claim to reach between two and three million people. In the mid-1980s the privately funded programs (items 3 and 4) only served fifty thousand and twenty thousand each year, respectively. The privately funded programs are successful in helping even those who cannot read at all. The way the government programs are set up all but guarantees that few people with less than fifth-grade reading skills will participate. The methods of recruitment and teaching, location of classrooms too far from where the students live, and similar problems prevent their participation. The military services rarely accept anyone with less than fifth-grade reading skills.[27]

Statistics show that even for those who do manage to enroll in Adult Basic Education programs, the programs themselves are near disasters.

1. At least 40 percent do not complete the program. (According to one source, "The dropout rate in adult education typically is between 50 and 70 percent."[28])

2. Only 30 percent of those who leave before completing the program do so because they have met their personal goals. More often they leave because of:
- inconvenient class schedules,
- inconvenient class location and transportation problems,
- the students moving elsewhere,
- job conflicts, or
- lack of interest.

3. Students in most of these programs remain for only fifty to one hundred hours and improve only one or two grade levels. And even that gain is suspect. Much of it is not retained.

4. Roughly twenty-four million have not completed eighth grade, and twenty-three million of these have not attended, or will not attend, ABE. This shows that these programs are not meeting their needs.[29]

With appropriate fanfare, President George Bush, senior, and a few congressional leaders proudly approved legislation in July 1991 for a $1.1 billion federal adult literacy program for the next four years.[30] As pointed out at the start of chapter 3 and in "The Cost of Solving Literacy Problems" section of chapter 12, even if the entire $275 million per year were going directly for teaching illiterates, it would be inadequate. As with all such programs, however, much of the funding was for administration, coordination, and additional, redundant research.

State and Local Literacy Programs

The percentages of functionally illiterate persons taught to read in local and state programs are also very small. Boston, for example, allocated $1 million for its literacy program in the early 1980s. With roughly 200,000 people who were illiterate or semiliterate this amounted to about $5 per nonreader per year. In addition to programs of the cities, there a few community based literacy programs which are very small, by comparison.

One of the most impressive state programs in the early 1980s, the California Literacy Campaign, allocated $2.5 million for their 5 million nonreaders. This amounted to only fifty cents per nonreader throughout the length of the program. The program was begun with federal funding, after which it had to depend precariously upon support from the state.[31]

In 1983, with some help from foundations and publishers, New York City set up the Literacy Assistance Center. Its purpose was to study the best ways to teach literacy and the length of time it takes the average student to learn to read and write. In 1986, Jacqueline Cook, the director, said, "illiteracy may be a tougher nut to crack than most people think." The research shows that the accepted standard of one hundred hours' instruction for one grade level of advancement may be overly optimistic. Only 30 percent of those tested so far moved up one grade after a year of study. Jacqueline Cook states,

> We are beginning to see that for many people, it may take up to 200 hours of instruction to move up a grade. That's a lot of hours,

and a lot of people become discouraged. The problem is only going to get worse as technology gets more complicated.[32]

Corporate Literacy Programs

Besides the government programs, some corporations teach reading skills to employees; others use groups like LVA to operate their programs. In most cases the students have the reading skills to be employable already, and they are only taught what they need to function more effectively in specific areas. This is also true of what is taught in programs in the military service.[33] David Harman, Professor of Education at Columbia's Teachers College, states,

> Economist Anthony Carnevale has calculated that while the tab for all forms of formal education combined reached $238 billion in 1985, employers spent a staggering $210 billion on employee training and education....
>
> Several surveys conducted over the past several years on the educational endeavors of the workplace have inadvertently shed additional light on the issue of literacy. While a few employers provide their employees with instruction in reading and writing skills—conventional literacy programs—a much larger number offer courses and programs carrying different titles that are, in fact, efforts to improve literacy. From courses in letter and report writing for corporate executives (sometimes called "executive communication"), through courses that seek to develop specialized vocabularies, to classes in expression, listening, speaking, and reasoning, the American workplace is constantly striving to improve the literacy abilities of its work force. Most of these efforts avoid the use of the term *literacy*, and those addressed by them are hardly thought of, or perceive themselves, as illiterate. However, it appears that there is a major and concerted effort to upgrade various aspects of literacy.[34]

A 1999 report shows statistics on the seriousness of the problem:

> The [American Management Association's] January survey of 1,054 member companies found that nearly 15 percent of

companies offer basic skills programs, up slightly from a year ago. Nine percent will even hire applicants who lack basic skills and then enter them in remedial training programs, up from 5 percent two years ago....

Nearly 36 percent of applicants lack the reading and math skills they need to do the jobs they seek, up from 23 percent in 1997, the group found.[35]

Adult Literacy Recruiting and Dropout Problems

Why do adult literacy programs have such difficulty recruiting students? Why do so few complete the course? Many scholars, such as Sir James Pitman, Godfrey Dewey Ed.D., Frank C. Laubach, Dr. Rudolph Flesch, and Kenneth Ives, have pointed out obstacles to the success of the conventional means to reduce English illiteracy. The primary obstacle to enrolling adult illiterates in reading classes is their (perhaps subconscious) desire to avoid any more of what was for them a confusing and self-image-shattering experience: trying and failing to learn to read English.

There are five secondary obstacles to adult literacy.

1. They are suspicious of strangers. As Frank C. Laubach explains, "First of all he has every reason to suspect that the teacher feels superior, for practically all educated people act superior. The illiterate dislikes this attitude of superiority as much as we do. He also has every reason to suspect an ulterior motive. Illiterates have been swindled and exploited and deceived by educated people so constantly that they are afraid of us—fear is their only defense."[36]

2. They think they are too old to learn to read.

3. They dread the time and effort required—as well they should. All present literacy classes require many months of tedious effort. Completing high school may require years of night school.

4. Publicly referring to poor readers and nonreaders as afflicted, disabled, or the target population hurts recruitment efforts. Even if nothing we do to attract reading program recruits is unkind, condescending, or "wrong," illiterates are usually observant enough to see if we consider them somehow deficient. If they think we consider them deficient, even if they are wrong in thinking so, they will avoid the embarrassment of revealing themselves.[37]

5. Illiterates are sensitive to their teacher's attitude. As Frank C. Laubach states,

> Illiterates know instinctively whether we love them as brothers or whether we look down upon them. Their own sense of inferiority makes them peculiarly sensitive to the slightest attitude of patronage....This is the reason you should sit down beside him as you teach; never stand above him....If you have an humble, loving spirit, your actions will take care of themselves.
> ...[T]hose who consciously or unconsciously insist upon keeping up the wall of class distinction find the illiterates unresponsive.[38]

Successful Adult Literacy Students

Chapters 6 and 7 and other sections of this chapter show how the difficulties of English spelling seriously hinder people's efforts at learning to read. For various reasons, most people who need help learning to read will not seek help—they often do not know where to seek help even if they should decide to do so. A large portion of those seeking help with reading will not be able or will not choose to continue until they become fluent readers. About half of native-born Americans and many immigrants *do* become fluent readers, however.

What are the characteristics of functionally illiterate adults who become fluent readers? Jonathan Kozol found that most of the students who become proficient readers after being unable to read as adults were those who were literate in another language. Most of them were also on the verge of being functional in our society—they only needed fluency in English to complete their quest for effectiveness. Such students had not lost hope as a result of injustice in our culture. They were, in effect, just moving from their previous realm of confidence into a new arena of potential opportunities.[39]

The Future of Literacy in the U.S.

The first step in understanding the future of literacy in the U.S. is developing a better understanding of exactly what is involved in functional literacy. Concerning the number of people in the U.S. who cannot read at all, we may be somewhat better off than we were one hundred years ago—or even twenty years ago. Although not true in other languages, in the past twenty years the number of people in the U.S. who cannot read at all has stayed the same or decreased somewhat. Functional literacy in the U.S., however, is decreasing because our society is becoming more complex. The rate at which literacy improves will control our economic strength among the family of nations.

The introduction of the computer has dramatically changed the job scene over the last twenty years. Available jobs in America are becoming more communication oriented and service oriented, compared to the manual-labor and product-oriented jobs in the past. At the same time, Kozol believes that all of evidence he has seen indicates that there will be even more illiterate adults within the next fifteen years or so.[40]

One reason functional illiteracy will increase is the growing number who cannot or will not be retrained for high-tech, decision-making, and communications jobs. People who cannot read the training manuals will be out in the cold. Many of the remaining manual-labor jobs will already be taken by persons (often immigrants) willing to work for much lower wages.

In 1982 Dorothy Shields, education director of the AFL-CIO union, stated, "By the 1990s anyone who doesn't have at least a twelfth grade reading, writing, and calculating level will be absolutely lost."[41] The "most comprehensive literacy study ever done by the U.S. Government" detailed earlier in this chapter and the "At Risk Report 20 Years Later" quoted in chapter 12 show that this is true—at least for the 48 percent of adults who cannot hold an above-poverty-level job as a result of their functional illiteracy. At a conference in the early 1980s sponsored by life insurance industry executives, Democratic Senator Paul Simon stated, "Unemployment is a permanent phenomenon. The demand for unskilled labor is going down; the pool of unskilled labor is growing."[42]

Because of raised expectations, those excluded from jobs in this century may be much less docile about their unemployment than previously. As you may know, social revolutions usually begin with those who feel unfairly excluded from "the good life." We must not ignore this potentially dangerous situation. It could wreak havoc in many areas in the U.S. We like to think that our nation is strong and stable, but throughout history, several "great nations" have crumbled. Some of these nations were "great" much longer than the U.S. has been. Those who do not learn from history are doomed to repeat it. Part of the violence in the streets now is directly attributable to anger over unemployment, part of which results from illiteracy. With more than two million illiterates being added to the population each year, how long do you think the illiterate unemployed will continue to meekly accept their situation? Chapter 3 outlines the effects of illiteracy on other nations, effects that may soon be felt in the U.S.

Another major aspect of the likely increase in illiteracy is the way illiteracy usually propagates from one generation to another. This is true for several reasons:

• Psychologists tell us that the first five years of a child's life are the formative years. If the parents are illiterate (or too busy or too disinterested), they do not read to their children. They do very few things that provide the early stimulation children need to help them reach their maximum intellectual potential.

• Illiterate parents are unable to help their children with homework or analyze problems in their children's schooling. Even if they could determine the problem, they are politically powerless to effect a change.

• Since illiterates are likely to associate mostly with other illiterates, their children will devalue the importance of reading because of the values of their peers.

Not only would increased literacy in the U.S. benefit our nation, but increased literacy in other nations can also benefit our nation—any increase in understanding between people of different cultures can be beneficial. We need worldwide literacy, and the most practical way to achieve it is to implement an easy-to-learn English spelling system.

Chapter 3
Worldwide Literacy

Advantages Illiterates Gain by Becoming Literate
Perhaps the best description of the advantages of literacy is that given by Frank C. Laubach.

We will repeatedly show in this book that if illiterates are taught in the proper manner, it is a delightful process for both student and teacher; it begets new faith and new vision in the learner; it destroys his sense of inferiority and frustration; it stirs him to new self-reliance; it destroys his defeatist complex; it makes him feel that he belongs to the class of society that triumphs over difficulties and does not live forever in despair. It has the same value for the illiterate that cultural education has for educated people in general. It gives him a new sense of mastery over his fate.

Besides, locked up in books are all the greatest secrets that the human race has discovered in the course of the last ten thousand years of civilization. Writers are constantly unearthing and presenting these secrets in new, fresh ways. Making a man literate pulls him from the edges of society, where he has lain stagnant mentally, into the current where he will be swept onward as a part of the great, moving course of human history. Some illiterates will never go far, but others may develop genius. Adults differ more widely than children do. There is many an Abraham Lincoln who awaits only the opportunity that Lincoln found in his log cabin, as he read a few books before the fire. Even if the new literate does not go far himself, the door has been unlocked for his children, and for his children's children.

The theory is often expressed that the masses will stop work with their hands if they become literate. That this is all nonsense is proved by the fact that the most literate countries in the world accomplish the most work.

…If…they are given information about their work, so that they can dignify their trades with new skill and catch the spirit of progress, then they will become far more efficient workers and they will enjoy what they are doing infinitely more.

…The right kind of reading matter constantly contributes new ideas for use in a man's own business and gives him the zest of discovery and the feeling of getting ahead. So reading delivers him from bondage to his toil and transforms it into fun. We say that a reading doctor is "up on his profession," while a doctor who does not read allows himself to fall behind the times. For, after all, reading is far and away the greatest means in the world by which people exchange their discoveries. Men pour onto the pages of books the finest results of their experiences, and other men may read these pages at their leisure. It is safe to say, therefore, that a thousand times as many progressive ideas are disseminated through the printed page as are spread in any other way. If this is true, learning to read multiplies a man's power to progress.[1]

Why Worldwide Literacy Is Desperately Needed

Since it would be difficult to find a more concise, yet all-inclusive way of stating the need, this section will consist entirely of quotations from two of Frank C. Laubach's books.

It is obvious that any attack on poverty and its associated problems must also include an all-out war on illiteracy, for this is the major root cause. Illiteracy exacts a tremendous toll in human terms. For the young adult it is a barrier and a burden that last a lifetime. It commits him to a future marked by personal deprivation, unemployment, social dependence, alienation and, in many cases, crime. There is no future for a person who does not possess the basic skills he needs to change his situation. He is held in place by forces that he has no capacity to change.

Society also pays a price, but it is not so personal. Our welfare rolls are filled with those who can do nothing but the most menial labor. When an illiterate is hired, it is because no one else can be found to do the work. When there is an economic slowdown, he is the first fired. Our jails and prisons are filled because the illiterate often turns to crime out of desperation. Illiteracy is a basic and just complaint coming out of our racial conflict. Conscience dictates that we do all in our power to make a change.

...There is a vast and ever-widening imbalance in our world. Dr. Barbara Ward, the famous economist, described this in her great books, *The Lopsided World,* and *The Rich Nations and the Poor Nations.* She says that we rich nations have the whip hand and have controlled the money and the tariffs so that the wealth of the world flows our way and saps from the poor nations all they have. Thus the rich get richer and the poor get poorer, and the end—perhaps nearer than we suspect—will be a world revolt more bloody than the French Revolution or the Russian Revolution or the Chinese Revolution.

Half the world goes to bed hungry every night. Because they are hungry, they are angry; and they are rising here, there, everywhere in revolt. Wherever hunger and wealth exist together the underprivileged are shouting and rebellious and often violent. Robbery and crime are on the increase in America until we are afraid to walk the streets at night in nearly every American city. We cry for more police, but neither police nor soldiers can hold back the breaking dikes if we allow hunger to continue to increase while we grow rich.

President Eisenhower's greatest statement was that all our military is merely negative—holding the line until we do the *positive things.*

That *positive thing* is to remove the terrible poverty and anguish that drive people to crime and irrational fury and war.

How shall we end poverty? Our first impulse is to distribute our surplus food and clothing. But we have tried that and it was never enough. Besides, the poor do not want to be paupers needing our charity. They want to come up to our level.

This is what the illiterate pauper says: *"Not charity but a chance. Not a coin in my hat, but a tool in my hand. If you give me a fish, you have fed me only one meal; If you teach me to fish, you have fed me a lifetime."*

That is what they want—to learn to fish and farm and make what they need—and they want to own what they make. They want to be independent. They want to know what we know. They want to be educated. Illiterates are nearly always hungry. Educated people nearly always have enough. So the hungry illiterate masses want education as the *only* door out of their desperate plight.[2]

It is true that [illiterates] have been in this state of destitution for thousands of years. But there are new factors in modern living that make these people more rebellious at their condition than ever before. The airplane, the radio, the cinema, and television have ushered us into the electronic age where illiterates can see for themselves the enormous economic superiority of literate countries. Every motion picture whips them into an ever rising determination not to tolerate this difference.[3]

English as a Worldwide Language

Scholars have stated that English is the ideal choice for a worldwide language. Dr. Mont Follick, a linguistics expert and member of parliament in England in the 1950s, states emphatically, "The English language itself is the most simple and the most unflexioned language that has ever been on earth. The only obstacle to the spread of English is the spelling." [4]

Frank C. Laubach's book, *Teaching the World to Read*, has a section that deals with proposed universal languages; Umskript is one of them. This section states,

> The literature promoting Umskript says, "Though English is the simplest in its grammar and syntax of any European language (with Danish a close second) the movement to make Basic English a world business language has little chance of success, so long as English spelling remains such a stumbling block...."

> [English] is the most irregularly spelled phonetic language on earth. Anybody therefore who could help bring system out of chaos in our spelling could meet a world demand....

> [Dr. Woodford Dulaney Anderson] gives numerous quotations from present day leaders who endorse English as the universal

language....He concludes that the weight of world scholarship favors English, reformed in spelling and grammar, rather than any other language.[5]

The remainder of this chapter is a list of the useful characteristics of English. It is based upon a lecture by Axel Wijk, a Swedish linguistics expert, at Manchester University on January 28, 1965, and data from Sir James Pitman's book, *Alphabets and Reading*.

Easy Grammar and Syntax

The need for a common auxiliary language for the whole world has become more urgent every year in the course of the present century....For a number of reasons English is undoubtedly the living language that is most suitable to fill this important role. For one thing, English is, though native speakers may perhaps find it hard to believe, a comparatively easy language to learn for foreigners at least as far as the everyday spoken and written forms of it are concerned. This is mainly due to its grammatical structure, which is far simpler than those of most other important languages, particularly so in comparison with French, German, Russian, or Spanish. We need only mention such advantages as:
- The absence of inflection for gender, case and number in the articles...
- simple ways of forming the plural,
- the absence of inflection in the adjective,
- the simple formation of tenses and other verbal forms, etc.[6]

Pitman states, "No other major language possesses such a simple grammar and syntax or combines the following advantages:
- ...[T]here are no arbitrary genders (except in such rare instances as referring to a ship or a machine as 'she').
- Agreement between adjectives and nouns is unnecessary;
- nouns have no cases except for the possessive ''s' for the genitive.
- The definite article has only one written form;
- verbs have very few inflexions and these tend to be regular.
- Very few verbs are irregular.

- Most words in common use have less than four syllables....
- Few modern languages are capable of such precision, flexibility, and subtlety, allied with brevity."[7]

Widespread Use

"No other language is more widely diffused throughout the five continents."[8] Laubach states, "No other language is used by [more people than English] unless it is Mandarin, which is spoken only by Chinese."[9]

"In many parts of the world a knowledge of English is essential if one is not to be debarred from communication with everyone except those who speak one's own very restricted, possibly tribal, tongue; without English or, dependent on the area, some other widely spoken and printed language, one's education is also likely to be gravely restricted because it is not economically feasible to write or translate many textbooks in a host of minor languages."[10] Because of the "influential position of the English-speaking peoples and their widespread distribution, English is vigorously taught in secondary schools all over the world and is by far the most important language studied in foreign countries."[11]

It is the main language of books, newspapers, airports and air-traffic control, international business and academic conferences, science, technology, medicine, diplomacy, sports, international competitions, pop music, and advertising. Over two-thirds of the world's scientists write in English. Three-quarters of the world's mail is written in English. Of all the information in the world's electronic retrieval systems, 80% is stored in English.[12]

English is the most widely spoken language in the history of our planet, used in some way by at least one out of every seven human beings around the globe. Half of the world's books are written in English, and the majority of international telephone calls are made in English. English is the language of over sixty percent of the world's radio programs.[13]

An October 16, 1997 report in *The Salt Lake Tribune* states, "English has become the first and only 'global language,'" and,

Worldwide Literacy

[E]ight languages account for fully half the world's people. (In order of size they are: Chinese, English, Hindi, Spanish, Russian, Bengali, Arabic and Portuguese.) The hundred biggest languages account for 95 percent of the world's people, and in some of the longest civilized places—the Middle East, Europe, East Asia—the surviving minority languages are counted only in the dozens. But in most places, many more "little languages" have survived: The United States and Brazil are home to hundreds, India and Indonesia to over a thousand each....

The native speakers of English number around 450 million: more than any other language except Chinese but less than 7 percent of the world's population. Count those who have learned English as a second language, however, and the total soars to 1.3-1.5 billion, far surpassing any potential rival.[14]

One visitor, returning to China in 1979, after a gap of 20 years, wrote: "...[T]oday, everyone is carrying a book of elementary English." Even if only 10% of these learners become fluent, the effect on totals is dramatic: the number of foreign learners is immediately doubled.[15]

There are more than 10,000 living languages in the world (as of 1997).[16] Since there are 191 nations in the world[17] (as of July 1999), this means that each nation uses an average of more than fifty languages. From a list of 166 nations there are 220 *official* languages, an average of 1.33 each. There are eighty-six different official languages. Among these eighty-six, only fifteen are used as official languages of more than one nation. Only four of these fifteen are used as the official language of more than six nations (English: 47, French: 31, Arabic: 21, Spanish: 20). English is an official or semiofficial language in over sixty-five nations, with a prominent place in another twenty nations.[18]

For the first time, in the year 2000, UN countries were asked to choose English, French, or Spanish as the language for their correspondence. The other three official languages of the UN, Russian, Chinese, and Arabic, cannot be read by most of the UN's word-processing programs. One hundred and eighty-five nations responded. One hundred thirty chose English, thirty-six chose French, and nineteen chose Spanish.

English is now, in effect, the international language of medicine. There are many foreign medical doctors in the U.S. Sensible spelling would help these doctors learn English and therefore avoid mistakes in reading medical information and communicating with their patients.[19]

Future language usage: By 2050 the three largest economies will be China, the U.S., and India. India now uses English as the common language for its multiplicity of language speakers, so two of the three will effectively be English-speaking for international purposes. China and Russia, however, already require all students to learn to speak English. English is already the working language of the European Union.[20]

Despite the widespread use of English, speakers of other languages need have no concern that English—or any global language—will ever cause the "language death" that was feared previously. Recent studies have shown that this almost never happens. Instead, people merely become bilingual (or multilingual) as necessary for their own benefit.[21]

Easy Adoption of New Words

English has an "extraordinary capacity for absorbing and developing new linguistic material."[22] "English has acquired the largest vocabulary of all the world's languages, perhaps as many as two million words, and has generated one of the noblest bodies of literature in the annals of the human race."[23] This makes English especially valuable for commerce and for technical usage of all kinds. Dewey states in his book *English spelliing: Roadblock to reading*, "English is already the official language of international aviation."[24] David Crystal, a Professor of Linguistic Science and author of several books including his book, *The Cambridge Encyclopedia of Language*, points out, "English is already recognized as the international language of the sea."[25] Despite these advantages, Wijk states,

> To all intents and purposes [English] must even now be regarded as the principal auxiliary language of the world. But for the great majority of foreigners the language is far too difficult to learn in its present written form. In order to make it more generally acceptable and serviceable as an international auxiliary language it is an indispensable requirement to subject its spelling to a radical and systemtic reform.[26]

Chapter 4
The Monetary Costs of Illiteracy

Five monetary costs are associated with the mistakes and inabilities of illiterates. It is difficult or impossible to assign an exact dollar value to many of these costs, since records that would associate these costs with illiteracy are rarely kept.

Five Monetary Costs of Illiteracy
1. Cost to taxpayers for government programs that provide services that primarily illiterates use.
2. Increased labor costs for government and private businesses.
3. Reduction in sales by businesses, since illiterates are not customers.
4. Cost of paying for (or preventing) injury or damage to:
   • illiterates or others,
   • government or private property, or
   • the environment.
5. Cost to national welfare because of the lost potential of the illiterates.

No attempt will be made to quantify the fifth monetary cost. Although it is one of the largest costs, it is the one to which it would be the most difficult to assign a dollar value. You've no doubt heard the saying, "A mind is a terrible thing to waste!" No one is likely to claim that an intellect like that of Newton or Einstein would be "wasted" by the difficulty and lack of logic in English spelling. As chapter 7 will show, however, some very bright people, many with above-average intelligence, never learn to read. Although they can get by better than other illiterates (because they *are* of above-average intelligence), their lack of reading ability severely limits their potential. It not only prevents their making a good living for themselves, but it also limits the contribution they could otherwise make in helping our nation compete successfully in world markets.

Table 4-1 shows the cost of several government programs used by illiterates (monetary cost number 1). Item 1 was not included because it costs a significant amount but because it is the only program in the list for the benefit only of illiterates. (Note that the federal funding was for a limited time and may be less now.) The table below summarizes the money spent in the early 1980s on literacy training (based upon table 4-1, item 1) versus what is needed and the results to be expected.

Federal tax money spent on ***adult literacy training***	$2.34 per year per taxpayer
Federal, state, & local taxes for ***adult literacy training*** *	$3.19 per year per taxpayer
Federal taxes spent on each adult illiterate for ***adult literacy training***	$4.58 per year
Federal, state, & local tax spent, each adult illiterate, ***literacy training****	$6.25 per year
Annual amount spent on literacy training: federal	$0.28 Billion
Federal, state, local*	$0.38 Billion
Annual minimum needed to significantly reduce illiteracy (1982 est. by the Executive Director of the National Advisory Council on Adult Education—a now defunct commission)	$5 Billion
Amount spent on each adult illiterate if $5 Billion is spent each year on literacy programs	$83 per year
Percentage of illiterate adults in all govt. and private literacy programs[1]	4 % max.
Percentage of illiterate adults involved in literacy programs who complete eighth grade	15 %
Percentage of total adult illiterates completing eighth grade:[2] 0.04 x 0.15 =	0.6 %

* Comparable 2004 figures, not readily available, may be even less.

Table 4-2 shows several increased labor costs because of illiterate or marginally literate employees or because of being unable to find qualified employees (monetary cost number two). Many items are "competition sensitive" or "company proprietary"—the type of information companies do not want known for competitive or legal reasons. Such costs can become very large for many American companies.

Table 4-1
The Monetary Costs of Illiteracy
Type 1: Cost to Taxpayers for Government Programs Providing Services That Many Illiterates Use

Item	Data Source*	Data Date	Cost
1. Adult literacy training (a) Federal (Creates National Inst. for Literacy, funds business and prison programs and Adult Basic Education)	*The Deseret News,* Salt Lake City, July 26, 1991, page A3, col. 1	July 26, 1991	$275 million per year
(b) Federal, state, and local combined	Hunter and Harman, page 100	1976	approx. $375 million per year
2. Child welfare costs and unemployment compensation due to illiterate adults unable to meet the employment standards	Senator George McGovern *Proceedings and Debates,* 95th Congress, Second Session	Sep. 1978	$6 billion per year, estimated
3. Prison maintenance of approx. 60% of the approx. 440,000 inmates of state and federal prisons** directly linked to illiteracy	U.S. Department of Justice Dr. Patricia Gold, John Hopkins University	Oct. 1983 Sep. 1984	$6.6 billion per year, estimated minimum
4. Court costs, law enforcement costs, and crime victim's costs in urban areas where 40% are unemployable for lack of literacy	*Illiterate America* by Jonathan Kozol, p. 14.	1985	unknown but must be many times the cost of prison maintenance
5. Industry and taxpayer costs of: (a) industrial equipment damage (b) workmen's compensation (c) industrial insurance for on-site accidents due directly to worker inability to read warning signs, chemical labels, machine operation manuals, etc.	*Illiterate America* by Jonathan Kozol, p. 14	1985	$20 billion per year, minimum
6. Health costs due to illiterate adults' inability to read material explaining preventative health measures, both physical and mental health	*Illiterate America* by Jonathan Kozol, p. 14	1985	unknown but obviously very large

* Sources 2 and 3 are quoted from *Illiterate America* by Jonathan Kozol, page 13.

** The 1986 population of *local jails* is up 23% in the last three years to 274,400 inmates.[3] Expenditures on these inmates would be similar. According to U.S. Department of Justice figures, total adults in custody (state and federal prisons and local jails) on June 30, 2002, was 2,021,223[4] or 4.59 times the 440,000 shown; 4.59 times the $6.6 billion shown is $30.3 billion. An April 23, 1996, report[5] shows the cost of prisons, jails, *and the parole and probation systems* is $40 billion, 60% of which is $24 billion.

Table 4-2
The Monetary Costs of Illiteracy
Type 2: Increased Labor Costs for Government and Business

Item	Data Source*	Data Date	Cost
1. Hundreds of thousands of entry-level and middle-level jobs remain unfilled for lack of applicants who can meet job requirements	Wall Street Journal	Oct. 16, 1978 Jan. 22, 1981	Cost of paying overtime to cover jobs for unfilled positions
2. Approx. 70% of the dictated correspondence must be retyped at least once due to secretaries' inability to spell and punctuate correctly.	American Council of Life Insurance, Washington, D.C.	1983	(This cost is now minimal due to computer spell-checking.)
3. Cost of correcting errors of illiterate employees, such as mailing a refund of $2,200 instead of the intended $22.00.	*Illiterate America*, by Jonathan Kozol, p. 14	1985	
4. The cost of useless or misleading answers to market research, polls, etc. by those who do not understand the written questionnaire	*Illiterate America* by Jonathan Kozol, p. 15	1985	Marketing firms spend millions of dollars to locate customers for present or for planned products and services
5. Bill collection costs, public disclosure information, and customer rights information as a result of mailings that are not understood	*Illiterate America* by Jonathan Kozol, p. 15	1985	
6. Legal costs due to the legal principle held in the U.S. in 1930 that "a deed executed by an illiterate person does not bind him" if its terms have not been read to him correctly	"Illiterate Americans and Nineteenth-Century Courts" By Edward Stevens, in *Literacy in Historical Perspective*, Daniel Resnick, editor	1983	This principle is not strictly enforced due to lack of legal help for illiterates. If it were strictly enforced, it would throw the legal system into chaos
7. Annual costs of illiteracy on lost productivity	*The Salt Lake Tribune*, Salt Lake City, October 8, 1995, page F8, col. 1-2	Oct. 8, 1995	$225 billion per year
8. About 35 percent of employees require training to upgrade their skills	"Press Misses Scary Story in Failing to Cover Literacy Adequately," *The Salt Lake Tribune*, Sep. 14, 1989, page A17[6]	Sep. 14, 1989	$30 billion, est., mostly for retraining high-level employees

* Sources 1, 2, and 6 are quoted from *Illiterate America* by Jonathan Kozol, pages 14 and 17.

The Monetary Costs of Illiteracy

No businessman or government official should ignore the magnitude of the items in table 4-2, particularly the last two items. The headline of the article from which item seven came was, "Illiteracy 'Crisis' Scares U.S. Executives" and ends by stating,

> Executives across America are learning literacy isn't something that can be taken for granted. An estimated 40 million adults in the United States—or about 1 in 5 workers—barely can read and write, according to a recent national study. Often the problem isn't immediately apparent in the workplace, because many people...are adept at concealing it.
> But the problem is showing up on the bottom line. According to a recent survey, about 90 percent of Fortune 1,000 executives say illiteracy is hurting productivity and profitability. It costs the U.S. economy about $225 billion a year in lost productivity, say experts.
> "It's a very serious economic problem," said Peter Coors, chief executive of the Colorado-based Coors Brewing Co. "I'd call it a crisis."[7]

Part of a company's literacy crisis stems from the need to recruit a workforce that has a better than average or at least an average literacy rate. A May 8, 1996, report in *The Salt Lake Tribune* shows that "One in three job applicants who were tested by major U.S. companies in 1995 lacked the reading or math skills to perform the jobs they sought."[8] This is from an annual survey by the American Management Association, a not-for-profit management training association based in New York. Only 3 percent of the almost one thousand companies responding to the survey said they hire anyone who is deficient in basic reading and math skills.

The third monetary cost, reduction in sales by businesses since illiterates are not customers, is also difficult to quantify. Three common examples are:

1. Illiterates spend almost no money attending public or private colleges, universities, or advanced-level training.

2. Most illiterates are excluded from the market for expensive homes, cars, and luxury items.

3. Illiterates buy few newspapers, magazines, or books.

Let's End Our Literacy Crisis

In 1997 the U.S. ranked only twenty-ninth in the world in per capita newspaper circulation (down from eighteenth in 1986).[9] About 45 percent of all adults, and 60 percent of adults in their twenties, do not read newspapers. About 35 percent of them *cannot* read newspapers. The less-distinguished newspapers are written at a tenth-grade level, but most are written at a higher grade level. Most news magazines are written at a twelfth-grade level or higher. The only new, major newspaper to succeed in the last few years (*USA TODAY*) relies upon more color, more graphics, and a simpler text for its success. Several newspapers have gone out of business lately due in large part to decreasing readership.[10]

Book publishers and booksellers are also feeling the effects of mass illiteracy. The U.S. published more different book titles than any other nation in 1986; by April 1997 four other nations published more books than the U.S.[11] Although the literacy rate was not the only factor, illiteracy played a major part in the declining sales of hardback books throughout the 1970s.[12] Americans bought thirty million fewer books in 1998 than in 1997; the sharpest decline was in the eighteen to twenty-five age group: down 20 percent.[13] On a typical day (in 1985, the latest date of readily available data) only 25 percent of U.S. adults read a book.[14] Among adults less than twenty-one years of age, 37 percent do not read books at all. The U.S. ranks twenty-fourth per capita (in 1985—it is undoubtedly lower now) in books produced among the nations of the world.[15]

It might be tempting to devalue the individual importance of the second and third monetary costs. However, companies do not absorb all the costs of increased labor and reduced sales. Instead, businesses pass on most of these costs to the customers in the form of higher prices. This not only reduces our standard of living, but it also makes it more difficult for U.S. firms to compete successfully with companies in other countries.

U.S. companies spend millions of dollars each year on monetary cost number 4, because of accidents and mistakes made by illiterate workers. Huge sums are spent for workmen's compensation, insurance, and lawsuits. In addition, a portion of each product, process, and manufacturing engineer's job is to design foolproof (illiterate- *and literate-*worker proof) tooling and processes to prevent accidents. Also, most larger companies have engineering groups whose sole functions are ensuring employee safety and preventing product loss. They work with all the other groups in preventing injury or damage and in investigating the cause of any accidents that do occur. They also recommend corrective actions to prevent similar events in the future.

Workplace Illiteracy: True Horror Stories

Monetary costs are just a small part of the picture concerning bodily injury. No amount of money can adequately compensate the family and friends of those killed or crippled in accidents. Money cannot compensate society for the contributions to humanity that some of those killed could have made. It may be tempting to dismiss monetary cost number four by saying, "It will never happen to me!" However, before doing so, consider the following examples:

1. In the Proceedings and Debates of the Second Session of the 95th Congress, September 1978, Senator George McGovern told of a young naval recruit who could not read the repair manuals for naval equipment. This recruit had caused $250,000 in damage to delicate naval equipment. The recruit had been trying to do repairs by using common sense and by following the pictures in the manual.

These Proceedings and Debates revealed that 30 percent of navy recruits are "a danger to themselves and to costly naval equipment." *The Boston Globe* on May 1, 1983, stated that 25 percent "of naval recruits read below 'the minimum level [required] to understand safety instructions.'" Serious safety concerns arise, for example, if personnel who cannot read repair manuals do the maintenance on the nuclear reactors on atomic submarines.[16]

2. A herd of prime beef cattle was killed in 1975 when an illiterate feedlot worker fed poison to the cattle. He thought he was adding a nutritional supplement to their feed.[17] What illiterate food-processing employee will, in the future, confuse a pesticide with a nutritional supplement in some mass-produced *human* food?

3. Reservation clerks, ticket agents, and other persons who deal directly with the public are usually highly literate and efficient. Airline employees directly concerned with airline safety are often much less literate. As an example, on May 5, 1983, three of the engines on an Eastern Airlines jumbo jet en route from Nassau to Miami went dead. The plane dropped three miles before the pilots averted disaster by getting one engine restarted! This occurred because two maintenance

workers "hadn't read" the instruction manual. It was not reported whether they neglected to read them or whether they had been unable to read and understand them.[18]

4. A major reason for the near-catastrophe in March 1979 at the Three Mile Island nuclear power plant was open valves that were left unsecured. A worker did not follow maintenance instructions.[19] Those who say, "A full-scale nuclear plant disaster is very unlikely," need only look a few years later at the Chernobyl incident. The Three Mile Island event could have affected millions of people in Pennsylvania, New York, and New Jersey.

Admittedly the events in the third and fourth examples cannot be identified with any *evidence* of inability to read. Remember however that, as chapter 2 shows, there are *at least* forty-two million functionally illiterate adults. When the unemployed are deducted, there are still well over thirty million functional illiterates in the workplace. The fact that there are millons of people in the work force that we do not know are illiterate makes hundreds of mistakes each day inevitable. The source and result of many of these mistakes may never be known.[20]

The Cost of Crime

The cost of crime is another cost of illiteracy, but it is difficult to evaluate. It affects all five costs listed at the start of this chapter. An April 23, 1996, Associated Press report in *The Salt Lake Tribune* on a survey done by the Justice Department and sponsored by the National Institute of Justice shows that "[c]rime costs Americans at least $450 billion according to the most comprehensive survey ever done."[21] This was the first survey that tried to measure the cost of child abuse, domestic violence, mental health care costs, reduced quality of life for victims, legal fees, lost work time, the cost of police work, and intangibles such as the affection lost for a murder victim's family, along with all the more commonly reported crime costs. The study did not include the cost of running prisons, jails, and the parole and probation systems, which would have added another $40 billion, bringing the total to almost $500 billion each year. Conservatively estimating that 30 percent of the $450 billion is directly linked to illiteracy, with 117.6 million taxpayers (as of December 1990), crime costs each taxpayer in the U.S. at least $1,150 a year in addition to all the other costs shown in this chapter.

What Is the Total Cost of Illiteracy?

If items 4 and 6 in table 4-1 (monetary cost number 1) are conservatively estimated at $10 billion and $5 billion, respectively, the total for the six items is $47.9 billion. The total of the number 2 monetary costs (table 4-2), other than the last two items, and the number 3 through 5 costs is *at least* in the tens of billions of dollars. Jonathan Kozol's book, *Illiterate America,* shows the 1985 estimated total cost of illiteracy in the U.S. was more than $100 billion per year.[22] This $100 billion would be higher fourteen years later—even if conditions had not worsened—but the last two items in table 4-2, totaling $255 billion, are recent findings that far exceed Kozol's estimates and must be added to the originally estimated $100 billion, giving a total of ***at least*** $300 billion. This is assuming that most of the cost of decreased productivity will be passed on to the consumer in the form of higher prices. These higher prices also make U.S. products less competitive in world markets, of course. The latest readily available figures show that in December 1990 there were 117.6 million workers over age sixteen in the U.S. labor force.[23] Using this number of taxpayers and the *minimum* total cost of $300 billion plus $1,150 per year additional crime costs, what is the total cost in 1999 of illiteracy, per taxpayer in the labor force?

The *minimum* cost of illiteracy of $300 billion per year
along with additional crime costs linked to illiteracy
totals at least $3,700 per taxpayer each year!

Chapter 5
The Human-Suffering Costs of Illiteracy

Millions of nonreaders and poor readers continually endure a multitude of problems and life-threatening dangers. Jonathan Kozol, in his book *Illiterate America*, gives a fuller explanation than can be presented in this chapter. A thoughtful, sensitive person cannot read Kozol's book without feeling compassion for illiterates over the depth and breadth of their problems. Kozol gives actual examples of people he knows and loves who have experienced the problems he describes.

The method of presenting the data in this chapter requires special consideration. It is important that you consider what effects the items below would have upon you instead of upon some nameless, faceless person you are not even sure exists. It is always easier to ignore problems, even serious ones, if they aren't happening to us or to someone we love.

Employment

1. Jobs lost upon discovering illiteracy. Today, even the most menial jobs require the ability to read. For example, janitors have been fired from their jobs because they could not read a note left for them after normal working hours, giving them special cleanup instructions.[1]

2. Low pay for low reading ability. Of 54.3 million adults aged sixteen years or more in 1970 who were out of school but not high school graduates, 75 percent earned less than $5,000 per year. Only 1 percent earned $15,000 per year or more, compared to 33 percent of the total population who earned $15,000 or more.

3. Pay tied to reading ability, not social class. Researchers Carmen Hunter and David Harman state, "Those who have completed high school have incomes about double those who have not completed grade school, and half again higher than those with eighth grade education. This situation prevails among all sectors of the population: men and women, white and black, and all age groups."[2]

4. Unemployment versus reading ability. The unemployment level for the "hard-core unemployed" (i.e., out of work for more than fourteen weeks) for 1975 when total unemployment was 9.2 percent:[3]

years of school completed	percent unemployed
0 to 4	35.6
5 to 8	35.2
9 to 11	28.3

5. Unemployment versus retraining. Of the eight million unemployed, the U.S. Department of Labor estimates that 75 percent lack the skills necessary to be retrained for high-tech jobs.[4]

Crime

This section refers only to the effects of illiteracy upon the crime rate. Chapter 6 explains the causes of illiteracy, many of which are also causes of crime. The inability to read well enough to hold a job providing an adequate income is also a cause of crime.

6. Percentage of functionally illiterate juvenile delinquents. Among juveniles appearing before the court, 85 percent are functionally illiterate.[5]

7. Percentage of nonreading first-time offenders. Florida Judge Charles Phillips stated in 1982, "Eighty percent of the new criminals who pass my desk would not be here if they had graduated from high school and could read and write."

8. Nonreading prison inmates. Up to 80 percent of prison inmates are nonreaders.[6]

The Human-SufferingCosts of Illiteracy

9. Education level among prison inmates. From the 1970 census of prisoners more than twenty-five years of age, 75 percent are not high school graduates. This compares to 38 percent of the total adult population that had not graduated from high school, and 35-42 percent of adults who had not completed ninth grade.[7]

Standard of Living

10. Income level versus education level. "In 1996 (the most recent year for which statistics are readily available) the average college graduate earned $36,980 a year," the average high school graduate earned $31,500, and the average high-school dropout earned $14,013.

Fifty percent of the heads-of-households who are officially below the poverty line read at less than an eighth-grade level.[8]

11. Functional illiterates on welfare. More than one-third of the mothers on welfare are functionally illiterate.[9]

An often unrecognized cause of homelessness: unemployment due to inability to read.

12. Education level versus percentage of families on welfare. There are twice as many on welfare with less than a sixth-grade education than there are with six to eight years of schooling. There are almost four times as many on welfare who have less than a sixth-grade education than there are who have completed nine to eleven years of school.[10]

Consumer Rights

13. Victimization of nonreaders by their landlords. Even the most basic needs are more uncertain for nonreaders and poor readers. An apartment to live in and fuel to keep it warm in winter are uncertain if the one signing the lease or receiving past due bill notices can't read. If a landlord knows the tenant can't read, he can, for example, tell the tenant that the lease allows his eviction if the baby cries and disturbs the neighbors. This could be done despite the landlord's real reason for wanting the tenant evicted. The tenant, fearing exposure as illiterate, will not risk challenging the landlord in an attempt to stand up for consumer rights he isn't sure he has. Even the loss of a place to live in winter is not as dreaded as the loss of dignity and self-respect.

14. Lack of understanding of insurance coverage. Insurance policies cannot be used for insuring against losses, the way they should be, for illiterate policyholders. This is true if the policyholders do not remember (or more likely were not told) all the details of the insurance coverage and cannot read the policy for themselves.

15. Lack of checking account equals loss of interest payments. Those who cannot read and write seldom keep their money in checking or savings accounts. Therefore they do not have the advantage of drawing any interest on the money they use for the daily necessities of life.[11]

Citizens' Rights

16. Democracy is denied to nonvoters and uninformed voters. One of a citizen's most basic rights is the right to vote. Most illiterates either do not vote or cast uninformed votes. Their knowledge of candidates is usually limited to paid political radio and television announcements and to events newsworthy enough to deserve air time. They usually have no other way of learning the facts about a candidate on issues that are most likely to affect them. They can't vote on issues that are in their best interests. Democracy, for them, is an unreachable ideal.

17. Loss of citizens' rights through lack of knowledge of them. Illiterates often do not know and exercise their rights as citizens. They can't read notices they receive from the Internal Revenue Service or from the welfare office. They must learn of their rights, deadlines they face, and things they must do by word of mouth or from the radio or television. They seldom know all their options. They must depend on people they often have reason to distrust to keep them informed. The rights that are written somewhere as theirs are just a hollow mockery if they don't know about them.

Education

18. Denial of the right to an education. A common present-day expectation of almost every U.S. citizen is that they will receive an education in public schools. This, more than any other "right," is of great importance to illiterates It is understandable that school officials, after reviewing the records, would decide that certain students are wasting a teacher's time and the school's budget for school materials. Believing that these students are not worthy of a teacher's time and that they are taking up space that more deserving students could use can be devastating to a teenager's self-respect. Such students drop out of school instead of insisting upon their right to an education. It is easier for all concerned to believe that the student has failed than that the educational system didn't do what it should for the student. In addition, parents, whether they can read or not, often are embarrassed and frustrated over their child(ren)'s having difficulty in school.

19. Children of the functionally illiterate lose educational rights. Children do not receive all the benefits that are due them from the school system if their parents can't read. Illiterate parents do not read letters from their children's teachers. Illiterate parents cannot study materials designed to help their children prepare for college, nor can they help their children with homework. They can't show their children the importance of an education by going to the classroom or by meeting the teacher. They fear they will embarrass themselves or their children with their inability to read or understand basic school subjects.

20. Embarrassment over the inability to read to children who request it. Illiterates must often suffer the embarrassment of having young children know their parent(s) can't read. For example, parents may try to help their first grader with their schoolwork by buying children's storybooks. When the children insist that their mother read the book, she may try to "fake it" by making up a story from the pictures. It then hurts to be told, "Mommy, that's not right." Even young children often know their parents can't read.[12]

21. **The cost of truancy**. Truancy is now such a serious problem that ordinances have been enacted allowing police in many U.S. cities to impose a $500 fine or thirty days in jail for the parents and suspension of drivers licenses of the students. Truancy costs include the cost of imposing curfews in many cities and, for example, the cost of over-

time pay for police in New Orleans. Enforcement of truancy laws in San Jose, California, increased police payroll costs by $1 million. Most truancy occurs because the truants have failed to learn to read. Better education significantly reduces both truancy and other forms of juvenile delinquency. When the students are better able to instruct and entertain themselves with reading they do not require such vast costs for social programs designed to keep them out of trouble.[13]

Basic Lifestyle Choices

22. Restaurant roulette: stick to basics or eat detested food. Illiterates can't always order what they want when they go to a restaurant. They may have to choose by pointing to something on the menu. If there are no pictures, they may not know what they have ordered until it arrives—and it may be something they do not like. They can't tell from a menu in the window what the price of items will be before they go inside. They must either order something basic they are sure the restaurant will have or depend upon the person they are with to order for them. Their choice is another hamburger and cola or something ordered for them that they hate.

23. Supermarket roulette: what is in this can? Illiterates are denied the choice of less expensive generic or unadvertised brands of food when grocery shopping. They have to buy products based on pictures on the package or buy labels they recognize from TV commercials. Even many nationally advertised brands are beyond their purchase. For example, how could they buy Campbell's soup and get what they want when every can looks the same? Most illiterates so dread prejudice—a dread that is all too often justified—that they will not ask for help in the supermarket. They therefore waste money on household items they can't use or on foods they detest. A typical example involves the welfare mother who buys a large can of Crisco thinking she is getting the chicken shown on the label. When she gets home, she finds she has a year's supply of Crisco. There is no money left to go back and buy something to cook in it for her hungry family.

24. Expense, time, and stress of traveling to pay bills. Illiterates cannot manage checking accounts, so they seldom pay bills by mail. This means they must spend several hours each month in time-consuming and often expensive travel, an added cost for every payment they make.

25. The dangers of travel. Travel is often difficult for illiterates. They endure risks that most of us could never imagine. Although they may learn to decipher many traffic signs and symbols, street signs they have never seen before are a complete mystery to them. Bus stop and subway station names are equally meaningless. Imagine your frustration at being lost in a foreign country with a language you know nothing about. A similar frustration or fear usually keeps most illiterates close to home.

26. Lack of choice of TV programs. Illiterates do not even have the luxury of deciding in advance what TV shows they will watch. They stick with weekly programs they know come on at a certain time. Alternatively, they find what they can by flipping through the channels, frequently missing programs that would be of more interest to them.

27. Inability to follow food preparation instructions. Illiterates can't follow the food preparation instructions on the items they purchase. They may want to avoid the monotony of always having the same food or the criticism of being a lazy, unimaginative cook. There is a danger, however, in purchasing some new food item or in trying a new recipe by following a friend's oral instructions. They run a high risk of wasting food for which replacement would be difficult or impossible because of limited finances. Even government food handouts become a mockery. If the recipients cannot read instructions, they cannot make a tasty meal from the surplus cheese, noodles, and powdered milk, for example.

28. The dilemma of having to trust someone who is untrustworthy. There is an obvious outcome of the examples in this chapter. Illiterates do not have even the most basic lifestyle choices that the rest of us have. They must rely upon others to choose for them. Because of their disability, illiterates can cite many times when wrong choices were made for them or times when they were cheated. They find themselves in the dilemma of having to trust people that they are not sure can be trusted. They are often paralyzed by not knowing the right word for the right thing at the right time. It is often a terrifying feeling.

Dangers and Health Risks

29. Medicine bottle precautions. Illiterates can't read precautions on a medicine bottle. The expiration date for safe usage, possible allergic reactions, sedative effects, who should not take it, and dosages thus may be a mystery to them.

30. Inability to read health pamphlets. Illiterates can't read health pamphlets and bulletins, and thus often do not know about the preventive health measures they describe. They often do not know, for example, the seven warning signs of cancer.

31. Inability to read product warnings. Illiterates can't read, for example, the warning sign on a pack of cigarettes. They may know that smoking is bad for them, but they can't read the details that would give them the determination to quit.

32. Unintended surgery through lack of understanding. Illiterates can't read waivers that they must sign before undergoing surgery, so they don't know their rights. They often do not understand the medical jargon and fear the unfamiliar atmosphere found in hospitals. They sometimes find, too late, that they've agreed to something that in the confusion was not adequately explained to them. Some women, for example, have found that by undergoing an unintended hysterectomy, they have forever been denied the basic privilege of motherhood.

33. Workplace injuries. Working with toxic chemicals can be a frightening job for anyone. It is especially so for someone who can't read package labels or the warning signs on the walls. The same is true regarding warning signs about machinery and other dangers. U.S. workers are more likely to be killed on the job than workers in other major industrialized countries (for example, thirty-six times more likely than in Sweden). One out of eleven U.S. workers will be killed or seriously injured at work.

34. Inability to use telephone directories. This example involves a simple task we often take for granted: looking up telephone numbers in the telephone book. Although some can find the name of a friend, far fewer have

An often unrecognized cause of accidents: inability to read warning signs.

the sorting skills to use the yellow pages. Even the emergency numbers on the first page are beyond recognition for many of them. Even if illiterates can remember an emergency number they can call, they may still be in trouble. If they are away from home, the inability to read street signs may keep them from explaining their location well enough to get timely help, for example, for a child who is choking.[14]

35. Death Rate of Children Tied to Mother's Education. A 1999 study by the World Bank showed that the average death rate for children under five years old whose mothers had no education was 144 per 1000 live births. This dropped to 106 per 1000 for mothers with a primary education only and to 68 per 1000 when the mothers had some secondary education also. When the infant's caregiver cannot read the directions on baby formula or medications, a wrong guess can lead to injury or death of the child. We have a moral obligation to prevent such tragedies, and making the directions on baby formula and medications easier to read by simplifying the spelling is an obvious first step. Those who protest that it would be too costly should be reminded that this improvement to our educational system would pay for itself by increased national productivity and by avoidance of all the problems associated with illiteracy.[15]

Let's End Our Literacy Crisis

Figure 6-1
A Dreadful Language?

I take it you already know
of tough and bough and cough and dough.
Others may stumble, but not you,
on hiccough, thorough, lough and through.
Well done! And now you wish perhaps,
to learn of less familiar traps?

Beware of heard, a dreadful word
that looks like beard and sounds like bird,
and dead: it's said like bed, not bead
for goodness' sake don't call it "deed"!
Watch out for meat and great and threat
(they rhyme with suite and straight and debt.)

A moth is not a moth in mother
nor both in bother, broth in brother,
and here is not a match for there
nor dear and fear for bear and pear,
and then there's dose and rose and lose
just look them up and goose and choose,
and cork and work and card and ward,
and font and front and word and sword,
and do and go and thwart and cart.

Come, come, I've hardly made a start!
A dreadful language? Man alive.
I'd mastered it when I was five.

T. S. Watt[1]

Notes:

First, this note is for those who do not promptly see the above poem as "tongue-in-check." T. S. Watt is gently poking fun at the perversity of English spelling hoping that we will briefly be "taken in" by his last verse. The humor comes from feeling foolish for briefly believing that he is serious. If Watt had an inborn talent for learning languages and was given the opportunity, he may have mastered *spoken* English by age five. Unless he was also a near-genius with a photographic memory who spent a year or two before age five reading English writings of all types, the spelling was not mastered by that age.

Second, as a mirror image of the first note, chapter 6 is included for those who do not see the proposals in this book as both serious and necessary. The perversity of English spelling is the logical, foundational cause of most English reading and spelling problems. This perversity of spelling is the driving force that demands correction of the problem.

Chapter 6
The Causes of Illiteracy

There are obviously many reasons why a particular nonreader cannot read English. Arranged in no particular order, some of these reasons may be:
- the nonreader or his parents or friends place little importance on learning to read;
- the nonreader is far more involved in numerous activities than in spending the time needed to learn to read, as explained more fully below;
- the nonreader goes to school hungry, frightened (over gang violence or classmates who bring weapons to school, for example), worried over problems at home or with schoolwork, or embarrassed (about failing to read aloud properly in class or about his old, ragged clothing, for example);
- the nonreader has poor eyesight, poor hearing, or learning problems;
- the nonreader doesn't like the teacher, or the teacher is not effective at teaching; or
- the teaching methods or textbooks used are not effective in teaching students to read.

In today's world, besides all the school and societal problems which hinder learning, there are *many* fun but time-consuming activities interfering with learning, which did not exist in simpler times—before the twentieth century. Some of these pleasurable activities include movies, television, musical concerts or recordings, video movies and games, newly developed sports, profitable full- and part-time jobs, and gang and other youth activities.

Like the items in Pandora's box, once these time-consuming or distracting activities have been loosed upon society, they cannot be taken back. It will be extremely difficult to get students to spend the long hours learning to read that were spent in more simple times. This is especially true if—due to teaching methods inferior to the memorization and dull drill used in prior centuries—the student is having difficulty learning. In this case, it will be very difficult, perhaps impossible, to persuade the student to spend time on an unpleasant and difficult activity rather than a multitude of readily available *pleasant* activities.

One or more of these reasons will apply to almost every student. There is only one hindrance to learning that affects every student: the spelling of words. This is also true in other languages, but only in English is the spelling such a hindrance to learning. If students of other languages encounter problems that various experts are blaming for U.S. illiteracy, it may slow their learning. They will still learn much faster than U.S. students because they do not have the added burden of overcoming the inconsistencies, lack of logic, and undependable sound-to-symbol and symbol-to-sound correspondences that are a part of English spelling. Note that symbol-to-sound and sound-to-symbol correspondences are mirror images in languages other than English, as will be explained in this chapter.

The Foundational Cause of English Illiteracy

Our confusing spelling system is the foundational or root cause of illiteracy. Whatever corrections are made to the educational system—even if it could be made perfect—there will still be students who cannot become proficient readers without extensive tutoring unless spelling is made logical and consistent. Most of us learned to read as young children and have forgotten any difficulties we had—we gloss over a multitude of traps for new learners.

Why Our Children Can't Read by Dr. Diane McGuinness gives a thorough, scientific explanation of the logic behind written languages. It explains the extreme difficulty of learning the English spelling system because of its adoption of so many words (and their spellings) from six other languages. Although the ideal spelling system uses symbols for *syllables*, this is completely unworkable with English. With its many consonant clusters, there are tens of thousands of different syllables. Few people can effectively use more than 2,000 language symbols. English must therefore use symbols for every sound, and students must be able to recognize and separate these sounds to learn to read.

Why Learning to Read English Is So Difficult

If a language does not hold strictly to a one-sound/one-symbol (phoneme/grapheme) correspondence, numerous problems occur. For example, a student may see a letter or letter combination when trying to read a word and—if the letter or letter combination represents more than one phoneme—not be able to recognize (read) the word, unless the word can be recognized by the context. The mirror image of this is that students may want to write a word they hear the teacher pronounce. If there is more than one letter or letter combination to represent a phoneme in the word, they do not know which to use, unless they have learned which is "correct." If there is not a strict phoneme/grapheme correspondence in a spelling system, there is no guarantee that if a certain grapheme represents a certain phoneme in a word (when reading), this phoneme will be represented (spelled) by this grapheme in a different word. In other words, there are far more ways of spelling a sound in English than there are ways to pronounce a letter or letter combination used in English. Even though there are 294 graphemes (single letters or two-, three-, four-, or five-letter combinations to represent a sound) in English, the worst of these has ten different pronunciations. Even though there are only 38 sounds to be spelled, the worst of these can be spelled in at least sixty different ways. This will be explained more fully later.

The number of phonemes in a language or dialect ranges from eleven in Rotokas (Indo-Pacific) and Mura (Chibchan) to 141 in !Xu (Khoisan). In a study of 317 languages, the number of vowel phonemes ranged from three to forty-six (a mean of 8.7); the number of consonant phonemes ranged from six to ninety-five[2] (a mean of 22.8). The number of phonemes in English varies depending upon which phonemes are considered both unique and essential. Some linguists may include as many as forty-five in their listing. This book demonstrates that only thirty-eight phonemes are needed for efficient communication. The average number of phonemes for the known languages of the world is about forty-five.

Appendix 3 gives a brief history of how the spelling of our English words evolved. An important part of the history is omitted. Prior to the mid-1700s, English people spelled words as they sounded. However, no one had settled upon a standard way of spelling the sounds. The common people, and even such authors as Shakespeare, might spell a word two different ways in the same paragraph. It was an awkward but easily readable system. But publishers wanted to standardize the spelling as a way to improve the quality of published work and to simplify the task of typesetters. Dr. Samuel Johnson—who, according to Dr. Thomas Lounsbury, in his book *English Spelling and Spelling Reform*, knew little about the pronunciation of words as related to their spelling and even less about the derivation of words—was a scholar chosen by the publishers to standardize the spelling. His dictionary was published in 1755. Although it was not the only dictionary at the time, it was well received by Johnson's peers, who also knew little about the relation of pronunciation to spelling. It was also accepted by the publishers—it met their need for standardization. It came to be accepted by later dictionary publishers as the authoritative work on the subject of the correct spelling of words—based not so much upon its technical merit as upon its acceptance by his peers and the publishers. But instead of standardizing the spelling of the sounds, as in other languages and as logic demands, he froze the spelling of the words; he listed a specific order of letters to represent each word. In many—if not most—cases, the letter order chosen was that used in the language of origin.

So the spelling Dr. Johnson devised was difficult to learn from the start. As you know, the pronunciation of words changes with time. So what was bad in the mid-1700s is much worse now. The grapheme-to-phoneme correspondence is now quite undependable

The rest of this chapter is, in effect, attacking our spelling. There may be an unconscious urge to become defensive when someone attacks our mother tongue, but here is the most important point to remember: you or I did not invent our ridiculous spelling, so we should not feel the need to defend it. Instead of being defensive, relax and enjoy the following. Our spelling is fully deserving of all the scorn.

Sounds per Symbol: Effect upon Reading

There are twenty-six letters in the English alphabet. Three letters—C, Q, and X—represent phonemes more often represented by other letters. Since we need symbols for thirty-eight phonemes and have only twenty-three letters representing unique phonemes, we need fifteen more graphemes. Ideally, (to avoid a cost of billions of dollars to replace hardware and software with twenty-six letters) we would use fifteen two-letter graphemes. English uses at least (since the data in this chapter only includes words found in a standard desk dictionary):

26	single letters
153	2-letter graphemes (71 vowels, 82 consonants)
98	3-letter graphemes (81 vowels, 17 consonants)
14	4-letter graphemes (11 vowels, 3 consonants)
3	5-letter graphemes (all vowels)
294	total graphemes

A few of these 294 graphemes represent only one phoneme. The worst, the *I* grapheme, represents nine different phonemes (seven vowels and two consonants), as well as being silent in some words. If all the pronunciations of the 294 graphemes are totaled, there are at least 653 of them. This is less than the 736 listed in the symbols-per-sound (spelling) tables (tables 6-2 and 6-3). Tables 6-2 and 6-3 include words made of combinations obvious to any reader familiar with English grammar and have therefore been omitted in this section concerned with reading. One example is combining the ED in past tense with vowels at the end of a word. The fact that this is a combination of ED following a vowel would not be immediately obvious verbally—instead, the entire word would be recognized in its context.

There are 621 example words in the appendix 1 tables plus the twenty-six single letters that are silent in some words. There are many silent vowels, most notably the *E* at the end of words. The second vowel is silent in most long vowel sounds (as in Mae Green tried roe glue) spelled with two vowels. An example of at least one word with a silent letter for each of the twenty-six letters (most letters have many others) is as follows: reAd, deBt, sCent, velDt, havE, halFpenny, siGn, rHyme, busIness, riJsttafel, Knot, taLk, Mnemonic, autumN, sophO-more, rasPberry, lacQuer, suRprise, aiSle, depoT, bUilt, savVy, Write, fauX pas, maYor, and rendeZvous. This gives a total of 647. The last six of the 653 mentioned earlier are the consonant sounds of *E, I, O,* and *U*: *I* sound like /j/ in *soldier, O* and *U* sound like /w/ in *choir* and *persuade, E* and *I* sound like /y/ in *azalea* and *opinion,* and *U* sounds like /f/ in one pronunciation of *lieutenant.*

Note that in table A1-3 all but two (*IU* and *UU*) of the twenty-five possible vowel digraph combinations (five beginning with and followed by a vowels) can be found in a standard desk dictionary with a single vowel sound. Most of these digraphs also have two sounds in some words.

Comparing English to Chinese Picture Writing

People often think that learning to read Chinese picture writing would be very difficult. They may say, "Maybe English is bad, but we only [!] need to learn 294 graphemes and 653 ways of using them. In Chinese, you have to learn thousands! You have to learn a different grapheme for every word!" In actuality, knowledge of only about 2,000 characters is required for basic literacy in modern Chinese.[3] Only a little more than half of Chinese words have more than one syllable. Only two types of sequences are used for most Chinese syllables, CV (consonant-vowel) and CVC (consonant-vowel-consonant). Most of the CVC syllables end in one of two sounds, /n/ or /ng/. There are very few consonant clusters in Chinese, and there are a grand total of about 1,280 "tonal" syllables. The meaning of a word can change with the tone or pitch of the syllable in tonal languages. As a result, Chinese has a very large number of homonyms—words with different meanings but with the same sound. This necessitates the use of about 200 "classifiers." A syllable sign and a classifier sign are therefore written together as compound signs for 90 percent of Chinese words.[4]

To Read English: Only Learn 294 Graphemes?

In addition to learning the 294 graphemes, you also must know which one of the phonemes each grapheme ***represents in each word.***

Although English is considered an alphabetic language, it is not that different from Chinese picture writing since it uses a specific group of letters in a specific order as a symbol for an entire word. The letter order for each word is unchanging (frozen), but the phonemes in many words have changed because the pronunciation of words changes with time. It is therefore necessary to memorize (or learn by repeated use) each grapheme *in each word*, *in proper order*! Unlike Chinese picture writing, learned by memory alone, the human mind recognizes similar graphemes in similar words and assumes the pronunciation is similar, but it often isn't. English spelling thus interferes with our logic and reasoning in learning to read because of its inconsistencies.

Tables 6-1 and A1-2 to A1-6 (appendix 1) show why reading English is so difficult. Appendix 1 tables show example words for table 6-1.

Summary of Table 6-1 and Tables A1-2 through A1-6 (in Appendix 1)

There is an average of at least*

Single Letters	Blends
4.0 pronunciations per consonant	1.4 pronunciations per consonant
9.2 pronunciations per vowel	2.2 pronunciations per vowel
5.0 pronunciations per letter	1.9 pronunciations per blend

Single Letters and Blends
294 total graphemes (see table, start of this section)
(26 single letters and 268 blends** to be learned***)
with a total average of 2.2 pronunciations each
(includes 26 silent letters and six vowels with consonant
sounds shown after the table at the start of the section)

* It is "at least" because capitalized words and many of the less-common pronunciations are not included in the tables. Some readers may feel that the tables contain some rare words and too many variations of pronunciations to strengthen the case against English spelling. The words you may consider rare have, in truth, been used by large numbers of people for many years (for example, studdingsail has been familiar to sailors for many years). Although many of the pronunciations may be unfamiliar to you, they are common enough to be included in dictionaries such as *The Shorter Oxford English Dictionary* and *Webster's New Collegiate Dictionary*. Three or four of the words in the tables may only be familiar to the relatively substantial number of linguists, lexicograhpers, and scrabble or other word game enthusiasts. Many more pronunciation variations could have been included, but in nearly all cases only those common enough to be included in standard desk dictionaries are included. Also, some may object that many of the variations in spelling are merely different combinations using silent letters. Organizing the silent letters as part of a specific grapheme, however, causes far fewer difficulties than considering the thousands of uses of silent letters in an unorganized individual manner. Also remember that there are *many* words with the same type of spelling as the example words in the tables. Writers must know every spelling variation in Tables 6-2 and 6-3 ***and its application to each individual word*** in order to correctly spell every word they want to write.

** The two-, three-, and four-letter blend totals include words ending in E or UE supposedly to change the pronunciation of the final vowel. These are listed in table A1-4.

*** It is possible to learn meanings of words without learning how to pronounce them correctly. Most non-English-speaking readers and most avid readers do this at least occasionally.

The Causes of Illiteracy

Table 6-1
The Number of Phonemes That Each of the 294 Graphemes Used in English Represents

Note: Only 38 graphemes are needed and each grapheme need only represent one phoneme! There are 647 phonemes listed below. Appendix 1 lists example words of 621 of them, and the text of this section lists examples of each of the 26 letters that are silent in a word.
The lowercase x represents one or more undesignated letters.

I	10	TH	4	EHEA	2	AT	1	IG	1	OUI	1
A	9	UxE	4	EIxE	2	AUGH	1	IGH	1	OUP	1
E	9	UA	4	EIG	2	AUT	1	II	1	OUS	1
O	9	UI	4	EIGH	2	AUX	1	IOU	1	OUSE	1
U	9	W	4	ET	2	AWE	1	ISxE	1	OUT	1
AxE	8	AxUE	3	EZ	2	AYO	1	JJ	1	OUX	1
X	8	AIxE	3	HA	2	BB	1	JU	1	OWxE	1
AU	7	AL	3	HEI	2	BD	1	KH	1	OYxE	1
C	7	AO	3	HOU	2	BH	1	KK	1	PB	1
EA	7	EAU	3	HY	2	BT	1	KN	1	PN	1
EI	7	EH	3	IAxE	2	CC	1	LC	1	PP	1
OU	7	EW	3	IC	2	CCH	1	LD	1	PPH	1
AH	6	EWE	3	IEU	2	CHM	1	LF	1	PS	1
ExE	6	EYE	3	IO	2	CHS	1	LH	1	PSH	1
EO	6	F	3	IT	2	CHT	1	LK	1	PT	1
IE	6	GG	3	K	2	CHTH	1	LM	1	QU	1
OUGH	6	GHT	3	LL	2	CK	1	LN	1	QUE	1
S	6	H	3	MN	2	CO	1	LO	1	RECA	1
Y	6	HE	3	ND	2	CT	1	LV	1	RH	1
Z	6	HI	3	OH	2	CZ	1	MB	1	RPS	1
AE	5	HO	3	OOH	2	DG	1	MH	1	RR	1
AI	5	HU	3	OUL	2	DI	1	MM	1	RT	1
AUxE	5	IA	3	OWA	2	DJ	1	MP	1	SL	1
AY	5	IS	3	OWE	2	DT	1	NG	1	ST	1
G	5	M	3	OY	2	ExUE	1	NGH	1	STR	1
GH	5	OA	3	P	2	EAxUE	1	NH	1	SW	1
J	5	OI	3	PHTH	2	EExE	1	NHW	1	TB	1
OxE	5	OIxE	3	R	2	EEW	1	NN	1	TCH	1
OE	5	PH	3	RS	2	EIGE	1	NT	1	TRE	1
OW	5	SH	3	SCH	2	EIGHE	1	O'E	1	TSW	1
T	5	SI	3	SSI	2	EIP	1	OAxE	1	TT	1
UE	5	TI	3	STH	2	EOU	1	OAT	1	TW	1
CH	4	UIxE	3	TS	2	ER	1	OEU	1	UAY	1
D	4	UO	3	TZ	2	ES	1	OG	1	UET	1
EAxE	4	WO	3	UxUE	2	ESxE	1	OGxE	1	UEU	1
EE	4	A'A	2	UH	2	EUxE	1	OIGxE	1	UEY	1
EU	4	AA	2	UY	2	EYxE	1	OIG	1	UOxE	1
EY	4	ACH	2	V	2	EYO	1	OIS	1	UOI	1
IxE	4	AG	2	WH	2	FF	1	OL	1	UOIxE	1
IxUE	4	AGH	2	YxE	2	FT	1	OOxE	1	UOY	1
IExE	4	AOU	2	AxU	1	GL	1	OR	1	VV	1
L	4	AW	2	AGxE	1	GM	1	OS	1	WxO	1
N	4	AYE	2	AIG	1	GN	1	OT	1	WxOxE	1
OxUE	4	B	2	AIGH	1	HAU	1	OU	1	WAI	1
OO	4	DD	2	AIOU	1	HEU	1	OUB	1	WR	1
OUxE	4	DH	2	ALF	1	HIxE	1	OUC	1	YE	1
Q	4	E'E	2	ANC	1	HL	1	OUE	1	ZH	1
SC	4	ED	2	AOH	1	HYxE	1	OUGHA	1	ZV	1
SS	4	EG	2	AS	1	IER	1	OUGHE	1	ZZ	1

79

Symbols per Sound: Effect upon Spelling

As normally used in English-speaking countries, the word *spelling* refers to the specific, unvarying sequence of letters used to represent a word. In other languages, spelling is simply the matching of phonemes and graphemes.

If you think learning to read English is difficult consider *spelling* English words! Two phonemes (/h/ as in *hat* and /th/ as in *then*) have only (!) four spellings, but most of them have *many*. The /u/ as in *nut* is spelled at least sixty different ways!

Roughly 20 percent of English words are spelled phonemically—if you use *one* consistent (the most common) spelling of each phoneme in the 10,161 most common words. This is based upon Dewey's study as reported in his book *Relativ Frequency of English Speech Sounds*. Claims that English is more than 20 percent phonemic are true only if more than one spelling of some of the phonemes is allowed. The problem is that you must memorize (or learn by repeated use) which words are phonemic, the same as you must learn the spelling of unphonemic words. There is no dependable way of knowing which word is spelled phonemically and which isn't. Also, hundreds of words have alternate pronunciations and alternate spellings. The alternate spellings have no necessary relationship to the pronunciation either. To be intellectually honest with themselves, anyone objecting to spelling reform by defending the frozen spelling we now use would also have to defend a far more extensive reason for confusion in word meaning as related to spelling: using the same spelling for thousands of words with the same sound and spelling that have more than one meaning!

How Can Anyone Defend English Spelling?

English spelling is so inconsistent, illogical, and confusing that it should not be defended. Most of the time people do not defend it. Much of what is considered a defense of English spelling is, in truth, a counterattack against the ideas that attack it. Or we assume it can't (or won't) be changed. Since most of us do not want to be bothered with too much change in our lives, we simply dismiss it from our minds.

The Causes of Illiteracy

Also, if we learned it as a child, we assume other people can, too. So we give it little thought other than when we have to look up a spelling in a dictionary. Speakers of most other languages do not have to use a dictionary to find spellings.

If you couldn't read, and if you discovered these facts about our spelling, you probably would be upset to say the least. You would be upset to find that you had needlessly blamed yourself for your present state, as most illiterates do. Are you upset to find that roughly 92 million people—almost one-half of the adult population of the U.S.—are affected? You probably are if you have given thoughtful attention to chapters 4 and 5.

The next two pages dramatically show why spelling English words is even more difficult than learning to read.* Table 6-2 lists 433 spellings of the fourteen vowel phonemes. Table 6-3 lists 303 spellings of twenty-four consonant phonemes. This gives a total of 736 spellings of the thirty-eight phonemes. The number beside the letters at the head of each column is the number of different spellings in the column.

Summary, Tables 6-2 and 6-3

*There is an average of at least***

12.6 ways of spelling each consonant phoneme,
30.9 ways of spelling each vowel phoneme, and
19.4 ways of spelling each phoneme.

The extremes are:

(vowel) 60 ways of spelling the *U* phoneme, as in *nut*,
(consonant) 26 ways of spelling the *S* phoneme, as in *sun*,
(vowel digraph) 42 ways of spelling *AE* phonemes, as in *Mae*,
(consonant digraph) 22 ways of spelling *SH* phonemes, as in *ash*.

---

* This is especially true since a person can recognize (read) a word without being able to remember its spelling later.

** See the * note in the "Summary of Tables 6-1..." above.

Let's End Our Literacy Crisis

Table 6-2: Spelling of the Vowel Sounds ** 1 of 2

A-23	47 conscIEncE	O-33	142 mullEIn	190 hurrAH
1 mAt	48 lIEUtenant	95 wAs	143 lunchEOn	191 tALk
2 bAA	49 fOEtid	96 bazAAr	144 gorgEOUs	192 extrAOrdinary
3 mA'Am	50 connOIsseur	97 mA'Am	145 connoissEUr	**193 hAUl**
4 hAvE	51 bUry	98 ArE	146 gingHAm	194 becAUsE
5 lApsE	52 gUEst	99 bArqUE	147 **HErb**	195 cAUGHt
6 harAngUE	53 gUEssEd	100 yACHt	148 veHIcle	196 sAW
7 drACHm	I-41	101 serAGlio	149 **HUmble**	197 **AWE**
8 **AErial**	54 imAging	102 shAH	150 fIrst	198 exHAUst
9 diaphrAGm	55 imAgE	103 cAlm	151 engInE	199 HOrs d'oeuvre
10 dAHlia	56 cAEsura	104 pharAOnic	152 IrOn *	200 sOft
11 plAId	57 shillelAGH	105 faux pAS	153 specIAL	201 gOnE
12 sALmon	58 shillelAH	106 eclAT	154 collegIAtE	202 tOrqUE
13 AUnt	59 mountAIn	107 nAUtical	155 allegIAncE	203 brOAd
14 lAUghEd	60 captAInEd	108 becAUsE	156 mischIEvous	204 memOIr *
15 prAYer	61 yesterdAY	109 sErgeant	157 patIEncE	205 turquOIsE
16 thErE	62 prEtty	110 hEArt	158 fashIOn	206 sOLder
17 bEAr	63 collEgE	111 burEAUctacy	159 conscIOUs	207 cOUgh
18 thEIr	64 hEAr	112 HAbitant	160 peopLE *	208 fOUGHt
19 chERt	65 bEEn	113 HOnor	161 criticisM *	209 tOWArd
20 lIngerie	66 forEHEAd	114 lIngerie	162 sOn	210 sqUAll
21 merIngUE	67 forfEIt	**115 hOp**	163 sOmE *	211 sWOrd
22 gUArantee	68 forEIGn	116 gOnE	164 OnE *	OI-12
23 gUImpE	69 pigEOn	117 cOnnEd	165 tOngUE	212 lAWyer
E-30	70 billET doux	118 catalOgUE	166 cupbOArd	**213 OIl**
24 Any	71 monEY	119 demijOHn	167 dOEs	214 nOIsE
25 AtE	72 rendEZvous	120 memOIr *	168 avOIrdupois	215 pOIGnant
26 **AErial**	73 exHIbit	121 repertOIrE *	169 porpOIsE	216 cOIGnE
27 sAId	74 rHYthm	122 patOIS *	170 cOLOnel *	217 bOY
28 sAYs	**75 bId**	123 lOUgh	171 blOOd	218 gargOYlE
29 bEd	76 gIvE	124 cOUghEd	172 rOUgh	219 emplOYEd
30 allEgE	77 bIsqUE	125 nOUGHt	173 tOUchEd	220 qUOIn
31 lEdgE	78 marrIAges	126 knOWledge	174 thorOUGHly	221 turqUOIsE
32 chEqUE	79 marrIAgE	127 gUArd	175 cOULd	222 bUOY
33 hEAd	80 vICtuals	128 About	176 pillOWcase	223 bUOYEd
34 clEAnsE	81 carrIEd	129 nuisAncE	**177 bUd**	OO-13
35 dEBt	82 sIEvE	130 shillelAGH	178 pleasUrE	224 plEUrisy
36 kEElson	83 chassIS	131 verandAH	179 jUdgE	225 silHOUette
37 phlEGm	84 petIT	132 captAIn	180 brUsqUE	226 wOlf
38 EH	85 wOmen	133 captAInEd	181 piqUAnt	**227 gOOd**
39 thEIr	86 chamOIS	134 blANC mange	182 lacqUEr	228 pOOH
40 forEHEAd	87 misTREss	135 restAUrant	183 liqUEUr	229 wORsted
41 lEOpard	88 bUsy	136 becAUsE	184 bUHr	230 bOUIllon
42 bellES lettres	89 minUtE	137 hEr	185 liqUOr	231 caoutchOUC
43 rendEZvous	90 plagUEY	138 wErE	186 boatsWAIn	232 cOULd
44 rHEtoric	91 bUIlt	139 ocEAn	187 martYr	233 pUll
45 vanIlla	92 plagUY	140 hEArsE	AU-24	234 sUrE
46 frIEnd	93 mYth	141 burEAUcrat	189 fAlsE	235 brUsqUE
*, ** See table 6-3	94 apocalYpsE		188 bAll	236 tissUE

Table 6-2: Spelling of the Vowel Sounds ** 2 of 2

OU-13			
237 cAOUchouc	286 EYrE	335 kInd	384 sOUl
238 sauerkrAUt	287 convEYEd	336 fInE	385 cOUrsE
239 glAOUr	288 EYOt	337 shIItake	386 thOUGH
240 HOUr	289 HEIr	338 IrOn *	387 knOW
241 IOUd	290 lingerIE	339 oblIqUE	388 tOWArd
242 hOUsE	291 bouqUET	340 dIAmond	389 OWE
243 renOUncE	**EE-30**	341 indICt	390 qUAhog
244 dOUBt	292 AEon	342 pIE	391 qUOth
245 bOUGH	293 mE	343 sIGn	392 qUOtE
246 plOUGHEd	294 thEsE	344 sIGnEd	393 sWOrd
247 nOW	295 E'En	345 hIGH	**UE-40**
248 brOWsE	296 EAsy	346 sIGHEd	394 cAOUtchouc
249 allOWEd	297 lEAve	347 ISland	395 lEEward
AE-42	298 lEAgUE	348 IIsIE	396 manEUver
250 fAding	299 bEEp	349 chOIr *	397 dEUcE
251 fAdE	300 chEEsE	350 cOYote	398 crEW
252 plAgUing	301 vEHicle	351 gUIding	399 brEWEd
253 plAgUE	302 EIther	352 gUIdE	400 rHEUmatic
254 mAElstrom	303 recEIvE	353 bUY	401 rHUbarb
255 champAGnE	304 recEIPt	354 gUYEd	402 lIEU
256 dAHlia	305 pEOple	355 bY	403 jIUjitsu
257 mAIn	306 demEsnE	356 tYpE	404 dO
258 rAIsE	307 kEY	357 dYE	405 mOvE
259 arrAIGn	308 kEYEd	**OE-36**	406 shOE
260 strAIGHt	309 diarrHEa	358 pharAOH	407 manOEUvre
261 hALFpenny	310 skI	359 chAUffeur	408 tOO
262 gAOl	311 marInE	360 mAUvE	409 lOOsE
263 gAOlEd	312 antIqUE	361 hAUTboy	410 wOOEd
264 gAUging	313 grIEf	362 fAUX pas	411 pOOH
265 gAUgE	314 bellIEvE	363 platEAU	412 sOUp
266 dAY	315 debrIS	364 yEOman	413 rOUtE
267 plAYEd	316 esprIT	365 sEW	414 dOUchEd
268 mAYOr	317 amOEba	366 sEWEd	415 denOUEment
269 mElee	318 qUAY	367 gHOst	416 thrOUGH
270 thErE	319 sqUEAk	368 mustachIO	417 brOUGHAm
271 E'Er	320 mosqUIto	369 nO	418 cOUP
272 stEAk	321 trustY	370 mOrE	419 rendezvOUS
273 matinEE	**IE-37**	371 O'Er	420 rendezvOUSEd
274 thEGn	322 mAEstro	372 rOgUE	421 ragOUT
275 EH	323 assegAI	373 cOAl	422 billet dOUX
276 vEIn	324 AISlE	374 cOArsE	423 flU
277 sEInE	325 bAYou	375 bOATswain	424 rUlE
278 rEIGn	326 AYE	376 dOE	425 blUE
279 rEIGnEd	327 hEIst	377 imbrOGlio	426 impUGn *
280 grEIGE	328 hEIGHt	378 colOGnE	427 bUHl
281 slEIGH	329 gEYser	379 OH	428 frUIt
282 wEIGHEd	330 EYE	380 yOLk	429 crUIsE
283 dossiER	331 rHIno	381 dOOr	430 bUOy
284 berET	332 rHInEstone	382 apropOS	431 tWO
285 prEY	333 rHYolite	383 depOT	432 WhO
	334 rHYmE		433 WhOsE

Let's End Our Literacy Crisis

Table 6-3: Spelling of the Consonant Sounds ** 1 of 2

B-7	D-8	F-11	G-9	H-4
434 Bad	441 BDellium	**449 Fan**	460 eCzema	**469 Had**
435 ruBBer	**442 Dim**	450 saFE	**461 Get**	470 Jai alai
436 eBBEd	443 aDD	451 oFF	462 eGG	471 WHo
437 roBE	444 faDE	452 stuFFEd	463 beGGEd	472 WHich *
438 BHang	445 DHow	453 oFTen	464 GHost	
439 cuPBoard	446 seemED	454 lauGH	465 GUide	
440 hauTBoy	447 wouLD	455 haLF	466 plaGUE	
	448 meZzo	456 telePHone	467 eXam *	
		457 saPPHire	468 eXHibit *	
		458 lieUtenant		
		459 Veldt		

J-14	K-26		L-16	
473 spinaCH	487 Can	500 KHaki	513 victuAL	521 siLHouette
474 eDucation	488 aCCount	501 chuKKa	514 victuALLer	522 aLL
475 granDEur	489 saCCHarine	502 faLCon	515 musCLE *	523 traveLLEd
476 juDGment	490 CHaos	503 taLK	516 intaGLio	524 kiLN
477 briDGE	491 aCHE	504 Quit	517 buHL	525 iSLand
478 solDIer	492 piCK	505 QUay	**518 Lad**	526 aiSLE
479 aDJust	493 loCKEd	506 antiQUE	519 miLE	527 nesTLE *
480 Gem	494 laCQUer	507 foRECAstle	520 peopLE *	528 knoWLedge
481 saGE	495 aCQUire *	508 visCount		
482 gorGEOus	496 bisCUit	509 eXcept		
483 exaGGerate	497 louGH	510 neXt *		
484 reGIon	**498 Kin**	511 eXHibit *		
485 Jam	499 baKE	512 noXIous		
486 haJJi				

M-11	N-20		P-7	R-15
529 draCHM	540 stuDDINGsail	550 doNE	560 hiccouGH	567 quandARy
530 phleGM	541 opENing	551 ipecacuaNHa	561 haLFPenny	568 coLOnel
531 caLM	542 siGN	552 diNNer	**562 Pin**	**569 Ran**
532 Man	543 viGNette *	553 plaNNEd	563 roPE	570 puRE
533 criticisM *	544 KNot	554 habitaNT	564 shePHerd	571 they'RE
534 coMB	545 MNemonic	555 guNWale	565 suPPer	572 centRE *
535 hoME	546 coMPtroller	556 reasONing	566 flaPPEd	573 RHyme
536 MHo	**547 Nab**	557 PNeumatic		574 RHEumatism
537 duMMy	548 maNana *	558 demeSNE		575 coRPS
538 shaMMEd	549 haNDsome	559 knoWN		576 meRRy
539 hyMN				577 refeRREd
				578 diaRRHea
				579 hoRS d'oeuvre
				580 moRTgage
				581 WRite

The Causes of Illiteracy

Table 6-3: Spelling of the Consonant Sounds ** 2 of 2

S-26		T-16	V-9	W-11
582 City	595 liSTen	608 deBT	624 oF	633 mariJUana
583 miCE	596 iSTHmus	609 yaCHT	625 haLVE	634 chOir
584 PSalm	597 miSTRess	610 indiCT	626 nePHew	635 OnE *
585 woRSted	598 SWord	611 hopED	**627 Van**	636 memOIr *
586 Sad	599 TSar	612 velDT	628 haVE	637 repertOIrE *
587 SCene	600 boaTSWain	613 askED	629 we'VE	638 patOIS *
588 coaleSCE	601 walTZ	614 niGHT	630 saVVy	639 bivOUac
589 SCHism	602 Xi	615 PHTHisic	631 Wedeln	640 perUade
590 mouSE	603 neXt *	616 receiPT	632 rendeZvous	**641 Win**
591 diSHonest	604 eXHibition	**617 Tan**		642 WHelk
592 raSPberry	605 pretZel	618 faTE		643 WHale *
593 leSS	606 scherZo *	619 THyme		
594 kiSSEd	607 piZZicato *	620 buTTon		
		621 TWo		
		622 scherZo *		
		623 piZZicato *		

Y-9	Z-22		CH-10	NG-7
644 azalEa	653 sacrifiCE	664 cloTHES	675 Cello	685 haNDkerchief
645 courtEOus	654 CZar	665 TSar	**676 CHin**	**686 siNG**
646 viGNette *	655 scorES	666 TZar	677 niCHE	687 wiNGEd
647 unIon	656 iS	667 belloWS	678 riGHTeous	688 giNGHam
648 halleluJah	657 diSCern	668 Xylophone	679 tenSIon	689 mah joNGG
649 bouiLLon	658 raiSE	669 eXam *	680 naTure	690 haraNGUE
650 tortiLLa	659 diSHonor	670 eXHibit *	681 maTCH	691 iNK *
651 maNana *	660 buSIness	**671 Zoo**	682 maTCHEd	
652 Yes	661 raSPberry	672 raZE	683 posTHumous	
	662 sciSSors	673 buZZ	684 quesTIon	
	663 aSTHma	674 whiZZEd		

SH-22		"Soft" TH-7	"Hard" TH-4	ZH-12
692 oCeanic	704 nauSEous	714 CHTHonic	721 eisteDDfod	725 rouGing
693 oCEan	**705 SHed**	715 trouGH	722 eDH	726 garaGE
694 maCHine	706 penSIon	716 drouGHT	**723 THem**	727 loGGia
695 mustaCHE	707 SKi	717 eightH	724 baTHE	728 Jardiniere
696 marCHIoness	708 iSSue	718 PHTHisic		729 meaSure
697 fuCHSIa	709 miSSIon	719 THin		730 occaSIon
698 speCIal	710 negoTiate	720 bliTHE		731 fiSSIon
699 PSHaw	711 naTIon			732 equaTIon
700 Sure	712 luXury *			733 luXurious *
701 faSCism	713 noXIous *			734 aZure
702 SCHist				**735 muZHik**
703 conSCience				736 braZIer

* The capitalized letters make another sound in addition to the one at the head of the column.
** Does not include capitalized words and words not in a standard desk dictionary

All of the spellings in Tables 6-2 and 6-3 can be found in a standard desk dictionary, but there are *far* more spellings of the phonemes!

Professor Julius Nyikos of Washington and Jefferson College in Washington, Pennsylvania, did a very extensive study of all the different ways of spelling *forty* English phonemes. He reported his findings on pages 146-163 of *The Fourteenth LACUS* (Linguistic Association of Canada and the United States) *Forum 1987* in an article titled "A Linguistic Perspective of Functional Illiteracy."

His study showed that if "practically all dictionary words" from six desk dictionaries (not unabridged) are included, there are **1, 768 ways of spelling forty English phonemes**—and 1,120 ways if only "words classified as common" are included. *This many additional spellings would include graphemes over and above the 294 shown in Table 6-1.*

Julius Nyikos was born and raised in Hungary at a time when it was rare for children to have preschool training in any facet of literacy. Yet without exception, he and his classmates became proficient readers of Hungarian **in first grade**. Building on the basis of literacy skill in Hungarian, at the age of ten he and all his classmates learned to decode Latin in one week and German in less than one week. They could accurately sound out any word in the language. As a result of having no hindrance from the writing system, the students went from simple decoding to proficient reading with relative speed and efficiency.

During his university years, Nyikos majored in German and Finno-Ugric Hungarian linguistics and developed a keen interest in the comparative study of orthographies (spelling systems). He had studied the English language for four years in high school. He observed that English spelling flies in the face of logic—a radical departure from the writing systems he knew. It took years to fully master English.

He came to the United States in 1949, but it took two years of intensive immersion in English to re-enter his field of foreign language teaching. As both a linguist and a learner, he observed the needless complexity of English spelling, particularly as he added Finnish to his linguistic repertoire: he learned to decode Finnish in just a few classes.

His LACUS article is a very scholarly and persuasive defense of his belief that functional illiteracy in English is primarily due to the spelling. As a result of our spelling "non-system," as he calls it, no method of teaching can be completely successful. He quotes the National Academy of Education's Commission on Reading (Anderson, et al., 1985) as saying, "It is unrealistic to anticipate that some one critical feature of instruction will be discovered which, if in place, will assure rapid progress in reading (4)." This is because, like the Bullock report (see page 117) they did not consider spelling reform.

What Is the Logic Behind Our Problems?

Noah Webster argued against the effort to freeze spelling in the introduction to his 1806 English dictionary. On page vi he states,

> Every man of common reading knows that a living language must necessarily suffer gradual changes in its current words, in the significations of many words, and in pronunciation. The unavoidable consequence then of fixing the orthography [spelling] of a living language, is to destroy the use of the alphabet. This effect has, in a degree, already taken place in our language; and letters, the most useful invention that ever blessed mankind, have lost and continue to lose a part of their value, by no longer being the representatives of the sounds originally annexed to them. Strange as it may seem, the fact is undeniable, that the present doctrine that no change must be made in writing words, is destroying the benefits of an alphabet, and reducing our language to the barbarism of Chinese characters instead of letters.[5]

Some linguists may consider this an overstatement, but English is by far the most inconsistent and illogical of the alphabetic spelling systems and therefore the hardest to learn.

Tables 6-1 through 6-3 summary: when reading, you will see 294 or more single letters or letter combinations (graphemes) to represent thirty-eight sounds (phonemes). Each of these 294 graphemes represents one to ten different phonemes and silent letters, and can be pronounced (read) in an average of 2.2 ways (650 grapheme/phoneme correspondence sets divided by 294 graphemes). When spelling, each of the thirty-eight phonemes that you may want to spell may be spelled from four to sixty different ways using one of the 294 graphemes used in English and can be spelled an average of 19.4 ways (736 phoneme/grapheme correspondence sets divided by thirty-eight phonemes).

How Bad *Is* the Cause of Our Problems?

How We Must Learn English Spelling

As Kenneth Ives states in his book *Written Dialects N Spelling Reforms: History N Alternatives*,

> A book giving a system of rules for pronouncing English runs to 128 pages of rules with many exceptions. (Wijk, 1966) It is so involved that one writer complains it "would require a linguistic Ph.D. with an encyclopedic memory" to use it for writing. A computerized attempt to use a set of 203 spelling rules was able to spell correctly only 49% of a list of 17,000 common words (Hanna et al, 1966)....English is the only language whose dictionaries routinely supply pronunciation for all root words. (Wijk, 1960: 7)[6]

Most Americans are surprised to learn that pronunciations are usually omitted from foreign language dictionaries. They are not needed because the spelling adequately represents the pronunciation. They are even more surprised to learn that students of other languages do not have spelling classes throughout most of grade school, as our students do. "As explained by a Spanish student: 'In Spain the teacher tells us the sounds of the letters and then we can write or read any thing we can say.'"[7]

Page four of M. M. Dougherty's *Instant Spelling Dictionary* states that comprehensive spelling rules are included. Then page 258 says, "Since English is a mixture of words from many languages, there is no set of rules that will cover the spelling of all English words."[8]

Edward Rondthaler of the American Language Academy pointed out, "A 1986 round table of British linguists called by eminent scholars to discuss the underlying pattern of English spelling concluded, not surprisingly, that only one rule in our spelling is not watered down with exceptions: No word in English ends with the letter V."[9] Since *Webster's Ninth New Collegiate Dictionary* lists the words *rev* and *spiv*, there are therefore *no* invariable English spelling rules. If you cannot learn to spell by rules, then you must learn by memorization and repetition. Many inconsistencies could be highlighted. Some examples are the

The Causes of Illiteracy

different sounds of the double *C*s in occasional and accident (pronounced like *K* and like *KS*, respectively) or the double *G*s in egg, exaggerate, and suggest (pronounced like *G*, *J*, or *GJ*, respectively). Perhaps the most impressive English spelling inconsistency is the following:

> Fill each of the blanks with *the exact same* letters to make words, chosen so that the sound of the letters is *different in every word.*
> 1. t_____
> 2. tr_____
> 3. th_____
> 4. th_____t
> 5. thr_____
> 6. thor_____
> 7. b_____
> 8. c_____
> 9. hicc_____
> 10. I_____
> 11. n_____t
> 12. sh_____
>
> Note 1: No. 2 has two more pronunciations. Nos. 6 and 11 each have one more pronunciation. The additional pronunciations of these three words are pronunciations in one of the other twelve.
>
> Note 2: If No. 2 is made plural, there are six accepted pronunciations
>
> tr_____s
> tr_____s
> tr_____s
> tr_____s
> tr_____s
> tr_____s

See table 6-4 for the "dirty dozen" of English pronunciation. How many different ways could we pronounce the eight remaining if we remove Numbers 2, 6, 11, and 12? (Numbers 2, 6, and 11 each have more than one pronunciation. Number 12 is common only in Scotland.) According to the laws of statistics, when there are eight pronunciations, any one of which can be used in eight different words, there are eight to the eighth power (in other words, 8 x 8 x 8 x 8 x 8 x 8 x 8 x 8) or 16,777,216 ways of pronouncing the eight words. This is assuming we haven't learned the one "correct" pronunciation of each of these eight words. As Ives states,

> Even if we compare only [the] common words a second grade pupil would meet: "though, through, ought," a sentence with these three words could be pronounced 27 different ways, from its own examples. With "rough, cough" [the] possibilities reach 3,125!

No wonder Johnny cannot read what he sees, nor spell what he hears, with accuracy [and] confidence! When we ask him to do so, he feels we are asking him a multiple choice question to which there is no *reasonable* answer. [And] he is right. Each word must be learned separately, by memory, [and] in two forms, written [and] spoken, with no necessary, systematic correspondence between them. He must, in effect, become bilingual in his native tongue![10]

Comparative Difficulty of English versus Other Alphabets

Noah Webster's advice on spelling was ignored, and the destruction of the benefits of an alphabet has continued. After 159 years of the type of changes Webster warned of, linguistics scholar Samuel Noory stated it this way:

> Any way these irregularities are added up, however, the net result, I believe, would repeat a truth already inferred—to wit, that English spelling is the most confusing alphabetic writing in use.... Even Chinese writing, the only system exceeding English spelling for complexity, is being changed to a phonetic alphabet of thirty letters.[11]

English may be less complex than Chinese writing, but it is more confusing, at least for some students. The reason is that Chinese students learn strictly by memory, but English students occasionally see some logic in English spelling and therefore look for similar logic elsewhere. Failure to find logic in English spelling is confusing and frustrating. Ives tells of a significant study by Rozin in this regard:

> The most unusual effort of this medium centered approach was probably "American children with reading problems can easily learn to read English represented by Chinese characters." (Rozin, 1971)[12]

The Complex Logic Our Spelling System Requires

This section gives a brief explanation of why learning to read English is so difficult. A more complete explanation can be found in chapters 1-7 of *Why Our Children Can't Read* by Dr. Diane McGuinness. These chapters refer to numerous studies in the last ten to fifteen years proving the difficulty of learning to read English. Chapter 7 explains the types of logic involved in understanding English spelling. All students must learn to read English by learning every individual word by rote memorization or by repetition, but learning is especially confusing for those children who are too young to understand the complex logic involved.

As stated previously, there are tens of thousands of different syllables in English. Unlike other languages, which have few syllable patterns, according to Dr. McGuinness, English has fifteen different syllable patterns: CV, CCV, CCCV, CVC, CCVC, CCCVC, CVCC, CVCCC, CCVCC, CCVCCC, CCCVCCC, VCCC, VCC, VC, and V. It is not known if CCCVCC was left out purposely or not. If it was accidently omitted, there are *sixteen* syllable patterns. There are two or more syllables in most English words.[13] Each syllable can have any of the fifteen or sixteen patterns. If each vowel and each consonant in these syllables always represented the same sound (one-to-one mapping, an "equivalence" relationship), there would be nothing in the logic of these syllables that would be beyond the abilities of most four- or five-year-olds, but they do not.

English spelling also has one-to-one mapping where one phoneme is represented by one digraph (two letters)—since there are not enough letters to represent all the phonemes. Almost half of English sounds are represented by digraphs.[14] But the real confusion comes since there is also one-to-many and many-to-one mapping, i.e., one phoneme is represented by many different graphemes (for spelling), and one grapheme represents many phonemes (for reading). This requires a type of logic that most children do not develop until they are eleven or twelve years old. As a result, to learn English spelling, children in kindergarten and grades one through four must be taught to read in carefully controlled steps, building types of logic they do not understand upon a logic they do understand. And until they are eleven or twelve years old, it is usually a waste of time to try to get them to understand the logic of it— they just have to be helped to learn. The types of logic required for one-to-many and many-to-one mapping are (1) the logic of "classes" (categories where objects or events that are similar are grouped together) and "relations" (where objects share some features but not all features, e.g., all poodles are dogs, but all dogs are not poodles) and (2) "propositional logic," which involves combining both the classes and relations types of logic. This requires the ability to think of the same item in more than one combination at the same time., These combinations require the use of relational terms such as "and," "or," "not," "if—then," and "if and only if" in formal statements of propositional logic The problem of digraphs can be stated as:

If an h follows the letter t, **then** say /tt/ (thin) or /th/ (then); but **if** any other letter or no letter follows the letter t, **then** say /t/ (top, ant).[15]

What Does All This Mean to Us, Today?
Perhaps Sir James Pitman sums it up best:

> It would be simple to fill many pages with the iniquities of English spelling, to draw attention to the mute characters in words like knot, scene, lamb, gnaw, hymn, and build or to list words with alternate spellings, but I hope I have included enough to convince anyone who may not previously have thought much about the subject that the pages over which their eyes skim so effortlessly and efficiently are in fact fraught with inconsistency and illogic, that there is a sizeable divergence between hearing and reading, between the language of the ear and the language of the eye; that no English man can tell how to pronounce a word in his mother tongue if he has only seen that word written and not heard and memorized it; that no English man can tell how to spell a word which he has only heard spoken and never seen written.[16]

You have, no doubt, heard the saying, "A picture is worth a thousand words." Since multiple requests to reprint a Duffy business cartoon from the early 1990s were ignored, it is hoped that you will visualize the following word picture. If you do, we can both profit; the author can save further correspondence time, and the reader can "get the picture." Imagine that you are a lawyer preparing a legal brief and you can't remember how to spell an important word that you need. You can't guess at the spelling well enough to find it in the dictionary and your computer spell checker can't help you. You have been struggling for ten or fifteen minutes to find the spelling and your deadline for preparing the brief is approaching. It is after normal office hours and everyone except your law partner has left for the day. Your partner walks past your office and greets you, intending to keep walking. You say,

"There is a word here that I can't spell."

He casually says, "Look it up," as he walks past your door sipping a cup of coffee.

You frustratedly shout, "How can I look it up if I don't know to spell it?"

This outburst from someone who is normally so calm and quiet startles your partner. He jerks his hand and spills coffee all over the front of his shirt. You apologize profusely. He understands your frustration, forgives you, and hurries off to the executive lounge to change his shirt. What do you do now? You still do not know how to spell this important word for your legal document.

We may have clues, by comparing with words we know, but we will not *know* until we consult a dictionary if we can guess the spelling well enough to find it!

The final aspect of English spelling to be examined is:

With our constantly changing language, why do we allow ourselves to be saddled with a frozen spelling that was not even consistent when frozen?

We can always put up the feeble excuse, "That's the way we've always spelled it." As we consider the great diversity of ways of spelling English sounds shown in the previous tables, however, being honest with ourselves demands the admission that, as the next chapter proves,

**there is no logical,
DEFENSIBLE
reason for it!**

Summary

The figure is a summary of tables 6-1 through 6-3. It shows the graphemes *used* versus graphemes *needed* in English and N'wenglish (see chapter 8). Note that the words in these tables represent many other words. Each word in tables A1-2 through A1-6 represents other words in which the graphemes have the sound shown. Each word in

Let's End Our Literacy Crisis

tables 6-2 and 6-3 represents other words in which the highlighted phoneme is spelled thesame way.

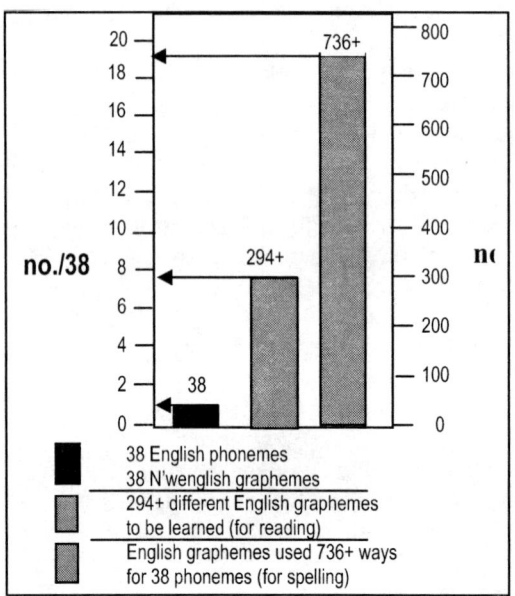

Perhaps the use of almost eight times as many English graphemes to represent the thirty-eight English phonemes as are needed makes no significant impact upon you. Perhaps even the use of more than nineteen times as many spellings of the English phonemes as are needed does not make a lasting impression. The reader is challenged, however, to complete one final exercise. Scan tables 6-1 through 6-3 keeping this in mind:

The phonemes and graphemes in the words in white (in black boxes) plus a grapheme for the sound of TH in thin are all we need for efficient communication The words in black are not only **unnecessary**, they are **counterproductive** to efficient communication. The inconsistency and lack of logic add a confusion factor that interferes with communication.

The Causes of Illiteracy

Table 6-4
The Dirty Dozen: The Twelve Sounds of OUGH

The plan, though thoroughly thought through, was all for nought when the rough trough full of cough and hiccough medicine made from a hemlock tree bough floated down the shough into a Scottish lough and sank to the bottom.

The sound of OUGH to fill the blanks in the box at the start of the last section of this chapter is the same as the underlined sound in the common words following them, below. (Note that except for the first column, common pronunciations are in the same column.)

1. tOUGH	cUFF		
2. trOUGH	clOTH	sO	AWFul
3. thOUGH		sO	
4. thOUGHt			bAll
5. thrOUGH	sUE		
6. thorOUGH	nUt	sO	
7. bOUGH	nOW		
8. cOUGH			AWFul
9. hiccOUGH	UP		
10. lOUGH	lOCK		
11. nOUGHt	nOt		bAll
12. shOUGH	LUKE		

The sound of *OUGHS* in *troughs* rhymes with the underlined sounds.

1. lAWS
2. cOUGHS
3. frOZE
4. trAUVZ (*AU* as in *haul*)
5. clOTHS (*TH* as in *thin*, *S* as in *sit*)
6. clOTHS (*TH* as in *then*, *S* as in *has*)

A Second Form of Dirty Dozen:
Words with a Single Consonant before OUGH

In addition to the word *ought*, by adding a *T* after *OUGH*, there are a dozen words (thirteen, if you include the Manx word **jough*—Manx is the form of Gaelic used on the Isle of Man*)* with a single consonant before *OUGH*.

bough	*mough (rhymes with *bough*)
cough	*pough (rhymes with *dough*)
dough	rough
*fough (pronounced *fu*, *u* as in *nut*)	sough (rhymes with *bough* or *rough*)
hough (rhymes with *lock*)	tough
lough (rhymes with *lock*)	wough (rhymes with *dough*)

* These words are found only in the *Oxford English Dictionary*. *Mough* and *pough* are obsolete words.

Let's End Our Literacy Crisis

Table 6-5
Using Logic to Spell English Will Confuse

Human beings try to learn things by association: comparing new, unknown things with old, familiar things. The following words have two or more pronunciations of a letter *in the same word,* with no way of knowing (other than just *remembering*) which is which:

vowels	consonants	
mAndAted	SugarS	tenSionS
sEsamE	treaSureS	SeaS
InvIted	GorGe	GaraGe
cOmbO	THiTHer	CyCle
UnrUly	bouiLLon	coLoneL
indEpEndEncE	negoTiaTe	maNaNa
fOOtstOOl	piZZicato	meZZo

The table below is from *Fonetic English Spelling* by Traugott Rohner. Although most of the words in the list below have several words pronounced the same as the words on both sides of the period, you never know if a new word is like the one on the left or right side of the period—or different than both of them—such as gone, done, and bone!

Why should the *changing* of a single consonant change the pronunciation of a word, as in:

```
  bead . dead         fury . bury         plow . blow
 beard . heard        gone . done         quit . suit
  bomb . tomb         hear . pear        rough . dough
  bowl . fowl        horse . worse        soul . foul
breath . wreath       keen . been         toll . doll
 caste . paste     laughter . daughter    were . mere
   dew . sew          lose . hose         what . chat
    do . no           love . move         worm . form
  does . toes         maid . said         your . pour
  four . hour         mind . wind (air)   pour . sour
 treat . tread        sour . soup         pour . pout
  worn . worm         peak . pear       finger . ginger
```

Furthermore, why should the *addition* of a single consonant change the basic pronunciation of the word? For instance:

```
   bus . bush        gown . grown         now . snow
 eight . height      have . haven        road . broad
  even . seven       lose . close        face . facet[17]
```

Figure 6-2
Why English is So Hard

We'll begin with a box, and the plural is boxes.
    But the plural of ox should be oxen, not oxes.
Then one fowl is goose, but two are called geese.
    Yet the plural of moose should never be meese.
You may find a lone mouse or a whole lot of mice,
    but the plural of house is houses, not hise.
If the plural of man is always called men,
    why shouldn't the plural of pan be called pen?
The cow in the plural may be cows or kine.
    But the plural of vow is vows, not vine.
And I speak of foot and you show me your feet,
    but I give you a boot—would a pair be called beet?
If one is a tooth and a whole set are teeth,
    why shouldn't the plural of booth be called beeth?
If the singular is this and the plural is these,
    should the plural of kiss be nicknamed kese?
Then one may be that, and three may be those,
    yet the plural of hat would never be hose.
We speak of a brother, and also of brethren,
    but though we say mother, we never say methren.
The masculine pronouns are he, his, and him.
    But imagine the feminine she, shis, and shim!
So our English, I think you will all agree,
    is the trickiest language you ever did see!

Anonymous[18]

Note: Although this poem focuses on the formation of plurals instead of spelling, and although, in general, the ways of forming English plurals is somewhat simpler than many other languages (see second bulleted item in the Easy Grammar and Syntax subsection of chapter 3), the last line of the poem is still true (because of the spelling), and the poem can still be enjoyed.

Figure 6-3

Homophones

Wood yew believe that eye didn't no
about homophones until too daze ago?
That day inn hour class inn groups of fore,
we had two come up with won ore moor.

Mary new sicks; enough too pass,
butt my ate homophones lead thee class.
Then a thought ran threw my head,
"Urn a living from homophones," it said.

Aye guess eye joust sat and staired into space.
My hole life seamed two fall into plaice.
Hour school's principle happened too come buy,
and asked about the look inn my aye.

"Sur," said eye as bowled as could bee,
"My future rode aye clearly sea."
"Sun," said he, "move write ahead,
set sell on you're coarse. Don't bee misled."

Aye herd that gnus with grate delight.
Eye will study homophones both day and knight.
Fore weeks and months, threw thick ore thin,
Aisle persue my ghole. Aye no isle wynn.

modification
of a poem by
George E. Coon
source unknown

Note: This poem is a good example of the fact that readers can easily determine meaning from context. If the communication is long enough to establish the context, almost no one will be confused by words that sound alike being spelled differently than the reader is accustomed to seeing (the traditional spelling).

Part 2
The Solution

Important Note

Reading portions of this section before reading chapter 1 and all of part 1 is similar to having a vague health problem that you've been treating with expensive home remedies. You go to a doctor who finds that you have a life-threatening but easily curable illness. Instead of listening to the doctor explain your complicated illness and simple treatment, you insist only that the doctor tell you the cost of treatment. Although the treatment is less expensive than several more months of your home remedies, you decide to continue with what you know rather than learn what you need.

There is no question that English spelling reform is long overdue. The present practice of attempting to teach *all* American youth to read and spell English is the foremost example of conspicuous consumption of a nation's resources since the building of the pyramids. Unfortunately for many children, the belief is still widely held that our economy can still afford this cruel waste....

It would be unbecoming of educators not to attempt hundreds of new and devious approaches to the problem rather than advocating the one logical (and eventually inevitable) solution.[1]

Arthur W. Heilman, Ph.D.
Phonics in Proper Perspective

Chapter 7
The Only Proven Solution to Illiteracy

Seeing with an Unprejudiced View

The first step in solving any problem is to be sure you are seeing the problem and the solution with an unprejudiced view. The most perceptive statement concerning our failure to view our literacy problems properly is by Sir James Pitman in his book *Alphabets and Reading*:

> In my own long campaign in Parliament and elsewhere to have the effect of our alphabet(s) and spelling on the learning processes involved in learning to read tested in a large-scale investigation, the worst obstacle has been the inability of many people to objectify, to depersonalize the problem. They assume that because *they*, personally, managed to learn to read without the alphabet being "tampered with," it must have been easy for them and therefore it must be equally simple for others to do likewise. If children fail to learn to read, the fault must lie elsewhere—in poor teaching, the wrong method, overcrowded classrooms....As stated in the opening chapter of this book, all these and similar factors are of great relevance, but this is a poor reason for overlooking the medium in which reading is taught. Some of our educational pundits are not unlike the surgeons when Joseph Lister first urged the advantages of asepsis. To us the necessity for sterilization appears to be self-evident, but it

took Lister some twenty-five years before the surgical educationists of the day were prepared even to consider his simple remedy—and a further twenty-five for it to be generally applied. There was nothing, the pundits declared, wrong with their methods of operating; those who died shortly afterwards were as well served as those who lived—the fault must be lack of skill in the surgeon, or congenital weakness in the patient, or it was gangrene which was a *separate* matter altogether and impossible to cure...and so they continued to carry their instruments round in a velvet-lined morocco pocket-case and to sharpen their scalpels on the soles of their boots. Millions died needlessly just as, equally needlessly, millions of children have failed to read.[2]

Unrealistic Views of Illiteracy

Some people believe that literacy is an elitist idea held by people who have had too many years of indoctrination in sophisticated, snobbish colleges. These people will tell you that:

• The ordinary person can do many things we could never imagine.
• The ordinary person has many virtues we could never imagine.
• The ordinary person shows ingenuity and a basic hardihood that far exceeds that of many college graduates.
• Plans to educate people endanger these abilities whether they can read or not.

Some people believe that illiterates are doing well without us, so why should we burden them with our middle class ambitions and cultural constraints? Such people will ask, "Does literacy make anyone happy?" Perhaps Jeanne Chall, college professor and author, gives the best answer:

> Does literacy make men happy? Only highly literate people seem to ask [this] question. And only the well-educated seem to say that it does not. They are like the rich who doubt that money makes one happy. Significantly, such doubts come only after they have accumulated enough money and do not have to worry...And so with the highly literate. They doubt that literacy will contribute to the happiness of those who are not yet literate only because they them-

The Only Proven Solution to Illiteracy

selves use it so well and easily in living, working, playing, and in making choices.[3]

We use literacy so well that we've been blinded to the advantages and options such literacy brings us. Such idealization of ordinary, uneducated people might be possible for someone who has never lived with the advantages of a printing press. There is not one community in the U.S., no matter how isolated, where that holds true today. People who write such things should ask themselves, "Is literacy of so little value that I would be willing to give up my ability to distribute, in print, the ideas I just expressed?" Although they are ready to give away other people's ability to read and write, they are not ready to surrender their own.

Recently the idea has arisen that people can function very well today by receiving the information they need from radio and television. Many of the "Human-Suffering Costs" in chapter 5 show why the electronic media cannot meet all the needs. The following quotation should clinch the matter:

> We live in a world in which important events occur daily. These events affect our lives, directly and indirectly. None occurs in a vacuum. They all have contexts that need to be understood. To some limited extent the electronic media try to provide context, but the accent must be placed on the word limited. Time constraints force the reduction of even the most momentous occurrences to their most basic facts. Full understanding of present events requires literacy, which make it possible, in greater leisure, to fill the canvas with all the necessary background and detail.
>
> Literacy makes possible depth and breadth, the pursuit of inquiry in any direction. The illiterate must be satisfied with the knowledge supplied by others. They are prisoners of what is meted out, unable to pursue avenues of inquiry determined by themselves. Such inquiry in itself is a vital force in human development: it fuels invention and innovation, enabling the mind to expand and to reach into the future, guided by the accumulated records of the past.[4]

Let's End Our Literacy Crisis

A Proposed Solution in Other Nations

Even after people become convinced of the wisdom of changing, they may have one last means of resisting change. They may ask if other nations or other language groups have successfully made such a change. The hope is that they can say, "Other people don't make such changes, why should we?" In spelling reform, we can point to many extensive and successful changes. Spelling reform scholar Kenneth Ives points out that the Dutch have had

> an evolving spelling,...regularly adapted to Dutch speech. Dutch spelling was simplified in 1804 (Siegenbeek), in 1864 (DeVries-TeWinkel), and in 1934 (Marchant),...approximately every sixty years.
>
> Portuguese has been simplified in 1911, 1931, 1943, [and] in Brazil in 1973....
>
> Other language reforms, in over half a dozen countries, range from Turkish adoption of Latin script [in 1928] to [the] Israeli reforms in Hebrew in 1968. These [and] other examples indicate that language reforms can be planned [and] carried out, often with lasting benefits.[5]

Laubach explains that Spain, Russia, and Turkey adopted the findings of "competent academies" called together to consider spelling reform. About Turkey, he writes,

> Turkey began her famous literacy campaign almost immediately after Kemel Pasha became dictator and president. In 1928 he threw the Arabic script out of the schools and replaced it with a splendid Latin phonetic alphabet—and all this during the summer vacation! No textbook with the old script was permitted in the schools when they reopened in the fall.[6]

More significantly for English-speaking people, two spelling reform bills introduced by Dr. Mont Follick were almost enacted in England. As Sir James Pitman explains it,

> Follick believed passionately that his reform could establish

English as the world's major second language. It is not, however, for his own particular alphabet that he is likely to be best remembered, but rather for his two Private Member's bills in the House of Commons (1949 and 1952) advocating the need for reform, with which I am proud to have been closely associated. In fact he invited me to draft his second bill and to take charge of it as if it were I and not he who had been successful in the ballot. His first bill was defeated on a second reading by only 3 votes after a five-hour debate; his second bill achieved a majority of 12 votes and was also successful in Committee despite ministerial opposition. After a good deal of "horse-trading" by me behind the scenes, he was induced to withdraw the second bill in return for an offer by Miss Horsburgh, then Minister of Education, to pledge her interest and goodwill "towards proposals by a competent research organization to investigate possible improvements in the teaching of reading by means of a system of simplified spelling.[7]

Effects on the Teaching Method

Hope springs eternal in the human breast. There will always be optimists who will claim that, with time, reading ability in America will improve. There will always be those who claim that more adult illiterates will enroll in reading classes if we make enough money available to improve the literacy classes. There will always be those who believe you can solve any problem if you throw enough money at it.

Convincing the optimists of how unlikely it is that enough money will be appropriated and that more illiterates will eventually participate may be futile. A stronger argument focuses on the effect English spelling has on preventing millions of schoolchildren and adult nonreaders from learning to read. English spelling has numerous characteristics that affect the teaching methods that must be used, including the following.

Difficulties Imposed on Specific Subjects

Reading: The use of more than one sound per symbol makes reading difficult. The reader does not know which sound a certain letter or letter combination represents. The beginning English-speaking reader has the words stored in memory as sounds. If the letters do not suggest the pronunciation of a familiar word, the reader does not recognize (read) it. Immigrants learning to read English usually learn the meaning of English words by comparison with the spelling of the word in their language. The obvious difficulty immigrants have is in the correct pronunciation. They must have a teacher pronounce the words for them or else have a phonemic transcription or audio recording of the word.

Spelling and Writing: The use of more than one symbol per sound makes writing difficult. For each sound of each word that English-speaking persons want to write, they know there are several possibilities, but often do not know which is correct. As chapter 6 explains, there are more different ways to spell each sound than there are sounds that can go with each letter or letter blend. Therefore, spelling correctly is even more difficult than reading. More people can read correctly spelled printed matter than can write so others know exactly what they mean. This is true even if the writers can fluently express their thoughts orally.

Other Subjects: Since reading is necessary to understand the school books of every subject, those who cannot read well have difficulty in every subject.

Remedial Reading Classes

Most public schools in the U.S. have remedial reading classes, or remedial reading groups in classes, for almost every grade level. Remedial reading classes are also common in college. David Harman states,

> One indication of [functionally illiterate high school graduates] can be found among students in community colleges, all graduates of high schools. Over half of community college entrants, researcher John Roueche found, are lacking in adequate basic skills: "The most offered courses in American community colleges were remedial reading, remedial writing, and remedial arithmetic."...
>
> Community colleges do not have a monopoly on remedial reading courses for high school graduates: a number of Ivy League colleges also make such courses available to entering freshmen who are found to need them.[8]

A September 1997 report states that "almost one-third of college freshmen require remedial instruction."[9]

Are there remedial reading classes in other languages? Dr. Rudolph Flesch states,

> Do you know that there are no remedial reading cases in Germany, in France, in Italy, in Norway, in Spain—practically anywhere in the world except in the United States?[10]

Part of the reason is that the school systems in many other nations do not try to make high school or college graduation a possibility for every student, the way we do. It is also true that there is much less need for remedial reading classes in most other nations.

Beginning Reader Teaching Methods

There are two basic methods used in the United States: the look-and-say (whole word or whole language) method and the phonics method. (As Dr. McGuinness convincingly demonstrates in *Why Our Children Can't Read*, however, until the mid 1990s few teachers knew the correct way to use the phonics method.) There are, however, various combinations of these two methods. There are also continual efforts at finding and introducing slight variations that are hailed as "new" ways of teaching reading. Kenneth Ives, in his book, *Written Dialects N Spelling Reforms: History N Alternatives*, states,

> Reading would appear to be [the] most difficult [and] controversial subject to teach in school. [The] 1960 *Encyclopedia of Educational Research* devoted 151 pages to reading research, but only two to five pages for each of [the] other school subjects. Another study refers to "1,000 reading research studies completed each year." Most of this research is concerned with [the] teaching of spelling or with [the] problems created by it. (Dewey, 1971; 41)[11]

The number of research reports on reading difficulties has increased since 1960. There are now hundreds of books and about 3000 articles on reading published each year.[12]

A stroll up and down the aisles of any large university library looking at the hundreds of books on reading would be an enlightening experience for most people. An examination of the students' and teachers' books used in teaching adults to read also would be enlightening. Just the table of contents to the four Laubach Literacy Action books requires fourteen large pages, fully packed with all the different letters, letter groupings, spelling rules, etc., that the student must learn in order to achieve eighth-grade reading skill. It usually requires a minimum of one year to complete the four books using Laubach's one-teacher-to-one-student method.

Considering the previous sections of this chapter, anyone who sees the brevity of this section may think that any claims of adequately covering the subject are highly presumptive. The way that English spelling affects any of these teaching methods, however, can conclusively be stated in just one short quotation. As Dewey states it,

> [T]he currently accepted spellings of T.O. [traditional orthography, i.e., the way English words are now spelled] are the chief roadblock to learning to read and write....Most reading methods are essentially efforts to detour that roadblock, to put off facing the hard facts of T.O. as long as possible.[13]

Most, if not all the spelling methods for beginners start with the simpler words and groupings of similar words. To show them the full story, as presented in tables 6-1 through 6-3, would completely bewilder the students. They must learn every word, one at a time, either by memorization or by familiarization through repetition

The Subject Matter of Textbooks

Because of the reading methods used, the characteristics of English spelling affect what appears in schoolbooks. For the first three grades and for part of the fourth grade, the reading matter is insubstantial. For part of the fourth grade and for all higher grades, the content becomes more important. Up to fourth grade the student learns to read. Beginning in fourth grade, the student reads to learn.

Because of this, beginning in fourth grade, students who cannot read well start to have serious problems in getting by. They can only get by if they learn to fake it. Students who do not learn to read by the fourth grade can rarely catch up. As Kozol, a fourth- and fifth-grade teacher for a time, explains, the only separate classes normally taught for reading after the fourth grade are remedial classes. Students who do not learn how to recognize the more complicated words by knowing how the letter sounds combine into words by the fourth-grade seldom catch up with their classmates. The stigma of being a nonreader prevents many of them admitting their need for remedial classes.[14]

Since the subject matter of reading textbooks for the first four grades is insubstantial, the authors of these books are free to write in any way they choose. In the look-and-say reading books (the so called "Dick and Jane" readers), the writers try to repeat the words that are being taught in the story as much as possible. As Dr. Rudolph Flesch impressively shows in his book *Why Johnny Can't Read*, the so called stories, particularly as they are haltingly read by beginning readers in the classroom, are almost unbearably boring. If the reading student is experiencing the joy of learning to read, it alleviates the boredom somewhat. For those who don't get it, however, reading class is an experience they never want to repeat![15]

As *Why Our Children Can't Read* explains in chapters 3 through 5, if an ineffective teaching method is used, it does not matter that the reading material is more interesting and exciting than the "Dick and Jane" readers. The children still have to invent their own strategies for making sense of a completely bewildering array of different ways to spell the words.

General Effects of the Present System

Some of the general effects that the inconsistencies and lack of logic in English spelling have upon people are the following.

English versus Other Languages

The school systems in many countries have such high standards that only students who can learn quickly remain in school. Rudolph Flesch explains another important difference:

> Generally speaking, students in our schools are about two years behind students of the same age in other countries. This is not a wild accusation of the American educational system; it is an established, generally known fact....

What accounts for these two years? Usually the assumption seems to be that in other countries children and adolescents are forced to study harder. Now that I have looked into this matter of reading, I think the explanation is much simpler and more reasonable: Americans take two years longer to learn how to read—and reading, of course, is the basis for achievement in all other subjects.[16]

Frank C. Laubach believes even more time is lost: "It is estimated that two and one-half years are lost in the student's studies because of our chaotic spelling."

How does this compare to other languages? Laubach states, "Over 90 percent of the world's languages have one sound for a letter and one letter for a sound. In such languages learning to read is swift and easy, requiring from one to twenty days."[17]

Laubach Literacy International taught students to read in 300 different languages all around the world. In 295 of these languages (98 percent of them) the students could master reading and writing in less than three months.[18]

Rudolph Flesch points out how quickly children of other nations learn to read. Russian schoolchildren, for example, are taught to read forty-six of the 130 national languages of Russia—in first grade! There is no reading instruction, as such, after first grade.[19]

How Can We Improve the Educational System?

With the recent publicity of U.S. illiteracy there have been increasing cries for someone to do something to improve the educational system. Usually, one of the first solutions proposed is to spend more money on education. An example is columnist Cal Thomas' report for the Los Angeles Times Syndicate. "[T]he federal government spends $97 billion per year of our money on more than 760 education programs spread over 40 government agencies."[20] In order to influence state policies, the government returns a portion of the $97 billion to the states. Nina Rees, writing for Knight-Ridder News Service, states that while the amount "appears small—about 7 percent of the average state's total education budget—it still adds up to millions, if not billions, of dollars."[21]

Although more money—if spent correctly—can sometimes help, the U.S. has proven that this is not the solution. A September 10, 1993, news report in *The Salt Lake Tribune* states,

> The amount of money America spends on its public schools has soared as much as health-care costs, so that each household now spends an annual average of $2,348 in taxes to fund schools.
> A large part of the rise has fattened bureaucracy and there is no sign that the investment improved learning, according to a study released Thursday....
> "I know it's fashionable to talk about underinvestment in education, but as our study confirms, we've invested and invested heavily in education," said Samuel Brunelli, director of the council and president of The ALEC [American Legislative Exchange Council] Foundation. "This investment has not paid off in terms of student achievement...."
> In New Jersey, New York, the District of Columbia, and other places where taxpayers pay among the most for their schools, the students are among lowest achievers.[22]

Dr. William Bennett's 1994 book *The Index of Leading Cultural Indicators* shows the details of the relationship of expenditures and scholastic achievement, as indicated by Scholastic Aptitude Test (SAT) scores. Average SAT scores dropped from 975 in 1960 to 890 in 1980. Although the information in Bennett's book shows a slight rise (to about 900 in 1993), the SAT scores are still well below the 1960 level. In the mid-1980s the SAT test was changed in a way that many believe made it easier. Mensa would previously accept SAT and American College Test (ACT) test scores as proof of a high IQ; they no longer do. During the 1960 to 1993 time period the elementary and secondary school expenditures for education, in constant 1989 dollars, rose from 70 billion to 250 billion or more. Although many factors were involved, part of the reason was that a smaller share of the expenditures went for actual classroom instruction than during any comparable time in recent history.

Furthermore, the U.S. spends more per pupil than other nations (Bennett lists the expenditure—in decreasing order—of Canada, Italy,

West Germany, France, the United Kingdom, and Japan). According to 1993 U.S. Department of Education data, the U.S. expenditure per pupil was about $3,800, Canada spent about $3,500, and Japan spent about $2,200. Also, there is no correlation between the amount spent on education by the states in the U.S. and the results obtained in student performance. For example, in 1992 and 1993 the top five states in SAT scores, in order, were Iowa, North Dakota, South Dakota, Utah, and Minnesota, whose expenditure rankings, respectively were twenty-seventh, forty-fourth, forty-second, fifty-first, and twenty-fifth. On the other hand, the top five states in expenditures in 1992 and 1993, in order, were New Jersey, Alaska, Connecticut, New York, and the District of Columbia, with SAT score rankings, respectively, of thirty-ninth, thirty-first, thirty-third, fortieth, and forty-ninth.[23] Although this certainly does not prove that the more money spent the worse the results, no honest observer could conclude that spending more money will definitely improve educational performance.

Predictably, the major solution proposed was that schools should *raise their standards.* If standards were raised high enough, *every* student would have to spend more time each year in class and on homework. They would need help from their parents, as in Korea and Japan, or from private tutors. However, some students are seriously confused by the lack of logic in English spelling. What about these students? Does raising the standards help those in the school system who are having problems in their schoolwork?

If (1) these students were failing because they were simply not trying hard enough, if (2) they believed they could pass if they tried harder, and if (3) they were sufficiently motivated to want to pass, then raising the standards would have a good effect. It doesn't take a genius to figure out that not all students fit all three "ifs." What effect does raising standards have on students who are having trouble reading? Instead of helping them, it squeezes them out. When the poorer students are out of the schools, then the average grades of those left in schools will be higher. Everyone will pat themselves on the back for improving the school system by raising the standards. The gain, however, has only been possible at the expense (the human-suffering cost in chapter 5) of the troubled students.

Those who are wealthy enough can ensure that their children get into the good colleges by putting them into private high schools. Others manage to get their children into gifted and talented programs in the public schools. Many parents of students having reading problems are illiterate. Neither of these recourses is open to most illiterate parents.[24]

Grade Inflation

There were demands for higher standards following the National Commission on Excellence in Education's 1983 "Nation at Risk" report. Four factors caused this to result in grade inflation: (1) "commercial demands" for success in teaching (no governmental funding is received for a student excluded because of low grades), (2) pressure from parents, (3) pressure from students, and (4) pressure from college admitting officers who rely on class rank and grade-point averages. So instead of improving performance, the opposite actually occurred. Twice as many Cs as As were given in 1966, but in 1978 more As were given than Cs, and more than 20 percent of students entering college in 1990 averaged A minus or more. All this was despite the fact that educational achievement had dropped. An A minus or more was the average grade of 54 percent of students entering private universities.[25]

> Both the SAT and ACT, the two big college testing services, report evidence of grade inflation [as reported in September 1997].
>
> The percent of A-average students among SAT test takers has risen to 37 percent from 28 percent in the past decade. Among those all-A students, the SAT averages fell by 14 points over the same period.
>
> Among ACT takers, the percent of all-A students rose to 32 percent in 1996, up from 16 percent in 1970, with no improvement in scores over that time period.[26]

Can Fluent English Readers Read Unfamiliar English Words?

The most all-encompassing effect is Pitman's statement,

> [N]o Englishman can tell how to pronounce a word in his mother tongue if he has only seen that word written and not heard and memorized it; that no Englishman can tell how to spell a word which he has only heard spoken and never seen written.[27]

You may be able to make an educated guess at the spelling or pronunciation of an unfamiliar word, but you will not be certain until you find it in the dictionary. If you think the words "no Englishman" do not actually include everyone, consider note 1 on the same page as Pitman's quotation in the previous paragraph:

> Mensa, the exclusive society of top brains, whose members are claimed to score higher than 98 percent of the population in a standard intelligence test and to be "verbally skilled people of considerable insight," recently issued a handout that spoke of, "thrashing out their differencies;" "the principle Mensa tenet;" the many "proffessors" in Mensa's ranks; and its "completely independant journal."

These misspelled words had obviously been seen before, but (assuming they were not purposely misspelled as a joke—there is no indication this was the case) the spelling was forgotten or never learned. The lack of any logical, consistent rules of spelling reduces even "America's top brains" to dependence upon a dictionary or upon memory.

Final Effects of the Present System

Chapters 4 and 5 detail some of the final economic and human-suffering effects of the present system. Two additional quotations, by Sir James Pitman and Godfrey Dewey Ed.D., respectively, summarize some of these final effects:

Delinquency and Backwardness in Reading

Is it farfetched to postulate that a child's first wrestling with the vagaries of the English alphabet(s) and spelling may prepare the ground for doubt about the adult world of teachers and parents, and nurture emotional and temperamental traits that will later be expressed in truancy and worse? As we have seen, delinquency and backwardness in reading are old companions.[28]

Delinquency, Crime, and Self-Destructive Violence

While English is already the nearest to a worldwide *spoken* language, our traditional orthography not only handicaps English as a world *written* language, but in our own and other English-speaking nations puts an intolerable and too often traumatic burden on beginning learners. Even among those of our children and adults who do not become nonreaders, the traumas of an irrational alphabet often continue as hidden or unconscious antipathies for, and roadblocks to, effective reading habits, and even more effective roadblocks to writing. Nonreaders not only feel declassé, but also too frequently become victims of frustrations leading to delinquency, crime, and the self-destructive violence associated with political infantilism and susceptibility to demagoguery.[29]

Difficult for *All*, Impossible for Some

English illiteracy does not necessarily show lower intelligence. Researchers such as Sylvia Scribner and Michael Cole[30] in 1981 and Sir James Pitman concur. As Pitman expresses it,

> To begin with, it must be remembered that intelligence is not necessarily a passport to the easy acquisition of reading. Among the seventeen per cent of backward readers [in England in the mid-1960s] will be found a few with considerable intellectual potentiality and even a high level of linguistic ability and experience.[31]

In fact, a higher intelligence level often interferes with learning to read English. This is because the student looks for logic and is confused by so seldom finding any in English spelling.

Facts about English spelling presented in chapter 6 also show why learning to read and write is difficult for all and impossible for some.

Developing Problem-Solving Skills

One important skill students must develop in school is the ability to solve problems. Having such an ability helps the students throughout their lives, not only in solving specific problems, but also in having the self-confidence to try other worthwhile tasks. Learning to read English is one of the most challenging types of problem solving a child meets. As stated previously, whatever teaching method is used, the hard facts of English spelling are usually put off as long as possible. If this were not true, most of the student would be completely bewildered. As a result of teachers and school curricula postponing the difficulties, the students can learn logical, systematic ways of solving problems on subjects other than English spelling. This will enhance their ability to solve other types of problems when they are intellectually more mature.

Teaching English Reading

The types of problem-solving skills involved in learning to read English are shown in the following quotation:

> In many systems of teaching reading steps are taken to eliminate some of the irregular words until later. By careful selection a child may first be taught only the words that are phonetically reliable, but he cannot get very far! Before long he has to accept that, whereas *go*, *so*, and *no* are pronounced in the same way, this does not apply to *do* or *to* and *who* which have to rhyme with *shoe* which, however, does not rhyme with *goes* or with *does* (in a common pronunciation of the derivate from *do*) and what can be made of the *wh* in *who* and *whole*; of *one* and *bun*; of *all* and *ought*; *has* and *was*; and many other common words? It is true that secondary clues in the context will be a help, but searching for these in the early stages is impracticable when three-quarters of the adjoining words are misleading. Moreover too much frustrated searching may well form bad habits of irregular eye-movements and, as we saw in chapter 2, the reader must at quite an early stage gain some skill in analyzing the shapes of syllables and words and in relating them to the corresponding sounds and meanings. However carefully protected, the beginner soon has to grapple with a capricious diversity of mental associations or relationships. Up to a certain point he can rely on a logical relationship between the visual and spoken forms of words, and between different words that are made up of similar syllables, but he has no means of telling when the relationship is going to let him down. There is no alternative, with our present spelling, for the beginner but to memorize the numerous irregularities among the common words, to learn them by rote.[32]

The Need for Logic in Learning

As Edward Rondthaler and Edward Lias state,

> Systematic spelling takes full advantage of a well documented educational principle: logic stimulates thinking, thinking encourages learning, learning is facilitated when what is being learned "makes sense." A spelling that makes sense would open the door to literacy for more people, young and old, than all our remedial reading efforts put together. It would go a long way toward rescuing those who if not rescued will greatly magnify our social problems and undermine our democratic structure.[33]

A disturbing report was issued in 1972 by the National Foundation for Educational Research in Great Britain. As a result of this report, Mrs. Margaret Thatcher, the Secretary of State for Education and Science, set up a twenty-member committee to study reading and the use of English. In 1975 the committee, headed by Sir Alan Bullock, vice-chancellor of Oxford University, issued its report. The report was more than 600 pages and cost nearly £100,000 to produce. In his book *Regularized English*, Axel Wijk says this about the report:

> The most serious criticism that must be leveled against the Committee's report is, however, the fact that they have so completely failed to study and take account of the methods of teaching reading which are universally used in all other European languages. In all these languages phonic methods are almost exclusively predominant, due to the fact that they have all fairly regular spelling systems, whereas in the English-speaking countries reading is usually taught by the aid of mixed whole-word and phonic methods or to some extent even by a purely whole-word approach.
>
> Phonic methods, which presuppose a fairly regular spelling system, are distinctly superior to mixed whole-word and phonic methods, because they are the only ones which permit of a predominantly logical approach to the teaching of reading. It is of vital importance to realize that for practically all children of normal ability the use of a regular spelling system will make it possible and very much easier to learn to read and write. The most essential

advantage of such a spelling system is that it permits us to introduce the various phonic units more or less one by one, whereas with the mixed or the purely whole-word approach such a large number of different sounds and spelling units are introduced at the same time that there can be no question of trying to establish an immediate relationship between spelling and pronunciation, especially not in such a language as English which displays an unusually large number of irregular spellings among the commonest words in the language....

When they maintain that "there is no one method, medium, approach, device or philosophy that holds the key" to the solution of the reading problem, they overlook the fact that in all European languages except English phonic methods are almost exclusively predominant, due to the fact that they have all fairly regular spelling systems....

Since English differs from all other European languages in having such a large number of irregular spellings among the commonest words, it is extremely difficult, almost impossible, to apply exclusively phonic methods to the teaching of English reading. By replacing the irregular spellings by regular ones ... traditional English may be turned into a "phonetic" language, which can be taught in accordance with definite rules of pronunciation. It seems therefore that we are fully justified in saying that there is one reliable and efficient method of teaching reading, namely by the aid of a regular spelling system.[3]

Kenneth Ives quotes an earlier statement by Axel Wijk on this subject:

If an orthographic system for English could be devised which would be just as simple, regular and logical as those found in most other European languages, it would be possible for all English-speaking school children to save at least one year's work.

Perhaps even more important would be the fact that such a reform of English orthography would make it possible for English-speaking school children to learn to read and write in the same way as the children of other nations, i.e. by using and training their sense of logic instead of by training and relying mainly on their eye memory, learning words by heart without much reference to the sounds of the letters of which they are composed. The present lack of system constitutes a very serious obstacle to the development of the child's reasoning powers.[35]

Kenneth Ives adds,

> With traditional spelling having to be learned by rote, reading [and] writing in it are made difficult from [the] start. [The] usual result is dull drill, which discourages or destroys [the] child's curiosity [and] creativity about [the] world.[36]

In the last chapter of *English Spelling and Spelling Reform*, published in 1909, Dr. Lounsbury convincingly demonstrates the devastating effects that the lack of logic in spelling has upon beginning learners. Thomas R. Lounsbury, LL.D., L.H.D., emeritus professor of English, Yale University, shows himself to be a careful and thorough scholar through his writing.

Why It Is Difficult for All, Impossible for Some

Now, we get to the essence. What is the result of problems with English spelling? It can scarcely be stated more decidedly than Pitman expresses it:

> [T]he child is expected to take on a task that is formidable for all and for some impossible: to analyze what is scarcely analyzable, to conjure abstractions and generalizations from a printed medium whose associations are in fact neither invariable nor consistent and thus doubly irrational. Would it not be truer to say that the child is perplexed precisely because of his innate ability to reason, to analyze, abstract, and generalize?...
>
> It would scarcely be surprising if the simultaneous presentation of so many problems, so many contradictory concepts, did not merely put an over-severe strain on the memory of many five- or six-year-olds but also damaged the ability to reason logically and to form good habits of problem solving....
>
> Once a child has failed to surmount early instances of illogicality

it is arguable that he may stick at this point and that this prevents him from progressing and gives rise to a swelling sense of frustration, confusion, and disappointment that hampers further efforts. My hypothesis is that this is when many backward readers are born. The great majority of these children never succeed in overcoming their bad start.[37]

Dr. Diane McGuinness reaches a similar conclusion. She states that based upon numerous research projects over the past ten years or so, language development in children makes them unable to use a phonetic alphabet unless they are specifically taught the phonemes. Although phonemic awareness can be learned at any age, the earlier it is learned the better it is for children learning to read. When children are learning to read, their logical development makes it almost impossible to understand the complex structure of our spelling code. Although one-to-one mapping logic can be figured out by some students without any help, all other types of mapping must be explicitly taught. Each step must also be based upon something they have already learned—the context must be familiar. There is no other way for learning to continue smoothly and effectively.

Like adults, children have great difficulty paying attention to tasks they can't do or concepts they do not understand. Their limited capacity to hold information in their minds is very greatly diminished if the information does not make sense.[38]

English is among the most difficult 5 percent of the world's languages in one narrow respect: consonant clusters. It is neither the consonant clusters, however, nor the grammar and syntax of English that causes the most problems. It is spelling that presents students with problems that are:

difficult for all, impossible for some.

Special Note to Language Scholars

N'wenglish is referred to in this book as "perfect." What might be considered "linguistically perfect" by one scholar might not be considered perfect by another. N'wenglish is referred to as "perfect" only in the sense that each grapheme represents only one phoneme, and each phoneme is represented by only one grapheme. Spelling reform to achieve linguistic perfection, even if possible, would never be agreed to by all those who want to participate in designing a linguistically perfect spelling system. N'wenglish was designed to achieve the following primary goals: 1) regularization of our spelling, to ease the learning for beginning readers, and 2) minimum relearning for those who now read English. These goals require downgrading to secondary importance the goal of achieving linguistic perfection. In addition to one-grapheme-to-one-phoneme correspondence, linguistic perfection would also require, among other things, conforming to international standards and conventions.

The most used grapheme for most of our English vowel phonemes is not the same as the standard grapheme-phoneme correspondence in many other languages. Making English conform to international grapheme-phoneme correspondence standards should not be insisted upon for two reasons. First, a simple and logical alphabet such as N'wenglish can be learned so easily that its difference from international standards will be quickly forgotten as written communication between English-speaking people rapidly improves. Second, as chapter 3 shows, English is the best candidate for an international language.

People around the world who want to learn written English will accept the grapheme-phoneme system of those who already read English. A spelling system attempting to make English conform to international standards would not be accepted by hundreds of millions of people who now read English.

If (1) a shorter /u/, as in *battle*; (2) the *ER* sound; (3) accented versions of the /e/, as in *me*, /u/, as in *nut*, /er/, and /u/-/r/ (where the *U* is accented); (4) the /a/ in *father*, for those who do not rhyme it with *bother*; (5) *WH* as in *whale* (not the same as *wail*); and (6) two German and four French phonemes are omitted, the N'wenglish phoneme choices are exactly the same as the Pronunciation Symbols table in *Webster's Ninth New Collegiate Dictionary*. It seems obvious that the length of a phoneme and whether or not it is accented (items 1 and 3) should not control phoneme choices and that foreign phonemes (item 6) do not need separate graphemes. Furthermore, pronouncing the /a/ in *father* to rhyme with *bother* (item 4) will not prevent you from being understood. And, although phoneticists will correctly tell you that the *R* sound in *AR*, *ER*, and *OR* are different from /r/ at the start of a syllable, the *ER* and *WH* sounds (items 2 and 5) can easily be recognized—even by kindergartners—as blends of a vowel and /r/ or a blend of /h/ and /w/ once they learn to separate the phonemes in blends.

If these primary goals are achieved, N'wenglish will attain a more important, foundational goal of all written languages: making written communication easier and more understandable. Although linguists might want additional phonemes included in a new spelling system, a person with an untrained ear can easily recognize the sound system used in N'wenglish. They would have difficulty hearing some of the subtle sound differences that linguists might want to indicate. The key question in deciding which phonemes to include, however, must be, **"What is the minimum number of phonemes that the average person can easily recognize in order to communicate efficiently?"**

Chapter 8
The Proposed Solution

After this chapter you will know how to read and spell anything in N'wenglish (= N'w English = New English). Although you will be able to read N'wenglish with only a few stumbles after reading the next four pages, please resist the temptation to skip ahead to appendix 4 until you complete this and the next chapter. By trying appendix 4 prematurely, you will diminish the thrill you can experience by reading a new spelling system at a normal speaking rate without error the first time you try. By finishing this chapter (including the exercises) and chapter 9, much of the strangeness of the words will be gone. You will be able to read for meaning, the way reading *should be*.

The Logic behind the Proposed Solution

N'wenglish was developed with two goals: to make reading and spelling English as simple as possible and to keep the present English spellings wherever possible. No English spellings were kept, however, that would interfere with the goal of making reading and spelling as simple as possible. The logical reason behind the choice of each grapheme used in N'wenglish is shown in appendix 2. Thirty-one of the thirty-eight graphemes (81.6 percent) chosen for N'wenglish are the most used grapheme for that phoneme in English. If it were not for the pronunciation of *OE* and *F* in the words *does* and *of*, respectively, the

/z/ of the common words *is*, *was*, and plurals such as *bags*, and the /ee/ of words ending in *Y*, thirty-five (92 percent) would be the most used graphemes for the phonemes. The use of *ZH* as in the English word *muzhik* is unusual. It is more often spelled with an *S* as in *treasure*. The use of *AE* for the long *A* sound is somewhat unusual. The only two N'wenglish usages that are unlike English are the use of *TT* for the sound of *TH* as in *thin* and the use of *Q* instead of *QU*. All four (*ZH*, *AE*, *TT*, and *Q*) are a result of conflicts and inconsistencies in English. All four of these phonemes are among the least used English phonemes.

Vowels

Since we use "short" vowels (as in, "That pet did not run.") roughly four times as often as "long" vowels (as in, "They eat fried tofu."), the letters *A*, *E*, *I*, *O*, and *U* are used for short vowels. This leaves long vowels and "other" vowels to be represented by digraphs (two letters used together) or single letters with macrons (a line over the vowel). We only need four "other" vowels: *AU*, *OI*, *OO*, and *OU*. (The terms "short," "long," and "other" vowels are significant only as convenient grouping terms.) This gives a total of fourteen vowel phonemes.

Note that there are two long *U* sounds in English, those in *sue* and in *fuel*. English spelling does not distinguish between the long *U* sounds. N'wenglish spells the sound in *sue* as *UE* and the sound in *fuel* as *YUE*. The logic behind this can be seen by considering *fuel* as the word *yule* with an *F* sound in front. When the letter *Y* is used this way, it can be considered a consonant—the *only* way *Y* is used in N'wenglish. The consonant sound of *Y*, however, is actually the sound of the short *I* forming a diphthong with a following vowel. (Similarly, the consonant sound of the letter *W*—its *only* sound in N'wenglish—is the sound of *UE* forming a diphthong with a following vowel.)

Consonants

There are only twenty-four consonant phonemes needed for efficient communication. Eighteen phonemes are represented by the single consonant letters other than *C*, *Q*, and *X* (since they represent phonemes represented more often by other letters). Since we have billions of dollars' worth of typewriters, typesetters, computer keyboards, and software using *C*, *Q*, and *X*, economy demands that they be used. N'wenglish uses *C* only in *CH* for the first phoneme in the word *chip*, *Q* only for the *KW* phoneme blend (as in *quit*), and *X* only for the *KS* phoneme blend (as in *exit*).

There are more words in the dictionary with a *TH* sound as in *thin*, but words with the *TH* as in *then* occur about ten times as often in most English sentences. This is due to the common words *the, that, this*, etc. To make N'wenglish more easily readable by those who already read English, *TT* represents the lesser-used *TH* sound as in *thin*.

The *WH* sound as in *wheel* or *whale* (not properly pronounced the same as *we'll* or *wail*, if understandability is the goal) is actually pronounced *HW* (air is expelled before a *W* sound). For the sake of those who already read English, however, and for consistency with other consonant digraphs, N'wenglish uses *WH*.

Details of the Proposed Solution

1. Use the single vowels (that is, *A*, *E*, *I*, *O*, and *U*) for the more-often-used short vowel sounds, as in "That pet did not run."

2. Add an *E* or a macron to the single vowels for the long vowel sounds, as in "Mae Green tried roe glue" or "Thā ēt frīd tōfū." Most publishers will use macrons since long vowels (9.1 percent of the phonemes used in most printed material, see appendix 1) will be half as long, saving them ink, paper, and labor.[1] Most handwritten material will use an added *E* for long vowels since a lowercase *E* is the easiest of all letters to write, and it is easier than having to pick up the pen, make a macron, and find your place again.

3. Use *AU*, *OO*, *OI*, and *OU* for the sounds in the words *haul*, *good*, *oil*, and *out*.

4. Use *TT* and *TH* for the sounds of *TH* in *thin* and *then*, respectively.

5. Use *C* only in *CH*, as in *chip*.

6. Use *SH* and *NG* as in *wishing*.

7. Use *ZH* for the sound of *Z* in *azure* or of *S* in *treasure*.

8. Use *Q* and *X* only for the sounds of *KW* and *KS*, as in the English words *quit* and *exit* (*qit* and *exit* in N'wenglish). A good memory word for the *KW* and *KS* twins is *quicksand* (*qixand* in N'wenglish). Use *KS* instead of *X* for plurals and possessives of words ending in *K*.

9. Use the graphemes that are the most used in English for all other

consonants (except for *F*, *S*, and *Y*, see table A2-1) as in, "Yes, Val 'Zip' Kim hid our big fan-jet win."

Table 8-1: The System in a Nutshell (N'wenglish Rules)

1. Each letter or combination of letters has only one sound, as in

M<u>ae</u> Gr<u>ee</u>n l<u>ied</u>, "J<u>oe</u> Bl<u>ue</u>, and K<u>e</u>vin 'T<u>o</u>p G<u>u</u>n' W<u>oo</u>d h<u>au</u>l <u>ou</u>r <u>oi</u>l."
    long vowels ∎ short vowels ∎ other vowels ▎diphthongs

Qit me<u>zh</u>uring fi<u>sh</u> <u>wh</u>ich yuez <u>th</u>is <u>t</u>tin box.

Consonant sounds represented by digraphs (two letters) are underlined. (It is *quit, measuring, use,* and *thin* in English. Underlining in these sentences is for highlighting only, not a rule of N'wenglish spelling. Consonant sounds represented by a single letter are not underlined.)

2. There are no silent letters and no double letters representing a single sound except *OO* and *TT*. A third double letter, *EE*, is used if digraphs instead of macrons are used for the long vowels.
3. All sounds must be shown except (1) the *NG* sound in *NK* and *NX* and (2) an *U* sound between a vowel other than *U* and *R* or *L*.
4. The spelling of trademarks and proper nouns other than the names of the months and the days of the week are unchanged from English.

Optional Rules

5. A slash (/) follows primary accented syllables unless the primary accent is on the last syllable. Hyphens are optional. Compound words may be spelled as one word or may be hyphenated.
6. N'wenglish spelling between slashes should follow proper nouns and trademarks if needed to show pronunciation.
7. The use of an apostrophe to show contractions (such as *can't* for *cannot*) is optional.
8. If needed for clarity, use the following spellings of these common homonyms. The less common homonyms, *if necessary,* can be distinguished by adding a synonym.

E = English, N = N'wenglish, S = singular, P = plural

E	N	E	N	E	N	E	N	E	N
boy	boi	burro	buroe	to	tue	ewe	iue*	your, S	Yoor
buoy	boih*/buei	burrow	buroew*	too	tueh*	yew	ihue*	your, P	yoor
flour	flour	sun	sun	two	tuew*	you, S	Yue	you're, S	Yoo'r
flower	flouur*	son	suhn*			you, P	yue	you're, P	yoo'r

*Different from other N'wenglish spelling. (The long *O* and *U* can also be spelled with macrons.)

The Proposed Solution

Now that you know the invariable sounds that each single letter and each digraph represents in N'wenglish, spelling is easy. Simply write the graphemes in strict left-to-right order representing each phoneme in strict first-to-last order. According to logic this seems so simple that it needs no explanation, but it needs to be stated because many English words do not follow this logical pattern and may mislead us. In N'wenglish there are only eight simple rules, four of which are optional, as shown in table 8-1. There are no exceptions or variations in any of the rules.

Optional rule 6 is important for easy readability and should be used for all except writing intended only for personal use. Although the pronunciation of N'wenglish is immediately obvious, often the placement of the accent is needed to make the word immediately recognizable. The use of an accent mark in English would be of as much or more value in English words as in N'wenglish words. The only reason we do not recognize the need is that we have not only memorized (or learned by repeated use) the pronunciation but also the accent placement of English words. If we are not familiar with a given English word, we must often try two or three accent placements before we can recognize the word. Use of the accent mark will also be of great value in programming computers for voice synthesis, since there are no reliable rules for placement of the accent in English words.

As you can see, there are differences between English and N'wenglish spelling other than which grapheme is used for which phoneme. Some N'wenglish spellings appear strange because they correct one or more of the following English spelling inconsistencies:

1. Some English words do not spell in strict left-to-right order. For example, the second vowel grapheme in *little* is on the wrong side of the *L*. It is *litul* in N'wenglish.

2. Some sounds, such as the second vowel in the word *spasm*, are not shown in English. In N'wenglish it is spelled *spazum*.

3. English uses one grapheme for two adjacent phonemes in some words and that same grapheme for only one of the phonemes in others. For example, the *NG* grapheme represents a different sound in the word *single* than in the word *singer*. They are *singgul* and *singer* in N'wenglish. The use of adjacent *G*s in the word *singgul* does not violate spelling rule 2. They are in different syllables. Similarly, the different pronunciations of Long Island is obvious from the N'wenglish spellings

Let's End Our Literacy Crisis

Long Island /Laung Ielund/ and Long Island /Laung Gielund/, and

4. As table 6-1 shows, many letters in English represent the same sounds as another letter. One of the most confusing is the S, C, Z inconsistency. The way N'wenglish solves the problem is best explained by the following example:

English	N'wenglish	English	N'wenglish
fleece	flees	sin	sin
piece	pees	sins	sinz
seize	seez	since	sins
tease	teez	sense	sens
lease	lees	cents	sens or sents
peace	pees	scents	sens or sents
peas	peez		
seas	seez		
teas	teez		

5. Plurals and past tenses are often shown by adding a suffix that has no relation to the pronunciation of the base word. Use of the suffix is according to complicated rules of doubling or not doubling final consonants and for dropping or not dropping final vowels, etc. Some examples of this inconsistency are:

Base Word			Plural or Past Tense	
English	N'wenglish	English Rule	English	N'wenglish
bat	bat	add *S*	bats	bats
bag	bag	add *S*	bags	bagz
dish	dish	add *ES*	dishes	dishuz
bus	bus	double last letter, add *ES*	busses	busuz
carry	karee	change *Y* to *I*, add *ES*	carries	kareez
judge	juj	add *D*	judged	jujd
hope	hoep	add *D*	hoped	hoept
laugh	laf	add *ED*	laughed	laft
hop	hop	double last letter, add *ED*	hopped	hopt
wade	waed	add *D*	waded	waedud
bat	bat	double last letter, add *ED*	batted	batud

Note: This completes the essentials needed to learn N'wenglish. The remainder of the chapter contains information regarding pronunciation and a comparison of N'wenglish with English and with previous spelling reform proposals. Information on pronunciation is included *only* to help you understand the sounds in the words you pronounce and those you hear others pronounce so you can accurately reproduce them in print. This will maximize the chance of people understanding what you write.

Understanding Pronunciation

For all practical purposes, *sens* and *sents* in item 4 in the previous section are the same. A phoneticist using specialized equipment could tell the difference, but unless the speaker purposely pronounces the word slowly and distinctly, the average person could not. If a person pronounces a word slowly and distinctly, the accent and pronunciation are usually different from when the word is used in normal speech. So when spelling N'wenglish, be sure to spell the words the way they are pronounced in normal speech. Sometimes, of course, we deliberately change the pronunciation of a word for emphasis. We might say, "It's dulish/us." if we like the taste, but if we are really enthusiastic about it we might say, "It's dee/lish/us!" by adding a second primary emphasis. (Only primary emphases are shown according to Spelling Rule 5.) Note the change in the vowel sound in the first syllable.

No one wants to be told how to pronounce their words—nor should they be. Some pronunciations, however, make it more difficult for people to understand us. This is because some speech patterns omit or change a phoneme which is needed to distinguish between similar words—such as omitting *R* phonemes at the end of syllables or of replacing the *R* phoneme with a *U* phoneme or by slightly extending the vowel prior to where the *R* phoneme should be (e.g., is it a *party* or a *potty*?).

In standard broadcast English, unaccented syllables are usually pronounced with a short *U* as in *nuts*. Less often, an unaccented syllable is pronounced with a short *I*. Sometimes unaccented syllables have another sound, but if in doubt use *U* in spelling unaccented syllables. Often the use of a sound other than *U* in unaccented syllables makes the speech sound artificial and pretentious, or regional and quaint.

Table 8-2 shows how the English phonemes are formed. The table is largely self-explanatory, but formation of some of the phonemes needs more explanation. The vowels are all "voiced"—the vocal cords hum—

and are formed by changing the shape of the tongue and mouth without restricting the flow of air. Drawings and explanations of the required shape of the tongue and mouth for pronouncing vowels are available (e.g., see "Phonetics" in the *Encyclopedia Britannica*). Although you undoubtedly know how to pronounce the vowels, practicing the following sounds in front of a mirror should help you understand how vowels are formed:

Sound	As In	Jaw Position	Lip Position	Tongue Position
ee	beet	close	smile	forward
i	bit		smile	forward
e	bet	to	smile	forward
a	bat		unrounded	mid
u	but	↓	unrounded	mid
o	lot	open	unrounded	back
au	law	to	least rounded	back
oo	look	↓	rounded	raised
ue	loon	close	most rounded	raised

The diphthongs are blends of sounds as follows:

Sound	As In	Combined Vowel Sounds
ae	bait	e + ee or e + i
ie	bite	o + ee or o + i
oe	boat	u + ue
yue	cute	i + ue
ou	bout	a + ue, a + oo, or a + u
oi	boil	au + ee, au + i, or au + u

In the Southern U.S., *AE*, *IE*, and *OE* are slightly prolonged single sounds. As previously explained, every syllable beginning with *Y* or *W* is a diphthong of *I* and the following vowel or of *UE* and the following vowel, respectively. Many vowel digraphs making more than one sound can be two sounds or a diphthong (e.g., *menial*: *meeneeul* or *meenyul*).

The consonants are formed by obstructing the airstream through the vocal tract. The most basic classifications of consonants are voiced and voiceless. As a learning exercise, alternately pronounce the two phonemes on the same line in table 8-2. Then note the position of your

The Proposed Solution

tongue and lips as you read aloud through the table. Most speakers raise the soft palate, sealing off the nasal cavity for all consonant phonemes except /m/, /n/ and /ng/. Note that /j/ and /ch/ are formed by briefly stopping the air flow by touching the tip of the tongue to the ridge just behind the front teeth, followed immediately by a *ZH* or *SH* phoneme. Note that the *F, TT, SH,* and *S* phonemes and their voiced equivalents restrict the air flow, but do not stop it. For the *V* and *F* phonemes the lower lip and the upper front teeth are lightly touching. For the *TH* and *TT* phonemes the air flows between the roof of the mouth and the upper front area of the tongue, which is pushed forward and raised to almost touch the ridge just behind the upper front teeth. Note the position of the tip of your tongue and the area just behind it as you pronounce the *S* and the *SH* phonemes. The tip of the tongue is almost against the ridge behind your upper front teeth for the *S* phoneme, but the tip is down very slightly, and the area behind the tip is raised for the *SH* phoneme. Note that the air flows along the sides of the tongue—with little restriction compared to other consonants—for the *L* phoneme. Likewise, there is little air flow restriction for the *R* phoneme—air flows around the tip of the tongue curled slightly up and back or by raising the back of the tongue slightly.

Although all the consonants except *W, Y* and the voiced stops *B, D, G,* and *J* can be said without a vowel, they are not syllables as the glossary shows. The fourteen consonants *M, N, NG, V, TH, ZH, Z, L, R, F, TT, SH, S,* and *H* can be called "continuants," since they can be a prolonged sound without a vowel (although someone would have to be able to see your face and hear you whisper to determine the unvoiced consonants). The *L, R, W,* and *Y* phonemes are often called "semivowels" since, unlike consonants, almost no "friction" is needed to say them. The *H, W,* and *Y* phonemes and the *Q* and *WH* blends occur only at the start of syllables. The *NG* phoneme and the *X, NK,* and *NX* blends can occur only at the end of syllables. The *H* phoneme can occur only before (1) a vowel, (2) the *Y* phoneme (as in *huge—hyuej* in N'wenglish), or (3) the *W* phoneme (in the *WH* blend).

Radio and TV have had a standardizing effect upon pronunciation. The adoption of N'wenglish will have even more of a standardizing effect upon the English-speaking population than radio and TV. This is because sounds are permanently recorded in written form instead of lasting for only a split second, as sounds do.

Table 8-2
How the English Phonemes Are Formed

sound	vocal cords hum			sound	vocal cords quiet
	mouth position				mouth position
	lips	tongue			
		tip	back		
B	closed	down	down	P	same as *B*
D	open	up **	down	T	same as *D*
G	open	down	sealed against soft palate	K	same as *G*
J	(same as the *D* plus the *ZH* sounds)			CH	same as *J* (*T* plus *SH*)
M	closed	down	down	The sounds above this ↑ line are made by briefly stopping the airflow through the mouth. There is airflow through the nose only in *M, N, & NG*.
N	open	up **	down	
NG	open	down	sealed against	
V	lower lip hits upper teeth	down	down	F	same as *V*
TH	open	forward almost to back of upper teeth	down	TT	same as *TH*
ZH	open, pushed forward	slightly down ***	down	SH	same as *ZH*
Z	open	almost to roof of mouth	down	S	same as *Z*
L	open	touch behind upper front teeth	down		
R	open	curled up & back	down		
		down ****	up & back		
vowels plus *w & y* *	slight variations in lips and tongue (air flow unrestricted)			H	slight closure in throat area

   * *W* and *Y*, considered consonants in N'wenglish, actually form a diphthong of a vowel preceded by *UE* and *I*, respectively.
  ** The tongue touches the roof of the mouth just behind upper teeth, sealing the mouth shut.
 *** The area just behind the tip is raised almost to the roof of the mouth.
**** This is the more common of the two alternates.

This does not mean that a "standard" speech should be imposed upon people. It also doesn't mean that a "standard" is needed for understanding a record of their pronunciation.

The Proposed Solution

Dr. Charles Kenneth Thomas, linguist and author, states,

> The truly sophisticated person recognizes that it is normal for the Bostonian, the Iowan, the New Yorker, and the Alabaman to speak each according to his own standard. He makes this observation without developing any undue sense of either superiority or inferiority in his own speech. With a little further acquaintance he may come to the conclusion that some Bostonians, some New Yorkers, some Iowans, and some Alabamans speak better than he does; others, not as well. No one area has a monopoly on "correctness."...
>
> Generally speaking, no dictionary should be used as the authority for the pronunciation of common words; the true authority lies in the speech around you. *Webster's New International*, for example, uses different symbols for the vowels of *damp* and *dance*. Do not therefore make the mistake of assuming that if you use the same vowel in *dance* as in *damp* you are speaking "incorrectly." A glance at Webster's "Guide to Pronunciation" will inform you that some people in some areas distinguish the vowel of *dance* from that of *damp*, and that others make no such distinction. The dictionary's function is to keep the categories straight, not to compel you to forsake the established usage of your community....
>
> The acquisition of good speech is part of the individual's adaptation to his social environment. Some types of speech mark the speaker as inferior. Unless he gives unmistakable evidence of superiority in other respects, some opportunities will be closed to him. The traditional American goal of rising in the world can rarely be achieved by speech improvement alone, but speech improvement often helps. Not all of us will become great public speakers, great actors, or great preachers. But most of us can adapt our speech to what the community accepts as normal, and be accepted as normal by our neighbors.[2]

Differences in Pronunciation We Will Hear

Among American speakers there are two major differences:
1. The first difference is retention or dropping of the *R* phoneme at the end of a syllable (or changing the *R* to a *U* phoneme). For clarity, all *writers* should include the *R*. Even the *R*-droppers know their location.

2. Some speakers omit the expulsion of breath before the /w/ in pronouncing words containing the *WH* blend (i.e., they pronounce *weather* and *whether*, *wail* and *whale*, *we'll* and *wheel* the same). Just as the *R*-droppers know, those who make no distinction between /w/ and /h/-/w/ know where the /h/-/w/ is located. To improve clarity, *writers* should show the *WH*.

This is a partial list of words that could be confused if no distinction is made between /h/-/w/ and /w/:

whale.wail	whence.wince	whicker.wicker
whaler.wailer	where.wear	whither.wither
whaling.wailing	whet.wet	whine.wine
what.watt	whether.weather	whir.were
wheal.we'll	whew.woo	whish.wish
whee.we	which.witch	whit. wit
wheel.we'll	whey.way	Whig.wig
when.win		

Speakers in England often pronounce vowels that Americans pronounce the same as the *A* in *hat* the way that Americans pronounce the *O* in *hot*. But other than a few isolated words that are different (such as pronouncing *been* to rhyme with *seen*), the only other major difference (besides the two differences in the previous paragraph) found in pronunciations in England is the distinction they make between the A in calm and father as opposed to the *O* in *comma* and *bother*. Accent placement of many British words is also different from the accent placement in the U.S.

Accents and Assimilations

The purpose of the remainder of this section on pronunciation is not to establish standards but to understand what we are hearing so that we can more easily represent the sounds. These examples are from Dr. Thomas's book, *An Introduction to the Phonetics of American English.*

> Variations in the level of energy we use in speaking have an important bearing on oral communication. We are accustomed to hearing some syllables pronounced with greater force than those which precede or follow them. If we do not hear such a variation, the speaking becomes monotonous, sometimes unintelligible. Occasionally,

The Proposed Solution

indeed, a difference in the degree of force may change the meaning: if we pronounce the syllables [of the word *insight*] with more energy in the first syllable than in the second, we pronounce the noun *insight*; but if we put more energy into the second syllable than the first, we pronounce the verb *incite*. Thus the energy level alone may have distinctive value, though ordinarily changes in the energy are accompanied by noticeable changes in the quality of the vowels as well. If, for instance, we add stress to the second syllable of *youngest* [*yungist* or *yungust* in N'wenglish], we change the meaning to that of *young guest* [note that the second vowel has changed]. If we add stress to the normally unstressed first syllable of *occur*, we may confuse the verb with the pigment ocher [*oe/kur* in N'wenglish, again note the change in the first vowel]....

A double assimilation takes place in the phrase *used to*. The verb *used* [*yuezd* in N'wenglish] has been assimilated to *use* [*yues* in N'wenglish], by the following [*T*], and has acquired the meaning "formerly accustomed." The unassimilated pronunciation, with looser juncture, has been kept for the meaning "utilized." Thus, *the pen he used to* [*yues tu* in N'wenglish] *write with* means the pen he was accustomed to write with; *the pen he used to* [*yuezd tue* in N'wenglish] *write with* means the pen he utilized for writing.

Something similar occurs in the phrases *have to* and *has to* when they denote compulsion. *That is all I have to* [*haf tu* in N'wenglish] *do* means that that is all I am compelled to do. *That is all I have to* [*hav tue* in N'wenglish] *do* means that that is all I have on hand at the moment to do. In the sentence, *That is all he has to do*, [*has tu* in N'wenglish] and [*haz tue* in N'wenglish] indicate the same distinction in meaning. The form [*yues tu* in N'wenglish] is fully established in standard speech; the assimilated [*haf tu* in N'wenglish] and [*has tu* in N'wenglish], despite their usefulness, still impress some conservatives as substandard....

Comparison of *sense* and *cents*, and *false* with *faults*, illustrates the falling together of originally distinct clusters. As the clusters [-*NTS*] and [-*LTS*] of *cents* and *faults* have weakened, [*T*] has intruded into the clusters [-*NS*] and [-*LS*] of *sense* and *false*, so that homophonous [words pronounced the same] pairs have developed. Only the laboratory phonetician, with instruments more sensitive than the human ear, can rightly decide whether to record both *sense* and *cents* as [*sens* in N'wenglish] or both as [*sents* in N'wenglish]; whether to record both *false* and *faults* as [*fauls* in N'wenglish] or both as [*faults* in N'wenglish]. For the practical purposes of daily speaking we distinguish *sense* from *cents*, and *false* from *faults*, in the same way that we distinguish *see* from *sea*: by context, not by sound.[3]

Exercise One

Transcribe the sentence below into N'wenglish. Refer to previous pages as much as you wish. This is a spelling test designed to emphasize the difference between English and N'wenglish, so it may be more difficult than ordinary reading material. This is an ideal preparation for reading appendix 4—words you find there will appear less unusual after this exercise. Your answer is correct if the differences from the answer at the end of this chapter are due to differences in the way you pronounce the words. (Adjacent bold words show different pronunciations of the same letters.)

A **single singer** in the **children's chorus won one** award for **his song**, written **by young** guest **conductor, cellist** "John Boy" Greenwood, an **exceptional example** of independence among American musicians, about an **unnatural type** of **city cop who, whenever** the need arose, proved that "blood is **thicker than** water" by taking his azure blue and his **jade green gems** and his "lynx links" gold chain necklace from his bank vault to quickly pay for his nephew's operation, the **first of** many that he needed to help him quit coughing whenever he pronounced the words *grasshopper, knighthood, however*, and *whoever*.

Understanding Those Who Pronounce Differently

Although N'wenglish will eventually have a standardizing effect, no one has to pronounce their words in a certain way to be understood. Frank C. Laubach points out that "[i]t is a linguistic axiom that what is understandable as speech is also understandable when written with a suitable phonetics."[4] Those who speak English can understand most people speaking English despite their pronunciation, dialect, or foreign accent. One main reason this is true is that we understand words in context, whether spoken or written.

Understanding written communication is easier than understanding spoken communication. This is because:

The Proposed Solution

1. When listening, if you miss a syllable or a word it is gone forever (unless it was recorded or you can ask the speaker to repeat the word), but the written word is permanent. We can examine written words at our leisure or examine them intently as long as needed.

2. The reader can look back at the context (just as the listener can remember what was said just before). The reader also can look ahead at the context, something not possible with spoken communication.

3. Perhaps most important, it is easy to see the starting and ending points of written words because of the spaces. With spoken words there is no such separation. Unless the speaker speaks slowly and purposely separates the words, many (if not most) of the words are run together. If we do not immediately recognize each word in the sentence, we may not know if one or more syllables from words both before and after the unrecognized word are a part of it.

Even those speakers who are often misunderstood, however, are usually familiar with the way people who are easily understood pronounce their words. If they want to be sure they are understood in writing, they can write using that pronunciation instead of their own. As Dewey points out, "As early as 1935, the British Broadcasting Corporation had successfully established a standard, 'Broadcast English,' for announcers."[5] A similar pronunciation is standard in the United States. Although large portions of the public do not pronounce their words according to the broadcast English standard, they are almost always familiar it.

Characteristics of the Proposed Solution

One initial concern about N'wenglish might be the length of the words. Because of the useless and confusing double consonants, the silent letters, and the two-, three-, four-, and even five-letter blends used for a single phoneme in English, the lengths of English and N'wenglish words are nearly the same. The length of N'wenglish words ranges from roughly 7 percent shorter than English if we use macrons but not accent symbols[6], to 4 percent longer if we use both digraphs and accent symbols. The ideal for readability—use of macrons and accent symbols—is almost identical with English in length.

Another concern is the spelling difference from English: 14.1 percent of the words in a list of all the different words in appendix 4 (other than capitalized and foreign words) are spelled the same as in

English. When frequency of usage is considered, the spelling is more similar: 29 percent of the one hundred most frequently used words (see table 9-2) are spelled the same. Also, 42.5 percent of a list of all the different words in appendix 4 are the same or with only one phoneme spelled differently.

Although every sample of writing will be somewhat different, most N'wenglish writing will be similar to appendix 4. There are 19,486 words and 7,991 consonant combinations (two or more adjacent letters) in appendix 4. Only 3.7 percent of the adjacent consonants are in different syllables (end of one syllable, start of the next). Of the 96.3 percent of the consonant combinations that blend into one syllable, 90.8 percent (or 87.4 percent of the total consonant combinations) are two-letter blends.

The frequency of occurrence of all combinations which make up 1 percent or more of the total of the 7,991 blends is shown in figure 8-1 in the next section of this chapter. The twenty blends in this figure (which include the *WH* blend and five phonemes) make up roughly 78 percent of the blends in appendix 4. Concerning the two sounds unlike English: (1) the *TT* phoneme makes up only about 4 percent of the total blends, and (2) the *Q* blend makes up less than 1 percent of the total. Note that only two three-letter blends (*RLD*, as in *world*, and *NGZ*, as in *things*) appear in the list—each of them occurs in only 1 percent of the consonant blends.

You Can Help End Our Literacy Crisis Workbook (see page opposite the title page) has a more complete table of consonant cluster usage frequency and lists 2,191 words that were found in a standard desk dictionary that are spelled the same in English and N'wenglish. Another dictionary would list additional words spelled the same in English and N'wenglish, and an unabridged dictionary would have even more.

This Proposal versus Previous Proposals

There is no readily available research on the acceptability of an extremely easy-to-learn spelling system—such as N'wenglish—to those who already read English. It may be that there is little, if any, such research. Research does reveal that no other spelling reform proposal approaches N'wenglish in simplicity. Furthermore, at no time the 1960s prior to has the American public—especially parents of school-age children—been so desperate to improve the teaching of reading. There has been no clamor for educators to succeed in teaching reading even if it requires going outside

The Proposed Solution

previously determined limits regarding the type of solution they are willing to try. Many scholars and spelling reform advocates assume that the public would never accept a phonemic spelling system. As a result, most educators and politicians want to maintain the status quo as opposed to implementing anything too different. The tiny proportion of educators and politicians advocating improving our spelling either advocate simplifying a few hundred words at a time or a spelling system with inconsistencies to make it more like English. However, those who already read would not look favorably on such a procedure. The reasons are obvious: those in positions of authority can already read; simplifying a few hundred words at a time would not only require many years to complete the process, everyone would have to know two spellings of certain words until the process is complete—the traditional spelling and the simplified spelling. Adoption of a spelling system with inconsistencies in it to make it more like English would not only be resisted by present readers for the same reasons as mentioned earlier, it would not be sufficiently easier than English to justify the effort required by new learners and their teachers.

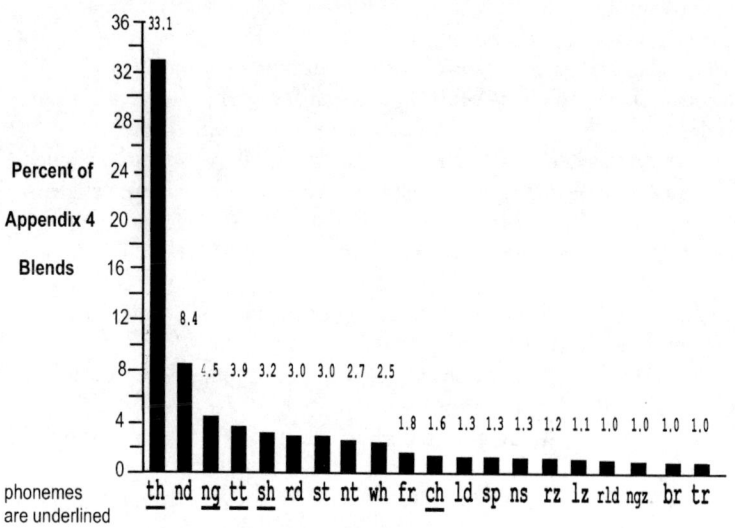

Figure 8-1
Frequency of Occurrence of Two or More Adjacent Consonants

Let's End Our Literacy Crisis

Exercise Two

Transcribe the following sentence into English. What is unique about the English transcription? (See the answer at the end of this chapter.)

Ie due not noe wher fam/ulee dok/turz uqierd ilej/ublee purplex/ing hand/rieting; nevurthules, extruoer/duneree formusue/tukul intulekchual/utee, kounturbal/unsing indusiefurubil/utee, transunden/tuliezuz inturkumyuenukae/shun'z inkompruhen/subulnus.

Testimonial letters for the initial teaching alphabet (i.t.a., a simplified spelling system popular in the 1960s) in Sir James Pitman's book *Alphabets and Reading* point out the rapid learning possible with a simpler spelling of English words. The letters may also cause the reader to ask if we should adopt the spelling system referred to in the letters or some other proposed system instead of N'wenglish. I.t.a. was never intended to permanently replace English spelling—as N'wenglish is—but to show beginners that they can read. With the psychological help of knowing that they *can* read, they are ready—usually in the second grade—to switch over to learning English spelling. The switchover was usually easier than the bewilderment of initially learning English spelling. But since the change to English spelling was a problem for some students, i.t.a. has been abandoned in most—if not all—areas.

I.t.a. would help many schoolchildren if used as a stepping stone to English spelling, since it is designed with several inconsistencies to make it more like English spelling. It would do little as a stepping stone for adult illiterates, however, who would still have to spend hundreds of hours learning English spelling—which most are unwilling or unable to do. See appendix 6 for a detailed listing of the inconsistencies of i.t.a.

There are five types of proposed spelling reforms:

1. Augmented—adding symbols to the 26 letters so there is one letter for each sound (for example, i.t.a.).

2. Diacritical—adding marks above or below letters to distinguish sounds.

3. Digraphic—using the existing 26 letters and combinations of them to represent all the sounds—the method used in English and N'wenglish.

4. Color codes—using colors to indicate different sounds.

The Proposed Solution

5. Non-Romanic—adopting an entirely new alphabet with a new symbol for each sound, such as that proposed by George Bernard Shaw.

Appendix II of Sir James Pitman's book *Alphabets and Reading* shows details on eight augmented, three diacritical, eight digraphic, and five non-Romanic alphabets proposed between 1568 and 1968. Although no color code alphabets are shown, the text gives a brief description of four of them. It seems clear that the huge costs of replacing all printing equipment rules out all but the digraphic proposals. A comparison of the eight digraphic proposals and N'wenglish shows that only N'wenglish is strictly a one-sound-per-symbol and one-symbol-per-sound system. The other eight proposed spellings range (1) from one to seven letters that have more than one pronunciation—several letters have as many as three pronunciations; (2) from two to thirteen phonemes that are spelled with more than one grapheme—some phonemes are spelled with as many as six different graphemes; and (3) from one to twelve more spellings than N'wenglish that are not the most used in English.

There have been a few spelling reform proposals since the publication of Pitman's list, but like those on his list, they contain several inconsistencies. Presumably the inconsistencies in all the proposed spelling systems are to make them more like English and therefore more acceptable to those who already read English. All such inconsistencies, however, make the spelling system more difficult for new learners and largely defeat the original purpose of designing a new system. A brief reference to the relative frequency of phonemes usage chart in appendix 1 shows that N'wenglish cannot be much simpler than it now is. A simpler alphabet is listed on the chart, but far fewer of the phoneme-grapheme pairs are the same as those most used in English. As a result, the alphabet would be much more difficult for present readers of English to learn. The small gain in simplicity of the alphabet does not justify the additional learning required. Appendix 6 shows details of how N'wenglish is superior to all other known spelling reform proposals.

Scholars and researchers may profit from endless speculation that a proposed alphabet may prove inadequate if tested on enough different combinations of thousands of words. Those who benefit from more research or who are too cautious about—or resistant to—change will no doubt want to examine other possibilities. They may want more precision in representing sounds, even though for the purpose of communication N'wenglish is more than adequate. The point, however, is that the chance of significantly improving upon N'wenglish, regardless of how much more research is done, is slight; the need for a solution to our literacy crisis is great and growing, and hundreds of millions of people will be hurt by our failure to act upon what we already know!

Exercise One Answer

U sing/gul sing/ur in thu chil/drun'z koer/us (or kaur/us) wun wun uwaurd fur (or faur) his saung, rit/un bie yung gest kunduk/tur, chel/ust "John Boi" Greenwood, an ixep/shunul igzam/pul uv indupen/duns (or indeepen/duns*) umung American myoozi/shunz (or myuezi/shunz), ubout an unach/urul tiep uv sit/ee kop hue, whenev/ur thu need uroez, pruevd that "blud iz ttik/ur thun (or than) wo/tur" bie taek/ing hiz azh/ur blue and hiz jaed green jemz and hiz "linx links" goeld chaen nek/lus from hiz bank vault tue qik/lee pae faur hiz nefyue'z opurae/shun, thu furst uv me/nee that hee need/ud tue qit kauf/ing when (or whun) hee prunounst thu wurdz gras/hopur, niet/hood, houev/ur, and hue/evur.

* Note four different pronunciations of the letter *E* in one English word (ee, e, u, silent)!

Exercise Two Answer

I do not know where family doctors acquired illegibly perplexing handwriting; nevertheless, extraordinary pharmaceutical intellectuality, counterbalancing indecipherability, transcendentalizes intercommunication's incomprehensibleness.

The thing that is unique about the English transcription is that each word has one more letter than the previous one. This is the only known instance in this book in which the English has a regularity to it that the N'wenglish does not. This is because it was *designed* to be that way.

Chapter 9
Effective Literacy Training

With N'wenglish, students are taught the phonemes and the graphemes that represent them. As a result they learn to pronounce any word—even "words" made from nonsense syllables and words they do not know! If they pronounce a word in their vocabulary, they recognize (read) the word. Although they can read words in sentences or phrases more easily because of the contextual clues, they can also read word lists. Reading word lists correctly is impossible for students of English spelling unless they have already learned every word in the list, because there is no dependable phoneme-grapheme correspondence. In short, N'wenglish students are taught a method by which they can decipher the word, rather than the whole-word, memory-work (or worse: guesswork) methods used with English that far too often lead to failure. N'wenglish bypasses the phonics versus whole-word or whole-language debate by making our words perfectly phonemic, so that teaching by phonics *can* be used. In other words, N'wenglish cures the root cause of the problem.

Dr. Diane McGuinness' book, *Why Our Children Can't Read*, refers to extensive research in the last ten years on teaching methods to be used to teach reading. She conclusively demonstrates that when the phonics method is used correctly it is far superior to other methods. The research she refers to is not the only research reaching that conclusion.

Let's End Our Literacy Crisis

For example, Dr. Patrick Groff, in his book *Decodable Words in Reading Textbooks, Why They Are Imperative*, says that even with our "messed-up" spelling system, a direct and systematic phonics teaching system is better than any other system. He also says that the whole language approach to teaching reading resulted in students in California being the least competent reading students in the nation prior to the 1995 California law mandating that words in the reading books must now be "decodable." This means the students must be taught, through phonics instruction, to sound out each letter in the word before seeing the word in a reading book. This also means that with our "messed-up" spelling system it can take *years* for the students to reach a point where they can accurately "decode" every word they see.

Whole language teaching depends upon the students to gain clues to the meaning of words from the adjacent words, that is, from the context. But this does not work if they do not know all of the adjacent words, and it does not always work even if they do.[1]

Dr. Diane McGuinness's book, *Why Our Children Can't Read*, is one of the best books in print for teaching students to read English. There are two problems, however. Chapter 8 of *Why Our Children Can't Read*, entitled "Beginning Reading Right," which teaches beginning readers *one* grapheme for each phoneme, states that learning the material in chapter 8 should take from four to eight months—depending on the age and aptitude of the child.[2] This agrees closely to the amount of time required to learn to read in other languages. But then the student must tackle the material in chapter 9, entitled "Mastering the Advanced Code in Reading, Writing, and Spelling," which can require many additional months for learning what are called "alternative spellings." The time spent learning these alternative spellings is time wasted—valuable time that puts our students far behind students in the rest of our increasingly competitive world.

The second problem is that many adults have great difficulty with any teaching method for learning a spelling system (i.e., English) that has already "defeated them." At present, less than 1 percent of adult nonreaders or poor readers ever receive enough instruction to achieve the equivalent of an eighth-grade reading skill after leaving grade school or high school. Most who *do* succeed in learning to read as adults require over a year of intensive one-on-one tutoring. Until an easy-to-learn spelling system such as N'wenglish is adopted, many millions of adult illiterates will not learn to read.

Requirements for an Effective Teacher

Almost anyone can effectively teach N'wenglish with only a day or two of preparation. If you are not a teacher by profession, you should plan on teaching only one student at a time. The only real requirement, other than being familiar with material in this book and the companion volume, *Let's End Our Literacy Crisis Workbook*, is to be enthusiastic and encouraging toward your students. You will also need to provide the simple teaching materials the students need, as explained here and in the companion volume. You will be able to prepare almost all of these materials from items you already have or from items you can purchase inexpensively. Note that table 9-2, at the end of this chapter, shows that by learning only one hundred words, the students will know about half the words they will see in most written material.

The companion volume has more complete teaching guidelines for young children, teenagers, and adults. It also has most of the beginning teaching materials you will need.

The Latest Scientific Studies on Dyslexia

Research reported by Dr. McGuiness tells parents that they should firmly believe that all students can be taught to read. The research data overwhelmingly show that present beliefs about dyslexia, developmental delays, and learning disabilities are incorrect. Basing your teaching upon these incorrect beliefs will keep you from expecting rapid progress. The research shows that if a student is having reading problems, you must quickly do something about it—the problem will *not* self-correct.[3]

Even if a child is diagnosed as having some sort of minimal brain disfunction, the child can still be taught to read. Medical doctors most familiar with these diagnoses will tell you that there is such a thing as attention deficit disorder, but it is much more rare than many people think. They will tell you that one in twenty students, at most, have true attention deficit disorder. A parent should never accept a diagnosis of any type of brain disfunction from a teacher or school administrator. Not all medical doctors are qualified to make such a diagnosis. Parents and guardians should insist upon receiving the evaluation of a medical doctor who is a specialist in minimal brain disfunction, perhaps even getting a second opinion from another specialist.

As Sir James Pitman, Dr. Diane McGuinness, Samuel Blumenfeld, and others have found, and as chapter 7 has shown, disruptive behaviors are often incorrectly diagnosed as some type of minimal brain disfunction. More often these behaviors are a result of the frustration of being unable to read.

The section on the psychology of learning at the end of this chapter highlights one of the biggest differences between teaching students to read in the U.S. prior to the twentieth century and now. Teachers and parents back then fully expected every student to learn to read—and the students knew it. As a result of this expectation and other factors, almost all of them *did* learn to read. In fact, in the early 1800s, in what is believed to be the first educational survey done in the U.S., it was found that only one in a thousand (0.1 percent) could not read—and write neatly—as reported by President Adams. Other differences (explained in chapter 6) include (1) hindrances to learning that did not exist prior to the twentieth century, (2) time-consuming pleasurable activities that did not exist before the twentieth century, and (3) present-day inferior teaching methods adopted partly because nearly all teachers and some students (especially older students) dislike the memorization and drills that students in simpler times were more willing to accept.

A diagnosis of *dyslexia* was often a result of the earliest, now disproven theory that it occurred in students who had visual problems. Several experiments showed that good readers were no better at visual tasks than poor readers. Poor readers of the same age and intelligence as good readers were just as good at copying English or Hebrew letters as the good readers and remembered the visual patterns of the Hebrew letters equally well. Furthermore, there was no evidence that poor readers reversed their letters more often than good readers.

Early belief that dyslexia was a result of an inferior verbal ability has brought out the question of which causes which: is the poor verbal ability the cause of reading problems, or does the poor reading ability cause the verbal problems? Reading can open a whole new world of verbal experience, which may expand the abilities of the good readers. Since the answer to which causes which is not presently known, age and intelligence matching of good and poor students cannot be used to prove anything about reading ability. Such matching is only good for excluding possibilities; it is equivalent to the first hurdle the researcher must cross.

Researchers tested the word retention of a group of four- and five-year-old students. There was no correlation between word memory and ability to read one and one-half years later. There *was* a correlation between the ability to remember words at the age of four or five and reading ability after two and one-half years—by which time the students had learned to read—causing the researchers to conclude that learning to read is what improved their memory.

It has been shown by reading match experiments that poor readers have poor phonological skills. They have difficulty detecting rhymes and initial consonant clusters, and they are poor at reading nonsense words, indicating that poor readers are hindered by their weakness in perceiving the sounds of English. Perception of the phonemes, however, can be learned. There have been experiments which compare those who can and cannot read and comparing readers' learning of a logographic (picture writing) script and an alphabetic script. The experiments indicate that the experience of learning an alphabetic script improves phonological skills *if the phoneme-grapheme correlation is dependable*—which in English it is not. Some students can manage in spite of the difficulties of English spelling. Others cannot manage the difficulties and give up.[4]

Recent studies by the American Association for the Advancement of Science have shown that countries with a complex, irregular spelling system have a higher incidence of dyslexia. The dyslexia rate of ten-year-old students in the U.S. is at least twice that in Italy, which has a simple spelling system. As mentioned earlier, authorities have claimed the problem is due to some type of brain disfunction. The question must be asked, "Do the brains of dyslexics in different countries have processing problems that are different?" A recent study of dyslexic adults who speak English, Italian, and French shows that this is not the case. Although the disorder manifests itself in different ways in the three languages, the neurological basis for dyslexia is the same.

Those who think the difficulties of spelling English have been exaggerated in chapter 6 (where 736 ways of spelling thirty-eight phonemes are listed) should make note of this statement by the American

Association for the Advancement of Science, "[T]here are 1,120 ways of representing 40 sounds (phonemes) [in English]." It also states, "[L]anguages with complex [spellings] are difficult for both dyslexics and non-dyslexics to read."[5]

An article entitled "Why English is hard on the brain" in the January 20, 1996, issue of *New Scientist* magazine tells of a seventeen-year-old boy raised in Japan by English-speaking parents. The boy, known as AS, has no trouble with university textbooks on physics written in Japanese, but he has great difficulty reading primary-school storybooks in English. He began attending a Japanese primary school when he was six years old. It was soon apparent that he was lagging behind his Japanese peers in English. When AS was thirteen, he was diagnosed as having dyslexia, the first person shown to be dyslexic in one language but not dyslexic in another.

Takeo Wydell of Brunel University in west London pointed out that if dyslexia were caused by impairments in a specific area of the brain, it should—in theory—affect all languages and that AS's case poses problems for those claiming that dyslexia is caused by a disorder in visual processing. This is clearly shown when comparing Japanese and English written languages. Japanese has three written forms: kanji, hiragana, and katakana. Kanji is composed of symbols which have a consistent meaning but have no phonetic value. Katakana and hiragana symbols represent a specific, unvarying sound. AS can read both kanji and katakana with no problems, showing that he has no problems with visual processing. AS can speak English "just like a native" English speaker, but he scored only half as well as the average person his age and could read only one in fifty "difficult" words. Wydell argues that if AS had difficulty with visual processing, it would show up even more in kanji. Wydell suspects that AS—and many other students—suffers from a type of dyslexia that mainly occurs in English. Wydell believes that the problem is the brain's ability to cope with the English language's complex mapping of phonemes to graphemes and the many irregularities. Kana letters, on the other hand, always sound the same.[6]

Teaching Principles and Overview

You cannot teach your students something you do not fully understand yourself. Few parents or teachers are fully informed about the sounds in our language—even though they may read fluently. So your first step is to be sure you know the phonemes used in N'wenglish. Review the section entitled "Understanding the Pronunciation of Words" in chapter 8 and practice until you can teach confidently. Learn the fourteen vowel sounds by practicing the memory aid sentences in part (3) of the "Do We Really Want to Solve the Literacy Crisis" section of chapter 1, table 8-1, or figure 11-1. Practice saying the continuants (/m/, /n/, /ng/, /v/, /th/, /zh/, /z/, /l/, /r/, /f/, /tt/, /sh/, and /s/) as a prolonged sound without a vowel (the last four are unvoiced, so someone who is close enough to see your face and hear you whisper could probably tell which phoneme you are saying). Practice the unvoiced stops (/p/, /t/, /k/, and /ch/) with just a puff of air. Practice saying /y/ and /w/ and the voiced stops (/b/, /d/, /g/, and /j/)—the only consonants that cannot be said without a vowel—with the very minimal /u/ (as in *nut*). The only other phoneme is represented by the letter *H*, which is just an exhalation before another phoneme.

You cannot teach merely by telling your students what they need to know. Students do not learn based upon what the teacher says or does but based upon what the teacher gets the students to do.

Teachers of beginning readers must be alert because they are custodians of their students' destiny. Since many things can go wrong, never assume that a student is using the correct strategy, even if the student seems to be reading fluently. Research shows that beginning readers are less likely to adopt an efficient strategy than an inefficient one. Once an insufficient strategy is adopted, many students will not change their reading strategy, no matter how inefficient it may become. Some very intelligent students go for years before their serious reading problem becomes evident.

There are other problems that impact reading ability. Severe speech disorders will cause students to have difficulty with an alphabetic writing system. Most teachers routinely request help for students they think may have speech problems.

Since visually scanning left to right across a row of text then moving down to the next line and scanning across again is an unnatural act, this skill is often slow to develop. It is almost impossible for some students to master without extra help. Such students may begin guessing at words because they do not see each letter in the word. The teacher should notify the parent, guardian, or a responsible adult if visual problems are suspected. The person notified should get help from an optometrist specializing in therapy for visual problems.[7]

Although parents can work with their child one on one, teachers must often deal with a class of twenty-five or thirty students. Most of the effective teaching of reading skills must be done in small groups so that the teacher can give individual help to the slower students. The normal maximum is about four preteens or six teenagers or older. Teachers must arrange for exercises for the entire class as well as for portions of the class while they monitor each student at some time during the week. Plan for ten to twenty minutes of group time every day, depending upon the age of the students.

The students will learn faster and will be less likely to develop reading problems if the teacher provides a variety of reading materials, stories, games, spelling words, and worksheets that are of interest to the students and that use all three skills: reading, writing, and spelling. The reading materials chosen must, quite obviously, correspond to the developing mastery of the students' reading skills. Teachers, however, should also read materials to the class that may be above the reading ability of the students. This would include interesting stories or poems, or stories that the teachers have invited students to invent and which the teachers transcribe. Materials provided for the students' reading, however, should *not* contain types of letter combinations that they have not been taught.

Present-day kindergarten teaching methods virtually guarantee that the students have learned exactly what they do not need and should not know. They have usually memorized letter names which will interfere with their attempts to learn to read and spell. This is because the present-day English letter names give little or no indication of what sounds the letters make. Most kindergartners are also taught many English "sight words." They have been set up for failure as a result of two things:

1. The names of the letters are just sounds to chant in sequence that provide no help in learning to read.

2. They learn to read by memorizing whole words by sight.[8]

The teacher should strongly discourage the use of the present English letter names. Teachers who show a letter *B* and ask what it is will probably get a chorus of "It's a bee!" Tell the students that "bee" is a letter name they need to forget for a while. They should be told that the present English letter names do not assist in learning to read or spell. Teach the students that the *sound* the letters make is what is important. Show the letter *B* and say that it is a "sound picture" for the sound /b/, and it is *always* spelled this way.[9]

Consider using the optional names for the alphabet as shown in the section titled "Letter Names," later in this chapter. The optional alphabet names should definitely be used if the students have not already learned the English alphabet names.

An overview of a good beginners' reading program is as follows:

1. *Phoneme awareness*. Students must learn the sound of the phonemes and the letter(s) that represents each one. They must learn to separate adjacent phonemes and blend separated phonemes.

2. *Alphabet principle*. The alphabet must be taught in the way it is *written:* from sound to print.

3. *Sound-to-symbol association*. Teach the students to relate the phonemes in words to each letter or digraph.

4. *Logic*. The training must proceed in a logical order from simple to complex. It must also meet the developmental needs of the students. It must include *all* of the different N'wenglish spellings of the phonemes.

5. *Curriculum*. Teaching materials must include all of the skill areas: phoneme analysis, segmenting, blending, reading, writing, and spelling, and the skill areas must be related in their *context*.

6. *Teaching style*. Teaching should be by example and by exposing the teaching materials to the students. Brief, clear explanations are necessary. Get the students involved in discovering ideas and concepts and in solving problems.

7. A *Fail-safe Method*. Ensure that the students are making progress by frequent monitoring.[10]

8. *The **critical** teaching component*. Be absolutely certain that each student masters each skill area before proceeding to the next skill area.[11]

The Correct Order for Teaching Reading Skills

1. *Teach the eighteen consonants represented by a single letter*.

2. *Teach these consonants at both the start and end of three phoneme words (CVC or consonant-vowel-consonant) and teach the five vowels represented by a single letter at the same time*.

3. *Teach segmenting, blending, and tracking*. Show the students

the way to separate phonemes in two- and three-phoneme words into isolated sounds: /k/ /a/ /t/, and the way to blend the sounds into a word: *kat.* Also, teach the students to listen for changes in the sound of a series of words in which one sound is different in each new word. This is called "tracking" or "chaining." The student should write at each step. The letters should be copied in sequence, and the sound each letter makes should be said aloud as the teacher dictates, sound by sound. Carefully explain that most words (other than *I, you,* and *a)* have both vowels and consonants, but ***all words have a vowel***—there are no exceptions.[12]

4. *Teach consonant clusters, both at the start and end of words with one of the five vowels they have learned.* After the students have mastered simple CV, CVC, and VC patterns and the one-to-one mappings have been mastered, introduce the consonant clusters. Carefully explain that consonant clusters are blends of two or more sounds and must never be confused with digraphs, which are two letters to represent one sound. All of the consonants in the consonant clusters at this point in instruction must be those represented by a single letter. The students can take what they have now learned and produce hundreds of new words—all using the same logic.[13]

5. *Teach students the consonant digraphs.* A completely new logic is involved with the consonant digraphs. This teaching must not begin until the students have mastered reading and spelling with single letters. Switching to a logic in which two of the letters the students have been using to represent separate sounds are combined to represent a single new sound causes a problem for them: a single letter is in two categories at the same time.

To be sure the students understand that a digraph represents *one sound,* they must go back and explore mouth and tongue actions and perform listening exercises. For example, after the students learn the /ch/ phoneme, the teacher can show them the /ch/ "sound picture." This must be both letters written on a single card or tile, *not* the letters on separate cards or tiles pushed together.[14]

6. *Teach redundant letters.* Since the letters *C, X,* and *QU* are used for sounds that are more often spelled with other letters, these three letters are redundant. As a result, *C* is used in N'wenglish *only* for the *CH* digraph, *X* is used *only* for the /ks/ sound, and *Q* (not *QU*) is used *only* for the /kw/ sound. Use the *KS* spelling for plurals and past tenses

of words ending in *K*. Note that *X* and *Q* are the opposite of digraphs in that a single letter represents two sounds. The redundant letters should merely be taught as representing their respective sounds. If a student notices that *X* and *Q* represent two sounds, compliment them for being so observant.[15]

7. *Teach vowel digraphs.* After the students have mastered the consonant digraphs, they should be ready for the more difficult vowel digraphs. They have learned five vowels that are represented by single letters. English has fourteen vowel phonemes. Mastery of N'wenglish spelling comes only after learning *all* the vowel phonemes. This is because some of the vowel sounds are a little difficult to tell apart. Accurate pronunciation of some of the vowels is more difficult than of most of the consonants, but it is important, because changing a vowel results in a new word or nonsense syllables.

There is no satisfactory way of classifying the vowels. They are simple or complex in terms of their sound patterns, but they are not "long" or "short." The *diphthongs* are complex in that two simple vowels are said in such rapid succession that they are *perceived* as a single sound. For example, one common pronunciation of the /oi/ diphthong is /au/ and /i/ said in rapid succession, even though it is not spelled that way. Do not try to classify the vowels for the students. If, for example, you refer to "long' and "short" vowels, it will confuse the students. They may think they should have noticed something about the vowels that they cannot recognize.[16]

Three of the vowel digraphs begin with the letter *O*: *OI*, *OO*, and *OU*. The last one is the *AU* phoneme. Prepare the letter tiles or cards with these symbols and the five vowels followed by *E* on a single card (don't prepare them by pushing two *O*s together, for example). In some parts of the U.S., the vowel sound in the words spelled (in English) with *AU* or *AW* (*caught* or *law*, for example) is pronounced the same as the *O* phoneme (as in *hot*), so the students may not hear the difference in the words. Since most English-speaking areas make a distinction, it should be taught as a separate sound. Even though the students may not speak that way themselves, their writing should show the distinction, so that their writing can be understood by others. Because of all the English words that begin with the letters *Y* and *W*, for ease of learning, N'wenglish treats these letters as consonants, although they are, in fact, diphthongs. The letter *Y* represents /i/ plus a vowel; the letter W is used for /ue/ plus a vowel..This is the only way they are used in N'wenglish. A special case is the *YUE* diphthong, which English spelling does not distinguish from the single sound *UE*.

8. *Teach multisyllable words.* More than 80 percent of English words have more than one syllable; this is due to compound words (such as *lampstand*) and to root words with prefixes, suffixes, or both. Two sets of skills are required for multisyllable words:

    1 The ability to separate words into syllables is easy for everyone.

    2 Decoding phoneme by phoneme *within* each syllable, remembering the phoneme sequences in the correct order, and developing the ability to spell each syllable one by one is more difficult.

Some students are initially overwhelmed at the multisyllable level because they do not know how to attack a long word—how to break it apart and then put it back together. As a result, everything must slow down at this level. Students must practice verbally isolating the syllables and also practice putting syllables into words.

The procedure for teaching multisyllables is to isolate the first syllable in the word and analyze the phonemes in it. Do this for each succeeding syllable, and keep track of the order of phonemes in all the syllables. The student should be allowed to make the choice of where the syllable boundaries are. There are no right or wrong ways to separate them.[17] The word *separate,* for example, can be correctly split in these ways:

/s/ /e/ — /p/ /u/ — /r/ /ae/ /t/
/s/ /e/ — /p/ /u/ /r/ — /ae/ /t/
/s/ /e/ /p/ — /u/ — /r/ /ae/ /t/
/s/ /e/ /p/ — /u/ /r/ — /ae/ /t/

9. *Teach comprehension.* Accuracy is more important than speed, according to the research reported by Dr. McGuinness. Even though they may be slow, accurate readers can understand what they read; fast but inaccurate readers cannot. This is contrary to what many teachers have believed for the last few years. The recent research shows that fluent reading *follows* accuracy—fluency does *not* come first, followed by improved comprehension. Teachers who tell their students not to sound out their words and not to slow down are preventing them from improving their comprehension rate.[18]

10. *Teach writing.* After the students begin to be comfortable with

their writing skills, they will find it both helpful and interesting to copy portions of stories from printed material. This copying engenders their pride of accomplishment and helps them develop various essential writing skills, such as leaving spaces between words, left-to-right sequencing, capitalization, and punctuation.[19]

Letter Names (Optional)

Knowledge of the English alphabet letter names gives almost no help in knowing the sounds of the letters. Table 9-1 and the paragraph that follows show why this is true.

English alphabet letter names have the following inconsistencies:

• Vowel names are the *less-used* long sounds.

• There's no order in vowel sounds in the names of consonants.

• There is no order in whether the vowel sound comes before or after the consonant sound.

• The *Y never* has the sound of the letter *W*—except in its name.

• Only 2 percent of words starting with *Q* give it the *KY* sound (as in its name) instead of a *KW* sound.

• The names of *H* and *W* give no hint of the phonemes' pronunciation.

By learning the N'wenglish alphabet, the student has an aid for referring to the *sound* of all twenty single consonants, all fourteen vowels, and all six consonant digraphs that represent phonemes. Each spelling of the alphabet names consists of both a vowel and a consonant. Be sure the student understands which part of the name is the vowel and which is the consonant by teaching them the pattern, as shown in table 9-1.

Learning alphabetical order is important for using dictionaries, telephone books, and all alphabetic listings. The order in which the alphabet is to be memorized (that is, *A*, *B*, *C*, *D*, etc.) should remain the same, except that in N'wenglish, *CH* replaces *C*.

Let's End Our Literacy Crisis

Table 9-1
The Pronunciation Used in Reciting the Alphabet

The example words are all in English spelling. Letters are capitalized and underlined, and the vowels are boxed ("short" vowels in black boxes and "long" vowels in white boxes) only to show the pattern or lack of pattern.

	Letter	N'wenglish Alphabet		As in	English Alphabet		As in
1	A	**A**	ng	bANG	A		fAding
2	B	B	ae	BAY	B	ea	BEAm
3	CH or C	CH	ae	CHAse	C	ee	exCEEd
4	D	D	ae	DAY	D	ee	DEEd
5	E	**E**	sh	mESH	E		mE
6	F	F	ee	FEE	e F		lEFt
7	G	G	ee	GEEse	G	ee	JEEp
8	H	H	ee	HE	(aech)		nATure
9	I	**I**	zh	vISIon	I		kInd
10	J	J	ie	JIve	J	ay	JAY
11	K	K	ie	KInd	K	ay	CAse
12	L	L	ie	LIE	e L		ELf
13	M	M	au	MAUl	i M		hIM
14	N	N	au	NAUghty	N		IN
15	O	**O**	tt	gOTHic	O		tOE
16	P	P	oe	POst	P	ea	PEAce
17	Q *	Q	oe	QUOte	(kyue)		CUE
18	R	R	oe	ROE	o R		ARE
19	S	S	oo	SOOt	e S		mESS
20	T	T	oo	TOOk	T	ea	TEAm
21	U	**U**	th	mOTHer	y U		YEW
22	V	V	ue	VOO doo	V	ea	VEAl
23	W	W	ue	WOO	(dubyu)		(dubyu*)
24	X *	ue X		spOOKS	e X		vEX
25	Y	Y	oi	YOIcks ***	(wie)		WIde
26	Z	Z	ou	ZOUnds ***	Z	ea	ZEAl

	Digraph	As in		Comparing Alphabets		
27	AE (or Ā)	mAE			N'wenglish	English
28	EE (or Ē)	bEE		unrepresented letter sounds	none	G, H
29	IE (or Ī)	pIE	long vowels	sounds represented by wrong letter	none	Y sound in U; W sound in Y
30	OE (or Ō)	dOE				
31	UE (or Ū)	sUE				
32	AU	hAUl	other vowels	duplicated sounds	none	J (jee, jay = G, J); S (see, es = C, S)
33	OO	gOOd				
34	OI	OIl	diph-thongs			
35	OU	OUt				
36	NG	siNG				
37	NK *	piNK		phonemes represented besides the 26 letters	CH as itself	CH as H (aech)
38	NX *	lyNX	consonants			
39	SH	SHip		consonant blends	Q = KW; X = KS	Q = KY; X = KS
40	TH	THen				
41	TT	THin		maximum number of consonants with the same vowel****	3	8
42	WH *	WHen				
43	ZH	muZHik				

* consonant blends; all others are phonemes   ** or "double you"   *** oi and ou as in *oil out*
**** In poor reception conditions (radio, telephones, etc.), N'wenglish will be more easily understandable.

Effective Literacy Training

Teenage and Adult Teaching Guidelines

If not carefully monitored, students of any age may develop ineffective reading strategies. Students who have left school without learn to read English have an additional disadvantage: they may consider themselves somehow deficient because of their failure to learn to read. They believe this because, in their mind at least, most of their peers *did* learn. Most of the adult nonreaders have sat through four or more years in the public school system, giving them experiences of failure they have no desire to repeat. Experienced teachers may have limited success with a small class (no more than six students), but for many reasons Dr. Diane McGuinness strongly recommends one-to-one teaching. The caring atmosphere that will help ensure success can best be achieved through teaching someone that you know and are concerned about.

Besides sincerely caring for your student, the primary requirement is to be enthusiastic about how easy it is to learn N'wenglish and how exciting it will be if they can read anything they want. These are the keys to success. This is because they have likely spent years convinced that they could never learn to read well, and because reading, in public schools, was not exciting and fun, but frustrating and boring.

The teaching of students who have already been exposed to English reading classes must be aimed at choosing material they are interested in and be done by a method guaranteeing rapid progress. Most of the existing literacy classes require many months of effort, and only a few of the entering students complete their studies. So we must teach N'wenglish spelling in a nonthreatening way (minimum threat of embarrassment or of failure) that gives *rapid* results.

Since adults and teens who can't read are often easily discouraged, it is important for their teachers to understand some special principles and techniques, outlined in the companion volume. If you are to succeed in teaching older students, an understanding of these principles and techniques is an important first step.

As with teaching children, be certain that the student has mastered each part of the instruction before proceeding. The student should be able to consistently tell you the sound of each phoneme and identify the letter for that phoneme before proceeding. Simply tell the student the correct answer rather than calling attention to the error by saying, "It should be...." Pointing out the error may appear to express doubt in the student's ability. If the student hesitates for too long, simply state the answer instead of prompting him or her to guess. On the other hand, don't try too hard to avoid a period of silence. Give the student three or four seconds to think.

It is important to emphasize the necessity of mastering each grapheme before going to the next lesson. Explain why this is important; unlike English, reading N'wenglish is simply a matter of pronouncing what they see and combining the sounds—in order—into words. Regardless of what they learned or didn't learn about English, they cannot learn to read N'wenglish effectively without learning this.

Use flash cards for testing and review. To avoid boredom try to think of additional ways to teach a grapheme the students are having trouble with. But you should proceed to the next lesson only after the students can unfailingly read each grapheme in the lesson. This is particularly true for the vowels. Vowel sounds are more difficult to pronounce exactly, but explain that exact pronunciation of each vowel is important because if the vowel changes, the word changes or a nonsense syllable is produced. An example is pronouncing both words, *good* and *fued* (*good food* in English), using the same vowel sound.

After years of experience with English spelling, it may take some time for students to realize how dependable and unchanging N'wenglish spelling is. Once the students understand that each letter and each letter combination is always the same and they know what sound each of them stands for, learning should be rapid.

The Psychology of Learning

Those who are familiar with psychology know that self-image must be protected. Bad self-images can adversely affect people for their entire lives. More particularly, their potential will be severely restricted if they allow early childhood failures to convince them that they are mentally deficient in some way. Because English spelling is so difficult, some very smart people may never become good readers. What a teacher does is important, but what a teacher gets the student to do is much more important. The best way to get maximum performance from students is to be enthusiastic, positive, and caring and to show the students that you believe in their abilities.

We are usually limited in what we can do by what we believe we can do and what we believe other people think we can do. We are seldom what other people think we are. To some extent we are what we think we are. But often, we are what we think other people think we are. This is especially true of small children, who almost always live up to or down to what significant adults in their life think of them. Therefore, students must know there is nothing "wrong" with them that prevents learning. Instead—with English—the fault lies in an illogical, inconsistent spelling that causes problems for everyone. It is also vital for older schoolchildren and adults to know they no longer have to deal with a spelling system that has "defeated" them. They can make a new start with a spelling that *is* logical and consistent. A brief review of the testimonial letters for i.t.a. (initial teaching alphabet, see appendix 6) will verify this claim. See pages 191, 202-208, and 224-226 of Sir James Pitman's book *Alphabets and Reading*.

To illustrate, think about what happens when students get back something they have written and many of the words are circled as being misspelled. The next time they turn in something they have written, many of them will restrict themselves to words they think they know how to spell correctly rather than risk a low grade. By doing this, they often fail to use words that would more accurately and fully express their thoughts. They are frustrated by having to stop their train of thought and concentrate on how to spell the words or find other words they know how to spell rather than on accurately expressing themselves. Even worse is the embarrassment they feel when they misspell something orally or on the blackboard before the class—or having to explain the poor grades resulting from their spelling to their parents.

Every spelling error the students make is a visible sign of their inadequacy to all who see it. Every spelling error reduces whatever sense of self worth they may have left. For many students, spelling tests are worse than boring, they are torture. An expenditure of vast amounts of money, time and energy will make marginal improvements in the students' spelling, but it is not worth the money—when spelling reform is such an easier way—and it definitely is not worth the "wear and tear" on the students' egos.

Thoughtless teachers who ridicule students' spelling before the class reduce the students' self-esteem, especially if their self-esteem is already low for some reason. A simplified spelling system will lift such students out of the ranks of the low achievers, help them fit in with their peers and make them less prone to harassment and bullying. A simplified spelling system will, in short, reduce the discipline problems that interfere with learning.[20]

Table 9-2
The One Hundred Most Used English Words *
(listed in order from top of first column to bottom of second)

English	N'wenglish (where different)	English	N'wenglish (where different)
the	thee, thu	when	
of	ov, uv	him	
and		them	
to	tue	her	hur
a	ae, u	war	waur
in		your	Yoor (singular)
that		your	yoor (plural)
it		any	enee
is	iz	more	moer
I	le	now	nou
for	faur	its	
be	bee	time	tiem
was	woz, wuz	up	
as	az	do	due
you	Yue (singular)	out	
you	yue (plural)	can	kan
with	witt	than	
he	hee	only	oenlee
on		she	shee
have	hav	made	maed
by	bie	other	uthur
not		into	intue
at		men	
this		must	
are	or	people	peepul
we	wee	said	sed
his	hiz	may	mae
but		man	
they	thae	about	ubout
all	aul	over	oevur
or		some	sum
which		these	theez
will	wil	two	tuew
from		very	veree
had		before	bufoer
has	haz	great	graet
one	wun	could	kood
our		such	
an		first	furst
been	bin	upon	
no	noe	every	evree
their	thaer	how	hou
there	thar	come	kum
were	wur	us	
so	soe	shall	shal
my	mie	should	shood
if		then	
me	mee	like	liek
what	whot	well	wel
would	wood	little	litul
who	hue	say	sae

* See the notes at the end of the book: chapter 8, note 6. Note that 29 percent of the words in this table are spelled the same in English and N'wenglish. These one hundred words constitute 54.3 percent of the individual words found in the 100,000-word sample. The first ten words make up 26,677 of the entire 100,000 words (i.e. 26.677 percent).

Chapter 10
Advantages and Supposed Disadvantages of This Proposal for Worldwide Use

Advantages of Implementing This Proposal

Several advantages of implementing N'wenglish apply to some extent to anyone who learns to read it. The first item, of course, is of particular interest to present nonreaders or poor readers. No attempt has been made to rank the advantages beyond listing the most important item first, since what is important varies significantly from one person to another.

1. Avoidance of the costs of illiteracy: The main advantage of implementing N'wenglish for those who cannot read English, or who can't read well, will be avoidance of the costs of illiteracy explained in chapters 4 and 5, and in item 21, later in this section.

2. No embarrassing mispronunciations: We will never again be embarrassed by mispronouncing a word while reading in public.

3. No embarrassing misspellings: We will never again be embarrassed by misspelling something we have written.

4. Unaided correct spelling: We may want to consult a dictionary to see what the preferred pronunciation is. We will never again, however, have to consult a dictionary for the correct spelling of a word we know how to pronounce or to record the way we have heard someone pronounce it.

5. Unaccented syllables are usually obvious: Chapter 8 shows that a *U* can be in an accented or an unaccented syllable in English or N'wenglish. In a N'wenglish word of more than one syllable, the syllable with the *U* (or less often, with an *I*) is more likely to be unaccented than a syllable with another vowel. In English spelling, an unaccented syllable could have any vowel letter in it.

6. Easy learning of pronunciation: Students will learn correct pronunciation much more easily not only from hearing people speak but also by seeing the words recorded phonemically. Speech is fleeting—miss hearing a word for any reason and (if it is not recorded) it is gone forever. Written words are permanent—they can be read at leisure or studied intently for whatever length of time is necessary.

7. Pronunciation standardization: As time goes by, the preferred pronunciation of all the words we use will become more and more familiar to us. N'wenglish will have much the same standardizing effect upon speech as the widespread use of radio and television had in the twentieth century. N'wenglish will probably have even more of a standardizing effect than radio and television because, unlike sounds, written words are permanent and can be studied. N'wenglish will provide guidance in pronunciation now lacking. As Pitman states it,

> A rational phonetic spelling will do much to steady our language in the perilous seas upon which it is now embarked, for, in these days of universal literacy, the visual language exercises a remarkable influence on the spoken language. It is the one constant standard, common throughout the world: the more phonetic it is, the more uniform will pronunciation tend to be. When men first began to write, they wrote as they spoke; now they tend to speak as they write—and we cannot blame them.[1]

8. No forgetting of N'wenglish words: There are few, if any, people who do not sometimes forget how to spell an English word. We must ask someone or consult the dictionary. Over time, people usually forget many spellings. This will never happen with N'wenglish. If you know how to pronounce a word, you know how to spell it.

9. Shorter words equal cost savings: The form of N'wenglish using the macron to indicate the long vowels is roughly 7 percent shorter than English. Printing companies already have or can easily

*Advantages and Supposed Disadvantages
of This Proposal for Worldwide Use*

obtain hardware or software for printing macrons. For these companies, both labor costs and paper and ink costs can be reduced by 7 percent. With millions of dollars spent on printing every year, the savings will be significant.

10. N'wenglish syllables are obvious: Pronunciation is more difficult if the division into syllables is not immediately obvious. Syllables are often difficult to determine in English because of silent letters, words where all the sounds aren't shown, words where sounds are not spelled in strict first-to-last order, and standardized plural and past tense spellings, as the second section of chapter 8 shows.

11. N'wenglish is easy to typeset: Because of the obvious split into syllables, N'wenglish is easy to typeset. English syllables are not obvious. Therefore, the place at which words can be broken at the end of a line has been standardized. Syllabification of English has been frozen, the same as the spelling has been. If we are not using a computer for typesetting, we must consult a dictionary to find where syllable can be broken in a new word or if we forget where the English word can be split.

12. N'wenglish distinguishes between *YUE* and *UE*: English spelling does not show whether the *Y* sound is present before the *UE* sound or not. Readers must learn which "long *U*" sound a word has.

13. N'wenglish has no confusing heteronyms: Heteronyms are words with the same spelling but with different pronunciations and meanings; homonyms are words with the same pronunciation but with different spellings and meanings. Although homonyms are unlikely to cause any confusion in N'wenglish (see Optional Rule 8 in table 8-1 and item 6 at the end of this chapter), any confusion resulting from homonyms in N'wenglish is easily offset by the lack of heteronyms.

14. Immigrants can more easily learn N'wenglish: The inconsistencies and lack of logic in English spelling hinder immigrants from learning English more than any other feature. This causes some immigrants to give up in their effort to learn English. The ease of N'wenglish will encourage them to complete their learning. A quotation by Pitman explains why this is true:

> Students, especially when they learn to read English before they can speak it, often complain of the difficulties of English pronunciation, but the spelling is what they really mean, because this fails to

offer reliable clues to how words should sound and, worse, proffers countless false clues....

Foreigners learning English are faced with the same conundrums and illogicality as face the English-speaking child learning to read...but with the additional difficulty that they possess no store of spoken words to which to relate the words they are given to read.[2]

15. N'wenglish is an excellent candidate for worldwide language: As several scholars have pointed out, English is already the most used spoken auxiliary language in the world. Written English, however, is totally unsuitable as a worldwide language. Most languages other than English are almost perfect (one-for-one letter- or letter-blend-to-sound correspondence). N'wenglish, however, *is* perfect—completely consistent and logical one-for-one correspondence. N'wenglish therefore opens the English-speaking countries to all the economic, cultural, and political advantages that come from easy communication with other countries.

16. N'wenglish distinguishes singular from plural *you*: In the same way that the English word *I* refers to a singular person, the word *you* in N'wenglish is capitalized to show the singular. When the word *you* refers to more than one person (or no differentiation is needed), it is not capitalized. Contractions of the words *you* and *I* are capitalized or not capitalized in the same way.

17. N'wenglish uses no unnecessary double letters for a single sound: The use of double letters in English is unnecessary and confusing. In N'wenglish there are no double letters except *OO* and *TT*—and *EE* if macrons are not used.

18. N'wenglish has no silent letters: The use of silent letters makes an immediate location of syllable splits much more difficult. In addition, silent letters require additional labor, paper, and ink.

19. N'wenglish avoids some British spelling problems: British spelling is different from U.S. spelling for a few words. Since N'wenglish is completely phonemic, it avoids these spelling inconsistencies

20. N'wenglish encourages writing and vocabulary building: Many people do not like to write. Many people fear being embarrassed by misspelling because they can't look up words or don't want to take the time. N'wenglish will encourage people to express themselves.

*Advantages and Supposed Disadvantages
of This Proposal for Worldwide Use*

Looking up words in the dictionary will be easy, reading will be easy, and therefore vocabulary building will be much easier.

21. English-speaking nations' productivity will rise: English-speaking nations will be on more of an equal economic base with nations that now have higher literacy rates. In our increasingly competitive world, low productivity due to employee illiteracy is a severe trade disadvantage. Unless the quality of our labor force improves to match that of some of the more literate nations, the trade disadvantage will increase. As other nations begin catching up with English-speaking nations technologically, if their literacy rate is better a substantial competitive advantage may soon become apparent.

22. Enabling immigrants to learn English more easily will help stop cultural alienation: In most big cities there are areas where English is not widely used. Because of the difficulty immigrants have in learning English, civil rights advocates are pushing for bilingual (or multilingual) teaching in the grade schools. Besides the huge expense, this can have disastrous effects: multilingual teaching will tend to maintain the cultural and political separation instead of drawing us together as a nation as a common language would help accomplish. Nineteen or more states are now considering laws to make English the official language. Legislation of this type, however, will not reduce the difficulty immigrants have in learning English. It is a problem not found in other nations and little understood by U.S. citizens.

23. Computer speech synthesis and written transcriptions of speech will be easier with N'wenglish: Preparation of software for converting written words into understandable audible sounds (speech synthesis) or for transcribing spoken words into written words will be much easier. This is because of the much shorter and invariable listing of phoneme-grapheme correspondences that would need to be programmed.

24. No variant spellings in words pronounced the same: Besides the unphonemic spellings of many English words, there is the confusion of hundreds of variant spellings. Often both (or all) of the variant spellings of a word are unphonemic.

25. Early grade-school books will be more interesting for student *and* teacher: The reading books in the first four grades in school are concerned with teaching reading. Therefore they may stress some words, letter combinations, or sound patterns by repetition and severely restrict the vocabulary. This is true of schools using the "look and say" method, in which an average of only about four hundred words each year is taught by memory in the first three or four grades. As chapter 8 of Dr. Rudolph Flesch's book *Why Johnny Can't Read* convincingly shows, this results in "stories" that are almost unbearably boring.[3] "Whole language" books may be less boring, but they are just as confusing if the students are not learning to read. In N'wenglish grade schools, all the books used can be concerned only with content. Books can be chosen based upon how interesting and helpful they are.

26. Teachers (and students) need not spend hundreds of hours on reading and spelling: This will free them for more productive studies and put them on a par with students of other nations.

27. By "hearing" authors' dialect, reading will be more interesting: We'll not only know what the authors are saying, but also to an extent how they are saying it. We'll know the major regional variations that make listening to speakers from other areas so interesting.

Supposed Disadvantages That Really Aren't

People may have developed some misconceptions if they have not carefully researched the effects of English spelling. Certain items, upon brief examination, may seem disadvantages of spelling reform, although they are not. The supposed disadvantage also may be counterbalanced (or even overbalanced) by a corresponding advantage.

Will Existing Writings Become Inaccessible?

Conventional wisdom states that if a completely different spelling system is adopted, all the existing material in English will become inaccessible. However, learning a new language will not make us unable to understand our first language. Learning a new way of spelling will not erase all memory of English spelling. Nor would the printing of new books suddenly cause all the existing books to self-destruct. The truth is this: all the existing books in English are *already* inaccessible *to illiterates*.

After N'wenglish is implemented, everyone will read. People who now read English will keep their books written in English and read either English or N'wenglish. Libraries will keep their books in English. All others will read only N'wenglish, unless they choose also to learn

Advantages and Supposed Disadvantages of This Proposal for Worldwide Use

English, similar to English literature scholars who must learn Middle English to read Chaucer and other writers of his era. Lawyers, English scholars, historians, and all those whose vocation or hobby requires extensive research through written material of the past—if it is not of sufficient interest to make reprinting in N'wenglish economically feasible—would learn English spelling as a college (or possibly high school) elective course.

All the books that are so important that they have a readership large enough to make reprinting economically feasible for the publishers will be reissued in N'wenglish. Competition among printers for their share of the market suddenly swollen with millions of previous nonreaders will ensure such an event. In the same way that we currently see "Now in HDTV!" preceding certain television programs, we will soon see advertisements by bookstores declaring, "Now in N'wenglish!" Many libraries have few books that are fifty years old or more. Many libraries sell outdated and least used books to make room for new ones. Often the books they sell are only one or two years old. The average age of books in a bookstore is much less than that of books in a library. Few books in a bookstore are so eagerly sought that they will be reprinted for more than a year or two.

Is a Standard Pronunciation Required?

A second supposed disadvantage of spelling reform based on phonemic spelling (such as N'wenglish) is that it would require a fixed standard of pronunciation, which we do not have. This line of thinking is a fallacy. We understand each other's spoken words. We will understand the written transcription of words even more easily than spoken words because of the permanent-versus-fleeting aspect mentioned in Advantage 6 in this chapter and the fact that written words are separated by spaces. It is often difficult to know the start and end of *spoken* words because they are run together unless the speaker purposely speaks slowly and distinctly. So, basing our spelling upon pronunciation would not require that we all pronounce words the same to be understood. No one wants to be told how to pronounce their words—nor should they be. As stated earlier however, people's speech will become more standardized as time goes by. This will occur both by choice and by the same process as occurred through the widespread use of radio and television begun in the twentieth century.

Will Linguistic History Be Lost?

A third and much less convincing supposed disadvantage of spelling reform is that reformed spelling would destroy the etymological or linguistic history of words. Samuel Noory shows that "today's spelling is in many respects as much an offspring of fancy as of design."[4] He gives several examples, in his book *Dictionary of Pronunciation*, in which spelling is not based on historical roots. Also, etymologists themselves would prefer to see English spelled phonemically, and thus, from this point forward, have a dynamic history of the language. As it is, we have 250 years of repetition of a "snapshot" of spelling the way many words *were* pronounced—a static history. As mentioned earlier, adoption of N'wenglish spelling would not result in the instantaneous destruction of all books written in English. Therefore, the question must be asked, "How much more static history of a mid-1700s spelling freeze do we need?" A much more pertinent question must be asked. Let us grant for a moment that the etymological history of present English spelling is *very* valuable. Should we let the desire for etymological data by a limited number of scholars cause us to keep a spelling system that is causing a severe problem for hundreds of millions of people around the world?

Must We Standardize Plural and Past-Tense Spelling?

The final supposed disadvantage to be considered is that a phonemic spelling would hinder the recognition of the plural and past-tense forms of words. This also is untrue. If the plurals and past tenses were shown with a standard prefix, the reader might recognize them as plural or past tense a millisecond sooner. When the reader's eyes reach the end of a word, however, if the word has been recognized (read), the reader knows that the word is plural or past tense not only by knowing the word but also by the context. And as explained before, the ability to decide the pronunciation from the spelling helps in recognizing the word.

*Advantages and Supposed Disadvantages
of This Proposal for Worldwide Use*

Although this should be enough to dismiss the argument, a more thorough explanation is needed. The argument has philosophical overtones affecting our overall view of languages.

Philosophical Overtones of Frozen Spelling

Since there are four *spellings* of plurals (adding *S* or *ES* to words not ending in *S* or *Y*, adding *SES* to words ending in *S*, and changing *Y* to *I* and adding *ES*) and only three *sounds* of plurals (*S*, *Z*, or *UZ*), spelling phonemically *reduces* irregularity—and improves clarity. (Words in which plurals are not constructed in this manner would be essentially the same length in English and N'wenglish.) One source (who will probably appreciate remaining anonymous if he carefully examines this chapter) states that the actual differences in sound are "irrelevant."

Let's analyze this statement.

If written communication were the primary form of communication (that is, if all spoken communication were just a way of turning the written words into sounds)

and if everyone who had a need to read English knew exactly what sounds every S added to show plurals stood for, the statement might have some validity. Neither "if" is true, however, and the first "if" is the exact opposite of the truth.

Regarding the first "if," the spoken language is primary for these reasons:

1. Almost everyone learns to speak their native language before learning to read it.

2. Human beings act as talkers and listeners much more than as readers and writers; 90 percent of all human communication is through speech.[5] (Note, however, that written words can be disseminated to more people more easily than spoken words, and the value of what is communicated by written words is often greater, so the last paragraph of the first section of chapter 3, which points out the great value of the written word, is also true.)

3. David Crystal point out that, "No community has ever been found to lack spoken language, but only a minority of languages have ever been written down."[6]

4. Writing is simply a way of making spoken words or vocal ideas in the mind permanent for later use by the writer or someone else that

the writer wants to communicate with but cannot (or does not desire to) speak to.

5. Whether a language has a written form is irrelevant to the characteristics of the language itself. Many unwritten languages are as highly structured, as rich in vocabulary, and as efficient for communication as languages that are written.

As Aristotle expressed it, "Spoken words are the symbols of mental experience and written words are the symbols of spoken words."[7]

Regarding the second "if," both beginning readers (especially immigrants trying to learn English) and adult illiterates are badly confused by written words that give no hint of how they are pronounced. Since most English words are learned in spoken form first, if the written word does not suggest how it is to be pronounced, it often cannot be recognized (read).

Why Do Some Scholars Oppose Our Proposed Solution?

Most scholars insist upon precision and "exactitude" (as they should). A few scholars insist upon "pedantic exactitude." This is insistence upon maintaining "high standards of scholarship" for the purpose of *displaying* their scholarship. N'wenglish will not require the scholarship of remembering complex spellings and spelling rules. We must not misjudge motives, however. We must not casually attribute all scholarly opposition to spelling reform to pedantic exactitude.

Most opposition to spelling reform comes from a natural human resistance to change. It also comes from overlooking the real purpose of a written language. Scholars (like the rest of us) can easily isolate themselves from the monetary and human-suffering costs of illiteracy to such an extent that they may even fail to see that

> **the purpose of writing is to COMMUNICATE IDEAS,**
> ***not* to display an ability to remember complex spelling**
> **rules and traditional spellings of thousands of words.**

Dr. Lounsbury presents a devastating attack against all the common objections to spelling reform mentioned earlier as well as the objection of spelling homonyms the same in his book *English Spelling and Spelling Reform*. He convincingly demonstrates that the real motiva-

*Advantages and Supposed Disadvantages
of This Proposal for Worldwide Use*

tion in opposing spelling reform is the natural human tendency to resist change—even change for the better. Although Dr. Lounsbury convincingly disproved the objections to spelling reform, his book is a scholarly one which was evidently not as widely circulated as it should have been. As a result, present-day references to spelling reform still dredge up these same disproven objections as sufficient, in themselves, to dismiss any further consideration of spelling reform. Perhaps another reason his book had no lasting influence is that, although he vehemently attacked what he recognized as ridiculous arguments against spelling reform, he did not take the next logical step of proposing a solution to the problem by advocating a specific spelling reform proposal. This book does.

Real Disadvantages for Worldwide Usage

Having looked at four supposed disadvantages, we now turn to any real disadvantages there may be.

1. Learning a new spelling method requires time and effort. In all honesty, those who carefully research objections to and results of spelling reform must admit that this is the only substantial objection to spelling reform. Human beings simply resist change. People would prefer to endure the inconvenience of the known than the improvements of the unknown, in far too many cases. If the "inconvenience" affected only those deciding whether to change, it would be excusable even though unwise. Unfortunately, for illiteracy, the ones deciding whether to change are "inconvenienced" (a mild word considering chapter 5 data) much less than the illiterates. As William Dwight Whitney states, "It is the generations of children to come who appeal to us to save them from the affliction which we have endured and forgotten."[8]

The overriding fact about this disadvantage is that if you have carefully read chapters 8 and 9, done the exercises, and unprejudicially tried appendix 4, this disadvantage no longer applies to you. You can already read N'wenglish!

2. Speed-reading will require a few months of familiarization. Most people read silently a little faster than they can read aloud, while speed-readers can read silently several times faster. Few people are speed-readers, at least compared with the number of nonreaders. Those who learn N'wenglish will read N'wenglish at a normal speaking rate, or a little faster, as soon as they learn N'wenglish. It will take a few months of practice before speed-readers can return to their former reading rates on N'wenglish.

Because of the unphonemic nature of English, many scholars believe that English must be taught in whole-word chunks. Dr. Diane McGuinness, Rudolph Flesch, and others have convincingly disproved this and explained why the student must have a phonemic base for reading.[9] An important fact that explains why speed-reading is possible and why Rudolph Flesch is correct in emphasizing phonemic reading, even for irregularly spelled words, is explained by Dr. Miriam Balmuth of Hunter College of The City University of New York and author of *The Roots of Phonics*:

> For writing purposes, therefore, each word to be recorded must be separated into the speech sounds of which it is composed. The characters for those speech sounds are then set down in the same sequence in which they are produced in the spoken word. The reader of such a system must perceive each character in turn, blend their sounds in strict sequence, and so reconstruct the original word.
>
> This procedure would be tedious for a written selection of any length if a fortunate process did not generally take place. That is, with repeated experience, the string of characters seems eventually to be perceived as a whole unit—almost as a logogram—making the process a good deal easier than it would be if every word had to be sounded out anew each time. Exactly how this occurs is not yet clear. There is evidence that, despite this apparently unified perception, the blending of individual units continues to take place, although at an extremely rapid rate.[10]

3. Puns based upon English heteronyms will not be possible. Puns have been described as the lowest form of humor. Puns based upon homonyms (words with different meanings but the same pronunciation) will still be possible. The cheap sight gags based upon heteronyms (words pronounced differently but spelled the same) will not be possible.

4. A small number of reading experts will have to find other jobs. Those who are employed by the major reading textbook compa-

*Advantages and Supposed Disadvantages
of This Proposal for Worldwide Use*

nies to research and produce new material concerned with teaching reading will have to find more interesting work. They could scarcely do otherwise.

5. Reading textbook companies will no longer be able to sell a new, very expensive reading textbook series every few years. Printing many other types of books in N'wenglish will take up much of the slack in the reading textbook companies. The only problem (for them) is that they will be on an equal competitive footing with any competitors with the same printing capabilities. (This is a disadvantage only for the textbook companies. It is an advantage to taxpayers paying for "new, improved" textbooks every few years.)

6. Words that are homonyms in English will be spelled the same in N'wenglish. Although the absence of heteronyms will be a counterbalancing advantage in N'wenglish, the absence of different spellings for words pronounced the same in N'wenglish but with different meanings (homonyms) will be a minor disadvantage.

(1) Those opposing spelling reform often exaggerate the "problem" of homonyms, but there are relatively few homonyms (compared to the size of the average adult vocabulary), and the vast majority of homonyms can be distinguished by context or by grammar (whether verb, noun, adjective, etc.). Those who wish to magnify the problem of homonyms will complain that when using phonemic spelling you cannot distinguish between the homophones. They fail to mention, however, that when *speaking*, those same words are indistinguishable. Traugott Rohner, in his book *Fonetic English Spelling*, prepared a list of the homonyms among the five hundred most common words from the *Teacher's Book of 30,000 Words*. There were *seventy sets* of homonyms in the list. Frequency data from the 30,000-word list was not available, so Dewey's more complete 100,000-word list frequency data (see chapter 8 notes for data on this word list) were used. There were 10,161 different words in Dewey's 100,000-word list (as compared to a "typical educated adult vocabulary" of roughly 70,000 words—see the "Reading 'Textbooks'" section of chapter 11). There were more than 78,633 words (i.e., 78.6 percent) in the list that occurred more than ten times (1,027 different words). There were 87,358 root words (1,131 different words) that occurred more than ten times (since root words include individual words appearing ten times or

less). The following tabulation shows how often the words in these seventy sets of homonyms appear among the 87,358 root words from the 100,000-word sample:

Number of homonyms FROM EACH SET Found in the 87,358 words	No. of sets	No. of words
None*	2	0
one	54	54
two	13	26
three (to, too, two)	1	3
Total	70	83

* since this was a different word list than that used for the homonyms

This shows that most words in the list of seventy sets of homonyms are in the list because there is an infrequently used word (i.e., less than ten occurrences, or 0.01 percent of the 100,000 words) that sounds like a common word. And since it is common, of course, it is less likely to be misunderstood. More significantly, only six homonym sets have any reasonable likelihood of being misunderstood, but only the words in one of the sets (the words *to*, *too*, and *two*) are among the 87,358 words. Stated differently, seven out of eight words (or 87.36 percent, to be more exact) in typical English written material will not contain any confusing homonyms, and the frequency of any one confusing homonym appearing in typical written material will be less than 0.01 percent of the words (ten out of 100,000). See the companion volume, *Let's End Our Literacy Crisis Workbook*, for a list of the seventy homonym sets and additional information on homonyms and heteronyms. See the bottom of table 8-1 for the spelling of possibly confusing homonyms.

(2) Concerning context, Edward Rondthaler and Edward Lias state:

> Context will clarify the meaning [of homonyms in written material]—just as it does in our speech. For example:
> "Come heer to heer the music."
> There's nothing new in using context to clarify meaning. We do it all the time:
> "That gold mine is mine."
> "Bank at the bank on the bank."

*Advantages and Supposed Disadvantages
of This Proposal for Worldwide Use*

Context is stronger than spelling. If I write
"Come hear to here the music."
you know exactly what I mean. Thousands of words with just one spelling have numerous definitions. The word *point* has 86; *set* has 115![11]

(3) Charles C. Fries, author of *Linguistics and reading,* as quoted by Dewey, states,

> As against a few hundred homophones [homonyms] now distinguished more or less fortuitously by different spellings, there are in [English spelling] many thousands of words of like sound *and* spelling (homographs), and there is no demand to create artificial distinctions of these. A few suggestive examples are:
>
> bay (a color, a tree, a part of a building, a body of water, a prolonged bark)
> fair (good weather, impartial, an exposition)
> right (a privilege, opposite of left, opposite of wrong)
> sound (a condition, a noise, a body of water)
> spring (a season, a leap, an elastic device)
> state (to express in words, a condition, a unit of government)…
>
> Fries reports that for the 500 most used words of English the *Oxford Dictionary* records 14,070 separate and different meanings—an average of 28 different meanings for each word.[12]

Those who object to spelling reform because of spelling homonyms the same in N'wenglish—to be intellectually honest—would have to object even more strongly to the thousands of English words (as opposed to a few hundred homonyms) spelled and pronounced the same with *many* different meanings!

(4) Dr. David Crystal in his book *The Cambridge Encyclopedia of Language* provides the clincher: "Normal speech proves to be so rapidly and informally articulated that in fact over half the words cannot be recognized in isolation—and yet listeners have little trouble following it, and can repeat whole sentences accurately."[13]

Chapter 11
How to Implement This Proposal

No one would want to have a dictator impose spelling reform in English-speaking countries. However, for sheer efficiency you can't beat Kemel Pasha's methods. What is needed is something more efficient than legislative procedures and less drastic than dictatorial decree. We need a method in which the people decide what they want and implement it directly. The method presented here meets these requirements.

At this point in the book, it is important to stay open-minded. All the other chapters are filled with easily verifiable facts. You need only compare the conclusions in this book with those in the books listed in the bibliography and many similar ones to see for yourself. But this chapter is proposing a method to solve the problem in the very near future. The most significant point to remember, however, is that although it has not been attempted in the U.S., it has been proven effective in every other alphabetic language in the entire world.

Long experience in industry has shown that unless a proposed change shows immediate benefits and ease of implementation, it will be resisted. There have been many situations in which workers say that a proposed change will not work, and they will tell you why, if you give them a chance. (Anyone can give you reasons why something *won't* work.) This is despite the fact that all the objections may have been extensively researched and disproven beforehand. Many readers will assume that spelling reform would be an impossibly difficult task. Such persons may look at the three simple steps put forth here and assume that the proposed solution is naive wishful thinking. Once that assumption is made, it is difficult to allow room for conflicting information. Human beings detest being wrong, even about something which we have merely *assumed* to be true. So before we begin, let's look at some proven facts on similar events in the past.

The method proposed in this chapter is designed as a grass-roots operation by the masses, depending upon the flow of information. Two quick examples will be very informative. In the 1960s there was a best-selling book—a large book which had little if any appeal due to its attractiveness or even due to a proven usefulness—entitled *How to Avoid Probate*. I know; I bought one based upon newspaper and magazine advertising, as did many other people.

Another example more like this book is a best seller of the 1950s entitled *Why Johnny Can't Read* by Dr. Rudolph Flesch. As you've heard many times, word-of-mouth advertising is the most effective. *Why Johnny Can't Read* made a hit with parents and, based upon word-of-mouth advertising and subsequent actions, changes were temporarily made in teaching methods. Teaching methods have gone back to being more like they were before the book was issued. This is because Rudolph Flesch's proposed methods improved, but did not solve, the problems with English spelling.

There have been several instances in American history in which the public acted, *en masse*, when the motivation was sufficient. The evidence in part one of this book indicates that we have reached that point again, this time concerning public education.

Although some may object that the author involved in writing a book purporting to solve the literacy problem in English-speaking countries should be an expert in linguistics and education, no honest inquirer can deny that not only are engineers (such as the author of this book) qualified by training, practice, and disposition to research and analyze, but they can also often evaluate situations more accurately than the experts. This is true because many—if not most—experts feel obligated to defend the past practices of their profession. The primary outcome of these practices is to maintain the status quo. Stated differently, one need not be an expert in linguistics or education to be able to accurately evaluate and correlate the writings of scholars who *are* experts. Furthermore, over eighteen years of researching the subject and delving into areas that Ph.D. programs seldom—if ever—examine, should lend credence to the author's proposals.

The change to spelling our words logically is analogous to Louis Pasteur's experience. Pasteur was a chemist who, based upon experimental evidence in studying cholera, tried to promote the use of vaccines. The medical community scoffed, "He's not a physician. What does he know of medicine?" They made the mistake, however, of challenging Pasteur to demonstrate his anthrax vaccine on sheep in an attempt to humiliate and embarrass him. Fortunately for the world, Pasteur accepted the challenge and proved that vaccines work as he claimed. Will you do what is "fortunate for the world" and accept the challenge to prove that logic and consistency in spelling will solve the major literacy problem of English-speaking people?

Practically every major innovation or invention has been met with the laughter of skeptics. Before it happened, we were told that man would never fly and that escaping earth's gravity was impossible. Even after working models were demonstrated of such major inventions as the telephone, television, and the horseless carriage, many of them were dismissed as only novelties with no practical value. There will always be small-thinking, negative-minded people who find it more convenient (less work for them) to avoid change, even if change is badly needed. They will say it cannot be done.

Those who are intellectually honest, however, know that when numerous experts agree that a certain change is needed, everyone should take heed, especially if the agreed-upon course of action has been found to be logical and practical not only by the experts but also by unbiased outsiders who do not have a vested interest in avoiding change. Skeptics will tell you that most Americans are only interested in their jobs, hobbies, and entertainment. It is, however, a self-defeating policy to believe the negative thinkers who say the American public is too self-absorbed to do what is in their own best interest. What is proposed in this chapter can happen. It can start small and grow, or it can happen very quickly in many places at once if we will just have the courage of our convictions and take action.

The Method

N'wenglish can be implemented with just three simple, simultaneous steps:

Let's End Our Literacy Crisis

Step One

Teach nonreading adult friends or relatives to read N'wenglish or locate someone who will do so. It may take nonreaders as long as five or six months to learn, but it will not require six solid months of the teacher's time. The real need is to provide ronreaders with

1. enthusiasm and encouragement,
2 needed materials, and
3. a small amount of initial instruction. You do not have to be a professional educator to do this.

Nonreaders and poor readers who are exposed only to English after step two begins will need to be taught N'wenglish the same as present day illiterates. Most of these new readers will enthusiastically join you in all three steps. Don't fail to ask!

Step Two

Contact your local school-board director and explain that beginning within two years, you want first graders to be taught N'wenglish, first and second graders taught N'wenglish the second year, first through third graders the third year, etc. This will provide a twelve-year interim period—until beginning students graduate from high school—in which the colleges, publishers, and businesses can prepare for widespread use of N'wenglish according to their own timetable. In this way, the decisions can be made in the executive branch of government upon direct insistence of the public, avoiding the long delays inevitable in legislation.

Another advantage of dealing with the local school-board directors is that they are more accessible to the average person than one's legislators. In addition, local school-board directors are much more likely to be responsive to the desires of the public than are legislators. Unlike when dealing with legislators, the public does not have to engage in an unfair competition with lobbyists to get its wishes enacted.

Those who learn only English after step two begins (those above first grade when step two begins) will learn N'wenglish the same as other English readers. Those who can read English can learn N'wenglish from this book or by studying figure 11-1, which will soon be on most book and magazine title pages and newspaper mastheads.

Step Three

Much more effective than any direct action you can take as an individual is the value of your recommendation. Those who are most concerned will want to purchase extra copies of this book to give to persons who might not be willing to purchase one for themselves. If everyone who sees the value of N'wenglish will recommend to three others not familiar with N'wenglish that they carefully and open-mindedly read this book, and if each of them does the same, simple arithmetic shows that in ten levels of recommendations, every English-speaker in the world will be exposed to ideas that will bring about the "Reformation of the 21st Century." Since there will always be those who cannot be motivated to action, regardless of how worthy the cause, you can overcome their inaction by telling more than three others—obviously, the more the better.

A Clarification of the Method

It is important to note that what is proposed here is not a change in the curricula. Therefore approval of any teachers' organizations, school boards, or textbook selection organizations for a curricula change is not needed. All that is being proposed is that words in books used in the existing curricula at long last be spelled in a logical, consistent, scientifically-designed way instead of the present inconsistent and confusing way. As explained in the School Considerations section later in this chapter, it will very soon become apparent that the students' curricula will need to be improved by making more advanced reading materials available and making materials presently presented in later grades available. This will make the English curricula more competitive with that of other nations. These curricula changes can be determined in each individual school by those responsible for such changes.

Objections to spelling reform have been covered previously, but to clarify exactly what is being proposed, further comment on one of these objections—the objection based upon pronunciation—is needed. A common form of the objection was found on the Internet on May 3, 2004, in which the author of the Website stated that no one would stand for letting another person's pronunciation be used as the standard for a phonemic spelling. The Website also stated that *whatever* phonemic spelling was adopted, it would represent only the pronunciation of one group of speakers. The objection to spelling reform represented by this line of thought is based entirely upon most English speaker's belief that only one spelling is correct and all others are wrong. This is *not* the case with what is proposed here.

As stated in chapter 8, it is a linguistic axiom that what is understandable as speech is also understandable when written with a suitable phonetics. In fact, as other portions of this book have shown, it will be *more easily* understandable when written than when spoken. This is true for at least three reasons: (1) the inclusion of spaces between words not present in the spoken words, (2) the ability to study the written words as long as necessary whereas spoken words must be comprehended in the split second in which they are spoken (unless there is an audio recording which can be replayed), and (3) the ability to study the context both before *and after* a written passage—which is impossible with spoken words since the context after a misunderstood word hasn't been spoken yet or has been spoken and not understood because of puzzling over the misunderstood word.

As a result, this book proposes that everyone be allowed to spell their words the way *they* pronounce them. No one can—or should—force us to pronounce our words in a certain way. No one can—or should—force us to spell our words in a certain way. If writers want to improve their chances of being understood, they may choose to spell their words the way they hear radio and television announcers pronounce them (Standard Broadcast English). They may not pronounce the words that way themselves, but almost everyone is familiar with that pronunciation. If they fail to spell a few words according to Standard Broadcast English, the context will indicate which words they are spelling. This freedom of spelling will also apply to those who choose to continue spelling as they do now.

The spelling reform proposed in this book is *only* as follows. Beginning within a couple of years, the phonemic spelling proposed will be adopted in the school system, first grade in the first year, first and second grade in the second year, and continuing to add a grade each year. Beginning within a couple of years, a large and growing proportion of *all new* publications will use the phonemic spelling proposed here. If a publishing company decides it wants to limit its readership only to those who understand the present spelling system, no one will force it to publish using the system proposed here. Market pressures will, of course, ensure that it will soon begin to publish at least a portion of its publications in the new spelling system. As stated earlier, until such time as almost everyone is using the new spelling system, the publishers will be in the profitable position of being able to sell their publications in both versions.

Basically, what this means is this: *no one*—readers, writers, or publishers—will be forced to spell their words in a certain way. The only change being made is that after over two and one-half centuries of confusion, we are finally implementing a logical, efficient, invariable, scientifically designed way of indicating English sounds. This will have no effect on other languages, but from this point on, if we accept a foreign word into our vocabulary, all the sounds in that word will be spelled with the *N'wenglish* way of spelling them.

Reading Textbooks

Although two years may seem like a short timeframe in which to begin such a change, it is only our experience with present reading textbooks that makes this seem quick. Teaching students to read English is so difficult that a dozen or more major textbook companies employ reading experts. These reading experts perform research and then write reading textbooks, teachers' guides, exercise books, and promotional materials. This process can easily require three to five years. N'wenglish reading books do not require this approach.

The students will not require reading textbooks, as such. Reading material provided to N'wenglish students can concentrate entirely upon the content. This is the beauty of teaching N'wenglish. Children should be given children's classics and subjects of interest to them in the age range being taught. Textbooks for English reading classes must be carefully limited in vocabulary and word repetition. Such limitations are unneeded in N'wenglish.

There need be no limitations upon:

1. Subject matter—except that it is interesting, informative, helpful to the student, and acceptable to parents and guardians; those who are most responsible for a student's welfare should insist on being involved—and have a right to do so.

2. Vocabulary—except that it should consist mostly of words in the

vocabulary of children of the age being taught. This gives much leeway. The average six-year-old in the first grade has a listening and speaking vocabulary of more than 24,000 words.[1] By the third grade, the number of words students know by sound, according to studies by the late Dr. Robert H. Seashore of Northwestern University, has reached 44,000 words. This is an astonishing number considering that with the "look and say" reading method, students may memorize only about 400 words each year by sight.[2] Dr. Seashore estimates that the vocabulary of college graduates is 157,000 words.[3]

3. Word repetition—there does not need to be any concern with repeating any given word or words a certain number of times. The repetitiveness in the "look and say" readers is not for vocabulary building but to fix in the students' minds the appearance of words they already know by their sound.

Reading Books for Four Months—Then School Books

The first three or four months of the first grade can be reserved for children's classics and other stories of interest to first graders. The content of beginning students' books is not just to give them interesting and varied reading matter to use in developing their reading skills. A more important purpose of the content of beginners' books is to develop in students a love for reading and learning.

After the first three or four months, students can begin learning all the other school subjects, the same as is done in the non-English-speaking world. They can begin learning some third- and fourth-grade subjects that formerly had to wait until the students could read. Using school books that were formerly used in higher grades usually will not require that the books be rewritten. All that is required is to transpose them into N'wenglish.

Thus, what may have appeared at first glance to be a huge problem in preparing textbooks turns out to be practically no problem at all. The typesetters who work for publishing companies will be able to transpose into N'wenglish as fast as they can type. We will be able to do the same, that is, write or type in N'wenglish while reading English. More importantly, however, computer software developers will be able to easily develop a program for transposing English into N'wenglish; the program required to do so is very simple.[4]

Implementing This Proposal

Governmental Considerations

Upon the urging of the citizenry, the local school-board members must go up the chain of command for this change to occur. The final authority for the local school board will usually be the state secretary of education. A grass-roots change will occur if enough school-board members insist upon what is best, overall, for their districts.

Ideally, most states will decide to order new reading books and begin the new system within the first year after learning the advantages to be gained. Very little works ideally, however, when tens of millions of people are involved. If most of the states agree, the federal government will be obligated to support (or at least not oppose) the wishes of the people. Otherwise the decision of what is best for their citizens rests entirely with the states.

There are enough benefits to implementing N'wenglish that many states will have the courage of their convictions. They will decide to implement N'wenglish despite what the other states do, if they remember these facts:

1. It will not take away the reading ability of those in their state who already read English. Instead, it will give them another spelling method that they can learn in only an hour or two.

2. It will enable millions of children and adults to read who otherwise would not read.

3. It will affect schoolchildren in their state who could have learned English by depriving them of that opportunity until they can take elective English spelling classes in college. (It could be as early as high school if there is enough demand to include it in the curriculum.) This will not be a problem for two reasons:

    a. States deciding to adopt N'wenglish will see to it that students receive most of the reading material they need and desire. Also, competition for sales dollars will ensure that private companies both within the state and elsewhere will provide for the pupils' needs and desires and for those of the newly literate adults in the state.

    b. The reading demands of most students in grade school and high school are not so sophisticated that the students will want (or even know about) English publications in other states that are in so little demand in their own state that it is not feasible to reproduce them in N'wenglish.

As time goes on, even if most states do not immediately decide to switch to N'wenglish, more states will adopt N'wenglish. This will be based upon the results gained in all the states with the initial foresight to adopt N'wenglish.

Newly literate adults will probably be even more vocal in urging the school boards to adopt N'wenglish than those who teach them to read. They will know by experience both the benefits of reading and the human suffering caused by not being able to read. Most illiterates in the United States have sat it out in school for at least eight years. They will have no desire to take a chance on subjecting their friends and family to the same frustrations they endured because of being unable to read English in school.

Private Sector Considerations

The details of when and how newspapers, magazines, and books are gradually converted over to N'wenglish should be left to the publishing companies. The publishers can do market surveys and decide what is in their financial best interest. In anything so complicated and varied, any effort at legislating requirements for publishers would inevitably result in hurting many of them. This much is certain: publishers will be as eager to sell material in N'wenglish as new readers will be to buy it. During the twelve-year interim period when N'wenglish is becoming increasingly widespread, the publishers will be in the profitable position of selling the same printed material in two versions.

The Interim Period

During the twelve-year period when N'wenglish is being adopted, one grade at a time into all twelve grades of public school, both English and N'wenglish materials will be published. The publishing houses will reprint in N'wenglish many books they believe are marketable. After the twelve-year period, the publishers will have many years in which to test the market. Based on these studies they will introduce other books, magazine articles, and pamphlets that were previously published in English. The advertising phrase "Now in N'wenglish" will, over time, become more and more familiar.

How to Implement This Proposal

One method of handling the interim period would be for newspapers and magazines to write 8 or 10 percent of their articles in N'wenglish the first year, 15 or 20 percent in N'wenglish the second year, etc.

At first it might be desirable to write some articles using both systems. The headlines of the articles could be in both English and N'wenglish, with articles the publishers believe will be most interesting and important written in N'wenglish. This would be one way of gradually switching more readers to N'wenglish. The only accommodation needed for those who can now read only English would be inclusion of figure 11-1 on all the magazine and book title pages and newspaper mastheads.

Dictionaries

Eventually complete dictionaries will be published in N'wenglish. The initial dictionaries for those who read English, however, need only be a cross-reference—N'wenglish words in alphabetical order with the corresponding English spelling. The glossary of appendix 4 words in part one, section three, of the companion volume is an example of such a cross-reference. Existing dictionaries, of course, already have the English-to-N'wenglish cross-reference since they show pronunciation.

School Considerations

Within twelve years colleges will be ready to teach English spelling in the same way that the Middle English of Chaucer's time is now taught. Everything else will be in N'wenglish. After twelve years there will not be any further advantage in using English for newly printed material. (People who now read English will still be able, however, to read books in English they already own or that are in libraries.) Those studying to be attorneys, historians, or English literature scholars, or preparing for vocations and hobbies requiring extensive research into past documents are among the very few who will need to learn the old English spelling.

Long before the twelve-year interim period is over, research will be completed for taking advantage of the ease of learning N'wenglish. Two big improvements can be made in the public school curricula of English-speaking countries to bring them up to the scholastic levels of other counties. First, the subjects taught can be moved down a grade level or two because of earlier reading abilities. Also, if individual children and their parents *choose* to do so, and if their linguistic ability permits it, some children should be allowed to start first grade as early as four years of age. As Pitman explains it,

> It has so far been widely accepted that children are not ready to start learning to read until they have a mental age of six and a half (see page 26). This may be true when children are faced at the outset with words spelt in the orthodox manner but with i.t.a. it would seem that a lower mental age is sufficient for a start to be made—provided, as has been argued earlier, that pupils possess an adequate level of linguistic ability. This is borne out by the research findings in Oldham, an area in which children were eligible for the infants school in the school year during which they reach their fourth birthday; four-year-olds in Oldham were learning to read i.t.a. with such ease that the whole question of reading readiness in relation to mental age demands to be reconsidered.
>
> Eventually it will be necessary to devise new tests of reading accuracy, speed, and comprehension because the existing tests are based on standards expected of children taught with all the frustrations of orthodox spelling. These tests are very suitable for attainments of children taught with the orthodox medium and have had to be used, by default, for the comparative research between it and i.t.a., but they do not reflect the higher norms to be expected when the use of i.t.a. becomes wide spread, any more than recognized tests of human physical performance in famine areas can be expected to be adequate elsewhere.[5]

Second, the process of teaching all phases of communication in English can eventually be combined and improved. Perhaps Pitman explains it best:

> [T]he advantage of allowing young children to write as they speak is that it assists teachers in detecting bad speech habits. If a child writes [Ie shood ov ben—this is the N'wenglish transliteration; i.t.a. characters are not available], it very clearly indicates that he hears and has learned to say the words wrongly. When it is explained that the sentence should be written [Ie shood hav ben], an

How to Implement This Proposal

> **Figure 11-1**
> **Format for Use on**
> **Magazine and Book Title Pages and Newspaper Mastheads**
> **N'wenglish Spelling Rules**
>
> 1. Each letter or combination has only one sound, as follows ("short," "long," and "other" vowels are only convenient grouping terms and have no other significance):
>   **5 short vowels**: use *A, E, I, O,* and *U* for the more-often-used sounds, as in "That pet did not run."
>   **5 long vowels**: add an *E* to the vowels (*AE, EE, IE, OE,* or *UE*) or use macrons (a line over the vowels) for the less-often-used sounds, as in "Mae Green tried roe glue" or "Thā ēt frīd tōfū."
>   **4 other vowels**: use A*U, OO, OI,* and *OU* for the sounds, as in "Haul good oil out."
>   **18 consonant sounds represented by a single letter**: use the letters that are used most often (except for *F, S,* and *Y,* entirely because of the very common word "of" and such words as *bags* and *pity*), as in "Yes, Val 'Zip' Kim hid our big fan-jet win."
>   **6 consonant sounds represented by digraphs** (two letters): (1) use *TH* and *TT* for the sounds, as in "then" and "thin," respectively; (2) use *C* **ONLY** in *CH* as in "chip;" (3) use *SH* and *NG* for the sounds, as in "wishing;" (4) use *ZH* as in "muzhik" for the sound of *Z* as in "azure" or of *S* as in "treasure."
>   **use *Q* and *X* ONLY as follows**: use *Q* (not *QU*) for the *KW* sound as in "quit" and *X* for the *KS* sound, as in "exit" (*qit* and *exit* in N'wenglish). "Quicksand" is spelled "qixand" in N'wenglish. Use *KS* instead of *X* for plurals and possessives ending in *K*.
>   A **memory aid** for the above is:
>   Mae Green lied, "Joe Blue and Kevin 'Top Gun' Wood haul our oil." Qit mez-huring fish which yuez this ttin box. (It is "Quit," "measuring," "use," and "thin" in English spelling.)
> 2. There are no silent letters and no double letters which make a single sound except *OO* and *TT* —and *EE* if macrons aren't used.
> 3. All sounds must be shown except (1) the *NG* sound in *NK* and *NX* and (2) a *U* sound between a vowel (other than *U*) and *R* or *L*.
> 4. The spelling of trademarks and proper nouns except the names of the months and days are unchanged.
> **Optional Rules**
> 5. A slash (/) follows primary accented syllables unless the primary accent is on the last syllable. Hyphens are optional. Compound words may be spelled as one word or may be hyphenated.
> 6. N'wenglish spelling between slashes follows proper nouns and trademarks if needed to show pronunciation.
> 7. The use of an apostrophe to show contractions (such as *can't* for *cannot*) is optional.
> 8. To avoid confusion with common synonyms, spell the following English words with the N'wenglish spelling shown in parentheses: *buoy* (*boih* or *buei*), *burrow* (*buroew*), *flower* (*flouur*), *son* (*suhn*), *too* (*tueh*), *two* (*tuew*), *ewe* (*iue*), *yew* (*ihue*), and the following **singular** nouns as shown: *you* (*Yue*), *your* (*Yoor*), and *you're* (*Yoo'r*).

improvement is being fostered in the child's diction as well as in his writing. Children with bad speech behaviour are often the victims of poor auditory discrimination; when corrected orally they still fail to hear their mistakes. Their visual discrimination is however usually perfect and when they are able to see their own mispronunciations put on paper in i.t.a. and then corrected in i.t.a. they soon become aware of the differences they need to listen for....Until recently teachers have acted on the supposition that their chief purpose is to teach reading and that improvement of "language" is a by-product; it can now, however, be argued that, with the removal of all the clutter that impedes children when learning to read, we shall come to recognize that their chief purpose is to teach "language" (including speech) and that reading and writing are but the visual half.[6]

International Considerations

Eventually most, if not all, of the English-speaking world will adopt N'wenglish, but how will it affect the United States if other English-speaking nations do not adopt N'wenglish as soon as we do? Assuming the nations not adopting N'wenglish want to sell their books, magazines, etc., in the United States, they will print them in N'wenglish. Citizens of those nations must spend an hour or two learning N'wenglish if they want to read U.S. publications. Also, material printed only in English in other countries after the United States adopts N'wenglish will be paraphrased and printed in N'wenglish by American publishing companies if it is of enough importance and if there is a sufficient market for it. So, in short, the hesitancy of other countries in adopting N'wenglish will adversely affect only their own citizenry.

Perhaps equally or even more likely is the converse: what if other English-speaking nations adopt N'wenglish before the United States? The exact same conditions as in the previous paragraph will occur. As nation after nation discovers the advantages of N'wenglish, eventually the U.S. will adopt N'wenglish based on its success elsewhere.

Why Implementing This Method Is Critical

Many educational activists will point to the superior success, on the average, of private schooling or home schooling and state that governmental funding should be allowed to be used for private or home schooling, where it would be more effective. The most recent U.S. presidents and vice presidents, as well as about half of U.S. congressmen and many state governmental officials—and a higher percentage of public school teachers than among the general public—send their children to private schools, but taxpayers who want to send their children to private schools cannot get tax benefits to do so. Parents claim—quite correctly—that it is unfair for them to have to pay twice for educating their children, if their public school is failing to educate them properly: once for the cost of the private schooling and once for the taxes used only for funding public schooling that their children will derive no direct benefit from.

Teachers, teachers' unions, and educational authorities will proclaim loudly that diverting some of the tax money for private schooling will "destroy" the public school system, because it is already underfunded, despite the fact that U.S. schools already spend far more per student than other nations and all but the most expensive private schools. What is overlooked, however, is that if public school funding is reduced, it will be only because there are fewer public school students, as students transfer to private schools and home schools.

Teachers correctly claim that part of the reason for the better performance of private schools is that public schools must accept and try to teach all students, but private schools can flunk out the poorer students and can expel students who are serious discipline problems. Parents of students who must leave a private school, however, will enroll them in another private school and provide the help needed to see that they succeed in their new school.

Others will state that if we would just go back to phonics instruction, we could solve all the problems. They will claim—quite correctly—that any whole-word instruction before the student knows what sounds each of the letters makes and how to blend the sounds will teach the student the habit of guessing at words—a habit that is hard to break. Dr. McGuinness's book, as explained in chapters 6 and 9 of this book, goes a long way in proving the truth of this claim *if* phonics is taught in the correct way.

Most adults who learned to read in grade school have forgotten the difficulty they had in learning to read. Many of those who learn to read as adults—usually with a year or more of one-on-one tutoring—

as well as those who learned to read as children will tell you that if they can learn to read with our present system, then anyone else can too, because (some of them may tell you) they are not particularly brilliant intellects.

All the earlier arguments have validity, but they all miss the point. As Sir James Pitman and several other scholars have shown, and as Dr. McGuinness's book has verified, English spelling is so difficult that a certain percentage of people will never be able to learn to read it fluently. And it is *not* strictly dependent only upon the student's intelligence. No one knows what percentage of students this applies to. As stated previously, however, with hundreds of millions of English-speaking people around the world, even if it is only 0.01 percent, that is still hundreds of thousands of people being hurt. There are millions more who can learn to read present English, but only with extensive one-on-one tutoring.

An equally significant point to remember is that all native-born and immigrant students except the most brilliant require two to two and one-half years to learn to read. They must learn one at a time, by rote memorization or by repetition, the reading vocabulary they need to succeed in life. This is time that should be used in learning the facts and skills they need to enable them to compete with students of other nations who do not have the hindrance of such an inconsistent and illogical spelling system.

Unless *you*, dear readers, are willing to spend a maximum of an hour or two of your time to learn a new spelling system and a few minutes to lobby those in positions of authority to take the compassionate action proposed in this chapter, our nation will continue plodding along, fighting the symptoms of illiteracy but never solving the problem. We will continue spending money every five years or so for "new, improved" reading books with minor variations of numerous failed teaching methods rather than what is proposed here: simpler, less expensive reading books that will not have to be replaced until they physically wear out. The functional illiterates will continue to be hurt, and our students will remain near the bottom, academically, among the industrialized nations of the world.

Chapter 12
Summary and Challenge

Chapter 10 listed the primary objections raised to spelling reform based upon the supposed disadvantages of changing English spelling. It showed that none of these supposed objections apply to N'wenglish. Two final objections to implementing changes in anything affecting literacy need to be considered: (1) the need for further research and (2) the impossibility of a quick fix for illiteracy.

To avoid the pain of change, many scholars, social scientists, and politicians often advocate more research. Although many scholars and researchers will profit from additional research, we should not automatically attribute such calls for additional research to a conscious profit-motive attitude on their part. In truth, most people sincerely want to be sure that any change made is the right change—especially one as far-reaching as changing the way that hundreds of millions of people read.

Is More Research Needed?

As Jonathan Kozol points out in his book *Illiterate America*, very-much-more-than-"enough" research has already been done. From his research we know that it is time to act upon what we already know, instead of doing more research that will only serve to confirm previous findings. Kozol points out that in these research programs, all the funds that are spent (or all but a tiny portion) go into the pockets of the researchers or into the accounts of their university or company. Nonreaders in America would have been helped significantly more if the money used for the research had been spent directly on teaching them to read.

Is a Quick Fix Possible?

One major reason that scholars, social scientists, and politicians want more research is their knowledge that solving illiteracy is such a complicated problem. This leads us to the second objection: the impossibility of a quick fix. A large portion of David Harman's book *Illiteracy: a National Dilemma* is devoted to showing the difficulty of solving the illiteracy problem. Chapter 4 of his book shows the strong influence students' cultural environment, particularly their family, has upon their desire to learn to read. If children never see their parents reading, it is understandable if they see little importance in reading. Reading ability is just something their schoolteacher wants them to develop. It has little or no relation to their lifestyle and goals, particularly if their peer group places little importance on it.

Television also has a strong influence in molding lifestyles. There may be occasional pitches for literacy in commercials. In the television programs themselves, however, the story line is much too action oriented to be slowed by showing a main character quietly reading for any length of time. If some "egghead" secondary character does spend time reading, that character is often more of a target for ridicule than a role model to be followed.

Years later, as adults, illiterate children may begin to see the advantages of literacy. By that time, however, they have developed the self-image of someone who "can't" learn to read. Or they don't have the time and opportunity to learn to read. Chapter 5 of David Harman's book then expands upon their desire to learn to read and shows the extreme importance of motivation if people are ever to become proficient readers. Examples of several different types of literacy programs are shown in chapter 6 of Harman's book. The success or failure of each of these different programs can be largely tied to the amount of motivation in the students.

Summary and Challenge

Impossibility of a Quick Fix Using Traditional Methods

All this is presented to verify Harman's assertion that the problems of illiteracy are so diverse that a quick fix is an unreasonable expectation. Similar to the Bullock Report discussed in chapter 7 of this book, Harman does not mention (and presumably has not considered) spelling reform. His assertion that the problems of illiteracy are very diverse and complicated is correct. Although most people try to end illiteracy by attacking the problems associated with illiteracy, they are attacking the *symptoms* of the "disease of illiteracy" rather than the *cause* of the illiteracy. There are many symptoms. There is only one root cause of the disease: our confused and illogical spelling method.

Our huge national deficit almost guarantees that we will not spend the minimum of $5 billion each year needed to significantly reduce illiteracy by combating the symptoms. Even if we did spend $5 billion on literacy programs, the difficulty of English spelling is such a strong demotivator that millions would still lack the motivation necessary to become proficient readers.

As pointed out by Ben Wood, former Director of Bureau of Collegiate Educational Research of Columbia University in his foreword to Godfrey Dewey's book *English spelling: Roadblock to reading*, the difficulty of English spelling even makes many people who can read, dislike reading. David Harman refers to those who can read but seldom do so with apparent puzzlement: "The numbers of people who are capable of reading but don't is as baffling a problem as the numbers of people who are unable to read."[1]

All this points out the importance of two actions:
1. We must motivate those learning N'wenglish by helping them find reading material of interest and value to them.
2. We must remove the demotivation that adult illiterates experienced in trying to learn English by stressing the great ease of learning N'wenglish.

Understanding the Problem

It would be easy for those of us who can read to decide that the problems documented in this book are not widespread since they do not apply to us. Can we be sure, however, that tens of millions of English-speaking people around the world do not have these problems? If you have been reading newspaper articles concerning illiteracy in the U.S. over the last several years, you are aware of the increasing concern. Perhaps you have devalued the seriousness of the problem reported in these newspaper articles for one or more of the reasons in chapter 2. Perhaps the way the articles were written concealed the size of the problem.

Anne C. Lewis, a freelance writer on education concerns, says there are "two big problems" the press makes in its coverage of illiteracy. The first mistake is confusing adult illiteracy problems with problems in the public schools. It is typical to blame the adult literacy problems on the schools and then go no further—as if fixing the blame will somehow result in solving the problem. Blaming the schools accomplishes nothing because, she pointed out, roughly 70 percent of the workforce in the year 2000 was already in the workforce and therefore permanently out of public schools. Furthermore, she says, thirty million or more Americans read so poorly they could "bring the whole economy crashing down." With the rapidly accelerating technology in the workplace and its demands, for example, for reading the operating manuals and for retraining, previous levels of illiteracy are no longer acceptable. She says the press rarely makes this known.

The second mistake in illiteracy coverage in the press is that it is far too often only concerned with boring stories of an occasional adult illiterate who can now read thanks to the efforts of some selfless volunteer. This type of coverage too often lulls the public into believing that is all there is to the problem of adult illiteracy.[2]

Business, media, and governmental leaders most aware of the problem, however, know there is more to it. They do not devalue the seriousness of illiteracy in the U.S. For example:

> An ill-educated citizenry threatens the United States' ability to remain competitive in world markets more than any of the other more frequently cited causes of unproductive work places.
>
> That, according to Geneva Steel President Joseph A. Cannon, was one of the main themes of the prestigious Eighth American Enterprise Institute World Forum he recently attended in Beaver Creek, Colo....
>
> The forum's discussion about the sad state of U.S. education

particularly interested Mr. Cannon....[I]n the one session about education which stands out in his mind, "they didn't talk about worker productivity. They didn't talk about new inventions. They didn't talk about government-industrial policy. They just talked about education. That was everyone's concern."

U.S. children rated about 14th out of 15 nations on mathematic skills....

Mr. Cannon said the average IQ of Japanese students is increasing while that of their counterparts in the U.S. is declining.

"This is a crisis and people have said it is a crisis for years," said Mr. Cannon. "But it's only getting worse....We spend more on education per capita than almost any nation in the world. People say, 'Well, spend some more money.' That does not appear to be the answer."[3]

The Cost of Solving Literacy Problems

Perhaps your first concern when you started reading this book was, "Sure, we need to solve our literacy problems, but the voters will never agree to such expenditures." Solving problems can cost money, but the cost savings from reducing the effects of the problem can often counterbalance the preventive costs.

[Harold L.] Hodgkinson [of the Institute for Educational Leadership in Washington] notes that it costs the taxpayers about $3,500 a year [it was projected at $8865 for each public elementary and high school student for the 2002-2003 school year][4] to educate a child or a college student. It costs them about $20,000 a year to house a prisoner....[Data from an April 4, 1996, article in *The Salt Lake Tribune*[5] shows it costs California an estimated $40,000 per year for food, guards, and capital costs to house a prisoner.]

To those who argue that there's no proven relationship between dropout rates and prison populations, Hodgkinson replies: Perhaps a direct relationship can't be proved. But consider this: Minnesota, with the best graduation rate in the country (90.6 percent), ranks 49th among the states in prisoners per 100,000 population, and there is an uncanny inverse relationship between dropout rates and prisoner population in all 50 states....

A Department of Justice study last April showed that 63 percent of the inmates released from prisons are rearrested for a serious crime within three years....Hodgkinson argues that given the high recidivism rate in prisons, the most cost-effective strategy is to keep people out of jail in the first place. And since there is very little return on investment in prisons, the best way to reduce criminal expenditures is to invest in education.[6]

The $20,000 per year, per prisoner mentioned earlier is just a small portion of the money spent on crime. (In the first place, the cell to hold a prisoner costs a minimum of $100,000 to construct.)[7] Also, the cost of crime is only a small part of the monetary costs of illiteracy.

Adult Illiteracy

People and organizations have been issuing warnings about the process of learning to read English for decades. A significant warning found May 1, 2004, on The Simplified Spelling Society's Web site (www.spellingsociety.org) stated, "English speaking adults always come near the bottom in international studies on literacy." Although improvements have been made, nothing approaching the level of changes needed has ever been seriously suggested. What is more important, even if the American public would be willing to have their taxes raised enough to ensure that most schoolchildren learn to read, this would not help the millions of adult nonreaders and poor-readers. Many people will claim that, with time, the teaching of adult illiterates will improve. Many people personally involved in adult literacy programs can justifiably take pride in the dozens of people they have personally helped and the thousands of people, collectively, that have been helped. It is often difficult for these people, as it is for all of us, to see the complete situation or the "big picture." Let's be brutally honest: there are fifty to ninety million functionally illiterate adults in the U.S. (depending on whose definition you use), and the number of adult illiterates is growing by more than two million each year.

Today, less than 1 percent of adult illiterates are learning to read and then going on to complete the equivalent of eighth grade. An absolute minimum of $5 billion would be needed to even make a dent in reducing the number of adult illiterates, and this would only amount to about $83 per adult illiterate per year. Even an extreme optimist would not believe that an $83 per person expenditure would be enough if the optimist is at all familiar with present-day adult literacy courses. Most adult illiterates do not have or (for reasons this book covers) will not devote long periods for learning to read English. In truth, the number of illiterates is growing and will continue to grow until an easily mastered spelling system such as N'wenglish is adopted.

The main reason that even a $5 billion expenditure on adult literacy each year would be inadequate is that even after adult illiterates learn to read, they often still cannot get a good job. Most desirable jobs require at least a high school diploma. Because of job or family responsibilities, many illiterates who learn to read cannot or will not devote the many months or years of effort needed to get a high school diploma. Usually, if students do not, as young children, spend the large amount of time required to learn what is necessary to gain a high school diploma, they never will. This is why it is so important that learning these subjects in the normal school curriculum must not be hindered by poor reading skills brought on by an inconsistent and illogical spelling system. Adopting a logical, consistent, simple spelling system will solve the problem—anything else is just fighting the symptoms

Human-Suffering Costs

John Corcoran taught high school in California for eighteen years without being able to read. Mr. Corcoran told how he felt as if something were wrong with him that prevented him from being able to read. He spoke of the emotional pain that belief caused him. Even his wife did not understand his pain until she could compare his personality and actions before and after he learned to read. When Mr. Corcoran was forty-eight years old he finally decided to try, once more, to learn to read. For the first thirty days, and almost twenty hours of one-on-one tutor time, he did not believe he would ever learn to read. Finally his tutor got through to him, and he began to learn. As is true of most adult nonreaders, it required him a little over a year to complete his reading course.Mr.   John Corcoran explained that the U.S. is in denial. As a help people in general, and as teachers in particular, we are too embarrassed to admit the scope of our illiteracy. Mr. Corcoran told of how all through grade school and high school his teachers never once heard him read or spell a word correctly, and yet they continued to call on him to read and spell as if they hadn't noticed. Not one teacher ever offered the one-on-one that he so desperately needed, perhaps out of fear that, like so many of his previous teachers, they would be unable to help him, or because they were busy with other tasks. It was easier to assume that perhaps he could read and spell better than his oral responses indicated or that he would soon learn on his own. When Mr. Corcoran got the one-on-one help he needed, he not only learned to read but he also went through four years of self study and then another hundred hours of very intensive instruction, bringing him to a college level of skill. He worked with first lady Barbara Bush on the literacy problem and served from 1994 to 1997 on the board of the National Institute for Literacy. He knows by firsthand knowledge how badly the U.S. public underestimates the illiteracy problem and the damage it does to nonreaders.

John Corcoran, the high school teacher who could not read, is a testimony to the ability of illiterates to hide—and the emotional turmoil of doing so.

Mr. Corcoran said that, to hide his embarrassment over being unable to read, he became the class clown "having too much fun to waste time on learning to read." He said that other nonreaders he knew were just as disruptive. As testimonial letters for i.t.a. in Sir James Pitman's book *Alphabets and Reading* point out, the frustration of feeling stupid or inferior usually results in discipline problems. Students would rather be considered a tough troublemaker not interested in reading than be seen as trying and failing to learn. He explained that being unable to read causes very low self-esteem, and the *only* way to build up the nonreaders' self-esteem is to teach them to read! As he stated it, "A crying child begs, 'Tell them not to hurt us anymore—teach us to read!'" Mr. Corcoran said he feels strongly that every American who can read—in particular, every teacher—has a moral obligation to help their fellow citizens learn to read.

Summary and Challenge

Chapter 5 listed and briefly explained the human-suffering costs of illiteracy. In relation to the human suffering resulting from illiteracy, Michael Harrington wrote,

At this point, I would beg the reader to forget the numbers game. Whatever the precise calibrations, it is obvious that these statistics represent an enormous, an unconscionable amount of human suffering....They should be read with a sense of outrage.[8]

A Nation at Risk

The National Commission on Excellence in Education, after observing the literacy crisis and the falling standards in high school and college, warned us on April 26, 1983, "Our nation is at risk." One of the statements from the report states,

If an unfriendly foreign power had attempted to impose on America the mediocre educational performance that exists today, we might well have viewed it as an act of war.[9]

In *Illiterate America*, Kozol ends chapter 3, "The Price We Pay," by agreeing that, as the National Commission on Excellence in Education stated, our nation is at risk because of illiteracy. Kozol points out that after the "Nation at Risk" report was issued, the Secretary of Education may not really have understood the nature of the risk. Kozol says we are, in effect, held captive by the actions or our fellow citizens. As a result *every* citizen—even the most wealthy and those who think they are most removed from the problem—will be forced to pay a "formidable price" for illiteracy.[10]

We have no choice but to pay a "formidable price" because of illiteracy, but will the money be spent in "fighting the disease or in fighting the symptoms of the disease?" Will we solve the problem in the most logical way and simplify the spelling, or will we continue spending money on the resulting illiteracy?

As Kozol expresses it, in a society that the common citizens did not create, our President and our leaders have enabled the growth of illiteracy by their "malign neglect." Kozol then asks the all important question, will we show the courage and character to solve a problem that so many nations poorer than the U.S. have found it natural to solve—the illiteracy that is putting us all at risk?[11]

There have been some improvements since the 1983 "Nation at Risk" report, but are we still at risk? Many recent reports show that we are. Chapter 1 listed several such reports. The following quotation shows some examples of the difficulty U.S. companies are having with illiteracy:

> The talk of a nation at risk is no idle rhetoric. One recent survey of Fortune 500 firms found that 58 percent of the companies surveyed had a problem finding employees with even the most basic skills. In fact it has been established that 20 percent of our nation's present work force is functionally illiterate.
>
> Motorola reports that only 20 percent of its applicants could successfully pass a simple, fifth-grade level test of arithmetic and a seventh-grade test of written comprehension. New York Telephone, likewise, reports that only 16 percent of its applicants could pass a fifth-grade level exam for an entry level position. According to a General Motors spokesman, 87 percent of its employees are incapable of performing tasks beyond a fifth-grade level.
>
> These workers are competing against a highly educated work force in Japan, where a high school education has been roughly equated with a college education in the United States.[12]

What is our position in 1990 and later? It is summed up in the following quotation:

> It's been seven years since the "Nation at Risk" report raised a national alarm about our schools. Reform efforts have lifted minimum standards in many communities. But those standards are not nearly high enough to meet the needs for economic survival....
>
> If this situation goes unremedied for another decade, this nation is doomed to decline. We simply cannot survive as a first-class economic power in the information age with "minimal" capacity to acquire and communicate facts, information, concepts or ideas.[13]

The optimists among the readers of this book will have noticed that most of the previous quotes are from the 1990s. They will say, "I'm sure we have made improvements since the 1990s." An April 20, 2003, report entitled "'At Risk' Report 20 Years Later" by Fredreka Schouten for Gannet News Service stated that following the "A Nation at Risk" report of April 26, 1983, there was a movement to improve the schools, raise standards, and hold both students and teachers accountable for academic performance. Notwithstanding, experts claim that twenty years of effort have yielded no dramatic change.

The reading scores of 9-year-olds have shown little or no change between 1983 and 2002, and almost 60 percent of high school seniors scored below basic on recent U.S. history tests. Also, high school seniors scored near the bottom in a recent twenty-three nation math and science academic competition. Despite the fact that some experts believe changes made a few years ago to the SAT made the test easier, average 2002 SAT scores on the verbal portion are virtually unchanged from 1983 scores. Performance on the American College Testing exam only improved slightly: 20.8 in 2002 versus 19.9 in 1983.

Phyllis Eisen, vice president of the Manufacturing Institute, said that about half of the money manufacturers spend on training employees is for remedial work. She also said that after twenty-five years of school reform, manufacturers have a feeling of despair about employees. Few job applicants have the basic knowledge they need, and too many job applicants cannot even read the application form. Deborah Wadsworth, president of Public Agenda said businesspeople are profoundly unhappy with job applicants.

Although 78 percent of teachers believe public school graduates have the skills to succeed in the workplace, only 41 percent of employers agree. Furthermore, only 47 percent of college professors believe these graduates are ready for college.

Finally, in Schouten's report Education Secretary Rod Paige said, "I don't think we can sustain our international leadership unless we achieve better performance in our educational system. The consequences are dire."[14]

Our condition is much worse than it was in 1887. Even that far back, however, the need was easily recognizable. Sociologist William Sumner stated,

I have two boys who are learning to spell. They often try to spell by analogy, thus using their brains and learning to think. Then I have to arrest them, turning them back from a rational procedure, and impose tradition and authority. They ask me "Why?" I answer "Because your father and others who have lived before you have never had the courage and energy to correct a ridiculous old abuse, and you are now inheriting it with all the intellectual injury, loss of time, and wasted labor which it occasions. I am ashamed that it should be so." (Robertson [and] Cassidy, 1954; 363)[15]

Summary

Some of the conclusions from the facts presented in this book are:

1. "[M]any of our children, even some of the brightest, find their sense of logic unable to cope with the illogic and disorderliness of English spelling."

2. Less than 1 percent of adult illiterates are learning to read then going on to complete the equivalent of eighth grade, which is still inadequate for getting a good job.

3. There is a "pressing demand for a much higher level of literacy in the United States as we move from a manufacturing economy into a sophisticated high-tech economy of services and communication."

4. There is a growing "awareness of the connection between illiteracy and our mounting social problems: dropout, crime-in-the-streets, hard core unemployment and poverty."

5. There is the "largely overlooked but very serious fact that illiteracy is a real threat to democracy. Those voters who depend on the spoken word alone...are easily deluded and manipulated."

6. There is a widespread "acceptance of English as the emerging [worldwide language] of international communication....A reduction in language barriers can open diplomatic, commercial, civic, and societal doors that are now scarcely ajar."

7. There is recognition "of the fact that traditional spelling tends to promote the mispronunciation of English....A better fit between sight and sound should not only reduce illiteracy but lead to greater stability of pronunciation, to less chance of misunderstanding, and to more reliable communication overall."[16]

Summary and Challenge

8. Illiteracy costs everyone (the illiterates: human suffering; taxpayers: cost of social programs; consumers: higher prices for consumer goods; the nation: the competitive edge in world markets). Spelling reform will cost less than illiteracy now costs.

9. English spelling and the effect it has upon learning are much worse than most people realize.

10. Based upon this and previously presented evidence, perhaps the most important conclusion is this: whatever improvements may be devised for teaching reading to schoolchildren, none of these will have a significant effect on adult nonreaders. The only *practical, permanent* solution to illiteracy—*for everyone*—is spelling reform.

Scholars have been advocating English spelling reform ever since the spelling was frozen in the mid-1700s. When the first significant English dictionary was issued in 1755, the spelling system was not a logical, scholarly, designed system. No one had gone to the effort of simply finding the phonemes used in English and deciding which letter(s) would most logically and efficiently represent these phonemes. It was merely a cataloguing of specific ways of spelling individual *words*, as they were then pronounced, or as the foreign words we've adopted into English were spelled in their original language.

N'wenglish will freeze the spelling of the phonemes, thus restoring to our alphabet the true purpose of an alphabet. The purpose of an alphabet is *not* to provide the writer with weird-shaped strokes to be combined sequentially, Chinese-picture-writing-style, into representations of words. In such a system we must remember the sequential arrangement of these "strokes" for the twenty thousand to seventy thousand words we normally use. Or we must refer to a dictionary, *if* one is handy *and if* we can find the word we need. Such a system is as much a hindrance as it is a help to communication. The true purpose of an alphabet is simply to provide a visual recording of the sounds that combine to form the words and meanings that we want to express.

In one narrow aspect of the problem—book sales—the question is not, "Will we spend additional money for students' textbooks and books for the general public?" That has already been decided; we will. The question is, "What books will we spend the money on?" Will we spend money for tons of books that tens of millions of Americans (30 to 50 percent of our population) will never read, or will we spend money for books that everyone can read?

Some of these new books will be spelling books. The method by which spelling is taught may change slightly, but the spelling itself does not. As Edward Rondthaler and Edward Lias state, "[Spelling] is the only branch of learning that has undergone no serious update or repair since before the 16th Century. Other disciplines receive continuous updating. But not spelling."[17]

One final quote should provide the proper perspective to the problem. Arthur W. Heilman, Ph.D., an internationally known expert on reading instruction ends his book *Phonics in Proper Perspective* with the following statement:

> The many alternative approaches available for cracking the code might be interpreted as evidence that mastering the English system of writing poses a formidable challenge. There is no question that English spelling reform is long overdue. The present practice of attempting to teach *all* American youth to read and spell English is the foremost example of conspicuous consumption of a nation's resources since the building of the pyramids. Unfortunately for many children, the belief is still widely held that our economy can still afford this cruel waste.
>
> Without doubt, the most patriotic and educationally sound endeavor that reading teachers, and their teachers, could follow would be to set a date a few years in the future and decline henceforth to teach another child to read traditional English writing. The brief delay suggested would provide time for a federal commission to devise a sweeping and thorough spelling reform of English.
>
> This suggestion is not likely to be followed since man is a thinking animal; and he is now busily thinking of numerous "new approaches" to teach archaic English. Furthermore, the federal government has indicated its willingness to raise the ante in support of education. It would be unbecoming of educators not to attempt hundreds of new and devious approaches to the problem rather than advocating the one logical (and eventually inevitable) solution.[18]

Fighting the Disease

Why fight the inevitable? When one shot of penicillin (spelling reform) will cure the disease (illiteracy), why spend billions of dollars on the symptoms? Why spend money on aspirin to reduce the fever (better reading textbooks), decongestants to combat excess mucus (better methods of teaching reading), oxygen therapy to ease breathing (publicizing and funding adult literacy programs), and research to find better methods of combating symptoms (educational research) if the disease can be cured?

It is long past time for America to have the courage and the foresight to do what several less-developed nations have done. It is long past time to do what dozens of educators, linguists, and scholars have advocated for centuries—fight the disease, not the symptoms, and make our spelling perfectly phonemic with N'wenglish.

David Harman may be correct in saying that a quick fix is impossible. If he is correct, however, it is only because our resistance to change prevents us from doing what should be done, not because there is no solution. The "fix" can be as "quick" as we, the American people, insist that it must be. There were undoubtedly many scholars in Turkey who said it "couldn't be done" or that a quick fix was impossible. Kemel Pasha's "shot of penicillin" cured Turkey's spelling problems in only one summer!

A newspaper editorial shortly after the news that 48 percent of U.S. adults are now functionally illiterate stated, "For many who are unplugged from society's basic communications and lack of rudimentary intellectual skills, life must be a constant source of bewilderment and frustration. No wonder alienation, poverty, anger and violence abound." It ends by stating,

> [T]he dismal findings of this comprehensive study should galvanize leaders to place even more emphasis and resources into reading.
>
> Can the United States afford to do that? Can the United States afford *not* to do that?
>
> Forget about the federal budget deficit, the economy, unemployment and health care reform. Until this nation can begin to cope with the literacy deficit, the hope of solving its other challenges will be dim.[19]

Challenge

As Edward Rondthaler and Edward Lias explain,

> The genius of alphabet, the one-to-one, sound-to-letter correspondence, is largely obscured in our writing. English is by far the most erratically spelled of modern languages....It is indeed a major factor in creating our mass of adult English-speaking functional illiterates....
>
> It is difficult to understand why a nation bearing the enormous social and economic burden of illiteracy has made no serious effort to eradicate its root cause. It is to our public shame and embarrassment that more than 40 countries have a higher percentage of literates than we. Yet we refuse to challenge our spelling. We accept it as a "given." We struggle along blindly, desperately using what are no more than remedial measures; never attacking the underlying source of the trouble.[20]

More than anything else, this book is a test of your resolve.

WILL YOU:

A. Do what you know should be done (if you've carefully read this entire book) and
   a. make arrangements today to begin teaching a friend, relative, or acquaintance who is functionally illiterate to read N'wenglish,
   b. contact today your local school board, and
   c. recommend today a careful reading of this book to three or more friends who haven't read it yet.

OR WILL YOU:

B. Take the easy way out and say,
   a. "(sigh) It probably won't work,"
   b. "I don't want to get involved. I don't have time," or
   c. any of a dozen other excuses?

Try as we might, we cannot avoid making a choice. By failing to choose A we are automatically, unavoidably choosing B. It may at first seem that the proposals in chapter 11 are somewhat naive, but who is more naive, someone who has spent the last eighteen years studying the lifetime research of numerous linguistic and educational experts, or those who know little about the subject other than what they have read here? This is especially pertinent since, if the reader so chooses, much of what is presented here can be assumed to be inaccurate. It may be that chapter 11 is the product of wishful thinking, but wishing we would finally solve our literacy problems cannot be considered wasted effort, except by those who have assumed spelling reform is unnecessary and impractical, perhaps mostly because they do not want to have to contend with too much change in their lives—regardless of how much help it would be to people who, unlike themselves, cannot read.

The Final, *Irrefutable* Arguments

This section will expand upon the practical meaning of the last paragraph of Dr. Heilman's quote in the summary section of this chapter.

Many educational and governmental officials will tell you progress is being made in solving our literacy crisis, assuming they are knowledgeable enough and honest enough to admit that a crisis exists. New plans and new books come out frequently. On the Larry King Live program on CNN on November 8, 1999, a book to be published in late 1999 was announced: Dr. William Bennett's book *The Educated Child*. From Dr. Bennett's description, the book is obviously an excellent attempt at solving educational problems—one of the better approaches presently available. It contains suggestions that every parent should implement with their children to ensure they get the best education presently available, and it addresses educational problems other than learning to read. There are at least two problems, however, that the book will not solve: (1) it attacks symptoms of the illiteracy problem rather than the foundational, root cause, like almost every other book or plan proposed in the last thirty-five years and (2) many parents will never follow the excellent advice offered.

Fighting the symptoms versus fighting the disease has been adequately addressed, but the problem of all—or even a majority of—parents' not doing what educational experts recommend is equally problematic. Parents' failure to do what many authorities believe to be best cannot be solely ascribed to lack of love and concern for their children's welfare. Even if *all* parents were to buy and read Dr. Bennett's book, understand it, and agree with it (which, of course, they cannot do if their own literacy skills are lacking), many would not benefit from doing so. Many parents must spend so many hours working just to maintain a reasonably decent standard of living that they do not have the time or energy to do the things necessary to ensure an adequate education for their children. Many of these time-consuming activities would be largely unnecessary if learning to read were as easy as it is in other languages.

In short, new plans and new books which "attempt hundreds of new and devious approaches to the problem rather than...the...logical solution" will continue to appear. The fact of their appearance is obvious; the reason why authorities propose their particular plans is much less obvious. Ask any people in positions of authority in education or government and they will tell you they want to solve our literacy crisis—and most of them *do* want to solve the problem. One or more of Dr. Samuel Blumenfeld's books explain why some people in positions of authority really do not want the masses to be as literate as they and their friends and relatives are. Some of Dr. Blumenfeld's more enlightening books are *Is Public Education Necessary?*, *The Whole Language/OBE Fraud,* and *The New Illiterates*. Whether or not you believe Dr. Blumenfeld there is one obvious conflict of interest—at least on a subconscious level: if everyone could become fluent readers in the first half of first grade (or in kindergarten) as they do in most other countries, our need for existing governmental services of all kinds would be greatly lessened.

You will notice that even though the experts come up with many "new and improved" educational ideas, none of them go outside the limits of what is taught in teachers' colleges. When they tell you that they really do want to solve our educational problems, what they do not tell you is that they want to solve them only in ways *they* decide. Among other things, this is not only because they want to claim the credit, but also because they do not want a system that is *too* efficient, or our need for their continued services, i.e., their job, would be lessened. The experts feel, of course, that *they*, rather than the uneducated masses, should decide which changes to make.

One should not be too surprised at this; it occurs in all professions. Some of the most influential spelling-reform advocates in the U.S are sincere in their desire to simplify our spelling. Shortly after contacting some of them, the author could see that although they want to improve our spelling, they want to do so with the systems *they* designed or that they have been advocating. Many of them have little interest in studying alternative proposals.

Summary and Challenge

There are, of course, those who can read about the emotional and physical pain and suffering that hundreds of millions of illiterates and functional illiterates around the world must endure—such as described in chapter 5 of this book or in Jonathan Kozol's book *Illiterate America*—and ignore what they have read. All those, however, who are absolutely sincere and passionate in their desire to solve our literacy crisis will be eager and willing to consider *all* reasonable chances of doing so—whether or not it is a method that they've personally designed or advocated.

Since most people in present-day America are very busy, even those who are most passionate about solving our literacy crisis need to be cautious of one common tendency. Most people have a strong inclination to leave many important and complicated decisions to so-called experts. You must be cautious about asking "experts" their opinion on spelling reform. You will find many, who do not want spelling reform. You will also find many—who know far less about the subject than you do, if you have carefully read this entire book—who will authoritatively tell you that "spelling reform will not work." They will even give you convincing-sounding reasons why it will not work, if you let them. What they will not do, however, is refute—point by point—the facts that are clearly stated in this book. They can't.

There are those who will see the title of this section and take it as a personal challenge. They will proclaim loudly that the arguments here *are* refutable. Examine carefully what they say, however. It is standard practice to attack the messenger instead of refuting the message. This attack usually takes the form of name-calling, attacking the messenger's qualifications, or dismissing the message as "unworkable" or some other claim which is unproven and perhaps even more inflammatory. Name-calling or dismissing the ideas of the messenger without refuting the ideas, point by point, should never be accepted by those who are truly passionate about solving the problem. In this case, "the messenger" has honestly evaluated and correlated the lifetime work of numerous scholars. "The messenger" is delivering the message of these scholars—in a way that engineers, by training and by temperament, are uniquely qualified to do, and in a way that educational and governmental authorities interested in maintaining the status quo will never do.

The bottom line is this: will we allow our governmental and educational officials to continue wasting our tax money on, as Dr. Heilman stated earlier in this chapter, "the foremost example of conspicuous consumption of a nation's resources since the building of the pyramids"? Or will we insist that we do what other nations have done and solve the problem, once and for all? Stating the problem in its most basic form: will we allow those responsible for the future of our children, our friends, and our nation to continue to be irresponsible by wasting our tax dollars on, as Heilman also said, "hundreds of new and devious approaches to the problem rather than advocating the one logical (and eventually inevitable) solution"?

Dr. Lounsbury's irrefutable defense of spelling reform in 1909 was largely unseen by the masses and ignored by those in positions of authority more interested in keeping the status quo than in solving problems. Due to technological advances and other changed conditions, the problem is much more urgent now. Anyone who is truly interested in solving our literacy crisis is hereby challenged not to ignore the unanswerable arguments in this book.

If you've read this far and still aren't sure, please read appendices 6 and 7 and excerpts of Dr. Lounsbury's book in the companion volume, *Let's End Our Literacy Crisis Workbook*. Also check the material in the bibliography, particularly (1) Blumenfeld's excellent and detailed history of methods for teaching reading in the U.S., *The New Illiterates* and his book *The Whole Language/OBE Fraud*, (2) portions of Dr. William Bennett's book *The De-Valuing of America* which refer directly to educational problems; and (3) Dr. Bennett's book *The Index of Leading Cultural Indicators*, which, perhaps more than any other book in print, will convince you of the need for immediate action on our educational problems. Verify for yourself that the quotations in this book are used correctly and that the data and conclusions in this book are correct. The need is so great that if such research on your part will spur you to action, then it will be well worth the expenditure of time both for you and for over a billion English-speaking people all around the world.

If you've ever tried to multiply or divide using Roman numerals, you have a small foretaste of the need to make our spelling logical. N'wenglish is destined to replace English in the same way that Arabic numerals replaced Roman numerals.

The Beginning

APPENDIX

Contents

An Introduction to the Appendices 215
Appendix 1
   Table A1-1
      Relative Frequency of the English Phonemes 219
   Tables A1-2 through A1-6
      (Example words for all the pronunciations of
      the 294 English Graphemes in Table 6-1) 220
Appendix 2
   Table A2-1
      Usage Frequency of Letters for English Phonemes 227
   Table A2-2
      Choice of Graphemes to Represent Each Phoneme 228
Appendix 3
      Why English Spelling Is So Bad 229
Appendix 4
      Thu Good Nuez uv John 231
Appendix 5
      Creative Problem Solving... 267

Appendix 6
    Comparing Our Proposal with Other Proposals..................273
Appendix 7
    There Really a Literacy Crisis? 285

An Introduction to the Appendices

Individual Notes for Each Part of the Appendix

Appendix 1

Table A1-1: This table shows the usage frequency of each of the phonemes, the most basic sounds, in normal English speech. It shows that since all the phonemes represented by digraphs (two letters) in N'wenglish are among the least used, the choice of letters to represent each phoneme cannot be significantly shortened or simplified.

Tables A1-2 through A1-6: Although there are many silent letters in the letter combinations shown, treating them each silent letter as part of a letter grouping is far easier than trying to remember the hundreds of silent letters in individual words, because there are ***no*** invariable rules for when a letter is silent. Also, it is important to remember that each example word shown in these tables represents many other words using the same pronunciation pattern. The fact that there is only one pronunciation shown for a certain letter combination does not mean that these are rare pronunciations. For example, although there is only one pronunciation for *AUGH*, it represents words such as *taught* and *daughter*, in addition to the example word shown. (This is an extension of table 6-1, which only shows the *number* of pronunciations of each letter and letter combination.)

Table A1-2: This table does not list words for the following phonemes which have only one example word: *IE* as in *fIne*, *YUE* (a blend of the Y and UE phonemes) as in *cUte*, B as in ***B**ag*, K as in ***K**in*, P as in ***P**in*, R as in ***R**an*, or V as in ***V**an*.

Table A1-3: To condense the table, the digraphs are not in strict alphabetical order from one part of the table to another.

Table A1-4: To condense the table, the following were omitted: *OUGH* as in *d**OUGH*** (OE), *A_E* as in *A**t**E* (*AE*) and *A**t**E* (*E*), and *E_E* as in *wE**rE*** (*U*).

Appendix 2

Table A2-1: Table A1-1 shows how often the phonemes appear in English spoken and written usage. This table shows what letter or letter combination is used to represent these sounds—how they are spelled. The numbers in both parts of the table are percentages and should total 100 percent on each horizontal row. The shaded boxes are sounds of letter(s) in the left column used more often than the sounds in black boxes. The black boxes show the representation of the sound chosen for N'wenglish. To condense the table, the following vowel spellings were omitted: *U* pronounced *YOO* as in *during* is 2.5 percent, *O* pronounced *WU* as in *one* is 2.3 percent, and the following letters are silent the percentage of the time shown: *A*, 0.1; *E*, 25.7 (because of silent *E* at the end of words and in unaccented syllables); *I*, 0.6; *O*, 0.2.

Table A2-1 Notes: * These are letter sounds occurring less than ten times in the 100,000 word sample (chapter 8, note 6, the next note below, and tables A1-2 through A1-6). Three vowels have other consonant sounds: *E* has a *Y* sound (*azalea*), *I* has *J* and *Y* sounds (*soldier, opinion*), and *U* has *F* and *W* sounds (*lieutenant, persuade*). The letter *G* also has a *ZH* sound (*garage*), S has a *CH* sound (*tension*), *X* has *GZH*, *KSH*, *SH*, and *Z* sounds (*luxurious, luxury, anxious*, and *xylophone*), *CH* has a *J* sound in one pronunciation of *spinach*, *TH* has *T* and *CH* sounds (*thyme* and *posthumous*), and *SH* (not shown in the table) has *Z* and *S* sounds (*dishonor* and *dishonest*)—all occurring less than ten times in the 100,000-word sample. ** This is calculated from the 1,027 most used words from a 100,000-word sample containing 10,161 different words. These 1,027 words comprise 78.6 percent of the 100,000 words and include all words occurring more than ten times (more than 0.01 percent of the total). *** Only the consonant sounds with more than one spelling in the 100,000-word sample are shown.

An Introduction to the Appendices

Table A2-2: This table shows the letter(s) chosen to represent each phoneme in N'wenglish and why each was chosen. More significantly, the table shows that *most* (92 percent if it were not for the two common spellings *of* and *does*) of the letters chosen are the ***most used*** letters for the phoneme used in English spelling.

Appendix 3

This appendix is a supplement to the first part of chapter 6. It explains part of the reason that English spelling is so inconsistent and illogical: the historical development of the language as an amalgamation of parts of the language—and spelling—of all the nations that conquered or occupied England prior to the thirteenth century.

Appendix 4

This appendix is included as somewhat of a final test of reading ability. It is written at what is called—in English—an adult reading level. (Reading levels are essentially meaningless in N'wenglish—if persons can read N'wenglish, they can read anything written in N'wenglish. If they encounter a word not in their vocabulary, they can correctly pronounce the word and may be able to determine the meaning from the context.) Many first- and second-grade students, and perhaps most third-grade or higher students, will have nearly all of the words in appendix 4 in their vocabulary.

This short book was chosen for transliteration into N'wenglish because tens of millions of the readers of this appendix will already have a copy of it in English. This eliminates the need to also print the English version here. It was also chosen because the main motivation for learning to read for hundreds of millions of people throughout the last several centuries is so that they could read the collection of sixty-six books (the *Bible*) from which this book was chosen and because this book, The Good News (which is the meaning of the word *gospel*) of John, is one of the favorite books in the collection.

Appendix 5

This appendix demonstrates that people often do not adequately research solutions to problems before settling upon a solution to implement.

The problems in this appendix are just a very small part of a book entitled *Creative Growth Games* by Eugene Raudsepp (see Bibliography). The reader should not discount the value of attempting to solve these problems.

Appendix 6

This appendix compares N'wenglish to other proposed spelling systems. The reader will naturally be tempted to believe that the author is advocating his system precisely because it is *his* system. This appendix proves that this is not the case. The facts speak for themselves. No spelling system could be found in which—like N'wenglish—(1) there is only one spelling per phoneme, (2) each grapheme is pronounced in only one way, **and** (3) over 80 percent of the graphemes used are the same as the ***most used*** graphemes for those phonemes in English.

Appendix 7

This appendix is a point-by-point refutation of the first chapter of a recent book claiming there is not literacy crisis. It is included for all those who question the accuracy of information included primarily in chapters 1 and 2. of this book.

Appendix 1

Table A1-1: Relative Frequency of the English Phonemes *

Note that only two phonemes are used less often than *TT*, the only N'wenglish usage that is different than English usage. Note also that *ZH* and *AE*, the only two N'wenglish usages that are somewhat unusual in English, are the least used consonant phoneme and one of the least used vowel phonemes. The shaded segments are phonemes (other than the long vowels) represented by digraphs. This shows that the number of letters used to represent English words with N'wenglish cannot be reduced much.

* This chart is based upon table 16 of *Relativ Frequency of English Speech Sounds* by Godfrey Dewey Ed.D., which is based upon a 100,000-word sample of a variety of written material. Table 16 and chapter 8, note 6 (of this book), list the types of written materials in the word sample.

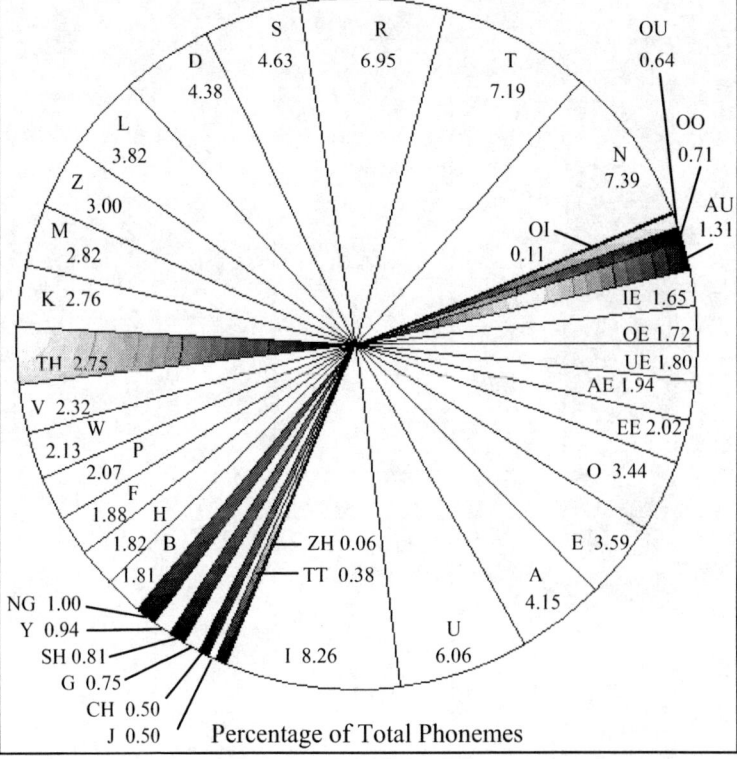

Percentage of Total Phonemes

Let's End Our Literacy Crisis

Table A1-2
All of the Single Letters in English **

Sound: As in: Letter	A mat	AE Mae	E bed	EE beet	I bid	O hop	OE doe	U bud	UE sue	AU haul	OO good
1 A	mAt	fAde	Any		homAge	fAther	cupolA	About		bAll	
2 E	thEre	mElee	bEd	mE	sErious	Entree		silEnt			
3 I	merIngue		vanIlla	skI	pIg	lIngerie		AprIl			
4 O			wOmen		sOd	bOne	cOnnect	dO		sOft	wOlf
5 U			bUry		bUsy			hUb		flU	pUll
6 C	K (kin) Cat	CH (chip) Cello			G (get) eCzema			S (sit) City		SH (ship) oCean	
7 D	Dim	J (jam) graDuate	T (tap) hopeD							**Notes:** * Y and W have both vowel and consonant sounds. ** All but F, J, and V are also silent in many words (see table 6-2)	
8 F	Fan	V (van) oF									
9 G	Get	J (jam) Gem			K (kin) Girsh			ZH (azure) garaGe			
10 H	Had	TH (thin) eightH									
11 J	Jet		H (hot) Jai alai		Y (yet) halleluJah			ZH (azure) Jardinière			
12 L	Lad		R (ran) coLonel		Y (yet) bouilLon		Horizontally across from each consonant in the left column is an example of that letter with the sound shown just above it. Beside the representation of the sound, in parentheses, is a common English word with that sound. See paragraph 2, section 4, chapter 6 for more examples.					
13 M	Man		UM (bum) spasM				^				
14 N	Nap		NG (sing) iNk		NY (maNana) maNana		^				
15 Q	KW (quit) Quit		K (kin) Quay		KY (cute) Queue		^				
16 S	Sat		CH (chip) tenSion		SH (ship) Sure			Z (zip) waS		ZH (azure) uSual	
17 T	Tap		CH (chip) naTure		SH (ship) negoTiate			ZH (azure) equaTion			
18 W*	Win		UE (sue) cWm *		V (van) Wedeln						
19 X	KS (tacks) taX		GZ (exam) eXam		GZH (luxurious) luXurious			K (kin) eXcept		KSH (luxury) luXury	
20 Y*	Yet		EE (beet) burY *		I (pit) mYth *		IE (pie) slY *	U (hut) phYsician *			
21 Z	Zip		D (dim) meZzo		S (sat) pretZel			T (tap) piZzicato		ZH (azure) aZure	

Appendix 1

Table A1-3, Part 1 of 3
Partial* Listing of *Two-Letter* Blends with a Single* Vowel Sound

Sound→ (bold caps) Blend ↓	mAt	mAElstrom	bEd	sEE	YUE *
27 AA	bAA				
28 A'A	mA'Am				
29 AE	AErial	**mAElstrom**	AEsthetic	AEon	
30 AG	diaphrAGm				
31 AH	dAHlia	dAHlia			
32 AI	plAId	mAIn	sAId		
33 AL	sALmon				
34 AO		gAOl			
35 AU	AUnt	gAUging			
37 AY	prAYer	dAY	sAYs		
38 EA	bEAr	stEAk	brEAd	EAsy	
39 EE		matinEE	kEElson	**sEE**	
40 E'E			E'Er	E'En	
41 EG		thEGn	phlEGm		
42 EH		**EH**	**EH**	vEHicle	
43 EI	thEIr	vEIn	hEIfer	recEIpt	
44 EO			lEOpard	pEOple	fEOd
45 ET		ballET			
46 EU					fEUd
47 EW					fEW
48 EY		prEY		kEY	
49 EZ			rendEZvous		
51 HE			rHEtoric	diarrHEa	
54 HU					HUmor
58 IE		lingerIE	frIEnd	grIEf	
59 II				shIItake	
61 IS				debrIS	
62 IT				esprIT	
64 OE			fOEtid	phOEbe	
66 OI			connOIsseur		
71 UA	gUArantee				
72 UE		gUEst			dUE
74 UI				mosqUIto	
76 UY				plagUY	

* Does not include capitalized words and words not in a standard desk dictionary. The *YUE* sound is a blend of the consonant *Y* and the *UE* sound. The blends are arranged and numbered alphabetically. Many of the blends in the left column also appear in part(s) 2 and/or 3 of this table.

Table A1-3, Part 2 of 3
Partial* Listing of *Two-Letter* Blends with a Single Vowel Sound

Sound→ (bold caps) Blend ↓	pIn	pIE	pOp	dOE	sUE
27 AA			bazAAr		
28 A'A			mA'Am		
29 AE	cAEsura				
30 AG			serAGlio		
31 AH	shillelAH		shAH		
32 AI	mountAIn	assegAI			
33 AL			cALm		
34 AO			pharAOnic		
35 AU			nAUtical	chAUvinist	
37 AY	yesterdAY	bAYou			
38 EA	hEAr		hEArt		
39 EE	bEEn				
43 EI	wEIrd	hEIght			
44 EO	pigEOn			yEOman	
45 ET	billET doux				
46 EU					manEUver
47 EW				sEW	crEW
48 EY	monEY	gEYser			
49 EZ	rendEZvous				
50 HA			HAbitant		
52 HI	exHIbit	rHIno			
53 HO			HOnor	gHOst	
54 HU					rHUbarb
55 HY	rHYthm	rHYolite			
56 IA	marrIAgeable	dIAmond			
57 IC	vICtuals	indICt			
58 IE	carrIEd	**pIE**			
60 IO				mustachIO	
61 IS	chassIS	ISland			
62 IT	petIT				
63 OA				cOAt	
64 OE				**dOE**	shOE
65 OH			demijOHn	**OH**	
66 OI			reservOIr		
67 OO				dOOr	schOOl
68 OU			lOUgh	bOUlder	yOUth
69 OW			knOWledge	knOW	
70 OY		cOYote			
71 UA			gUArd	qUAhog	
72 UE					**sUE**
73 UH					bUHl
74 UI	bUIlding	gUIding			crUIsing
75 UO				qUOth	bUOy
76 UY		bUY			
77 WO				sWOrd	tWO

* Does not include capitalized words and words not in a standard desk dictionary.

Appendix 1

Table A1-3, Part 3 of 3
Partial* Listing of *Two-Letter* Blends with a Single Vowel Sound

Sound→ (bold caps) Blend ↓	sUn	hAUl	gOOd	OIl	OUt
31 AH	verandAH	hurrAH			
32 AI	captAIn				
33 AL		tALk			
34 AO		extrAOrdinary			
35 AU	restAUrant	**hAUl**			sAUerkraut
36 AW		sAW		lAWyer	
38 EA	ocEAn				
43 EI	mullEIn				
44 EO	lunchEOn				
46 EU	connoissEUr		plEUrisy		
50 HA	gingHAm				
51 HE	HErb				
52 HI	veHIcle				
53 HO		HOrs d'oeuvre			
54 HU	HUmble				
56 IA	specIAl				
58 IE	mischIEvous				
60 IO	fashIOn				
63 OA	cupbOArd	brOAd			
64 OE	dOEs				
66 OI	avOIrdupois			**OIl**	
67 OO	blOOd		**gOOd**		
68 OU	rOUgh	cOUgh	cOUld		**OUt**
69 OW	pillOWcase	tOWard			nOW
70 OY				bOY	
71 UA	piqUAnt				
72 UE	gUErilla		tissUE		
73 UH	bUHr				
75 OU	liqUOr				
77 WO		sWOrd			

* Does not include capitalized words and words not in a standard desk dictionary.

Let's End Our Literacy Crisis

Table A1-4
Partial* Listing of *Three-or-More-Letter* Blends with a Single* Vowel Sound

78 ACH	drACHm (A)	yACHt (O)			
79 AGH	shillelAGH (I)	shillelAGH (U)			
80 AOU	cAOUtchouc (UE)	cAOUtchouc (OU)			
81 AYE	**AYE** (AE)	**AYE** (IE)			
82 EAU	burEAUcracy (O)	platEAU (OE)	burEAUcrat (U)		
83 EIG	rEIGn (AE)	forEIGn (U)			
84 EWE	sEWEd (OE)	brEWEd (UE)	**EWE*** (YUE)		
85 EYE	convEYEd (AE)	kEYEd (EE)	**EYE** (IE)		
86 HEI	**HEI**r (AE)				
87 HOU	silHOUette (OO)	**HOU**r (OU)			
88 IEU	lIEUtenant (E)	lIEU (UE)			
89 OOH	pOOH (UE)	pOOH (OO)			
90 OUL	cOULd (U)	cOULd (OO)			
91 OWA	tOWArd (OE)	tOWArd (AU)			
92 OWE	**OWE** (OE)	allOWEd (UE)			
93 EHEA	forEHEAd (E)	forEHEAd (I)			
94 EIGH	slEIGH (AE)	hEIGHt (IE)			
95 OUGH*	nOUGHt (O)	thorOUGH (U)	thrOUGH (UE)	fOUGHt (AW)	bOUGH (OU)
96 A_E	hAvE (A)	fAdE (AE)	imAgE (I)	nuisAncE (U)	fAlsE (AU)
97 E_E	thErE (A)	thErE (AE)	allEgE (E)	thEsE (EE)	collEgE (I)
98 I_E	marInE (EE)	gIvE (I)	fInE (IE)	engInE (U)	
99 O_E	gOnE (O)	mOrE (OE)	sOmE (U)	mOvE (UE)	gOnE (AU)
100 U_E	minUtE (I)	pleasUrE (U)	rUlE (UE)	sUrE (OO)	
101 Y_E	apocalYpsE (I)	tYpE (IE)			
102 AI_E	millionAIrE (A)	rAIsE (AE)	AIslE (IE)		
103 AU_E	gAUchE (OE)	becAUsE (O)	becAUsE (AU)	becAUsE (U)	gAUgE (AE)
104 EA_E	clEAnsE (E)	plEAsE (EE)	milEAgE (I)	hEArsE (U)	
105 EI_E	sEInE (AE)	recEIvE (E)			
106 IA_E	marrIAgE (I)	collegIAtE (U)			
107 IE_E	conscIEncE (E)	patIEncE (U)	belIEvE (EE)	sIEvE (I)	
108 OI_E	porpOIsE (U)	turquOIsE (AU)	nOIsE (OI)		
109 OU_E	cOUrsE (OE)	scOUrgE (U)	rOUtE (UE)	hOUsE (OU)	
110 UI_E	gUImpE (A)	gUIdE (IE)	crUIsE (UE)		
111 A_UE	harAngUE (A)	plAgUE	bArqUE (O)		
112 I_UE	merIngUE (A)	antIqUE (EE)	bIsqUE (I)	oblIqUE (IE)	
113 O_UE	catalOgUE (O)	rOgUE (OE)	tOngUE (U)	tOrqUE (AU)	
114 U_UE	brUsqUE (U)	brUsqUE (OO)			

* Doesn't include proper nouns and words not in a standard desk dictionary. The highlighted letters are pronounced the same as the letters in parentheses (parentheses), as in *mAn*, *mAElstorm*, *sEt*, *sEE*, *pIn*, *pIE*, *tOp*, *tOE*, *sUn*, *sUE*, *hAUl*, *gOOd*, *OIl*, and *OUt*. The OUGH blend also represents seven sounds that are blends of more than one phoneme, i.e., *augh* as in *trough*, *uek* as in *shough*, *auf* as in *cough*, *uf* as in *rough*, *ok* as in *lough*, and *up* as in *hiccough*. Yue is a blend of two phonemes.

Appendix 1

Table A1-5
Partial* Listing of *Two-or-More-Letter* Blends with a Single Consonant Sound

115 CH	spinaCH (J)	maCHine (SH)	CHaos (K)	CHip (CH)	
116 DD	eisteDDfod (TH)	aDD (D)			
117 DH	DHow (D)	eDH (TH)			
118 ED	seemED (D)	askED (T)			
119 GG	exaGGerate (J)	suGGest (GJ)*	eGG (G)		
120 GH	hiccouGH (P)	trouGH (TH)	GHost (G)	lauGH (F)	louGH (K)
121 LL	tortiLLa (Y)	aLL (L)			
122 MN	MNemonic (N)	hyMN (M)			
123 ND	haNDkerchief (NG)	haNDsome (N)			
124 PH	telePHone (F)	shePHerd (P)	nePHew (V)		
125 PH	hoRS d'oeuvre (R)	woRSted (S)			
126 SC	faSCism (SH)	viSCount (K)	diSCern (Z)	SCene (S)	
127 SH	diSHonest (S)	diSHonor (Z)	SHip (SH)		
128 SI	buSIness (Z)	penSIon (SH)	tenSIon (CH)		
129 SS	sciSSors (Z)	fiSSion (ZH)	iSSue (SH)	leSS (S)	
130 TH	posTHumous (CH)	THyme (T)	THem (TH)	THin (TT)	
131 TI	equaTIon (ZH)	quesTIon (CH)	acTIon (SH)		
132 TS	TSar (S)	TSar (Z)			
133 TZ	walTZ (S)	TZar (Z)			
134 WH	WHelk (W)	WHo (H)			
135 GHT	riGHTeous (CH)	drouGHT (TH)	niGHT (T)		
136 SCH	SCHism (S)	SCHist (SH)			
137 SSI	miSSIon (SH)	fiSSIon (ZH)			
138 STH	iSTHmus (S)	aSTHma (Z)			
139 PHTH	PHTHisic (TH)	PHTHisic (T)			

* This table does not include capitalized words and uncommon words. Several of the words in this table (in addition to *GG*, no. 119) represent a blend of two or more phonemes in addition to the single phoneme shown. There are alternate pronunciations of several words in the table. The sound in parentheses is as in the words *Dip, Fan, Get, Jet, Kin, Lad, Man, Nap, Pan, Ran, Sat, Tap, Van, Win, Zip, CHip, SHip, THin (TT), THen (TH), siNG,* and *muZHik.*

Let's End Our Literacy Crisis

Table A1-6
Partial Listing of Blends with Only One Common Pronunciation*

Vowels

140 faux pAS (O)	140 faux pAS (O)	180 billet dOUX (UE)	200 chEEsE (EE)
141 eclAT (O)	141 eclAT (O)	181 misTREss (I)	201 demESnE (EE)
142 chERt (A)	142 chERt (A)	182 qUAY (EE)	202 dEUcE (UE)
143 bellES lettres (E)	143 bellES lettres (E)	183 bouqUET (AE)	203 EYrE (AE)
144 sIGn (IE)	144 sIGn (IE)	184 liqUEUr (U)	204 rHInEstone (IE)
145 O'Er (OE)	145 O'Er (OE)	185 plagUEY (EE)	205 rHYmE (IE)
146 imbrOGlio (OE)	146 imbrOGlio (OE)	186 qUOIn (OI)	206 lISlE (IE)
147 sOLder (AU)	147 sOLder (AU)	187 bUOY (OI)	207 cOArsE (OE)
148 wORsted (OO)	148 wORsted (OO)	188 boatsWAIn (U)	208 colOGnE (OE)
149 apropOS (OE)	149 apropOS (OE)	189 strAIGHt (AE)	209 lOOsE (UE)
150 depOT (OE)	150 depOT (OE)	190 cAUGHt (AU)	210 brOWsE (OU)
151 dYE (IE)	151 dYE (IE)	191 grEIGE (AE)	211 gargOYlE (OI)
152 arrAIGn (AE)	152 arrAIGn (AE)	192 gIAOUr (OU)	212 qUOtE (OE)
153 hALFpenny (AE)	153 hALFpenny (AE)	193 rendezvOUSEd (UE)	213 WhOsE (UE)
154 blANC mange (U)	154 blANC mange (U)	194 wEIGHEd (AE)	214 chEqUE (E)
155 pharAOH (OE)	155 pharAOH (OE)	195 brOUGHAm (UE)	215 lEAgUE (EE)
156 hAUTboy (OE)	156 hAUTboy (OE)	196 plOUGHEd (OU)	216 cOIGnEd (OI)
157 fAUX pas (OE)	157 fAUX pas (OE)	197 plAgUing (AE)	217 turqUOIsE (OI)
158 AWE (AU)	158 AWE (AU)	198 WhO (UE)	
159 mAYOr (AE)	159 mAYOr (AE)	199 champAGnE (AE)	

Consonants

218 raBBit (B)	238 mariJUana (W)	257 diNNer (N)	276 WRite (R)
219 BDellium (D)	239 KHaki (K)	258 habitaNT (N)	277 muZHik (ZH)
220 BHang (B)	240 chuKKa (K)	259 bivOUac (W)	278 rendezVous (V)
221 deBT (T)	241 KNowledge (N)	260 cuPBoard (B)	279 buZZ (Z)
222 aCCount (K)	242 faLCon (K)	261 PNeumatic (N)	280 saCCHarine (K)
223 piCK (K)	243 wouLD (D)	262 suPPer (P)	281 draCHM (M)
224 laCQuer (K)	244 haLF (F)	263 PSalm (S)	282 fuCHSia (SH)
225 indiCT (T)	245 siLHouette (L)	264 receiPT (T)	283 yaCHT (T)
226 CZar (Z)	246 taLK (K)	265 bouQUet (K)	284 giNGHam (NG)
227 juDGment (J)	247 caLM (M)	266 RHyme (R)	285 guNWHale (N)
228 solDIer (J)	248 kiLN (L)	267 meRRy (R)	286 saPPHire (F)
229 aDJust (J)	249 coLOnel (R)	268 moRTgage (R)	287 PSHaw (SH)
230 velDT (T)	250 haLVe (V)	269 iSLand (L)	288 antiQUE (K)
231 oFF (F)	251 coMB (M)	270 liSTen (S)	289 coRPS (R)
232 oFTen (F)	252 MHo (M)	271 SWord (S)	290 miSTRess (S)
233 intaGLio (L)	253 duMMy (M)	272 hauTBoy (B)	291 eTCH (CH)
234 phleGM (M)	254 coMPtroller (N)	273 buTTon (T)	292 boaTSWain (S)
235 siGN (N)	255 siNG (NG)	274 TWo (T)	293 CHTHonic (TH)
236 buHL (L)	256 ipecacuaNHa (N)	275 saVVy (V)	294 foRECastle (K)
237 haJJi (J)			

* This table does not include capitalized words and uncommon words. Several letter combinations shown also represent two or more phonemes in addition to the single phoneme shown. The letters in parentheses represent the same sounds as shown in the notes to tables A1-4 and A1-5.

Appendix 2

Appendix 2, Table A2-1
Usage Frequency of Letters for English Phonemes **

Vowels

No. of Occur-rences ***	Sound → As in → Letter or Digraph ↓	A mat	AE Mae	E bet	EE bee	I pit	IE pie	O pot	OE doe	U sum	UE sue	AU haul	OO good	OI oil	OU out	YUE few
20,808	A	50.0	8.6	2.9		0.3		8.7	*	24.0		5.4				
0	AE	*	*	*	*	*										
28,068	E	*	*	13.6	13.0	5.1		*		42.6						
1,131	EE		*	*	71.0	29.0										
16,031	I	*		*	1.0	77.2	16.1	*		5.1						
225	IE		*	15.1	53.3	*	12.9			18.7						
19,214	O					0.2		12.7	14.6	52.1	8.9	8.7	0.3			
64	OE			*	*				17.2	82.8	*					
3,407	U			*		3.0				78.9	1.9		5.1			8.6
153	UE			*						*	59.5		*			40.5
169	AU	*	*					*	*	10.1		89.9			*	
998	OO							*	*	27.3			72.7			
63	OI			*				*		*				100		
2,763	OU							*	5.4	18.8	28.8	*	2.9		44.3	

Consonants ***

No. of Occur-rences	Letter or Digraph	Sound as in	%	Sound as in	%	Sound as in	%	Sound as in	%	Sound as in	%
8,148	F	V of	54.8	F fan	45.2						
1,816	G *	G get	89.7	J gem	10.3						
12,754	S *	Z bags	59.1	S pits	40.1	SH sure	0.4	ZH measure	0.4		
238	X *	KS exit	69.7	GZ exam	15.6	K except	14.7				
4,465	Y	EE pity	47.1	Y yet	29.8	IE by	21.3	I myth	1.2	U physician	0.2
369	CH *	CH chip	96.5	SH machine	1.8	K chorus	1.7				
1,546	NG	NG sing	93.1	NJ plunge	5.4	NGG finger	1.5				
389	TH *	TH then	88.6	TH thin	11.4						

*, **, *** and another note: See second page of An Introduction to the Appendix.

This table shows that most of the letters used to represent a phoneme in N'wenglish (all but highlighted letters in column 4) are the *most used* letters for the phoneme in English.

Appendix 2, Table A2-2
Choice of Graphemes to Represent Each Phoneme

↓ **ENGLISH PHONEME** (the underlined sound).
　　↓ Percent of the time the underlined letter(s) in column 1 represent this phoneme in English *
　　　↓ Minimum number of other phonemes the underlined letter(s) in column 1 represent in English **
　　　　↓ **N'WENGLISH SPELLING**
　　　　　↓ The underlined letters in column 1 significantly more often represent this

					Reason for Choice/Comment
m**A**t	50.0	8	**A**		
m**E**t	13.6	8	**E**	n**U**t	due to illogical use of *E* in unaccented syllables
p**I**n	77.2	9	**I**		
p**O**p	12.7	8	**O**	n**U**t	due to illogical use of *O* in unaccented syllables
p**U**p	78.9	8	**U**		
M**AE**	0.0 ***	4	**AE**		Letters besides *AE* for this phoneme conflict with other choices.
n**EE**d	71.0	3	**EE**		
p**IE**	12.9	5	**IE**	b**EE** *	from changing *Y* to *I* and adding *ES* or *ED* for plural or past tense
d**OE**	17.2	4	**OE**	p**U**p *	based entirely upon the common word *does*
s**UE**	59.5	4	**UE**		
h**AU**l	89.9	6	**AU**		
g**OO**d	72.7	3	**OO**		
s**OI**l	100.0	3	**OI**		
s**OU**r	44.3	6	**OU**		
Bat	100.0	1	**B**		
Dim	100.0	3	**D**		
Fan	45.2	1	**F**	**V**an	based entirely upon the common word *of*
Get	89.7	4	**G**		
Hat	100.0	2	**H**		
Jet	100.0	3	**J**		
Kin	100.0	1	**K**		
Lad	100.0	3	**L**		
Man	100.0	2	**M**		
Nap	100.0	3	**N**		
Pan	100.0	1	**P**		
Run	100.0	1	**R**		
Sat	40.1	5	**S**	**Z**ip	due to *is*, *was*, and plurals such as *bags*
Tap	98.9	4	**T**		
Van	100.0	0	**V**		
Wet	100.0	3	**W**		
Yet	29.8	5	**Y**	b**EE**	from words ending in *Y*, but *Y* must be used for consonant use
Zip	100.0	5	**Z**		
CHip	96.5	3	**CH**		
SHip	100.0	2	**SH**		
THin	11.4	3	**TT**		necessary since *TH* is used in words such as *thin* and *then* in English
THen	88.6	3	**TH**		
mu**ZH**ik	100.0	0	**ZH**		Other letters used for this phoneme more often have other sounds.
si**NG**	93.1	2	**NG**		

* Based upon table A2-1. Note the small number of occurrences of *IE* and *OE*.
** This excludes uncommon and capitalized words but includes words besides those on table A2-2
*** Although it does not occur in table A2-2, when *AE* occurs, it has this sound.

Appendix 3
Why English Spelling Is So "Bad"*

"Just before the beginning of the Christian Era, the inhabitants of the British Isles were illiterate Celtic peoples, with no written language. Fifty-five years after the birth of Christ, when Julius Caesar commenced the conquest of the islands, he found a number of hardy, adventurous Vikings from Iceland and Norway living among the Celts, who had adopted some of the Norse words into the Celtic tongue. Four centuries after Caesar's conquest, the islands were under Roman domination, and the language of the rulers, the soldiers, the merchants, and the law was spoken Latin, which differed considerably from the elaborate written Latin of Caesar and Cicero.

"Naturally, the language of the natives was greatly modified during this occupation, but it was never completely Romanized; in fact, the Celtic tongue is used in Wales down to the present day.

"At the beginning of the fifth century the Romans withdrew from England, which was soon overrun and conquered by the Angles and Saxons, Germanic tribes from the region south of Denmark. During the next six hundred years, the language of the island natives was greatly altered by the necessity of understanding and using the language of their new rulers. The fusion of tongues that grew out of this condition became known as Anglo-Saxon. It was spoken quite generally, but very little of it was written.

"Then, in 1066, William the Conqueror from Normandy made himself king of England, and for the next three hundred years the

Let's End Our Literacy Crisis

language of the court, laws, and trade became Norman French. So during these years the speech of the common man was again enriched by the inclusion of hundreds of words of Norman and French origin.

"Thus for hundreds of years the spoken language of these island people grew, changed, and developed. All the laws and literature of each period were written only in the language of the rulers.

"It was not until the year 1256, thirteen hundred years after Caesar's invasion of the islands, that the first public document was written in what we call English—it was the language of the common man, compounded through the centuries of Celtic, Norse, Icelandic, [Latin], Anglo-Saxon, German, Danish, and French words!

"Having grown in this manner, with its roots in the languages of so many different lands, English has the richest vocabulary in the world. It has many synonyms for most of its words. Note, for instance, the sources of the synonyms for *growth,* used quite naturally within these few paragraphs; *grow* from Anglo-Saxon, *change* from Celtic through Old French, *alter* and *modify* from French, *develop* and *vary* from Latin."

Unfortunately, English also inherited many types of orthography, and so is as difficult in spelling as any alphabet language in the world. English is unusually rich in vowel sounds, many more sounds than letters. When spoken English was put into written form, using Roman letters, there were only five Roman vowels....Seven of the pure English vowel sounds are not found in Latin at all....

There were a few phonetic experts in those days, but they made a sorry tangle of it. We are still struggling to get out of that tangle.

* Frank C. Laubach, *Teaching the World to Read* (New York: Friendship Press, 1947) pp. 100-102.

Appendix 4
Thu Good Nuez uv John[1]

In thu bigin/ing wuz thu Wurd, and thu Wurd wuz witt God, and thu Wurd woz God. Hē wuz in thu bigin/ing witt God. Aul ttingz wur mād bī Him, and wittout Him nutt/ing wuz mād that woz mād. In Him wuz līf, and thu līf wuz thu līt uv men. And thu līt shīnz in thu dork/nus, and thu dork/nus did not komprihend it.

Ther wuz u man sent frum God, hūz nām wuz John/Jon/. This man kām fur u wit/nus, tū bar wit/nus uv thu Līt, that aul ttrū him mīt bulēv. Hē wuz not that Līt, but wuz sent tū bar wit/nus uv that Līt.

That wuz thu trū Līt which givz līt tū evrē man hū kumz intū thu wurld. Hē wuz in thu wurld, and thu wurld wuz mād bī Him, and thu wurld did not nō Him. Hē kām tū Hiz ōn, and Hiz ōn did not risēv Him. But az me/nē az risvēd Him, tū them Hē gāv thu rīt tū bikum chil/drun uv God, ē/vun tū thōz hū bulēv in Hiz nām: hū wur bōrn, not uv blud, nor uv thu wil uv thu flesh, nor uv thu wil uv man, but uv God.

And thu Wurd bikām flesh and dwelt umung us, and wē biheld Hiz glōr/ē, thu glōr/ē az uv thē ōn/lē bigot/un uv thu Foth/ur, fool uv grās and trūtt. John bōr wit/nus uv Him and krīd out, sāing, "This wuz Hē uv hūm Ī sed, 'Hē hū kumz af/tur mē iz prifurd bifōr mē, for Hē wuz bifōr mē.'" And uv Hiz fool/nus wē hav aul risēvd, and grās fur grās. For thu lau wuz giv/un bī Moses/Mō/zuz/, but grās and trūtt kām bī Jesus/Jē/zus/ Christ/Krīst/. Nō wun haz sēn God at enē tīm. Thē ōn/lē bigot/un Sun, hū iz in thu boozum uv thu Foth/ur, Hē haz diklard Him.

And this iz thu testumō/nē uv John, when thu Jews/Jūz/ sent prēsts and Levites/Lē/vīts/ frum Jerusalem/Jurū/sulum/ tū ask him, "Hū or yū?" And hē kunfest, and did not dinī, but kunfest, "Ī am not thu Christ." And thā askt him, "Whot then? Or yū Elijah/Ilī/ju/?" And hē sed, "Ī am not." "Or yū thu Pro/fut?" And hē an/surd, "Nō." Then thā sed tū him,

"Hū or yū, that wē mā giv an an/sur tū thōz hū sent us? Whot dū yū sā ubout yurself?" Hē sed:

> "Ī am thu vois uv wun krī/ing in thu wil/durnus:
> 'Māk strāt thu wā uv thu Lord/Lōrd/,'

az thu pro/fut Isaiah/Īzā/u/ sed." And thōz hū wur sent wur frum thu Pharisees/Far/usēz/. And thā askt him, sāing, "Whī then dū yū baptīz if yū or not thu Christ, nor Elijah, nor thu Pro/fut?" John an/surd them, sāing, "Ī baptīz witt wotur, but ther standz Wun umung yū hūm yū dū not nō. It iz Hē hū, kum/ing af/tur mē, iz prifurd bifōr mē, hūz san/dul strap Ī am not wur/thē tū lūs." Thēz ttingz wur dun in Bethabara/Bettab/uru/ bēond thu Jordan/Jōr/dun/, wher John wuz baptīzing.

Thu next dā John sau Jesus kum/ing tōrd him, and sed, "Bihōld! Thu Lam uv God hū tāks uwā thu sin uv thu wurld! This iz Hē uv hūm Ī sed, 'Af/tur mē kumz u Man hū iz prifurd bifōr mē, for Hē wuz bifōr mē.' And Ī did not nō Him; but that Hē shood bē rivēld tū Israel/Iz/rēul/, tharfōr Ī kām baptīzing witt wotur." And John bōr wit/nus, sāing, "Ī sau thu Spir/ut disend/ing frum he/vun līk u duv, and Hē rimānd upon Him. And Ī did not nō Him, but Hē hū sent mē tū baptīz witt wotur sed tū mē, 'Upon hūm yū sē thu Spir/ut disend/ing, and rimān/ing aun Him, this iz Hē hū baptīzuz witt thu Hō/lē Spir/ut.' And Ī hav sēn and test/ufīd that this iz thu Sun uv God."

Ugen, thu next dā John stood witt tūw uv hiz disī/pulz. And looking at Jesus az Hē waukt, hē sed, "Bihōld thu Lam uv God!" And thu tūw disī/pulz hurd him spēk, and thā folōd Jesus. Then Jesus turnd, and sēing them fol/uwing, sed tū them, "Whot dū yū sēk?" Thā sed tū Him, "Rabbi/Ra/bī/" (which iz tū sā, when translā/tud, Tē/chur), "wher or Yū stāing?" Hē sed tū them, "Kum and sē." Thā kām and sau wher Hē wuz stāing, and rimānd witt Him that dā; for it wuz ubout thu tentt our. Wun uv thu tūw hū hurd John spēk, and fol/ōd Him, wuz Andrew/An/drū/, Simon/Sī/mun/ Peter'z/Pē/tur'z/ bruthur. Hē furst found hiz ōn bruthur Simon, and sed tū him, "Wē hav found thu Messiah/Musī/u/" (which iz translā/tud, thu Christ). And hē braut him tū Jesus. And when Jesus lookt at him, Hē sed, "Yū or Simon thu sun uv Jonah/Jō/nu/. Yū shal bē kauld Cephas/Sē/fus/" (which iz translā/tud, U Stōn).

Thu fol/uwing dā Jesus wont/ud tū gō tū Galilee/Gal/ulē/, and Hē found Philip/Fil/up/ and sed tū him, "Fol/ō Mē." Nou Philip wuz frum Bethsaida/Bettsā/idu/, thu sit/ē uv Andrew and Peter. Philip found Nathanael/Nuttan/yul/ and sed tū him, "Wē hav found Him uv hūm Moses in thu lau, and aulsō thu pro/futs, rōt—Jesus uv Nazareth/Naz/urutt/, thu sun uv Joseph/Jō/zuf/." And Nathanael sed tū him, "Kan enētting good kum out uv Nazareth?" Philip sed tū him, "Kum and sē." Jesus sau Nathanael kum/ing tōrd Him, and sed uv him, "Bihōld, an Israelite indēd, in hūm iz nō gīl!" Nathanael sed tū Him, "Hou dū Yū nō mē?" Jesus an/surd and sed tū him, "Bifōr Philip kauld yū, when yū wur undur thu fig tree, Ī sau yū." Nathanael an/surd and sed tū Him, "Rabbi, Yū or thu Sun uv God! Yū or thu King uv Israel!" Jesus an/surd and sed tū him, "Bikauz Ī sed tū yū, 'Ī sau yū undur thu fig trē,' dū yū bulēv? Yū wil sē grā/tur ttingz than thēz." And Hē sed tū him, "Mōst ushoor/udlē, Ī sā tū yū, hiraf/tur yū wil sē he/vun ōpun, and thē ānj/ulz uv God usend/ing and disend/ing upon thu Sun uv Man."

2

And thu tturd dā ther wuz u we/ding in Cana/Kā/nu/ uv Galilee, and thu muth/ur uv Jesus wuz thar. And bōtt Jesus and Hiz disī/pulz wur invī/tud tū thu we/ding. And when thā ran out uv wīn, thu muth/ur uv Jesus sed tū Him, "Thā hav nō wīn." Jesus sed tū hur, "Woomun, whot duz yoor kunsurn hav tū dū witt Mē? Mī our haz not yet kum." Hiz muth/ur sed tū thu sur/vunts, "Whotev/ur Hē sez tū yū, dū it." And ther wur set thar six woturpots uv stōn, ukaurd/ing tū thu manur uv pyoorufukā/shun uv thu Jewz, kuntā/ning twen/tē or ttur/tē gal/unz upēs. Jesus sed tū them, "Fil thu woturpots witt wotur." And thā fild them up tū thu brim. And Hē sed tū them, "Drau sum out nou, and tāk it tū thu mas/tur uv thu fēst." And thā took it. When thu mas/tur uv thu fēst had tās/tud thu wotur that wuz mād wīn, and did not nō wher it kām from (but thu sur/vunts hū drū thu wotur nū), thu mas/tur uv thu fēst kauld thu brīdgrūm. And hē sed tū him, "Evrē man at thu bigin/ing sets out thu good wīn, and when men hav wel drunk, then that which iz infir/ēur; but yū hav kept thu good wīn until nou." This bigin/ing uv sīnz Jesus did in Cana uv Galilee, and man/ufestud Hiz glōr/ē; and Hiz disī/pulz bulēvd in Him.

Af/tur this Hē went doun tū Capernaum/Kupur/nium/, Hē, Hiz muth/ur, Hiz bruthurz, and Hiz disī/pulz; and thā did not stā thar me/nē dāz.

And thu Pas/ōvur uv thu Jewz wuz at hand, and Jesus went up tū Jerusalem. And Hē found in thu tem/pul thōz hū sōld oxun and shēp and duvz, and thu munēchānj/urz dūing biz/nus. And when Hē had mād u whip uv kaurdz, Hē drōv them aul out uv thu tem/pul, witt thu shēp and thē oxun, and pōrd out thu chānj/urz' mun/ē and ōvurturnd thu tā/bulz. And Hē sed tū thōz hū sōld duvz, "Tāk thēz ttingz uwā! Dū not māk Mī Foth/ur'z hous u hous uv mur/chundīs!" And Hiz disī/pulz rimem/burd that it wuz rit/un, *"Zēl fur Yoor hous haz ēt/un Mē up."* Then thu Jewz an/surd and sed tū Him, "Whot sīn dū Yū shō tū us, sēing that Yū dū thēz ttingz?" Jesus an/surd and sed tū them, "Distroi this tem/pul, and in ttrē dāz Ī wil rāz it up." Then thu Jewz sed, "It haz tā/kun faur/tē-six yirz tū bild this tem/pul, and wil Yū rāz it up in ttrē dāz?" But Hē wuz spēking uv thu tem/pul uv Hiz bo/dē. Tharfōr, when Hē had ri/zun frum thu ded, Hiz disī/pulz rimem/burd that Hē had sed this tū them; and thā bulēvd thu Skrip/chur and thu wurd which Jesus had sed.

Nou when Hē wuz in Jerusalem at thu Pas/ōvur, dyoor/ing thu fēst, me/nē bulēvd in Hiz nām when thā sau thu sīnz which Hē did. But Jesus did not kumit Himself tū them, bikauz Hē nū aul men, and did not nēd that enēwun shood tes/tufī uv man, for Hē nū whot wuz in man.

3

Ther wuz u man uv thu Phariseez nāmd Nicodemus/Nikudē/mus/, u rū/lur uv thu Jewz. This man kām tū Jesus bī nīt and sed tū Him, "Rabbi, wē nō that Yū or u tē/chur kum frum God; fur nō wun kan dū thēz sīnz that Yū dū unles God iz witt him." Jesus an/surd and sed tū him, "Mōst ushoor/udlē, Ī sā tū yū, unles wun iz bōrn ugen, hē kanot sē thu king/dum uv God." Nicodemus sed tū Him, "Hou kan u man bē bōrn when hē iz ōld? Kan hē ent/ur u se/kund tīm intū hiz muth/ur'z wūm and bē bōrn?" Jesus an/surd, "Mōst ushoor/udlē, Ī sā tū yū, unles wun iz bōrn uv wotur and thu Spir/ut, hē kanot ent/ur thu king/dum uv God. That which iz bōrn uv thu flesh iz flesh, and that which iz bōrn uv thu Spir/ut iz spir/ut. Dū not mor/vul that Ī sed tū yū, 'Yū must bē bōrn ugen.' Thu wind blōz wher it wish/uz, and yū hir thu sound uv it, but kanot tel wher it kumz from and wher it gōz. Sō iz evrēwun hū iz bōrn uv thu spir/ut." Nicodemus an/surd and sed tū Him, "Hou kan thēz ttingz bē?" Jesus an/surd and sed tū him, "Or yū thu tē/chur uv Israel, and dū not nō thēz ttingz? Mōst ushoor/udlē, Ī sā tū yū, Wē spēk whot Wē nō and tes/tufī whot Wē hav sēn, and yū dū not risēv Our wit/nus. If Ī hav tōld yū urtt/lē ttingz and yū dū not bulēv, hou wil yū bulēv if Ī tel yū he/vunlē ttingz? And nō wun haz usend/ud tū he/vun but Hē hū kām doun from he/vun, ē/vun thu Sun uv Man hū iz in he/vun. And az Moses lift/ud up thu sur/punt in thu wil/durnus, ē/vun sō must thu Sun uv Man bē lift/ud up, that hūev/ur bulēvz in Him shood not perish but hav itur/nul līf.

"For God sō luvd thu wurld that Hē gāv Hiz ōn/lē bigot/un Sun, that hūev/ur bulēvz in Him shood not perish but hav evurlasting līf. For God did not send Hiz Sun intū thu wurld tū kundem thu wurld, but that thu wurld ttrū Him mīt bē sāvd. Hee hū bulēvz in Him iz not kundemd; but hee hū duz not bulēv iz kundemd aulred/ē, bikauz hē haz not bulēvd in thu nām uv thē ōn/lē bigot/un Sun uv God. And this iz thu kondemnā/shun, that līt haz kum intū thu wurld, and men luvd dork/nus rath/ur than līt, bekauz ther dēdz wur ē/vul. For evrēwun hū duz ē/vul hāts thu līt and duz not kum tū thu līt, lest hiz dēdz shood bē ex-pōzd. But hē hū duz thu trūtt kumz tū thu līt, that hiz dēdz mā bē klir/lē sēn, that thā or dun in God."

Af/tur thēz ttingz Jesus and Hiz disī/pulz kām intū thu land uv Judea/Jūdē/u/, and thar Hē rimānd witt them and baptīzd. And John aulsō wuz baptīzing in Aenon/Ē/non/ nir Salim/Sā/lum/, bikauz ther wuz much wotur thar. And thā kām and wur baptīzd. For John had not yet bin ttrōn intū priz/un. Then ther urōz u dispyūt bitwēn sum uv John'z disī/pulz and thu Jewz ubout pyoorufukā/shun. And thā kām tū John and sed tū him, "Rabbi, Hē hū wuz witt yū bēond thu Jordan, tū hūm yū bōr wit/nus—bihōld, Hē iz baptīz-ing, and aul or kum/ing tū Him!" John an/surd and sed, "U man kan risēv nutt/ing unles it haz bin giv/un tū him frum he/vun. Yū yurselvz bar mē wit/nus, that Ī sed, 'Ī am not thu Christ,' but, 'Ī hav bin sent bifōr Him.' Hē hū haz thu brīd iz thu brīdgrūm; but thu frend uv thu brīdgrūm, hū standz and hirz him, rijoisuz grāt/lē bikauz uv thu brīdgrūm'z vois. Tharfōr this joi uv mīn iz foolfild. Hē must in/krēs, but Ī must dē/krēs.

"Hē hū kumz frum ubuv iz ubuv aul; hē hū iz ov thē urtt iz urtt/lē and spēks uv thē urtt. Hē hū kumz frum he/vun iz ubuv aul. And whot Hē haz sēn and hurd, that Hē tes/tufīz; and nō wun risēvz Hiz testumō/nē. Hē hū haz risēvd Hiz testumō/nē haz surt/ufīd that God iz trū. For Hē hūm God haz sent spēks thu wurdz uv God, fur God duz not giv thu Spir/ut bī mezh/ur. Thu Foth/ur luvz thu Sun, and haz giv/un aul ttingz intū Hiz hand. Hē hū bulēvz in thu Sun haz evurlast/ing līf; and hē hū duz not bulēv thu Sun wil not sē līf, but thu ratt uv God ubīdz aun him."

4

Tharfōr, when thu Lord nū that thu Phariseez had hurd that Jesus mād and baptīzd mōr disī/pulz than John (thō Jesus Himself did not baptīz, but Hiz disī/pulz), Hē left Judea and di-port/ud ugen tū Galilee. But Hē nēd/ud tū gō ttrū Samaria/Sumer/ēu/. Sō Hē kām tū u sit/ē uv Samaria which iz kauld Sychar/Sī/kor/, nir thu plot uv ground that Jacob/Jā/kub/ gāv tū hiz sun Joseph. Nou Jacob'z wel wuz thar. Jesus tharfōr, bēing wir/ēd frum Hiz jur/nē, sat thus bī thu wel. It wuz ubout thu sixtt our. U woomun uv Samaria kām tū drau wotur. Jesus sed tū hur, "Giv Mē u drink." For hiz disī/pulz had gaun uwā intū thu sit/ē tū bī fūd. Then thu woomun uv Samaria sed tū Him, "Hou iz it that Yū, bēing u Jew, ask u drink frum mē, u Samaritan/Sumer/utun/ woomun?" For Jewz hav nō dēl/ingz witt Samari-tanz. Jesus an/surd and sed tū hur, "If yū nū thu gift uv God, and hū it iz hū sez tū yū, 'Giv Mē u drink,' yū wood hav askt Him, and Hē wood hav giv/un yū living wotur." Thu woomun sed tū Him, "Sur, Yū hav nutt/ing tū drau witt, and thu wel iz dēp. Wher then dū Yū get that living wotur? Or Yū grā/tur than our foth/ur Jacob, hū gāv us thu wel, and drank from it himself, az wel az hiz sunz and hiz līv/stok?" Jesus an/surd and sed tū hur, "Hūev/ur drinks uv this wotur wil tturst ugen, but hūev/ur drinks uv thu wotur that Ī shal giv him wil ne/vur tturst. But thu wotur that Ī shal giv him wil bikum in him u wel uv wotur springing up intū evurlast/ing līf." Thu woomun sed tū Him, "Sur, giv mē this wotur, that Ī mā not tturst, nor kum hir tū drau." Jesus sed tū hur, "Gō, kaul yoor huz/bund, and kum hir." Thu woomun an/surd and sed, "Ī hav nō huz/bund." Jesus sed tū hur, "Yū hav wel sed, 'Ī hav nō huz/bund,' fur yū hav had fīv huz/bundz, and thu wun hūm yū nou hav iz not yoor huz/bund; in that yū spōk trū/lē." Thu woomun sed tū Him, "Sur, Ī pursēv that Yū or u pro/fut. Our foth/urz wur/shupt aun this mount/un, and yū sā that in Jerusalem iz thu plās wher wun aut tū wur/shup." Jesus sed tū hur, "Woomun, bulēv Mē, thē our iz kum/ing when yū wil nēth/ur on this mount/un, nor in Jerusalem, wur/shup thu Foth/ur. Yū wur/shup whot yū dū not nō; wē nō whot wē wur/shup, fur salvā/shun iz ov thu Jewz. But thē our iz kum/ing, and nou iz, when thu trū wur/shupurz wil wur/shup thu Foth/ur in spir/ut and trūtt; fur thu Foth/ur iz sēking such tū wur/shup Him. God iz Spir/ut, and thōz hū wur/shup Him must wur/shup Him in spir/ut and trūtt." Thu woomun sed tū Him, "Ī nō that Messiah iz kum/ing," (hū iz kauld Christ). "When Hē kumz, Hē wil tel us aul ttingz." Jesus sed tū hur, "Ī hū spēk tū yū am Hē."

And at this point Hiz disīpulz kām, and thā mor/vuld that Hē taukt witt u woomun; yet nō wun sed, "Whot dū Yū sēk?" or, "Whī or Yū tauking witt hur?" Thu woomun then left hur woturpot, went hur wā intū thu sit/ē, and sed tū thu men, "Kum, sē u Man hū tōld mē aul ttingz that Ī e/vur did. Kood this bē thu Christ?" Then thā went out uv thu sit/ē and kām tū Him. In thu mēntīm Hiz disī/pulz urjd Him, sāing, "Rabbi, ēt." But Hē sed tū them, "Ī hav fūd tū ēt ov which yū dū not nō." Tharfōr thu disī/pulz sed tū wun unuth/ur, "Haz enēwun braut Him enētting tū ēt?" Jesus sed tū them, "Mī fūd iz tū dū thu wil uv Him hū sent Mee, and tū finish Hiz wurk. Dū yū not sae, 'Ther or stil fōr muntts and then kumz thu hor/vust'? Bihōld, Ī sā tū yū, lift up yoor īz and look at thu fēldz, fur thā or aulred/ē whīt fur hor/vust! And hē hū rēps risēvz wāj/uz, and gath/urz frūt fur itur/nul līf, that bōtt hē hū sōz and hē hū rēps mā rijois tugeth/ur. For in this thu sāing iz trū: 'Wun sōz and unuth/ur rēps.' Ī sent yū tū rēp that fur which yū hav not lā/burd; uthur men hav lā/burd, and yū hav ent/urd intū ther lā/burz."

And me/nē uv thu Samaritanz uv that sit/ē bulēvd in Him bikauz uv thu wurd uv thu woomun hū test/ufīd, "Hē tōld mē aul that Ī e/vur did." Sō when thu Samaritanz had kum tū Him, thā urjd Him tū stā witt them; and Hē stād thar tūw dāz. And me/nē mōr bulēvd bikauz uv Hiz ōn wurd. And thā sed tū thu woomun, "Nou wē bulēv, not bikauz uv whot yū sed, fur wē hav hurd fur ourselvz and nō that this iz indēd thu Christ, thu Sāv/yur uv thu wurld."

Nou af/tur thu tūw dāz Hē di-port/ud frum thar and went tū Galilee. For Jesus Himself test/ufīd that u pro/fut haz nō on/ur in hiz ōn kun/trē. Then, when Hē kām tū Galilee, thu

Galileanz/Galulē/unz/ risēvd Him, having sēn aul thu ttingz Hē did in Jerusalem at thu fēst; fur thā aulsō had gaun tū thu fēst.

Sō Jesus kām ugen tū Cana uv Galilee wher Hē had mād thu wotur wīn. And ther wuz u sur/tun nō/bulmun hūz sun wuz sik at Capernaum. When hē hurd that Jesus had kum out uv Judea intū Galilee, hē went tū Him and begd Him tū kum doun and hēl hiz sun, fur hē wuz at thu point uv dett. Then Jesus sed tū him, "Unles yū sē sīnz and wun/durz, yū wil bī nō mēnz bulēv." Thu nō//bulmun sed tū Him, "Sur, kum doun bifōr mī chīld dīz!" Jesus sed tū him, "Gō yoor wā; yoor sun livz." And thu man bulēvd thu wurd that Jesus spōk tū him, and hē went hiz wā. And az hē wuz nou gōing doun, hiz sur/vunts met him and tōld him, sāing, "Yoor sun livz!" Then hē inqīrd uv them thē our when hē got be/tur. And thā sed tū him, "Yes/turdē at thu sev/untt our thu fē/vur left him." Sō thu foth/ur nū that it wuz at thu sām our in which Jesus sed tū him, "Yoor sun livz." And hē himself bulēvd, and hiz hōl hous/hōld. This ugen iz thu se/kund sīn that Jesus did when Hē had kum out uv Judea intū Galilee.

5

Af/tur this ther wuz u fēst uv thu Jewz, and Jesus went up tū Jerusalem. Nou ther iz in Jerusalem bī thu Shēp Gāt u pūl, which iz kauld in Hebrew/Hē/brū/, *Bethesda/Buttez/du/*, having fīv pōr/chuz. In thēz lā u grāt mul/tutūd uv sik pē/pul, blīnd, lām, parulīzd, wā/ting fur thu mū/ving uv thu wotur. For an ānj/ul went doun at u sur/tun tīm intū thu pūl and sturd up thu wotur; then hūev/ur stept in furst, af/tur thu stur/ing uv thu wotur, wuz mād wel uv whotev/ur dizēz hē had. And u sur/tun man wuz thar hū had an infur/mutē ttur/tē-āt yirz. When Jesus sau him lī/ing thar, and nū that hē aulred/ē had bin in that kundi/shun u laung tīm, Hē sed tū him, "Dū yū wont tū bē mād wel?" Thu sik man an/surd Him, "Sur, Ī hav nō man tū poot mē intū thu pūl when thu wotur iz sturd up; but whīl Ī am kum/ing, unuth/ur steps doun bifōr mē." Jesus sed tū him, "Rīz, tāk up yoor bed and wauk." And imē/dēutlē thu man wuz mād wel, took up hiz bed, and waukt. And that dā wuz thu Sabbath/Sa/butt/. Thu Jewz tharfōr sed tū him hū wuz kyoord, "It iz thu Sabbath; it iz not lau/ful for yū tū kar/ē yoor bed." Hē an/surd them, "Hē hū mād mē wel sed tū mē, 'Tāk up yoor bed and wauk.'" Then thā askt him, "Hū iz thu Man hū sed tū yū, 'Tāk up yoor bed and wauk?'" And thu wun hū wuz hēld did not nō hū it woz, for Jesus had wittdraun, u mul/tutūd bēing in that plās. Af/turwurd Jesus found him in thu tem/pul, and sed tū him, "Sē, yū hav bin mād wel. Sin nō mōr, lest u wurs tting kum upon yū." Thu man diport/ud and tōld thu Jewz that it wuz Jesus hū had mād him wel. And tharfōr thu Jewz pur/sikyūtud Jesus, and saut tū kil Him, bikauz Hē had dun thēz ttingz aun thu Sabbath. But

Let's End Our Literacy Crisis

Jesus an/surd them, "Mī Foth/ur haz bin wurk/ing until nou, and Ī hav bin wurk/ing." Tharfōr thu Jewz saut aul thu mōr tū kil Him, bikauz Hē not ōn/lē brōk thu Sabbath, but aulsō sed that God wuz Hiz Foth/ur, mā/king Himself ē/qul witt God.

Then Jesus an/surd and sed tū them, "Mōst ushoor/udlē, Ī sā tū yū, thu Sun kan dū nutt/ing ov Himself, but whot Hē sēz thu Foth/ur dū; fur whotev/ur Hē duz, thu Sun aulsō duz in līk manur. For thu Foth/ur luvz thu Sun, and shōz Him aul ttingz that Hē Himself duz; and Hē wil shō Him grā/tur wurks than thēz, that yū mā mor/vul. For az thu Foth/ur rā/zuz thu ded and givz līf tū them, ē/vun sō thu Sun givz līf tū hūm Hē wil. For thu Foth/ur juj/uz nō wun, but haz kumit/ud aul juj/munt tū thu Sun, that aul shood on/ur thu Sun just az thā on/ur thu Foth/ur. Hē hū duz not on/ur thu Sun duz not on/ur thu Foth/ur hū sent Him. Mōst ushoor/udlē, Ī sā tū yū, hē hū hirz Mī wurd and bulēvz in Him hū sent Mē haz evurlast/ing līf, and shal not kum intū juj/munt, but haz past frum dett intū līf. Mōst ushoor/udlē, Ī sā tū yū, thē our iz kum/ing, and nou iz, when thu ded wil hir thu vois uv thu Sun uv God; and thōz hū hir wil liv. For az thu Foth/ur haz līf in Himself, sō Hē haz giv/un tū thu Sun tū hav līf in Himself, and haz giv/un Him uttor/utē tū ex/ikyūt juj/munt aulsō, bikauz Hē iz thu Sun uv Man. Dū not mor/vul at this; fur thē our iz kum/ing in which aul hū or in thu grāvz wil hir Hiz vois and kum fōrtt—thōz hū hav dun good, tū thu rezurek/shun uv līf, and thōz hū hav dun ē/vul, tū thu rezurek/shun uv kondemnā/shun.

"Ī kan ov Mīself dū nutt/ing. Az Ī hir, Ī juj; and Mī juj/munt iz rī/chus, bikauz Ī dū not sēk Mī ōn wil but thu wil uv thu Foth/ur hū sent Mē. If Ī bar wit/nus uv Mīself, Mī wit/nus iz not trū. Ther iz unuth/ur hū barz wit/nus uv Mē, and Ī nō that thu wit/nus which Hē wit/nusuz uv Mē iz trū. Yū sent tū John, and hē bōr wit/nus tū thu trūtt. Yet Ī dū not risēv testumō/nē frum man, but Ī sā thēz ttingz that yū mā bē sāvd. Hē wuz thu burning and shī/ning lamp, and yū wur wil/ing fur u tīm tū rijois in hiz līt. But Ī hav u grā/tur wit/nus than John'z; fur thu wurks which thu Foth/ur haz giv/un Mē tū finish—thu verē wurks that Ī dū—bar wit/nus uv Mē, that thu Foth/ur haz sent Mē. And thu Foth/ur Himself, hū sent Mē, haz test/ufīd uv Mē. Yū hav nēth/ur hurd Hiz vois at enē tīm, nor sēn Hiz fōrm. And yū dū not hav Hiz wurd ubī/ding in yū, bikauz hūm Hē sent, Him yū dū not bulēv. Yū surch thu Skrip/churz, fur in them yū ttink yū hav itur/nul līf; and thēz or thā which tes/tufī uv Mē. And yū or not wil/ing tū kum tū Mē that yū mā hav līf. Ī dū not risēv on/ur frum men. But Ī nō yū, that yū dū not hav thu luv uv God in yū. Ī hav kum in Mī Foth/ur'z nām, and yū dū not risēv Mē; if unuth/ur kumz in hiz ōn nām, him yū wil risēv. Hou kan yū bulēv, hū risēv on/ur frum wun unuth/ur, and dū not sēk thē on/ur that kumz frum thē ōn/lē God? Dū not ttink that Ī shal ukyūz yū tū thu

Foth/ur; ther iz wun hū ukyūz/uz yū—Moses, in hūm yū trust. For if yū bulēvd Moses, yū wood bulēv Mē; for hē rōt ubout Mē. But if yū dū not bulēv hiz rī/tingz, hou wil yū bulēv Mī wurdz?"

6

Af/tur thēz ttingz Jesus went ōvur thu Sē uv Galilee, which iz thu Sē uv Tiberias/Tībir/ēus/. And u grāt mul/tutūd fol/ōd Him, bikauz thā sau Hiz sīnz which Hē purfōrmd aun thōz hū wur dizēzd. And Jesus went up aun u mount/un, and thar Hē sat witt Hiz disī/pulz. And thu Pas/ōvur, u fēst uv thu Jewz, wuz nir. Then Jesus lift/ud up Hiz īz, and sēing u grāt mul/tutūd kum/ing tōrd Him, Hē sed tū Philip, "Wher shal wē bī bred, that thēz mā ēt?" And this Hē sed tū test him, for Hē Himself nū whot Hē wood dū. Philip an/surd Him, "Tūw hun/drud denarii/dinar/ēī/ wurtt uv bred iz not sufish/unt for them, that evrē wun uv them mā get u litul." Wun uv Hiz disī/pulz, Andrew, Simon Peter'z bruthur, sed tū Him, "Ther iz u lad hir hū haz fīv bor/lē lōvz and tūw smaul fish, but whot or thā umung sō me/nē?" And Jesus sed, "Māk thu pē/pul sit doun." Nou ther wuz much gras in thu plās. Sō thu men sat doun, in num/bur ubout fīv ttou/zund. And Jesus took thu lōvz, and when Hē had giv/un tfanks Hē distrib/yūtud them tū thu disī/pulz, and thu disī/pulz tū thōz sit/ing doun; and lī/kwīz uv thu fish, az much az thā wont/ud. And when thā wur fild, Hē sed tū Hiz disī/pulz, "Gath/ur up thu frag/munts that rimān, sō that nutt/ing iz laust." Tharfōr thā gath/urd them up, and fild twelv bas/kuts witt thu frag/munts uv thu fīv bor/lē lōvz which wur left ōvur bī thōz hū had ēt/un. Then thōz men, when thā had sēn thu sīn that Jesus did, sed, "This iz trū/lē thu pro/fut hū iz tū kum intū thu wurld."

Tharfōr when Jesus pursēvd that thā wur ubout tū kum and tāk Him bī fōrs tū māk Him king, Hē diport/ud ugen tū u mount/un bī himself ulōn.

And when ēv/ning kām, Hiz disī/pulz went doun tū thu sē, got intū thu bōt, and went ōvur thu sē tōrd Capernaum. And it wuz nou dork, and Jesus had not kum tū them. And thu sē urōz bikauz u grāt wind wuz blō/ing. Sō when thā had rōd ubout ttrē or fōr mīlz, thā sau Jesus wauk/ing aun thu sē and drau/ing nir thu bōt; and thā wur ufrād. But Hē sed tū them, "It iz Ī; dū not bē ufrād." Then thā wil/inglē risēvd Him intū thu bōt, and imē/dēutlē thu bōt wuz at thu land wher thā wur gōing.

Thu fol/uwing dā, when thu pē/pul hū stood aun thē uthur sīd uv thu sē sau that ther wuz nō uthur bōt thar, ix/ept that wun which Hiz disī/pulz had ent/urd, and that Jesus had not ent/urd thu bōt witt Hiz disī/pulz, but Hiz disī/pulz had gaun uwā ulōn—houev/ur, uthur bōts kām frum Tiberias, nir thu plās wher thā āt bred af/tur thu Lord had giv/un ttanks—when thu pē/pul tharfōr sau that Jesus wuz not thar, nor Hiz disī/pulz, thā aulsō got intū bōts and

239

kām tū Capernaum, sēking Jesus. And when thā had found Him aun thē uthur sīd uv thu sē, thā sed tū Him, "Rabbi, when did Yū kum hir?" Jesus an/surd them and sed, "Mōst ushoor/udlē, Ī sā tū yū, yū sēk Mē, not bikauz yū sau thu sīnz, but bikauz yū āt uv thu lōvz and wur fild. Dū not lā/bur fur thu fūd which per/ishuz, but fur thu fūd which indoorz tū evurlast/ing līf, which thu Sun uv Man wil giv yū, bikauz God thu Foth/ur haz set Hiz sēl aun Him." Then thā sed tū Him, "Whot shal wē dū, that wē mā wurk thu wurks uv God?" Jesus an/surd and sed tū them, "This iz thu wurk uv God, that yū bulēv in Him hūm Hē sent." Tharfōr thā sed tū Him, "Whot sīn wil Yū purfōrm then, that wē mā sē it and bulēv Yū? Whot wurk wil Yū dū? Our foth/urz āt thu manna/man/u/ in thu dez/urt; az it iz rit/un, *'Hē gāv them bred frum he/vun tū ēt.'*" Then Jesus sed tū them, "Mōst ushoor/udlē, Ī sā tū yū, Moses did not giv yū thu bred frum he/vun, but Mī Foth/ur givz yū thu trū bred frum he/vun. For thu bred uv God iz Hē hū kumz doun frum he/vun and givz līf tū thu wurld." Then thā sed tū Him, "Lord, aul/wāz giv us this bred." And Jesus sed tū them, "Ī am thu bred uv līf. Hē hū kumz tū Mē shal ne/vur hung/gur, and hē hū bulēvz in Mē shal ne/vur tturst. But Ī sed tū yū that yū aulsō hav sēn Mē and dū not bulēv. Aul that thu Foth/ur givz Mē wil kum tū Mē, and thu wun hū kumz tū Mē Ī wil bī nō mēnz kast out. For Ī kām doun frum he/vun, not tū dū Mī ōn wil, but thu wil uv Him hū sent Mē. And this iz thu wil uv thu Foth/ur hū sent Mē, that uv aul Hē haz giv/un Mē Ī shood lūz nutt/ing, but shood rāz it up at thu last dā. And this iz thu wil uv Him hū sent Mē, that evrēwun hū sēz thu Sun and bulēvz in Hım mā hav evurlast/ing līf; and Ī wil rāz him up at thu last dā."

Thu Jewz then mur/murd ugenst Him, bikauz Hē sed, "Ī am thu bred which kām doun frum he/vun." And thā sed, "Iz not this Jesus, thu sun uv Joseph, hūz foth/ur and muth/ur wē nō? Hou iz it then that Hē sez, eĪ kām doun frum he/vun'?" Jesus tharfōr an/surd and sed tū them, "Dū not murmur umung yurselvz. Nō wun kan kum tū Mē unles thu Foth/ur hū sent Mē drauz him; and Ī wil rāz him up at thu last dā. It iz rit/un in thu pro/futs, *'And thā wil aul bē taut bī God.'* Tharfōr evrēwun hū haz hurd and lurnd frum thu Foth/ur kumz tū Mē. Not that enēwun haz sēn thu Foth/ur, ix/ept Hē hū iz from God; Hē haz sēn thu Foth/ur. Mōst ushoor/udlē, Ī sā tū yū, hē hū bulēvz in Mē haz evurlast/ing līf. Ī am thu bred uv līf. Yoor foth/urz āt thu manna in thu wil/durnus, and or ded. This iz thu bred which kumz doun frum he/vun, that u man mā ēt uv it and not dī. Ī am thu living bred which kām doun frum he/vun. If enēwun ēts uv this bred, hē wil liv furev/ur; and thu bred that Ī shal giv iz Mī flesh, which Ī shal giv fur thu līf uv thu wurld."

Thu Jewz tharfōr qor/uld umung themselvz, sāing, "Hou kan this Man giv us Hiz flesh tū ēt?" Then Jesus sed tū them, "Mōst ushoor/udlē, Ī sā tū yū, unles yū ēt thu flesh uv thu Sun uv Man and drink Hiz blud, yū hav nō līf in yū. Hūev/ur ēts Mī flesh and drinks Mī blud haz itur/nul līf, and Ī wil rāz him up at thu last dā. For Mī flesh iz fūd indēd, and Mī blud iz drink indēd. Hē hū ēts Mī flesh and drinks Mī blud dwelz in Mē, and Ī in him. Az thu living Foth/ur sent Mē, and Ī liv bikauz uv thu Foth/ur, sō hē hū fēdz aun Mē wil liv bikauz uv Mē. This iz thu bred which kām doun frum he/vun, not az yoor foth/urz āt thu manna, and or ded. Hē hū ēts this bred wil liv furev/ur." Thēz ttingz Hē sed in thu sin/ugog az Hē taut in Capernaum.

Tharfōr me/nē uv Hiz disī/pulz, when thā hurd this, sed, "This iz u hord sāing; hū kan undurstand it?" When Jesus nū in Himself that Hiz disī/pulz mur/murd ubout this, Hē sed tū them, "Duz this ufend yū? Whot then if yū shood sē thu Sun uv Man usend wher Hē woz bifōr? It iz thu Spir/ut hū givz līf; thu flesh pro/futs nutt/ing. Thu wurdz that Ī spēk tū yū or spir/ut, and thā or līf. But ther or sum uv yū hū dū not bulēv." For Jesus nū frum thu bigin/ing hū thā wur hū did not bulēv, and hū wood bitrā Him. And Hē sed, "Tharfōr Ī sed tū yū that nō wun kan kum tū Mē unles it haz bin giv/un tū him frum Mī Foth/ur."

From that tīm me/nē uv Hiz disī/pulz went bak and waukt witt Him nō mōr. Then Jesus sed tū thu twelv, "Dū yū aulsō wont tū gō uwā?" Then Simon Peter an/surd Him, "Lord, tū hūm shal wē gō? Yū hav thu wurdz uv itur/nul līf. And wē bulēv and or shoor that Yū or thu Christ, thu Sun uv thu living God." Jesus an/surd them, "Hav Ī not chōz/un yū, thu twelv, and wun uv yū iz u dev/ul?" Hē spōk uv Judas/Jū/dus/ Iscariot/Īskar/ēut/, thu sun uv Simon, fur it wuz hē hū wood bitrā Him, bēing wun uv thu twelv.

7

Af/tur thēz ttingz Jesus waukt in Galilee; fur Hē did not wont tū wauk in Judea, bikauz thu Jewz saut tū kil Him. Nou thu Jewz' Fēst uv Tabernaclez/Tab/urnakulz/ wuz at hand. Hiz bruthurz tharfōr sed tū Him, "Diport frum hir and gō intū Judea, that Yoor disī/pulz aulsō mō sē thu wurks that Yū or dūing. For nō wun duz enētting in sē/krut whīl hē himself sēks tū bē nōn ō/punlē. If Yū dū thēz ttingz, shō Yurself tū thu wurld." For not ē/vun Hiz bruth/urz bulēvd in Him. Then Jesus sed tū them, "Mī tīm haz not yet kum, but yoor tīm iz aul/wāz re/dē. Thu wurld kanot hāt yū, but it hāts Mē bikauz Ī tēs/tufī uv it that its wurks or ē/vul. Yū gō up tū this fēst. Ī am not yet gōing up tū this fēst, fur Mī tīm haz not yet fool/ē kum." When Hē had sed thēz wurdz tū them, Hē rimānd in Galilee.

But when Hiz bruth/urz had gaun up, then Hē aulsō went up tū thu fēst, not ō/punlē, but az it wur in sē/krut. Then thu Jewz saut Him at thu fēst, and sed, "Wher iz Hē?" And ther wuz much murmuring umung thu pē/pul kunsurn/ing Him, fur sum sed, "Hē iz u good Man"; uthurz sed, "Nō, aun

Let's End Our Literacy Crisis

thu kon/trerē, Hē disēvz thu pē/pul." Houev/ur, nō wun spōk ō/punlē uv Him fur fir uv thu Jewz.

Nou ubout thu mid/ul uv thu fēst Jesus went up intū thu tem/pul and taut. And thu Jewz mor/vuld, sāing, "Hou duz this Man nō le/turz, ne/vur having stu/dēd?" Jesus an/surd them and sed, "Mī dok/trun iz not mīn, but Hiz hū sent Mē. If enēwun wonts tū dū Hiz wil, hē shal nō kunsurn/ing thu dok/trun, wheth/ur it iz frum God or wheth/ur Ī spēk ov Mīself. Hē hū spēks frum himself sēks hiz ōn glōr/ē; but Hē hū sēks thu glōr/ē uv thu Wun hū sent Him iz trū, and nō unrī/chusnus iz in Him. Did not Moses giv yū thu lau, and yet nun uv yū kēps thu lau? Whī dū yū sēk tū kil Mē?" Thu pē/pul an/surd and sed, "Yū hav u dē/mun. Hū iz sēking tū kil Yū?" Jesus an/surd and sed tū them, "Ī hav dun wun wurk, and yū aul mor/vul. Moses tharfōr gāv yū surkumsizh/un (not that it iz frum Moses, but frum thu foth/urz), and yū sur/kumsīz u man aun thu Sabbath. If u man risēvz surkumsizh/un aun thu Sabbath, that thu lau uv Moses shood not bē brō/kun, or yū ang/grē witt Mē bikauz Ī hav mād u man kumplēt/lē wel aun thu Sabbath? Dū not juj ukaurd/ing tū upir/uns, but juj witt rī/chus juj/munt."

Then sum uv them frum Jerusalem sed, "Iz this not Hē hūm thā sēk tū kil? But look! Hē spēks bōld/lē, and thā sā nutt/ing tū Him. Dū thu rū/lurz nō indēd that this iz trū/lē thu Christ? Houev/ur, wē nō wher this Man iz from; but when thu Christ kumz, nō wun nōz wher Hē iz from." Then Jesus krīd out, az Hē taut in thu tem/pul, sāing, "Yū bōtt nō Mē, and yū nō wher Ī am from; and Ī hav not kum uv Mīself, but Hē hū sent Mē iz trū, hūm yū dū not nō. But Ī nō Him, fur Ī am from Him, and Hē haz sent Mē." Then thā saut tū tāk Him; but nō wun lād handz aun Him, bikauz Hiz our had not yet kum. And me/nē uv thu pē/pul bulēvd in Him, and sed, "When thu Christ kumz, wil Hē dū mōr sīnz than thēz which this Man haz dun?" Thu Phariseez hurd that thu pē/pul mur/murd such ttingz kunsurn/ing Him, and thu Phariseez and thu chēf prēsts sent of/usurz tū tāk Him. Then Jesus sed tū them, "Ī shal bē witt yū u litul whīl laung/gur, and then Ī gō tū Him hū sent Mē. Yū wil sēk Mē and not fīnd Mē, and wher Ī am yū kanot kum." Then thu Jewz sed umung themselvz, "Wher duz Hē intend tū gō that wē shal not fīnd Him? Duz Hē intend tū gō tū thu Dispur/zhun umung thu Greeks and tēch thu Greeks? Whot iz this tting that Hē sed, 'Yū wil sēk Mē and not fīnd Mē, and wher Ī am yū kanot kum'?"

Aun thu last dā, that grāt dā uv thu fēst, Jesus stood and krīd out, sāing, "If enēwun tturts, let him kum tū Mē and drink. Hē hū bulēvz in Mē, az thu Skrip/chur haz sed, out uv hiz hort wil flō riv/urz uv living wotur." But this Hē spōk kunsurn/ing thu Spir/ut, hūm thōz hū bulēv in Him wood risēv; fur thu Hō/lē Spir/ut wuz not yet giv/un, bikauz Jesus wuz not yet glōr/ufīd. Tharfōr me/nē frum thu

Appendix 4

kroud, when thā hurd this sāing, sed, "Trū/lē this iz thu Pro/fut." Uth/urz sed, "This iz thu Christ," but sum sed, "Wil thu Christ kum out uv Galilee? Haz not thu Skrip/chur sed that thu Christ kumz frum thu sēd uv David/Dā/vid/ and frum thu toun uv Bethlehem/Bett/luhem/, wher David woz?" Sō ther wuz u duvizh/un umung thu pē/pul bikauz uv Him. And sum uv them wont/ud tū tāk Him, but nō wun lād handz aun Him.

Then thē of/usurz kām tū thu chēf prēsts and Phariseez, hū sed tū them, "Whī hav yū not braut Him?" Thē of/usurz an/surd, "Nō man e/vur spōk līk this Man!" Then thu Phariseez an/surd them, "Or yū aulsō disēvd? Hav enē uv thu rū/lurz or thu Phariseez bulēvd in Him? But this kroud that duz not nō thu lau iz ukurst." Nicodemus (hē hū kām tū Jesus bī nīt, bēing wun uv them) sed tū them, "Duz our lau juj u man bifōr it hirz him and nōz whot hē iz dūing?" Thā an/surd and sed tū him, "Or yū aulsō frum Galilee? Surch and look, fur nō pro/fut haz uriz/un out uv Galilee." And evrēwun went tū hiz ōn hous.

8

But Jesus went tū thu Mount uv Ol/ivz. And ur/lē in thu maur/ning Hē kām ugen intū thu tem/pul, and aul thu pē/pul kām tū Him; and Hē sat doun and taut them. And thu skrībz and Phariseez braut tū Him u woomun kaut in udul/trē. And when thā had set hur in thu midst, thā sed tū Him, "Tē/chur, this woomun wuz kaut in udul/trē, in thu verē akt. Nou Moses, in thu lau, kumand/ud us that such shood bē stōnd. But whot dū Yū sā?" This thā sed, testing Him, that thā mīt hav sum/tting uv which tū ukyūz Him. But Jesus stūpt doun and rōt aun thu ground witt Hiz fing/gur, az thō Hē did not hir. Sō when thā kuntin/yūd asking Him, Hē rāzd Himself up and sed tū them, "Hē hū iz wittout sin umung yū, let him ttrō u stōn at hur furst." And ugen Hē stūpt doun and rōt aun thu ground. And thōz hū hurd it, bēing kunvik/tud bī ther ōn kon/chuns, went out wun bī wun, bigin/ing witt thē ōld/ust ē/vun tū thu last. And Jesus wuz left ulōn, and thu woomun standing in thu midst. When Jesus had rāzd Himself up and sau nō wun but thu woomun, Hē sed tū hur, "Woomun, wher or thōz ukyūz/urz uv yoorz? Haz nō wun kundemd yū?" Shē sed, "Nō wun, Lord." And Jesus sed tū hur, "Nēth/ur dū Ī kundem yū; gō and sin nō mōr."

Then Jesus spōk tū them ugen, sāing, "Ī am thu līt uv thu wurld. Hē hū fol/ōz Mē shal not wauk in dork/nus, but hav thu līt uv līf." Thu Phariseez tharfōr sed tū Him, "Yū bar wit/nus uv Yurself; Yoor wit/nus iz not trū." Jesus an/surd and sed tu them, "Ē/vun if Ī bar wit/nus uv Mīself, Mī wit/nus iz trū, fur Ī nō wher Ī kām from and wher Ī am gō-ing; but yū dū not nō wher Ī kum from and wher Ī am gōing. Yū juj ukaurd/ing tū thu flesh; Ī juj nō wun. And yet if Ī dū juj, Mī juj/munt iz trū; fur Ī am not ulōn, but Ī and thu Foth/ur hū sent Mē. It iz aulsō rit/un in yoor lau that thu testumō/nē uv tūw men iz trū. Ī am Wun hū barz wit/nus uv Mīself, and thu Foth/ur hū sent Mē barz wit/nus uv Mē." Then thā sed tū Him, "Wher iz Yoor Foth/ur?" Jesus an/surd, "Yū nō nēth/ur Mē nor Mī Foth/ur. If yū had nōn Mē, yū wood hav nōn Mī Foth/ur aulsō." Thēz wurdz Jesus spōk in thu trezh/urē, az Hē taut in thu tem/pul; and nō wun lād handz aun Him, fur Hiz our had not yet kum.

Then Jesus sed tū them ugen, "Ī am gōing uwā, and yū wil sēk Mē, and wil dī in yoor sin. Wher Ī gō yū kanot kum." Then thu Jewz sed, "Wil Hē kil Himself, bikauz Hē sez, 'Wher Ī gō yū kanot kum'?" And Hē sed tū them, "Yū or frum binētt; Ī am frum ubuv. Yū or ov this wurld; Ī am not ov thu wurld. Tharfōr Ī sed tū yū that yū wil dī in yoor sinz; fur if yū dū not bulēv that Ī am Hē, yū wil dī in yoor sinz." Then thā sed tū Him, "Hū or Yū?" And Jesus sed tū them, "Just whot Ī hav bin sāing tū yū frum thu bigin/ing. Ī hav me/nē ttingz tū sā and tū juj kunsurn/ing yū, but Hē hū sent Mē iz trū; and Ī spēk tū thu wurld thōz ttingz which Ī hav hurd frum Him." Thā did not undurstand that Hē spōk tū them uv thu Foth/ur. Then Jesus sed tū them, "When yū hav lift/ud up thu Sun uv Man, then yū wil nō that Ī am Hē, and that Ī dū nutt/ing ov Mīself; but az Mī Foth/ur haz taut Mē, Ī spēk thēz ttingz. And Hē hū sent Mē iz witt Mē. Thu Foth/ur haz not left Mē ulōn, fur Ī aul/wāz dū thōz ttingz that plēz Him." Az Hē spōk thēz wurdz, me/nē bulēvd in Him.

Then Jesus sed tū thōz Jewz hū bulēvd in Him, "If yū kuntin/yū in Mī wurd, then yū or Mī disī/pulz indēd. And yū shal nō thu trūtt, and thu trūtt shal māk yū frē." Thā an/surd Him, "Wē or Abraham'z/Ā/bruham'z/ disend/unts, and wur ne/vur in bondij tū enēwun. Hou iz it that yū sā, 'Yū wil bē mād frē?'" Jesus an/surd them, "Mōst ushoor/udlē, Ī sā tū yū, hūev/ur kumits sin iz u slāv uv sin. And u slāv duz not ubīd in thu hous furev/ur, but u sun ubīdz furev/ur. Tharfōr if thu Sun māks yū frē, yū shal bē frē indēd. Ī nō that yū or Abraham'z disend/unts, but yū sēk tū kil Mē, bikauz Mī wurd haz nō plās in yū. Ī spēk whot Ī hav sēn witt Mī Foth/ur, and yū dū whot yū hav sēn witt yoor foth/ur." Thā an/surd and sed tū Him, "Abraham iz our foth/ur." Jesus sed tū them, "If yū wur Abraham'z chil/drun, yū wood dū thu wurks uv Abraham. But nou yū sēk tū kil Mē, u Man hū haz tōld yū thu trūtt which Ī hav hurd frum God. Abraham did not dū this. Yū dū thu dēdz uv yoor foth/ur." Then thā sed tū Him, "Wē wur not bōrn uv faurnukā/shun; wē hav wun Foth/ur— God." Jesus sed tū them, "If God wur yoor Foth/ur, yū wood luv Mē, fur Ī prusēd/ud fōrtt and kām frum God; nor did Ī kum uv Mīself, but Hē sent Mē. Whī dū yū not undurstand Mī spēch? Bikauz yū or not ā/bul tū lis/un tū Mī wurd. Yū or ov yoor foth/ur thu dev/ul, and thu dizīrz uv yoor foth/ur yū wont tū dū. Hē wuz u mur/durur frum thu bigin/ing, and duz not stand in thu trūtt, bikauz ther iz nō trūtt in him. When hē spēks u lī, hē spēks frum hiz ōn rē/sōrsuz, fur hē iz u līr and thu foth/ur ov it. And bikauz Ī tel yū thu trūtth, yū dū not bulēv Mē. Which uv yū kunvikts Mē uv sin? And if Ī tel thu trūtth, whī dū yū not bulēv Mē? Hē hū iz uv God hirz God'z wurdz; tharfōr yū dū not hir them, bikauz yū or not uv God."

Then thu Jewz an/surd and sed tū Him, "Dū wē not sā rīt/lē that Yū or u Samaritan and hav u dē/mun?" Jesus an/surd, "Ī dū not hav u dē/mun; but Ī on/ur Mī Foth/ur, and yū dison/ur Mē. And Ī dū not sēk Mī ōn glōr/ē; ther iz Wun hū sēks and juj/uz. Mōst ushoor/udlē, Ī sā tū yū, if enēwun kēps Mī wurd hē shal ne/vur sē dett." Then thu Jewz sed tū Him, "Nou wē nō that Yū hav u dē/mun! Abraham iz ded, and thu pro/futs; and Yū sā, 'If enēwun kēps Mī wurd hē shal ne/vur tāst dett.' Or Yū grā/tur than our foth/ur Abraham, hū iz ded? And thu pro/futs or ded. Hūm dū Yū māk Yurself out tū bē?" Jesus an/surd, "If Ī on/ur Mīself, Mī on/ur iz nutt/ing. It iz Mī Foth/ur hū on/urz Mē, uv hūm yū sā that Hē iz yoor God. Yet yū hav not nōn Him, but Ī nō Him. And if Ī sā, 'Ī dū not nō Him,' Ī shal bē u līr līk yū; but Ī dū nō Him and kēp Hiz wurd. Yoor foth/ur Abraham rijoist tū sē Mī dā, and hē sau it and wuz glad." Then thu Jewz sed tū Him, "Yū or not yet fif/tē yirz ōld, and hav Yū sēn Abraham?" Jesus sed tū them, "Mōst ushoor/udlē, Ī sā tū yū, bifōr Abraham woz, Ī AM." Then thā took up stōnz tū ttrō at Him; but Jesus hid Himself and went out uv thu tem/pul, gōing ttrū thu midst uv them, and sō past bī.

9

And az Jesus past bī, Hē sau u man hū wuz blīnd frum burtt. And Hiz disī/pulz askt Him, sāing, "Rabbi, hū sind, this man or hiz par/unts, that hē wuz bōrn blīnd?" Jesus an/surd, "Nēth/ur this man nor hiz par/unts sind, but that thu wurks uv God shood bē rivēld in him. Ī must wurk thu wurks uv Him hū sent Mē whīl it iz dā; thu nīt iz kum/ing when nō wun kan wurk. Az laung az Ī am in thu wurld, Ī am thu līt uv thu wurld." When Hē had sed thēz ttingz, Hē spat aun thu ground and mād klā witt thu sulī/vu; and Hē unoin/tud thē īz uv thu blīnd man with thu klā. And Hē sed tū him, "Gō, wosh in thu pūl uv Siloam/Silō/um/" (which iz translā/tud, Sent). Sō hē went hiz wā and wosht, and kām bak sēing. Tharfōr thu nā/burz and thōz hū prē/vēuslē had sēn that hē wuz blīnd sed, "Iz not this hē hū sat and begd?" Sum sed, "This iz hē." Uth/urz sed, "Hē iz līk him." Hē sed, "Ī am hē." Tharfōr thā sed tū him, "Hou wur yoor īz ō/pund?" Hē an/surd and sed, "U Man kauld Jesus mād klā and unoin/tud mī īz and sed tū mē, 'Gō tū thu pūl uv Siloam and wosh.' And Ī went and wosht, and Ī risēvd sīt." Then thā sed tū him, "Wher iz Hē?" Hē sed, "Ī dū not nō."

Thā braut him hū faur/murlē wuz blīnd tū thu Phariseez. And it wuz u Sabbath when Jesus mād thu klā and ō/pund hiz īz. Then thu Phariseez aulsō askt him ugen hou hē had risēvd hiz sīt. Hē sed tū them, "Hē poot klā aun mī īz, and Ī wosht, and Ī sē." Tharfōr sum uv thu Phariseez sed, "This Man iz not frum God, bikauz Hē duz not kēp thu Sabbath." Uth/urz sed, "Hou kan u man hū iz u sin/ur dū such mir/ikulz?" And ther wuz u duvizh/un umung them. Thā sed tū thu blīnd man ugen, "Whot dū yū sā ubout Him bikauz Hē ō/pund yoor īz?" Hē sed, "Hē iz u pro/fut." But thu Jewz did not bulēv kunsurn/ing him, that hē had bin blīnd and risēvd hiz sīt, until thā kauld thu par/unts uv him hū had risēvd hiz sīt. And thā askt them, sāing, "Iz this yoor sun, hū yū sā wuz bōrn blīnd? Hou then duz hē nou sē?" Hiz par/unts an/surd them and sed, "Wē nō that this iz our sun, and that hē woz bōrn blīnd; but bī whot mēnz hē nou sēz wē dū not nō, or hū ō/pund hiz īz wē dū not nō. Hē iz uv āj; ask him. Hē shal spēk fur himself." Hiz par/unts spōk thēz wurdz bikauz thā fird thu Jewz, fur thu Jewz had ugrēd aulred/ē that if enēwun kunfest that Hē wuz Christ, hē wood bē poot out uv thu sin/ugog. Tharfōr hiz par/unts sed, "Hē iz uv āj; ask him."

Then thā ugen kauld thu man hū wuz blīnd, and sed tū him, "Giv God thu prāz! Wē nō that this Man iz u sin/ur." Hē an/surd and sed, "Wheth/ur Hē iz u sin/ur or not Ī dū not nō. Wun tting Ī nō: that thō Ī wuz blīnd, nou Ī sē." Then thā sed tū him ugen, "Whot did Hē dū tū yū? Hou did Hē ōpun yoor īz?" Hē an/surd them, "Ī hav tōld yū aulred/ē, and yū did not lis/un. Whī dū yū wont tū hir it ugen? Dū yū aulsō wont tū bikum Hiz disī/pulz?" Then thā rivīld him and sed, "Yū or Hiz disī/pul, but wē or Moses' disī/pulz. Wē nō that God spōk tū Moses; az fur this fel/ō, wē dū not nō wher Hē iz from." Thu man an/surd and sed tū them, "Wī, this iz u mor/vulus tting, that yū dū not nō wher Hē iz from, and yet Hē haz ō/pund mī īz! Nou wē nō that God duz not hir sin/urz; but if enēwun iz u wur/shupur uv God and duz Hiz wil, Hē hirz him. Sins thu wurld bigan it haz bin unhurd ov that enēwun ō/pund thē īz uv wun hū wuz bōrn blīnd. If this Man wur not frum God, Hē kood dū nutt/ing." Thā an/surd and sed tū him, "Yū wur kumplēt/lē bōrn in sinz, and or yū tēching us?" And thā kast him out.

Jesus hurd that thā had kast him out; and when Hē had found him, Hē sed tū him, "Dū yū bulēv in thu Sun uv God?" Hē an/surd and sed, "Hū iz Hē, Lord, that Ī mā bulēv in Him?" And Jesus sed tū him, "Yū hav bōtt sēn Him and it iz Hē hū iz tauking witt yū." And hē sed, "Lord, Ī bulēv!" And hē wur/shupt Him. And Jesus sed, "For juj/munt Ī hav kum intū this wurld, that thōz hū dū not sē mā sē, and that thōz hū sē mā bē mād blīnd." And sum uv thu Phariseez hū wur witt Him hurd thēz wurdz, and sed tū Him, "Or wē blīnd aulsō?" Jesus sed tū them, "If yū wur blīnd, yū wood hav nō sin; but nou yū sā, 'Wē sē.' Tharfōr yoor sin rimānz."

10

"Mōst ushoor/udlē, Ī sā tū yū, hē hū duz not ent/ur thu shēp/fōld bī thu

Appendix 4

dōr, but klīmz up sum uthur wā, thu sām iz u ttēf and u rob/ur. But hē hū en/turz bī thu dōr iz thu shep/urd uv thu shēp. Tū him thu dōr/kēpur ō/punz, and thu shēp hir hiz vois; and hē kaulz hiz ōn shēp bī nām and lēdz them out. And when hē bringz out hiz ōn shēp, hē gōz bifōr them; and thu shēp fol/ō him, fur thā nō hiz vois. And u strān/jur thā wil bī nō mēnz fol/ō, but wil flē frum him, fur thā dū not nō thu vois uv strān/jurz." Jesus yūzd this ilustrā/shun, but thā did not undurstand thu ttingz which Hē spōk tū them.

Then Jesus sed tū them ugen, "Mōst ushoor/udlē, Ī sā tū yū, Ī am thu dōr uv thu shēp. Aul hū e/vur kām bifōr Mē or ttēvz and rob/urz, but thu shēp did not hir them. Ī am thu dōr. If enēwun en/turz bī Mē, hē wil bē sāvd, and wil gō in and out and fīnd pas/chur. Thu ttēf duz not kum ix/ept tū stēl, and tū kil, and tū distroi. Ī hav kum that thā mā hav līf, and that thā mā hav it mōr ubun/duntlē. Ī am thu good shep/urd. Thu good shep/urd givz Hiz līf fur thu shēp. But hē hū iz u hīr/ling and not thu shep/urd, wun hū duz not ōn thu shēp, sēz thu woolf kum/ing, lēvz thu shēp, and flēz; and thu woolf ka/chuz thu shēp and ska/turz them. Thu hīr/ling flēz bikauz hē iz u hīr/ling and duz not kar ubout thu shēp. Ī am thu good shep/urd; and Ī nō Mī shēp, and am nōn bī Mī ōn. Az thu Foth/ur nōz Mē, ē/vun sō Ī nō thu Foth/ur; and Ī lā doun Mī līf fur thu shēp. And uthur shēp Ī hav which or not uv this fōld; them aulsō Ī must bring, and thā wil hir Mī vois; and ther wil bē wun flok and wun shep/urd. Tharfōr Mī Foth/ur luvz Mē, bikauz Ī lā doun Mī līf that Ī mā tāk it ugen. Nō wun tāks it frum Mē, but Ī lā it doun ov Mīself. Ī hav pour tū lā it doun, and Ī hav pour tū tāk it ugen. This kumand Ī hav risēvd frum Mī Foth/ur."

Tharfōr ther wuz u duvizh/un ugen umung thu Jewz bikauz uv thēz sāingz. And me/nē uv them sed, "Hē haz u dē/mun and iz mad. Whī dū yū lis/un tū Him?" Uth/urz sed, "Thēz or not thu wurdz uv wun hū haz u dē/mun. Kan u dē/mun ōpun thē īz uv thu blīnd?"

Nou it wuz thu Fēst uv Dedikā/shun in Jerusalem, and it wuz win/tur. And Jesus waukt in thu tem/pul, in Solomon'z/Sol/umun'z/ pōrch. Then thu Jewz suroun/dud Him and sed tū Him, "Hou laung dū Yū māk us dout? If Yū or thu Christ, tel us plaen/lee." Jesus an/surd them, "Ie toeld yue, and yue due not buleev. Thu wurks that Ie due in Mie Foth/ur'z naem, thae bar wit/nus uv Mee. But yue due not buleev, bikauz yue or not uv Mie sheep, az Ie sed tue yue. Mie sheep hir Mie vois, and Ie noe them, and thae fol/oe Mee. And Ie giv them itur/nul lief, and thae shal ne/vur perish; neeth/ur shal eneewun snach them out uv Mie hand. Mie Foth/ur, hue gaev them tue Mee, iz grae/tur than aul; and noe wun iz ae/bul tue snach them out uv Mie Foth/ur'z hand. Ie and Mie Foth/ur or wun."

Then thu Jewz took up stoenz ugen tue stoen Him. Jesus an/surd them, "Me/nee good wurks Ie hav shoen yue frum Mie Foth/ur. For which uv thoez wurks due yue stoen Mee?" Thu Jewz an/surd Him, saeing, "For u good wurk wee due not stoen Yue, but for blas/fumee, and bikauz Yue, beeing u Man, maek Yurself God." Jesus an/surd them, "Iz it not rit/un in yoor lau, '*Ie sed, yue or godz'?* If Hee kauld them godz, tue huem thu wurd uv God kaem (and thu Skrip/chur kanot bee broe/kun), due yue sae uv Him huem thu Foth/ur sank/tufied and sent intue thu wurld, 'Yue or blas/fuming,' bikauz Ie sed, 'Ie am thu Sun uv God'? If Ie due not due thu wurks uv Mie Foth/ur, due not buleev Mee; but if Ie due, thoe yue due not buleev Mee, buleev thu wurks, that yue mae noe and buleev that thu Foth/ur iz in Mee, and Ie in Him." Tharfoer thae saut ugen tue seez Him, but Hee iskaept out uv ther hand.

And Hee went uwae ugen beeond thu Jordan tue thu plaes wher John wuz baptiezing at furst, and thar Hee staed. And me/nee kaem tue Him and sed, "John purfoermd noe sien, but aul thu ttingz that John spoek ubout this Man wur true." And me/nee buleevd in Him thar.

11

Nou u sur/tun man wuz sik, Lazarus/ Laz/urus/ uv Bethany/Bett/unee/, thu toun uv Mary/Mer/ee/ and hur sis/tur Martha/Mor/ttu/. It wuz that Mary hue unoin/tud thu Lord witt frae/grunt oil and wiept Hiz feet witt hur har, huez bruthur Lazarus wuz sik. Tharfoer hiz sis/turz sent tue Him, saeing, "Lord, bihoeld, hee huem Yue luv iz sik." When Jesus hurd that, Hee sed, "This sik/nus iz not tue dett, but for thu gloer/ee uv God, that thu Sun uv God mae bee gloer/ufied ttrue it." Nou Jesus luvd Martha and hur sis/tur and Lazarus. Soe, when Hee hurd that hee wuz sik, Hee staed tuew moer daez in thu plaes wher Hee woz. Then af/tur this Hee sed tue Hiz disie/pulz, "Let us goe tue Judea ugen." Hiz disie/pulz sed tue Him, "Rabbi, laet/lee thu Jewz saut tue stoen Yue, and or Yue goeing thar ugen?" Jesus an/surd, "Or ther not twelv ourz in thu dae? If eneewun wauks in thu dae, hee duz not stum/bul, bikauz hee seez thu liet uv this wurld. But if wun wauks in thu niet, hee stum/bulz, bikauz ther iz noe liet in him." Theez ttingz Hee sed, and af/tur that Hee sed tue them, "Our frend Lazarus sleeps, but Ie goe that Ie mae waek him out uv sleep." Then Hiz disie/pulz sed, "Lord, if hee sleeps hee wil get wel." Houev/ur, Jesus spoek uv hiz dett, but thae ttaut that Hee wuz speeking ubout taek/ing rest in sleep. Then Jesus sed tue them plaen/lee, "Lazarus iz ded. And Ie am glad for yoor saeks that Ie wuz not thar, that yue mae buleev. Nevur-thules let us goe tue him." Then Thomas/Tom/us/, hue iz kauld Didymus/Did/imus/, sed tue hiz fel/oe disie/pulz, "Let us aulsoe goe, that wee mae die witt Him."

Then, when Jesus kaem, Hee found that hee had aulred/ee bin in thu tuem foer daez. Nou Bethany wuz nir Jerusalem, ubout tuew mielz uwae. And me/nee uv thu Jewz kaem tue Martha and Mary tue kum/furt them kunsurn/ing ther bruthur. Then Martha, az suen az shee hurd that Jesus wuz kum/ing, went and met Him, but Mary wuz sit/ing in thu hous. Then Martha sed tue Jesus, "Lord, if Yue had bin hir, mie bruthur wood not hav died. But Ie noe that ee/vun nou, whotev/ur Yue ask uv God, God wil giv Yue." Jesus sed tue hur, "Yoor bruthur wil riez ugen." Martha sed tue Him, "Ie noe that hee wil riez ugen in thu rezurek/shun at thu last dae." Jesus sed tue hur, "Ie am thu rezurek/shun and thu lief. Hee hue buleevz in Mee, thoe hee mae die, hee shal liv. And hueev/ur livz and buleevz in Mee shal ne/vur die. Due yue buleev this?" Shee sed tue Him, "Yes, Lord, Ie buleev that Yue or thu Christ, thu Sun uv God, hue iz tue kum intue thu wurld." And when shee had sed theez ttingz, shee went hur wae and kauld Mary hur sis/tur see/krutlee, saeing, "Thu Tee/chur haz kum and iz kaul/ing for yue." Az suen az shee hurd that, shee uroez qik/lee and kaem tue Him.

Nou Jesus had not yet kum intue thu toun, but wuz in thu plaes wher Martha met Him. Then thu Jewz hue wur witt hur in thu hous, and kum/furting hur, when shee sau that Mary roez up qik/lee and went out, fol/oed hur, saeing, "Shee iz goeing tue thu tuem tue weep thar." Then, when Mary kaem wher Jesus woz, and sau Him, shee fel doun at Hiz feet, saeing tue Him, "Lord, if Yue had bin hir, mie bruthur wood not hav died." Tharfoer, when Jesus sau hur weeping, and thu Jewz hue kaem witt hur aulsoe weeping, Hee groend in thu spir/ut and wuz tru/buld. And Hee sed, "Wher hav yue laed him?" Thae sed tue Him, "Lord, kum and see." Jesus wept. Then thu Jewz sed, "See hou Hee luvd him!" And sum uv them sed, "Kood not this Man, hue oe/pund thee iez uv thu bliend, aulsoe hav kept this man frum die/ing?"

Then Jesus, ugen groen/ing in Himself, kaem tue thu tuem. It wuz u kaev, and u stoen lae ugenst it. Jesus sed, "Taek uwae thu stoen." Martha, thu sis/tur uv him hue wuz ded, sed tue Him, "Lord, bie this tiem ther iz u stench, for hee haz bin ded foer daez." Jesus sed tue hur, "Did Ie not sae tue yue that if yue wood buleev yue wood see thu gloer/ee uv God?" Then thae took uwae thu stoen frum thu plaes wher thu ded man wuz lie/ing. And Jesus lift/ud up Hiz iez and sed, "Foth/ur, Ie ttank Yue that Yue hav hurd Mee. And Ie noe that Yue aul/waez hir Mee, but bikauz uv thu pee/pul hue or standing bie Ie sed this, that thae mae buleev that Yue sent Mee." And when Hee had sed theez ttingz, Hee kried witt u loud vois, "Lazarus, kum foertt!" And hee hue had died kaem out bound hand and foot witt graev/kloethz, and hiz faes wuz rapt witt u klautt. Jesus sed tue them, "Lues him, and let him goe."

Then me/nee uv thu Jewz hue had kum tue Mary, and had seen thu ttingz Jesus did, buleevd in Him. But sum uv them went ther wae tue thu Phariseez and toeld them thu ttingz Jesus did.

Then thu cheef preests and thu Phariseez gath/urd u koun/sul and sed, "Whot shal wee due? For this Man wurks me/nee sienz. If wee let Him uloen liek this, evreewun wil buleev in Him, and thu Romanz/Roe/munz/ wil kum and taek uwae boett our plaes and nae/shun." And wun uv them, Caiaphas/Kae/ufus/, beeing hie preest that yir, sed tue them, "Yue noe nutt/ing at aul, nor due yue kunsid/ur that it iz ixpee/deeunt fur us that wun man shood die fur thu pee/pul, and not that thu hoel nae/shun shood perish." And this hee did not sae aun hiz oen ut-tor/utee; but beeing hie preest that yir, hee prof/usied that Jesus wood die fur thu nae/shun, and not fur that nae/shun oen/lee, but aulsoe that Hee wood gath/ur tugeth/ur in wun thu chil/drun uv God hue wur skat/urd ubraud. Then frum that dae aun thae plot/ud tue poot Him tue dett.

Tharfoer Jesus noe laung/gur waukt oe/punlee umung thu Jewz, but went frum thar intue thu kun/tree nir thu wil/durnus, tue u sit/ee kauld Ephraim/Ee/fraeim/, and ther rimaend witt Hiz disie/pulz. And thu Pas/oevur uv thu Jewz wuz nir, and me/nee went frum thu kun/tree up tue Jerusalem bifoer thu Pas/oevur, tue pyoor/ufie themselvz. Then thae saut Jesus, and spoek umung themselvz az thae stood in thu tem/pul, "Whot due yue ttink—that Hee wil not kum tue thu feest?"

Nou boett thu cheef preests and thu Phariseez had giv/un u kumand, that if eneewun nue wher Hee woz, hee shood ripoert it, that thae miet seez Him.

12

Then, six daez bifoer thu Pasoevur, Jesus kaem tue Bethany, wher Lazarus woz hue had bin ded, huem Hee raezd frum thu ded. Thar thae maed Him u sup/ur; and Martha survd, but Lazarus wuz wun uv thoez hue sat at thu tae/bul witt Him. Then Mary took u pound uv veree kaust/lee oil uv spiek/nord, unoin/tud thu feet uv Jesus, and wiept Hiz feet witt hur har. And thu hous wuz fild witt thu frae/gruns uv thee oil. Then wun uv Hiz disie/pulz, Judas Iscariot, Simon'z sun, hue wood bitrae Him, sed, "Whie wuz this frae/grunt oil not soeld fur ttree hun/drud denarii and giv/un tue thu poor?" This hee sed, not that hee kard fur thu poor, but bikauz hee wuz u tteef, and had thu mun/ee box, and yues tue taek whot wuz poot in it. Then Jesus sed, "Let hur uloen; shee haz kept this fur thu dae uv Mie ber/eeul. For thu poor yue hav witt yue aul/waez, but Mee yue due not hav aul/waez."

Then u graet me/nee uv thu Jewz nue that Hee wuz thar; and thae kaem, not fur Jesus' saek oen/lee, but that thae miet aulsoe see Lazarus, huem Hee had raezd frum thu ded. But thu cheef preests took koun/sul that thae miet aulsoe poot Lazarus tue dett, bikauz aun ukount uv him me/nee uv thu Jewz went uwae and buleevd in Jesus.

Thu next dae u graet mul/tutued that had kum tue thu feest, when thae hurd that Jesus wuz kum/ing tue Jerusalem, took branch/uz uv polm treez, went out tue meet Him, and kried out:
"Hosanna/Hoezan/u/!
*'Bles/ud iz Hee hue kumz in thu
naem uv thu* Lord!'
Thu King uv Israel!"
And Jesus, when Hee had found u yung daunk/ee, sat aun it; az it iz rit/un:
*"Fir not, daut/ur uv Zion/Zie/un/;
Bihoeld, yoor King iz kum/ing,
Sit/ing aun u daunk/ee'z koelt."*
Hiz disie/pulz did not undurstand theez ttingz at furst; but when Jesus wuz gloer/ufied, then thae rimem/burd that theez ttingz wur rit/un ubout Him and that thae had dun theez ttingz tue Him. Tharfoer thu pee/pul, hue wur witt Him when Hee kauld Lazarus out uv hiz tuem and raezd him frum thu ded, boer wit/nus. For this reez/un thu pee/pul aulsoe met Him, bikauz thae hurd that Hee had dun this sien. Thu Phariseez tharfoer sed umung themselvz, "Yue see that yue or ukom/plishing nutt/ing. Look, thu wurld haz gaun af/tur Him!"

And ther wur sur/tun Greeks umung thoez hue kaem up tue wur/shup at thu feest. Then thae kaem tue Philip, hue wuz frum Bethsaida uv Galilee, and askt him, saeing, "Sur, wee wish tue see Jesus." Philip kaem and toeld Andrew, and ugen Andrew and Philip toeld Jesus. And Jesus an/surd them, saeing, "Thee our haz kum that thu Sun uv Man shood bee gloer/ufied. Moest ushoor/udlee, Ie sae tue yue, unles u graen uv wheet faulz intue thu ground and diez, it rimaenz uloen; but if it diez, it produes/uz much graen. Hee hue luvz hiz lief wil luez it, and hee hue haets hiz lief in this wurld wil keep it tue itur/nul lief. If eneewun survz Mee, let him fol/oe Mee; and wher Ie am, thar Mie sur/vunt wil bee aulsoe. If eneewun survz Mee, him Mie Foth/ur wil on/ur.

"Nou Mie soel iz tru/buld, and whot shal Ie sae? 'Foth/ur, saev Mee frum this our'? But fur this pur/pus Ie kaem tue this our. Foth/ur, gloer/ufie Yoor naem." Then u vois kaem frum he/vun, saeing, "Ie hav boett gloer/ufied it and wil gloer/ufie it ugen." Tharfoer thu pee/pul hue stood bie and hurd it sed that it ttund/urd. Uth/urz sed, "An aenj/ul spoek tue Him." Jesus an/surd and sed, "This vois did not kum bikauz uv Mee, but fur yoor saek. Nou iz thu juj/munt uv this wurld; nou thu rue/lur uv this wurld wil bee kast out. And Ie, if Ie am lift/ud up frum thee urtt, wil drau aul men tue Mieself." This Hee sed, sig/nufieing bie whot dett Hee wood die. Thu pee/pul an/surd Him, "Wee hav hurd frum thu lau that thu Christ rimaenz furev/ur; and hou iz it Yue sae, 'Thu Sun uv Man must bee lift/ud up'? Hue iz this Sun uv Man?" Then Jesus sed tue them, "U litul whiel laung/gur thu liet iz witt yue. Wauk whiel yue hav thu liet, lest dork/nus oevurtaek yue, fur hee hue wauks in dork/nus duz not noe wher hee iz goeing. Whiel yue hav thu liet, buleev in thu liet, that yue mae bikum sunz uv liet." Theez ttingz Jesus spoek, and diport/ud, and wuz hid/un frum them. But thoe Hee had dun soe me/nee sienz bifoer them, thae did not buleev in Him, that thu wurd uv Isaiah thu pro/fut miet bee foolfild, which hee spoek:

>"Lord, hue haz buleevd our ripoert?
>
>And tue huem haz thee orm uv thu
>
>Lord bin riveeld?"

Tharfoer thae kood not buleev, bikauz Isaiah sed ugen:

>"Hee haz bliend/ud ther iez and hord/und ther hort,
>That thae shood not see witt ther iez,
>Nor undurstand witt ther hort,
>And turn ugen, and Ie shood heel them."

Theez ttingz Isaiah sed when hee sau Hiz gloer/ee and spoek uv Him. Nevurthules ee/vun umung thu rue/lurz me/nee buleevd in Him, but bikauz uv thu Phariseez thae did not kunfes Him, lest thae bee poot out uv thu sin/ugog; fur thae luvd thu praez uv men moer than thu praez uv God.

Then Jesus kried out and sed, "Hee hue buleevz in Mee, buleevz not in Mee but in Him hue sent Mee. And hee hue seez Mee seez Him hue sent Mee. Ie hav kum az u liet intue thu wurld, that hueev/ur buleevz in Mee shood not ubied in dork/nus. And if eneewun hirz Mie wurdz, and duz not buleev, Ie due not juj him; fur Ie did not kum tue juj thu wurld but tue saev thu wurld. Hee hue rijekts Mee, and duz not riseev Mie wurdz, haz that which juj/uz him—thu wurd that Ie hav spoek/un wil juj him in thu last dae. For Ie hav not spoek/un aun Mie oen uttor/utee; but thu Foth/ur hue sent Mee gaev Mee u kumand, whot Ie shood sae and whot Ie shood speek. And Ie noe that Hiz kumand iz evurlast/ing lief. Tharfoer, whotev/ur Ie speek, just az thu Foth/ur sed tue Mee, soe Ie speek."

13

Nou bifoer thu feest uv thu Pas/oevur, when Jesus nue that Hiz our had kum that Hee shood diport out uv this wurld tue thu Foth/ur, having luvd Hiz oen hue wur in thu wurld, Hee luvd them tue thee end. And sup/ur beeing end/ud, thu dev/ul having aulred/ee poot it intue thu hort uv Judas Iscariot, Simon'z sun, tue bitrae Him, Jesus, noeing that thu Foth/ur had giv/un aul ttingz intue Hiz handz, and that Hee had kum frum God and wuz goeing tue God, roez frum sup/ur, laed usied Hiz gor/munts, took u toul, and gurd/ud Himself. Af/tur that, Hee poerd wotur intue u baes/un and bigan tue wosh thu disie/pulz' feet, and tue wiep them witt thu toul witt which Hee wuz gurd/ud. Then Hee kaem tue Simon Peter. And Peter sed tue Him, "Lord, or Yue wosh/ing mie feet?" Jesus an/surd and sed tue him, "Whot Ie am dueing yue due not undurstand nou, but yue wil noe af/tur this." Peter sed

Appendix 4

tue Him, "Yue shal ne/vur wosh mie feet!" Jesus an/surd him, "If Ie due not wosh yue, yue hav noe port witt Mee." Simon Peter sed tue Him, "Lord, not mie feet oen/lee, but aulsoe mie handz and mie hed!" Jesus sed tue him, "Hee hue iz baethd needz oen/lee tue wosh hiz feet, but iz kumpleet/lee kleen; and yue or kleen, but not aul uv yue." For Hee nue hue wood bitrae Him; tharfoer Hee sed, "Yue or not aul kleen."

Soe when Hee had wosht ther feet, tae/kun Hiz gor/munts, and sat doun ugen, Hee sed tue them, "Due yue noe whot Ie hav dun tue yue? Yue kaul Mee Tee/chur and Lord, and yue sae wel, fur soe Ie am. If Ie then, yoor Lord and Tee/chur, hav wosht yoor feet, yue aulsoe aut tue wosh wun unuth/ur'z feet. For Ie hav giv/un yue an igzam/pul, that yue shood due az Ie hav dun tue yue. Moest ushoor/udlee, Ie sae tue yue, u sur/vunt iz not grae/tur than hiz mas/tur; nor iz hee hue iz sent grae/tur than hee hue sent him. If yue noe theez ttingz, hap/ee or yue if yue due them. Ie due not speek kunsurn/ing aul uv yue. Ie noe huem Ie hav choez/un; but that thu Skrip/chur mae bee foolfild, *'Hee hue eets bred witt Mee haz lift/ud up hiz heel ugenst Mee.'* Nou Ie tel yue bifoer it kumz, that when it kumz tue pas, yue mae buleev that Ie am Hee. Moest ushoor/udlee, Ie sae tue yue, hee hue riseevz huemev/ur Ie send riseevz Mee; and hee hue riseevz Mee riseevz Him hue sent Mee."

When Jesus had sed theez ttingz, Hee wuz tru/buld in spir/ut, and test/ufied and sed, "Moest ushoor/udlee, Ie sae tue yue, wun uv yue wil bitrae Mee." Then thu disie/pulz lookt at wun unuth/ur, purplext ubout huem Hee spoek. Nou ther wuz leen/ing aun Jesus' boozum wun uv Hiz disie/pulz, huem Jesus luvd. Simon Peter tharfoer nod/ud tue him, that hee shood ask hue it woz ov huem Hee spoek. Then, leen/ing bak aun Jesus' chest, hee sed tue Him, "Lord, hue iz it?" Jesus an/surd, "It iz hee tue huem Ie shal giv u pees uv bred when Ie hav dipt it." And having dipt thu bred, Hee gaev it tue Judas Iscariot, thu sun uv Simon. And af/tur thu pees uv bred, Satan/Saet/un/ ent/urd him. Then Jesus sed tue him, "Whot yue due, due qik/lee." Nou noe wun at thu tae/bul nue fur whot reez/un Hee sed this tue him. For sum uv them ttaut, bikauz Judas had thu mun/ee box, that Jesus had sed tue him, "Bie thoez ttingz wee need fur thu feest," or that hee shood giv sum/tting tue thu poor. Having riseevd thu pees uv bred, hee then went out imee/deeutlee. And it wuz niet.

Then, when hee had gaun out, Jesus sed, "Nou thu Sun uv Man iz gloer/ufied, and God iz gloer/ufied in Him. If God iz gloer/ufied in Him, God wil aulsoe gloer/ufie Him in Himself, and gloer/ufie Him imee/deeutlee. Litul chil/drun, Ie shal bee witt yue u litul whiel laung/gur. Yue wil seek Mee; and az Ie sed tue thu Jewz, 'Wher Ie am goeing, yue kanot kum,' soe nou Ie sae tue yue. U nue kumand/munt Ie giv tue yue, that yue luv wun unuth/ur; az Ie hav luvd

253

yue, that yue aulsoe luv wun unuth/ur. Bie this aul wil noe that yue or Mie disie/pulz, if yue hav luv fur wun unuth/ur."

Simon Peter sed tue Him, "Lord, wher or yue gocing?" Jesus an/surd him, "Wher Ie am goeing yue kanot fol/oe Mee nou, but yue shal fol/oe Mee af/turwurd." Peter sed tue Him, "Lord, whie kan Ie not fol/oe Yue nou? Ie wil lae doun mie lief fur Yoor saek." Jesus an/surd him, "Wil yue lae doun yoor lief fur Mie saek? Moest ushoor/udlee, Ie sae tue yue, thu rues/tur shal not kroe til yue hav dinied Mee ttree tiemz."

14

"Let not yoor hort bee tru/buld; yue buleev in God, buleev aulsoe in Mee. In Mie Foth/ur'z hous or me/nee dweling plaes/uz; if it wur not soe, Ie wood hav toeld yue. Ie goe tue pripar u plaes fur yue. And if Ie goe and pripar u plaes fur yue, Ie wil kum ugen and riseev yue tue Mieself; that wher Ie am, thar yue mae bee aulsoe. And wher Ie goe yue noe, and thu wae yue noe." Thomas sed tue Him, "Lord, wee due not noe wher Yue or goeing, and hou kan wee noe thu wae?" Jesus sed tue him, "Ie am thu wae, thu truett, and thu lief. Noe wun kumz tue thu Foth/ur ix/ept ttrue Mee. If yue had noen Mee, yue wood hav noen Mie Foth/ur aulsoe; and frum nou aun yue noe Him and hav seen Him." Philip sed tue Him, "Lord, shoe us thu Foth/ur, and it iz sufish/unt fur us." Jesus sed tue him, "Hav Ie bin witt yue soe laung, and yet yue hav not noen Mee, Philip? Hee hue haz seen Mee haz seen thu Foth/ur; soe hou kan yue sae, 'Shoe us thu Foth/ur'? Due yue not buleev that Ie am in thu Foth/ur, and thu Foth/ur in Mee? Thu wurdz that Ie speek tue yue Ie due not speek aun Mie oen uttor/utee; but thu Foth/ur hue dwelz in Mee duz thu wurks. Buleev Mee that Ie am in thu Foth/ur and thu Foth/ur in Mee, or els buleev Mee fur thu saek uv thu wurks themselvz. Moest ushoor/udlee, Ie sae tue yue, hee hue buleevz in Mee, thu wurks that Ie due hee wil due aulsoe; and grae/tur wurks than theez hee wil due, bikauz Ie goe tue Mie Foth/ur. And whotev/ur yue ask in Mie naem, that Ie wil due, that thu Foth/ur mae bee gloer/ufied in thu Sun. If yue ask eneetting in Mie naem, Ie wil due it. If yue luv Mee, keep Mie kumand/munts. And Ie wil prae thu Foth/ur, and Hee wil giv yue unuth/ur Help/ur, that Hee mae ubied witt yue furev/ur, ee/vun thu Spir/ut uv truett, huem thu wurld kanot riseev, bikauz it neeth/ur seez Him nor noez Him; but yue noe Him, fur Hee dwelz witt yue and wil bee in yue. Ie wil not leev yue aur/funz; Ie wil kum tue yue. U litul whiel laung/gur and thu wurld wil see Mee noe moer, but yue wil see Mee. Bikauz Ie liv, yue wil liv aulsoe. At that dae yue wil noe that Ie am in Mie Foth/ur, and yue in Mee, and Ie in yue. Hee hue haz Mie kumand/munts and keeps them, it iz hee hue luvz Mee. And hee hue luvz Mee wil bee luvd bie Mie Foth/ur, and Ie wil luv him and man/ufest Mieself tue him." Judas

Appendix 4

(not Iscariot) sed tue Him, "Lord, hou iz it that Yue wil man/ufest Yurself tue us, and not tue thu wurld?" Jesus an/surd and sed tue him, "If enee wun luvz Mee, hee wil keep Mie wurd; and Mie Foth/ur wil luv him, and Wee wil kum tue him and maek Our hoem witt him. Hee hue duz not luv Mee duz not keep Mie wurdz; and thu wurd which yue hir iz not Mien but thu Foth/ur'z hue sent Mee.

"Theez ttingz Ie hav spoek/un tue yue whiel beeing prez/unt witt yue. But thu Help/ur, thu Hoe/lee Spir/ut, huem thu Foth/ur wil send in Mie naem, Hee wil teech yue aul ttingz, and bring tue yoor rimem/bruns aul ttingz that Ie sed tue yue. Pees Ie leev witt yue, Mie pees Ie giv tue yue; not az thu wurld givz due Ie giv tue yue. Let not yoor hort bee tru/buld, neeth/ur let it bee ufraed. Yue hav hurd hou Ie sed tue yue, 'Ie am goeing uwae and kum/ing bak tue yue.' If yue luvd Mee, yue wood rijois bikauz Ie sed, 'Ie am goeing tue thu Foth/ur,' fur Mie Foth/ur iz grae/tur than Ie. And nou Ie hav toeld yue bifoer it kumz tue pas, that when it kumz tue pas, yue mae buleev. Ie wil noe laung/gur tauk much witt yue, fur thu rue/lur uv this wurld iz kum/ing, and hee haz nutt/ing in Mee. But that thu wurld mae noe that Ie luv thu Foth/ur, and az thu Foth/ur gaev Mee kumand/munt, soe Ie due. Uriez, let us goe frum hir."

15

"**Ie am thu true vien**, and Mie Foth/ur iz thu vien/dresur. Evree branch in Mee that duz not bar fruet Hee taeks uwae; and evree branch that barz fruet Hee pruenz, that it mae bar moer fruet. Yue or aulred/ee kleen bikauz uv thu wurd which Ie hav spoek/un tue yue. Ubied in Mee, and Ie in yue. Az thu branch kanot bar fruet ov itself, unles it ubiedz in thu vien, neeth/ur kan yue, unles yue ubied in Mee. Ie am thu vien, yue or thu branch/uz. Hee hue ubiedz in Mee, and Ie in him, barz much fruet; fur wittout Mee yue kan due nutt/ing. If enee wun duz not ubied in Mee, hee iz kast out az u branch and iz with/urd; and thae gath/ur them and ttroe them intue thu fier, and thae or burnd. If yue ubied in Mee, and Mie wurdz ubied in yue, yue shal ask whot yue dizier, and it shal bee dun fur yue. Bie this Mie Foth/ur iz gloer/ufied, that yue bar much fruet; soe yue wil bee Mie disie/pulz. Az thu Foth/ur luvd Mee, Ie aulsoe hav luvd yue; kuntin/yue in Mie luv. If yue keep Mie kumand/munts, yue wil ubied in Mie luv, just az Ie hav kept Mie Foth/ur'z kumand/munts and ubied in Hiz luv. Theez ttingz Ie hav spoek/un tue yue that Mie joi mae rimaen in yue, and that yoor joi mae bee fool. This iz Mie kumand/munt, that yue luv wun unuth/ur az Ie hav luvd yue. Grae/tur luv haz noe wun than this, that hee lae doun hiz lief fur hiz frendz. Yue or Mie frendz if yue due whotev/ur Ie kumand yue. Noe laung/gur due Ie kaul yue sur/vunts, fur u sur/vunt duz not noe whot hiz mas/tur iz dueing; but Ie hav kauld yue frendz, fur aul ttingz that Ie hav hurd frum Mie Foth/ur Ie hav maed noen tue yue. Yue hav not choez/un Mee, but Ie hav choez/un yue and upoint/ud yue that yue shood goe and bar fruet, and that yoor fruet shood rimaen, that whotev/ur yue ask thu Foth/ur in Mie naem Hee mae giv yue. Theez ttingz Ie kumand yue, that yue luv wun unuth/ur. If thu wurld haets yue, yue noe that it haet/ud Mee bifoer it haet/ud yue. If yue wur uv thu wurld, thu wurld wood luv its oen. Yet bikauz yue or not ov thu wurld, but Ie hav choez/un yue out uv thu wurld, tharfoer thu wurld haets yue. Rimem/bur thu wurd that Ie sed tue yue, 'U sur/vunt iz not grae/tur than hiz mas/tur.' If thae hav pur/sikyuetud Mee, thae wil aulsoe pur/sikyuet yue. If thae hav kept Mie wurd, thae wil keep yoorz aulsoe. But aul theez ttingz thae wil due tue yue fur Mie naem'z saek, bikauz thae due not noe Him hue sent Mee. If Ie had not kum and spoek/un tue them, thae wood hav noe sin, but nou thae hav noe ixkyues fur ther sin. Hee hue haets Mee haets Mie Foth/ur aulsoe. If Ie had not dun umung them thu wurks which noe wun els haz dun, thae wood hav noe sin; but nou thae hav seen and aulsoe haet/ud boett Mee and Mie Foth/ur. But this hap/und that thu wurd miet bee foolfild which iz rit/un in ther lau, '*Thae haet/ud Mee wittout u kauz.*' But when thu Help/ur kumz, huem Ie shal send tue yue frum thu Foth/ur, thu Spir/ut uv truett hue pruseedz frum thu Foth/ur, Hee wil tes/tufie uv Mee. And yue aulsoe wil bar wit/nus, bikauz yue hav bin witt Mee frum thu bigin/ing."

16

"**Theez ttingz** Ie hav spoek/un tue yue, that yue shood not bee maed tue stum/bul. Thae wil poot yue out uv thu sin/ugogz; yes, thu tiem iz kum/ing that hueev/ur kilz yue wil ttink that hee auf/urz God sur/vus. And theez ttingz thae wil due tue yue bikauz thae hav not noen thu Foth/ur nor Mee. But theez ttingz Ie hav toeld yue, that when thu tiem kumz, yue mae rimem/bur that Ie toeld yue uv them. And theez ttingz Ie did not sae tue yue at thu bigin/ing, bikauz Ie wuz witt yue. But nou Ie goe uwae tue Him hue sent Mee, and nun uv yue asks Mee, 'Wher or Yue goeing?' But bikauz Ie hav sed theez ttingz tue yue, sor/oe haz fild yoor hort. Nevurthules Ie tel yue thu truett. It iz tue yoor udvant/ij that Ie goe uwae; fur if Ie due not goe uwae, thu Help/ur wil not kum tue yue; but if Ie diport, Ie wil send Him tue yue. And when Hee haz kum, Hee wil kunvikt thu wurld uv sin, and uv rie/chusnus, and uv juj/munt: uv sin, bikauz thae due not buleev in Mee; uv rie/chusnus, bikauz Ie goe tue Mie Foth/ur and yue see Mee noe moer; uv juj/munt, bikauz thu rue/lur uv this wurld iz jujd. Ie stil hav me/nee ttingz tue sae tue yue, but yue kanot bar them nou. Houev/ur, when Hee, thu Spir/ut uv truett, haz kum, Hee wil gied yue intue aul truett; fur Hee wil not speek aun Hiz oen uttor/utee, but whotev/ur Hee hirz

Hee wil speek; and Hee wil tel yue ttingz tue kum. Hee wil gloer/ufie Mee, fur Hee wil taek uv whot iz Mien and diklar it tue yue. Aul ttingz that thu Foth/ur haz or Mien. Tharfoer Ie sed that Hee wil taek uv Mien and diklar it tue yue. U litul whiel, and yue wil not see Mee; and ugen u litul whiel, and yue wil see Mee, bikauz Ie goe tue thu Foth/ur." Then sum uv Hiz disie/pulz sed umung themselvz, "Whot iz this that Hee sez tue us, 'U litul whiel, and yue wil not see Mee; and ugen u litul whiel, and yue wil see Mee'; and, 'bikauz Ie goe tue thu Foth/ur'?" Thae sed tharfoer, "Whot iz this that Hee sez, 'U litul whiel'? Wee due not noe whot Hee iz saeing." Nou Jesus nue that thae dizierd tue ask Him, and Hee sed tue them, "Or yue inqier/ing umung yurselvz ubout whot Ie sed, 'U litul whiel and yue wil not see Mee, and ugen u litul whiel and yue wil see Mee'? Moest ushoor/udlee, Ie sae tue yue that yue wil weep and lument, but thu wurld wil rijois; and yue wil bee sor/uful, but yoor sor/oe wil bee turnd intue joi. U woomun, when shee iz in lae/bur, haz sor/oe bikauz hur our haz kum; but az suen az shee haz giv/un burtt tue thu chield, shee noe laung/gur rimem/burz thee ang/gwish, fur joi that u hyue/mun beeing haz bin boern intue thu wurld. And tharfoer yue nou hav sor/oe; but Ie wil see yue ugen and yoor hort wil rijois, and yoor joi noe wun wil taek frum yue. And in that dae yue wil ask Mee nutt/ing. Moest ushoor/udlee, Ie sae tue yue, whotev/ur yue ask thu Foth/ur in Mie naem Hee wil giv yue. Until nou yue hav askt nutt/ing in Mie naem. Ask and yue wil riseev, that yoor joi mae bee fool.

"Theez ttingz Ie hav spoek/un tue yue in fig/yurutiv lang/gwij; but thu tiem iz kum/ing when Ie wil noe laung/gur speek tue yue in fig/yurutiv lang/gwij, but Ie wil tel yue plaen/lee ubout thu Foth/ur. In that dae yue wil ask in Mie naem, and Ie due not sae tue yue that Ie shal prae thu Foth/ur fur yue; fur thu Foth/ur Himself luvz yue, bikauz yue hav luvd Mee, and hav buleevd that Ie kaem foertt frum God. Ie kaem foertt frum thu Foth/ur and hav kum intue thu wurld. Ugen, Ie leev thu wurld and goe tue thu Foth/ur." Hiz disie/pulz sed tue Him, "See, nou Yue or speeking plaen/lee, and yuez/ing noe fig/yur uv speech! Nou wee or shoor that Yue noe aul ttingz, and due not need that eneewun qes/chun Yue. Bie this wee buleev that Yue kaem foertt frum God." Jesus an/surd them, "Due yue nou buleev? Indeed, thee our iz kum/ing, ycs, haz nou kum, that yue wil bee skat/urd, eech tue hiz oen, and wil leev Mee uloen. And yet Ie am not uloen, bikauz thu Foth/ur iz witt Mee. Theez ttingz Ie hav spoek/un tue yue, that in Mee yue mae hav pees. In thu wurld yue wil hav tribyulae/shun; but bee uv good chir, Ie hav oevurkum thu wurld."

17

Jesus spoek theez wurdz, lift/ud up Hiz iez tue he/vun, and sed, "Foth/ur, thee our haz kum. Gloer/ufie Yoor Sun, that Yoor Sun aulsoe mae gloer/ufie Yue, az Yue hav giv/un Him uttor/utee oevur aul flesh, that Hee shood giv itur/nul lief tue az me/nee az Yue hav giv/un Him. And this iz itur/nul lief, that thae mae noe Yue, thee oen/lee true God, and Jesus Christ huem Yue hav sent. Ie hav gloer/ufied Yue aun thee urtt. Ie hav finisht thu wurk which Yue hav giv/un Mee tue due. And nou, Oe Foth/ur, gloer/ufie Mee tugeth/ur witt Yurself, witt thu gloer/ee which Ie had witt Yue bifoer thu wurld woz. Ie hav man/ufestud Yoor naem tue thu men huem Yue gaev Mee out uv thu wurld. Thae wur Yoorz, Yue gaev them tue Mee, and thae hav kept Yoor wurd. Nou thae hav noen that aul ttingz which Yue hav giv/un Mee or frum Yue. For Ie hav giv/un tue them thu wurdz which Yue gaev Mee; and thae hav riseevd them, and hav noen shoor/lee that Ie kaem foertt frum Yue; and thae hav buleevd that Yue sent Mee. Ie prae fur them. Ie due not prae fur thu wurld but fur thoez huem Yue hav giv/un Mee, fur thae or Yoorz. And aul Mien or Yoorz, and Yoorz or Mien, and Ie am gloer/ufied in them. And nou Ie am noe laung/gur in thu wurld, but theez or in thu wurld, and Ie kum tue Yue. Hoe/lee Foth/ur, keep ttrue Yoor naem thoez huem Yue hav giv/un Mee, that thae mae bee wun az Wee or. Whiel Ie wuz witt them in thu wurld, Ie kept them in Yoor naem. Thoez huem Yue gaev Mee Ie hav kept; and nun uv them iz laust ix/ept thu sun uv purd-ish/un, that thu Skrip/chur miet bee foolfild. But nou Ie kum tue Yue, and theez ttingz Ie speek in thu wurld, that thae mae hav Mie joi foolfild in them-selvz. Ie hav giv/un them Yoor wurd; and thu wurld haz haet/ud them bi-kauz thae or not ov thu wurld, just az Ie am not ov thu wurld. Ie due not prae that Yue taek them out uv thu wurld, but that Yue keep them frum thee ee/vul wun. Thae or not ov thu wurld, just az Ie am not ov thu wurld. Sank/tufie them bie Yoor truett. Yoor wurd iz truett. Az Yue hav sent Mee intue thu wurld, Ie aulsoe hav sent them intue thu wurld. And fur ther saeks Ie sank/tufie Mieself, that thae aulsoe mae bee sank/tufied bie thu truett. Ie due not prae fur theez uloen, but aulsoe fur thoez hue wil buleev in Mee ttrue ther wurd; that thae aul mae bee wun, az Yue, Foth/ur, or in Mee, and Ie in Yue; that thae aulsoe mae bee wun in Us, that thu wurld mae buleev that Yue hav sent Mee. And thu gloer/ee which Yue gaev Mee Ie hav giv/un them, that thae mae bee wun just az Wee or wun: Ie in them, and Yue in Mee; that thae mae bee maed pur/fikt in wun, and that thu wurld mae noe that Yue hav sent Mee, and hav luvd them az Yue hav luvd Mee. Foth/ur, Ie dizier that thae aulsoe huem Yue hav giv/un Mee mae bee witt Mee wher Ie am, that thae mae bihoeld Mie gloer/ee which Yue hav giv/un Mee; fur Yue luvd Mee bifoer thu foundae/shun uv thu wurld. Oe rie/chus Foth/ur! Thu wurld haz not noen Yue, but Ie hav noen Yue; and theez hav noen that

Appendix 4

Yue hav sent Mee. And Ie hav diklard tue them Yoor naem, and wil diklar it, that thu luv witt which Yue hav luvd Mee mae bee in them, and Ie in them."

18

When Jesus had spoek/un theez wurdz, Hee went out witt Hiz disie/pulz oevur thu Brook Kidron/Kid/run/, wher ther wuz u gord/un, which Hee and Hiz disie/pulz ent/urd. And Judas, hue bitraed Him, aulsoe nue thu plaes; fur Jesus auf/un met thar witt Hiz disie/pulz. Then Judas, having riseevd u band uv soel/jurz, and of/usurz frum thu cheef preests and Phariseez, kaem thar witt lant/urnz, taurch/uz, and we/punz. Jesus tharfoer, noeing aul ttingz that wood kum upon Him, went faur/wurd and sed tue them, "Huem or yue seeking?" Thae an/surd Him, "Jesus uv Nazareth." Jesus sed tue them, "Ie am Hee." And Judas, hue bitraed Him, aulsoe stood witt them. Then, az suen az Hee had sed tue them, "Ie am Hee," thae drue bak and fel tue thu ground. Then Hee askt them ugen, "Huem or yue seeking?" And thae sed, "Jesus uv Nazareth." Jesus an/surd, "Ie hav toeld yue that Ie am Hee. Tharfoer, if yue seek Mee, let theez goe ther wae," that thu saeing miet bee foolfild which Hee spoek, "Ov thoez huem Yue gaev Mee Ie hav laust nun." Then Simon Peter, having u soerd, drue it and struck thu hie preest's sur/vunt, and kut auf hiz riet ir. Thu sur/vunt's naem wuz Malchus/Mal/kus/. Then Jesus sed tue Peter, "Poot yoor soerd intue thu sheett. Shal Ie not drink thu kup which Mie Foth/ur haz giv/un Mee?"

Then thu band uv soel/jurz and ther kap/tun and thee of/usurz uv thu Jewz urest/ud Jesus and bound Him. And thae led Him uwae tue An-nas/An/us/ furst, fur hee wuz thu foth/ur-in-lau uv Caiaphas hue wuz hie preest that yir. Nou Caiaphas wuz hee hue gaev koun/sul tue thu Jewz that it wuz ixpee/deeunt that wun man shood die fur thu pee/pul.

And Simon Peter fol/oed Jesus, and soe did unuth/ur disie/pul. That disie/pul wuz noen tue thu hie preest, and went witt Jesus intue thu ko-ert/yord uv thu hie preest. But Peter stood at thu doer outsied. Then that uthur disie/pul, hue wuz noen tue hie preest, went out and spoek tue hur hue kept thu doer, and braut Peter in. Then thu sur/vunt gurl hue kept thu doer sed tue Peter, "Yue or not aulsoe wun uv this Man'z disie/pulz, or yue?" Hee sed, "Ie am not." And thu sur/vunts and of/usurz hue had maed u fier uv koelz stood thar, fur it wuz koeld, and thae waurmd themselvz. And Peter stood witt them and waurmd himself.

Thu hie preest then askt Jesus ub-out Hiz disie/pulz and Hiz dok/trun. Jesus an/surd him, "Ie spoek oe/punlee tue thu wurld. Ie aul/waez taut in thu sin/ugogz and in thu tem/pul, wher thu Jewz aul/waez meet, and in see/krut hav sed nutt/ing. Whie due yue ask Mee? Ask thoez hue hurd Mee whot Ie hav sed tue them. Indeed thae noe whot Ie sed." And when Hee had sed theez ttingz, wun uv thee of/usurz hue stood bie struk Jesus witt thu polm uv hiz hand, saeing, "Due Yue an/sur thu hie prccst lick that?" Jesus an/surd him, "If Ie hav spoek/un ee/vul, bar wit/nus uv thee ee/vul; but if wel, whie due yue striek Mee?" Then Annas sent Him bound tue Caiaphas thu hie preest.

And Simon Peter stood and waurmd himself. Tharfoer thae sed tue him, "Yue or not aulsoe wun uv Hiz disie/pulz, or yue?" Hee dinied it and sed, "Ie am not!" Wun uv thu sur/vunts uv thu hie preest, u rel/utiv uv him huez ir Peter kut auf, sed, "Did Ie not see yue in thu gord/un witt Him?" Peter then dinied ugen; and imee/deeutlee u rues/tur kroed.

Then thae led Jesus frum Caiaphas tue thu Praetorium/Preetoer/eeum/, and it wuz ur/lee maur/ning. And thae themselvz did not goe intue thu Praetorium, lest thae shood bee difield, but that thae miet eet thu Pas/oevur. Pilate/Pie/lut/ then went out tue them and sed, "Whot akyuzae/shun due yue bring ugenst this Man?" Thae an/surd and sed tue him, "If Hee wur not an eevuldue/ur, wee wood not hav diliv/urd Him up tue yue." Then Pilate sed tue them, "Yue taek Him and juj Him ukaurd/ing tue yoor lau." Tharfoer thu Jewz sed tue him, "It iz not lau/ful fur us tue poot eneewun tue dett," that thu saeing uv Jesus miet bee foolfild which Hee spoek, sig/nufieing bie whot dett Hee wood die.

Then Pilate ent/urd thu Praetorium ugen, kauld Jesus, and sed tue Him, "Or Yue thu King uv thu Jewz?" Jesus an/surd him, "Or yue speeking fur yurself, or did uth/urz tel yue this ubout Mee?" Pilate an/surd, "Am Ie u Jew? Yoor oen nae/shun and thu cheef preests hav diliv/urd Yue tue mee. Whot hav Yue dun?" Jesus an/surd, "Mie king/dum iz not uv this wurld. If Mie king/dum wur uv this wurld, then Mie sur/vunts wood fiet, soe that Ie shood not bee diliv/urd tue thu Jewz; but nou Mie king/dum iz not frum hir." Pilate tharfoer sed tue Him, "Or Yue u king then?" Jesus an/surd, "Yue sae riet/lee that Ie am u king. For this kauz Ie wuz boern, and fur this kauz Ie kaem intue thu wurld, that Ie shood bar wit/nus tue thu truett. Evreewun hue iz uv thu truett hirz Mie vois." Pilate sed tue Him, "Whot iz truett?" And when hee had sed this, hee went out ugen tue thu Jewz, and sed tue them, "Ie fiend noe fault in Him at aul. But yue hav u kus/tum that Ie shood rilees sum/wun tue yue at thu Pas/oevur. Due yue tharfoer wont mee tue rilees tue yue thu King uv thu Jewz?" Then thae aul kried ugen, saeing, "Not this Man, but Barabbas/Borab/us/!" Nou Barabbas wuz u rob/ur.

19

Soe Pilate then took Jesus and skurjd Him. And thu soel/jurz twist/ud u kroun out uv ttaurnz and poot it aun Hiz hed, and thae poot aun Him u pur/pul roeb. And thae sed,

Appendix 4

"Hael, King uv thu Jewz!" And thae struk Him witt ther handz. Pilate then went out ugen, and sed tue them, "Look, Ie am bringing Him out tue yue, that yue mae noe that Ie fiend noe fault in Him." Then Jesus kaem out, war/ing thu kroun uv ttaurnz and thu pur/pul roeb. And Pilate sed tue them, "Bihoeld thu Man!" Tharfoer, when thu cheef preests and of/usurz sau Him, thae kried out, saeing, "Krue/sufie Him, krue/sufie Him!" Pilate sed tue them, "Yue taek Him and krue/sufie Him, fur Ie fiend noe fault in Him." Thu Jewz an/surd him, "Wee hav u lau, and bie our lau Hee aut tue die, bikauz Hee maed Himself thu Sun uv God." Tharfoer, when Pilate hurd that saeing, hee wuz thu moer ufraed, and went ugen intue thu Praetorium, and sed tue Jesus, "Wher or Yue from?" But Jesus gaev him noe an/sur. Then Pilate sed tue Him, "Or Yue not speeking tue mee? Due Yue not noe that Ie hav pour tue krue/sufie Yue, and pour tue rilees Yue?" Jesus an/surd, "Yue kood hav noe pour at aul ugenst Mee unles it had bin giv/un yue frum ubuv. Tharfoer thu wun hue diliv/urd Mee tue yue haz thu grae/tur sin." Frum then aun Pilate saut tue rilees Him, but thu Jewz kried out, saeing, "If yue let this Man goe, yue or not Caesar'z/See/zur'z/ frend. Hueev/ur maeks himself u king speeks ugenst Caesar." When Pilate tharfoer hurd that saeing, hee braut Jesus out and sat doun in thu juj/munt seet in u plaes that iz kauld Thu Paev/munt, but in Hebrew, *Gabbatha/Gab/uttu/*.

And it wuz thu Prepurae/shun Dae uv thu Pas/oevur, and ubout thu sixtt our. And hee sed tue thu Jewz, "Bihoeld yoor King!" But thae kried out, "Uwae witt Him, uwae witt Him! Krue/sufie Him!" Pilate sed tue them, "Shal Ie krue/sufie yoor King?" Thu cheef preests an/surd, "Wee hav noe king but Caesar!" Soe then hee diliv/urd Him tue them tue bee krue/sufied. And thae took Jesus and led Him uwae.

And Hee, baring Hiz kraus, went out tue u plaes kauld thu Plaes uv u Skul, which iz kauld in Hebrew, *Gol-gotha/Gol/guttu/*, wher thae krue/sufied Him, and tuew uth/urz witt Him, wun aun ee/thur sied, and Jesus in thu sent/ur. And Pilate roet u tiet/ul and poot it aun thu kraus. And thu riet/ing wuz:

JESUS UV NAZARETH, THU KING UV THU JEWZ.

Then me/nee uv thu Jewz red this tiet/ul, fur thu plaes wher Jesus wuz krue/sufied wuz nir thu sit/ee; and it wuz rit/un in Hebrew, Greek, and Latin/Lat/un/. Then thu cheef preests uv thu Jewz sed tue Pilate, "Due not riet, 'Thu King uv thu Jewz,' but, 'Hee sed: Ie am King uv thu Jewz.'" Pilate an/surd, "Whot Ie hav rit/un, Ie hav rit/un."

Then thu soel/jurz, when thae had krue/sufied Jesus, took Hiz gor/munts and maed foer ports, tue eech soel/jur u port, and aulsoe Hiz tue/nik. Nou thu tue/nik wuz wittout seem, woe/vun frum thu top in wun pees.

Let's End Our Literacy Crisis

Thae sed tharfoer umung themselvz, "Let us not tar it, but kast lots fur it, huez it shal bee," that thu Skrip/chur miet bee foolfild which sez:

> *"Thae duvied/ud Mie gor/munts umung them,*
> *and fur Mie kloeth/ing thae kast lots."*

Tharfoer thu soel/jurz did theez ttingz. Nou ther stood bie thu kraus uv Jesus Hiz muth/ur, and Hiz muth/ur'z sis/tur, Mary thu wief uv Clopas/Kloe/pus/, and Mary Magdalene/Mag/duleen/. When Jesus tharfoer sau Hiz muth/ur, and thu disie/pul huem Hee luvd standing bie, Hee sed tue Hiz muth/ur, "Woomun, bihoeld yoor sun!" Then Hee sed tue thu disie/pul, "Bihoeld yoor muth/ur!" And frum that our that disie/pul took hur tue hiz oen hoem.

Af/tur this, Jesus, noeing that aul ttingz wur nou ukom/plisht, that thu Skrip/chur miet bee foolfild, sed, "Ie tturst!" Nou u ves/ul fool uv sour wien wuz sit/ing thar; and thae fild u spunj witt sour wien, poot it aun his/up, and poot it tue Hiz moutt. Soe when Jesus had riseevd thu sour wien, Hee sed, "It iz finisht!" And Hee boud Hiz hed, and gaev up Hiz spir/ut.

Tharfoer, bikauz it wuz thu Prepurae/shun Dae, that thu bod/eez shood not rimaen aun thu kraus aun thu Sabbath (for that Sabbath wuz u hie dae), thu Jewz askt Pilate that ther legz miet bee broe/kun, and that thae miet bee tae/kun uwae. Then thu soel/jurz kaem and broek thu legz uv thu furst and uv thee uthur hue wuz krue/sufied witt Him. But when thae kaem tue Jesus and sau that Hee wuz aulred/ee ded, thae did not braek Hiz legz. But wun uv thu soel/jurz pirst Hiz sied witt u spir, and imee/deeutlee blud and wotur kaem out. And hee hue sau it boer wit/nus, and hiz wit/nus iz true; and hee noez that hee iz tel/ing thu truett, that yue mae buleev. For theez ttingz wur dun that thu Skrip/chur shood bee foolfild, *"Not wun uv Hiz boenz shal bee broe/kun."* And ugen unuth/ur Skrip/chur sez, *"Thae wil look aun Him huem thae pirst."*

And af/tur this, Joseph uv Arimathea/Arimuttee/u/, beeing u disie/pul uv Jesus, but see/krutlee, fur fir uv thu Jewz, askt Pilate that hee miet taek uwae thu bo/dee uv Jesus; and Pilate gaev him purmish/un. Soe hee kaem and took thu bo/dee uv Jesus. And Nicodemus, hue at furst kaem tue Jesus bie niet, aulsoe kaem; and hee braut u mix/chur uv mur and al/oez, ubout u hun/drud poundz. Then thae took thu bo/dee uv Jesus, and bound it in strips uv lin/un witt thu spies/uz, az thu kus/tum uv thu Jewz iz tue ber/ee. Nou in thu plaes wher Hee wuz krue/sufied thar wuz u gord/un, and in thu gord/un u nue tuem in which noe wun had yet bin laed. Soe thar thae laed Jesus, bikauz uv thu Jewz' Prepurae/shun Dae, fur thu tuem wuz nirbie.

20

Thu furst dae uv thu week Mary Magdalene kaem tue thu tuem ur/lee,

Appendix 4

whiel it wuz stil dork, and sau thu stoen had bin tae/kun uwae frum thu tuem. Then shee ran and kaem tue Simon Peter, and tue thee uthur disie/pul, huem Jesus luvd, and sed tue them, "Thae hav tae/kun uwae thu Lord out uv thu tuem, and wee due not noe wher thae hav laed Him." Peter tharfoer went out, and thee uthur disie/pul, and kaem tue thu tuem. Soe thae boett ran tugeth/ur, and thee uthur disie/pul outran Peter and kaem tue thu tuem furst. And hee, stuep/ing doun and looking in, sau thu lin/un klauthz lie/ing thar; yet hee did not goe in. Then Simon Peter kaem, fol/uwing him, and went intue thu tuem; and hee sau thu lin/un klauthz lie/ing thar, and thu hank/urchuf that had bin uround Hiz hed, not lie/ing witt thu lin/un klauthz, but foeld/ud tugeth/ur in u plaes bie itself. Then thee uthur disie/pul, hue kaem tue thu tuem furst, went in aulsoe; and hee sau and buleevd. For az yet thae did not noe thu Skrip/chur, that Hee must riez ugen frum thu ded. Then thu disie/pulz went uwae ugen tue ther oen hoemz.

But Mary stood outsied bie thu tuem weeping, and az shee wept shee stuept doun and lookt intue thu tuem. And shee sau tuew aenj/ulz in whiet sit/ing, wun at thu hed and thee uthur at thu feet, wher thu bo/dee uv Jesus had laen. And thae sed tue hur, "Woomun, whie or yue weeping?" Shee sed tue them, "Bikauz thae hav tae/kun uwae mie Lord, and Ie due not noe wher thae hav laed Him." And when shee had sed this, shee turnd uround and sau Jesus standing thar, and did not noe that it wuz Jesus. Jesus sed tue hur, "Woomun, whie or yue weeping? Huem or yue seeking?" Shee, supoez/ing Him tue bee thu gord/nur, sed tue Him, "Sur, if Yue hav kar/eed Him uwae, tel mee wher Yue hav laed Him, and Ie wil taek Him uwae." Jesus sed tue hur, "Mary!" Shee turnd and sed tue Him, *"Rabboni/Ruboe/nie/!"* (which iz tue sae, Tee/chur). Jesus sed tue hur, "Due not kling tue Mee, fur Ie hav not yet usend/ud tue Mie Foth/ur; but goe tue Mie breth/run and sae tue them, 'Ie am usend/ing tue Mie Foth/ur and yoor Foth/ur, and tue Mie God and yoor God.'" Mary Magdalene kaem and toeld thu disie/pulz that shee had seen thu Lord, and that Hee had spoek/un theez ttingz tue hur.

Then, thu saem dae at eev/ning, beeing thu furst dae uv thu week, when thu doerz wur shut wher thu disie/pulz wur usem/buld, fur fir uv thu Jewz, Jesus kaem and stood in thu midst, and sed tue them, "Pees bee witt yue." And when Hee had sed this, Hee shoed them Hiz handz and Hiz sied. Then thu disie/pulz wur glad when thae sau thu Lord. Then Jesus sed tue them ugen, "Pees bee witt yue. Az Mie Foth/ur haz sent Mee, Ie aulsoe send yue." And when Hee had sed this, Hee breethd aun them, and sed tue them, "Riseev thu Hoe/lee Spir/ut. If yue furgiv thu sinz uv enee, thae or furgiv/un them; and if yue ritaen thu sinz uv enee, thae or ritaend."

But Thomas, kauld Didymus, wun uv thu twelv, wuz not witt them when

263

Jesus kaem. Thee uthur disie/pulz tharfoer sed tue him, "Wee hav seen thu Lord." But hee sed tue them, "Unles Ie see in Hiz handz thu print uv thu naelz, poot mie fing/gur intue thu print uv thu naelz, and poot mie hand intue Hiz sied, Ie wil not buleev."

And af/tur aet daez Hiz disie/pulz wur ugen insied, and Thomas witt them. Jesus kaem, thu doerz beeing shut, and stood in thu midst, and sed, "Pees bee witt yue." Then Hee sed tue Thomas, "Reech yoor fing/gur hir, and look at Mie handz; and reech yoor hand hir, and poot it intue Mie sied. And due not bee unbuleev/ing, but buleev/ing." And Thomas an/surd and sed tue Him, "Mie Lord and mie God!" Jesus sed tue him, "Thomas, bikauze yue hav seen Mee, yue hav buleevd. Bles/ud or thoez hue hav not seen and yet hav buleevd."

And true/lee Jesus did me/nee ut/hur sienz in thu prez/uns uv Hiz disie/pulz, which or not rit/un in this book; but theez or rit/un that yue mae buleev that Jesus iz thu Christ, thu Sun uv God, and that buleeving yue mae hav lief in Hiz naem.

21

Af/tur theez ttingz Jesus shoed Himself ugen tue thu disie/pulz at thu See uv Tiberias, and in this wae Hee shoed Himself: Simon Peter, Thomas kauld Didymus, Nathanael uv Cana in Galilee, thu sunz uv Zebedee/Zeb/idee/, and tuew uth/urz uv Hiz disie/pulz wur tugeth/ur. Simon Peter sed tue them, "Ie am goeing fishing." Thae sed tue him, "Wee or goeing witt yue aulsoe." Thae went out and imee/deeutlee got intue thu boet, and that niet thae kaut nutt/ing. But when thu maur/ning had nou kum, Jesus stood aun thu shoer; yet thu disie/pulz did not noe that it wuz Jesus. Then Jesus sed tue them, "Boiz, hav yue enee fued?" Thae an/surd Him, "Noe." And Hee sed tue them, "Kast thu net aun thu riet sied uv thu boet, and yue wil fiend sum." Soe thae kast, and nou thae wur not ae/bul tue drau it in bikauz uv thu mul/tutued uv fish. Tharfoer that disie/pul huem Jesus luvd sed tue Peter, "It iz thu Lord!" Nou when Simon Peter hurd that it wuz thu Lord, hee poot aun hiz out/ur gor/munt (for hee wuz war/ing oen/lee an un/durgormunt), and plunjd intue thu see. And thee uthur disie/pulz kaem in thu litul boet (for thae wur not for frum land, but ubout tuew hun/drud kyue/buts), drag/ing thu net witt fish. Then, az suen az thae had kum tue land, thae sau u fier uv koelz thar, and fish laed aun it, and bred. Jesus sed tue them, "Bring sum uv thu fish which yue hav just kaut." Simon Peter went up and dragd thu net tue land, fool uv lorj fish, wun hun/drud and fif/teettree; and aulthoe ther wur soe me/nee, thu net wuz not broe/kun. Jesus sed tue them, "Kum and eet brek/fust." And nun uv thu disie/pulz dard ask Him, "Hue or Yue?"—noeing that it wuz thu Lord. Jesus then kaem and took thu bred and gaev it tue them, and lie/kwiez thu fish. This iz nou thu tturd tiem

Appendix 4

Jesus shoed Himself tue Hiz disie/pulz af/tur Hee wuz raezd frum thu ded.

Soe when thae had eet/un brek/fust, Jesus sed tue Simon Peter, "Simon, sun uv Jonah, due yue luv Mee moer than theez?" Hee sed tue Him, "Yes, Lord; Yue noe that Ie luv Yue." Hee sed tue him, "Feed Mie lamz." Hee sed tue him ugen u se/kund tiem, "Simon, sun uv Jonah, due yue luv Mee?" Hee sed tue Him, "Yes, Lord; Yue noe that Ie luv Yue." Hee sed tue him, "Tend Mie sheep." Hee sed tue him thu tturd tiem, "Simon, sun uv Jonah, due yue luv Mee?" Peter wuz greevd bikauz Hee sed tue him thu tturd tiem, "Due yue luv Mee?" And hee sed tue Him,

"Lord, Yue noe aul ttingz; Yue noe that Ie luv Yue." Jesus sed tue him, "Feed Mie sheep. Moest ushoor/udlee, Ie sae tue yue, when yue wur yung/gur, yue gurd/ud yurself and waukt wher yue wisht; but when yue or oeld, yue wil strech out yoor handz, and unuth/ur wil gurd yue and kar/ee yue wher yue due not wish." This Hee spoek, sig/nufieing bie whot dett hee wood gloer/ufie God. And when Hee had spoek/un this, Hee sed tue him, "Fol/oe Mee." Then Peter, turning uround, sau thu disie/pul huem Jesus luvd fol/uwing, hue aulsoe had leend aun Hiz chest at thu sup/ur, and had sed, "Lord, hue iz thu wun hue bitraez Yue?" Peter, seeing him, sed tue Jesus, "Lord, and whot wil this man due?" Jesus sed tue him, "If Ie wil that hee rimaen til Ie kum, whot iz that tue yue? Yue fol/oe Mee." Then this saeing went out umung thu breth/run that this disie/pul wood not die. Yet Jesus did not sae tue him that hee wood not dic, but, "If Ie wil that hee rimaen til Ie kum, whot iz that tue yue?"

This iz thu disie/pul hue tes/tufiez uv theez ttingz, and roet theez ttingz; and wee noe that hiz testumoe/nee iz true.

And ther or aulsoe me/nee uthur ttingz that Jesus did, which if thae wur rit/un wun bie wun, Ie supoez that ee/vun thu wurld itself kood not kuntaen thu books that wood bee rit/un. Aemen.

[1] The Bible text in appendix 4 is adapted from *The New King James Bible—New Testament*. Copyright © Thomas Nelson, Inc. Used by permission.

Appendix 5
Creative Problem Solving

Although the solutions to the problems in this exercise are trivial compared to the seriousness of the illiteracy problem, the *solution* of the problems is not the point. The point is to help you discover something about *how* we solve problems.

These problems are adapted from the July 21, 1977 *Machine Design* magazine article "Games That Stimulate" by Eugene Raudsepp. The article includes one or more problems in each of thirteen very different types of problems. The purpose of these problems is to increase your creativity by giving you a chance to find innovative ways of solving problems, so give it a try. You will probably learn something valuable that will help with many of the problems you encounter.

Problem One

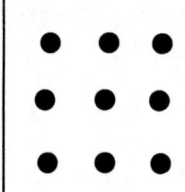

Connect all nine dots with the minimum number of straight lines. You cannot retrace any line and you cannot pick up your pen, pencil, etc. after completing one line and before starting another; that is, every line you draw must be connected to any other line you draw. Do not go through any dot more than once.

Problem Two

Ten coins are to be arranged into rows as shown at right. Move just two coins to another position so there are two rows containing six coins each when added horizontally or vertically.

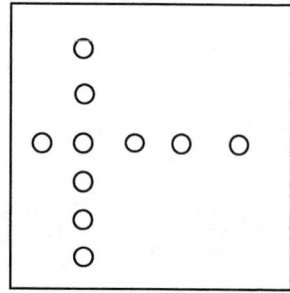

Problem Three

Using six kitchen matches, make four equilateral triangles. (You cannot cut, break, or bend the matches.)

Problem Four

Add one line to the roman numeral XI, and end up with the number ten. Try for at least three different solutions.

Appendix 5

(Solutions on following pages)

Problem Solutions

Problem One

If you unnecessarily limit yourself to drawing all the lines inside the box, you will need five lines. (There are many solutions with five lines.) If you unnecessarily limit yourself to drawing the lines through the center of the dots, it can be solved with four lines (fig. 1). If you unnecessarily limit yourself to leaving the paper unfolded, it can be solved with three lines (fig. 2). If you unnecessarily limit yourself to using a pencil or fine tip pen, it can be solved with one line plus some very fancy paper folding (fig. 3). If you unnecessarily limit yourself to a wide-tipped felt tip pen and some very simple paper folding, it can also be solved with one line (fig. 4). The ultimate solution however, is one line with no paper folding: use a brush wider than the width of the three dots. None of these solutions is prohibited in the statement of the problem.

Problem Two

Move the rightmost coin to the left of the leftmost coin and place the bottom coin on the middle coin. Most people (if they think of it) assume they cannot stack the coins, but the statement of the problem does not prohibit it.

Problem Three

See figure 5. Most people unnecessarily limit themselves to a two-dimensional solution. It cannot be solved in two dimensions.

Problem Four

If you unnecessarily limit yourself to straight lines, there are at least four solutions. The most obvious solution is to add a fraction bar between the X and the I: X/I. Solution 2: draw a line through the I changing it to a plus sign (ten plus nothing is ten). Solution 3: draw a horizontal line through both the X and the I separating it into a VI (six) and an upside-down IV (four), totaling ten. Solution 4: rotate the page ninety degrees clockwise and add a 1 below the I to yield X/1 (with the I becoming the crossbar). There are also at least three more solutions:

Appendix 5

(1) put a proofreader's delete mark (like a pigtail) through the I, leaving only the X; (2) place a square-root sign over the I (ten times the square root of one is ten); and (3) add the written word "ten" (still to be recognized as a single line) before XI making the X a times sign (ten times one is ten). The statement of the problem does not rule out any of these solutions.

As you probably discovered, we have a strong tendency to confine ourselves within nonexistent limits and to make baseless assumptions when attempting to solve problems. The longer we strive within these nonexistent limits, the more likely we are to think they cannot be exceeded.

Let's End Our Literacy Crisis

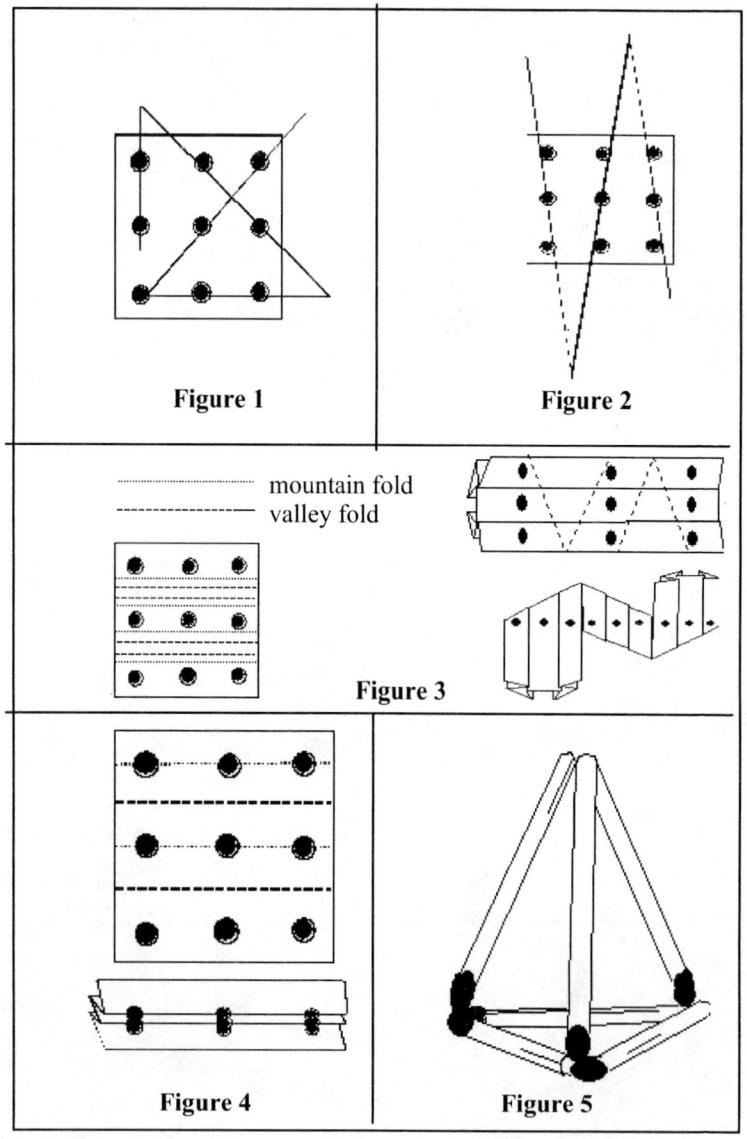

Appendix 6
Comparing Our Proposal with Other Proposals

Four chapters, a total of ninety-two pages, of Pitman's book *Alphabets and Reading* show the results of research and testimonial letters from teachers and school administrators concerning i.t.a. (initial teaching alphabet). There are 124 testimonial letters from administrators and teachers, totaling forty-five pages. Pitman states, "The letters are a small sample of teachers' opinions on the general effectiveness of i.t.a.…[T]hey are typical of the opinions held by a great many, almost certainly the majority, of the teachers involved in the experiment."[1]

Why Not Just Adopt i.t.a.?

Initial teaching alphabet was never intended as a reformed spelling system. As its name implies, i.t.a. was designed as a teaching method to give beginners the initial success in reading needed for a successful self-image. When they see they *can* read, they have the self-confidence to tackle the much more difficult English spelling. The change from i.t.a. to English is usually easy. This is because the i.t.a. letters which are deviations from a one-letter-for-one-symbol correspondence are designed to make i.t.a. more like English. Some students, however, do not find the changeover from i.t.a. to English easy, which is perhaps one of the reasons i.t.a. is seldom if ever used today.

Two great hindrances to the adoption of i.t.a. are:

1. Besides eighteen consonants and five short vowels that are unchanged, there are twenty-two new symbols. Billions of dollars' worth of

typewriters, printers, and computers would have to be converted to forty-five "letters." Besides the thirty-eight phonemes used in N'wenglish, i.t.a. uses new symbols for the *WH*, *UR*, and *YUE* blends, separate symbols for *A* as in *father* and *O* as in *bother*, a vowel sound that is intermediate between that of *A* and *O*, and two separate symbols for the *K* and *Z* sounds. I.t.a. also uses a new symbol for the *D* phoneme.

2. I.t.a. would be much less effective for adults because hundreds of hours (which students often cannot or will not invest) are still required to learn English after learning i.t.a.

In spite of advantages that i.t.a. may have, N'wenglish has all the same advantages and then some.

1. N'wenglish is much easier to learn than i.t.a.

  a. Students need not learn "rules" (and many exceptions) about which letter to use.

  b. N'wenglish has twenty-five single letters and fifteen digraphs; i.t.a. has forty-five single letters.

  c. N'wenglish is a perfect one-symbol-to-one-sound system.

2. No changeover to English is needed!

Summary of Spelling Reform Proposals

It seems clear that the huge costs of replacing all printing equipment rule out all but the digraphic proposals. Table A6-2, adapted from Appendix II of Sir James Pitman's book *Alphabets and Reading*, shows the essential characteristics of eight digraphic alphabets that have been proposed. Two are not strictly digraphic. Isaac Pitman, Sir James Pitman's father, was an early spelling reform advocate. His alphabet uses an accent mark above the *U* that represents the N'wenglish *UE* sound. Frank C. Laubach's alphabet uses a macron on *A*, *E*, *I*, *Y*, *OW*, *OO*, and *OU*.

The phonemes in table A6-2 that are represented by more than one letter or digraph are shaded. As you can see, three spelling systems have more than one spelling of two of the phonemes. Glossic, Anglic, The Simplified Spelling Society's system, Pitman's, and Laubach's have three, seven, eight, nine, and thirteen sounds, respectively, with more than one spelling. In addition, all eight alphabets use the same letter to represent more than one sound (the bold capitalized letters). Therefore, when reading, you would have to learn the correct pronunciations of words using duplicated letters. Table A6-1 shows these duplications. In this table the letter is followed by the sounds in N'wenglish that the letter represents.

Appendix 6

The *E*, *IE*, *O*, *OE*, *S*, and *Y* graphemes represent the *E*, *IE*, *O*, *OE*, *S*, and *Y* phonemes less often than some other sound. (See table A6-2 and appendix 2 table A2-1). This is true in N'wenglish and all eight other digraphic alphabets. In addition, the eight spelling systems have from two to thirteen more sounds than N'wenglish that are not represented by the most used grapheme in English (marked with asterisks in table A6-2).

As you can see from table A6-2, none of the eight alphabets has the logical and easily remembered order that

Table A6-1: Letters with More Than One Pronunciation
(The capitalized letters inTable A6-2)

N'wenglish		Simplified Spelling Soc.	
none		a:	a, o, ae
Glossic		e:	e, ee
d:	d, t	i:	i, ie
Pitman		u:	u, ue
a:	a, o, ae	y:	i, y
e:	e, ee	d:	d, t
u:	u, oo	Laubach	
d:	d, t	a:	a, o, oe
Anglic		i:	i, ie
a:	a, o, ae	o:	o, oe
e:	e, ee	y:	i, y
i:	i, ie	oo:	o, ue
d:	d, t	ou:	o, ou
Follick		o_e:	o, oe
i:	i, y	d:	d, t
uu:	ue, oo	World English Spelling	
New Spelling		a:	a, o
a:	a, o	d:	d, t
d:	d, t		

the N'wenglish alphabet has. Also, all of the other alphabets have (1) more pronunciations of the graphemes than N'wenglish, (2) more spellings of the phonemes than N'wenglish, and (3) more sounds represented by a grapheme that is not the most used in English than N'wenglish does. See the table titled Summary of Table A6-2 Vowels.

Two recent spelling reform proposals not included in appendix II of Sir James Pitman's book *Alphabets and Reading* are "Fonetic English" and "American Spelling." Fonetic English is a digraphic and diacritical (macrons for long vowels) spelling system with several inconsistencies. These include (1) the use of *X* for all seven sounds of *X* in English, (2) the use of *TH* for both English *TH* sounds, and (3) a different treatment of *X* and

Summary of Table A6-2 Vowels

Spelling System	Avg. No. of Pronunciations, Each Grapheme	Avg. No. of Spellings, Each Sound	No. of Graphemes That Aren't Most Used in English
N'wenglish	1.0	1.0	4
Glossic	1.0	1.1	6
Pitman	1.4	2.0	9
Anglic	1.4	1.6	7
Follick	1.2	1.1	9
Simp. Spell. Assoc.	1.6	1.7	6
New Spelling	1.1	1.2	4
Laubach	1.7	3.7	11
World Eng. Spell.	1.1	1.2	5

Let's End Our Literacy Crisis

the *YUE* diphthong at the start, middle, and end of words.

American Spelling is a digraphic spelling system similar to English and N'wenglish, but American Spelling has many inconsistencies to make it more like English, presumably to make it more acceptable to those who can already read English. It also has several rules (some with exceptions) to show pronunciations more precisely. American Spelling is designed as an alternative spelling system that, it is presumed, will eventually replace English spelling. The problem is that the student must learn both English and American Spelling during the transition period. (More likely, the student would need to learn English first and gradually learn American Spelling.) As the history of previous proposals of this sort decidedly shows, once someone has learned English, any desire also to learn alternative spellings that are not in widespread use is very greatly diminished.[2]

There are now eight spelling reform proposals on the Internet. Two of them, NuSpel and Reformed English, propose new (non-Romanic) alphabets and have little chance of adoption because of the huge cost of converting all present printing equipment. Two of them propose to solve the problem by adopting a set of spelling rules. The system proposed by The Simplified Spelling Society, based in Great Britain, is called Cut Spelling. Briefly stated, these rules are:

1. Cut letters irrelevant to the sound.
2. Cut unstressed vowels before *L*, *M*, *N*, and *R*.
3. Cut vowels in regular endings.
4. Write most double consonants single.
5. Substitute *F* for *GH* and *PH*, *J* for soft *G,* and *Y* for *IG*.
6. Write only proper names with capitals.
7. Write apostrophes only to link words.

As you can see, learning this system requires a knowledge of English that many do not have at present—knowledge of which letters are irrelevant, which syllables contain the stress, what comprises a regular ending, which double consonants should remain doubled, which words have a soft *G*, which words are proper names, etc. Although much simpler than English, it is still far more complicated than N'wenglish. The other spelling system proposing to solve the problem of English spelling by adopting spelling rules, Spelriet, is even more complicated than Cut Spelling. It lists forty-eight problems with English spelling and proposes fifty-three spelling rules as a solution to these problems. Although simpler than English, it would still require considerable effort to learn.

Appendix 6

Table A6-2: Eight Pre-1970 Diagraphic Proposals[3]
Part 1 of 2

- Column headings show originator and/or name of alphabet and year proposed.
- This table excludes letters used the same in all alphabets.
- Letters used for more than one phoneme are in bold capitals.
- Phonemes spelled with more than one letter are shaded.
- An asterisk precedes letters that are not the *most used* for the sound in English.
- The *UR* blend is shown by *'R* in Glossic.

N'wenglish Phoneme	Letters Used to Represent the Phonemes			
	A. J. Ellis (Glossic) 1870	R. E. Zachrisson (Anglic) 1932	Isaac Pitman 1897	Mont Follick 1934
I	i	**I**	i	**I**
* o	* aa, o	* **A**, aa, o	* **A**, aa, o	* o, aa
ae	* ai	* **A**, ae	* **A**, ai, ay	* ei
ee	ee	* **E**, ee	* **E**, ee	* ie
* ie	* ei	* **I**, ie	* ei	* ai
* oe	* oa	* o, oe	* o, oa	* ou
ue	* oo	* uu	* ú, oo	* **UU**
Au	au	au	* o, au, aw	* oa
Oo	* uo	oo	* **U**	* **UU**
Oi	oi	oi	* oi, oy	oi
ou	ou	* au	* ou, ow	* au
F	f	f	f	f
K	k	* k, x, qu	k	* c, k
r, (ur)	* r, ('r)	r	r	r
T	* t, **D**	* t, **D**	* t, **D**	t
* y	* y	* y	* y	* **I**
Ch	ch	ch	ch	* tsh
tt	th	th	th	th
th	* dh	* dh	th	* dh
nk	*ngk	nk	nk	* ngk
nx	*ngx	nx	nx	* ngx
wh	wh	wh	wh	* hu

Table A6-2: Eight Pre-1970 Diagraphic Proposals[3]
Part 2 of 2

- Column headings show originator and/or name of alphabet and year proposed.
- This table excludes letters used the same in all alphabets.
- Letters used for more than one phoneme are in bold capitals.
- Phonemes spelled with more than one letter are shaded.
- An asterisk precedes letters that are not the *most used* for the sound in English.

N'wenglish Phoneme	Letters Used to Represent the Phonemes			
	Simplified Spelling Society 1938	Frank Laubach 1966	New Spelling 1955	World English Spelling, 1968
i	* **I, Y**	* **I, Y**	i	i
* o	* **A**, o, aa	* **A, O**, aa, ah, **ŌO, OU, O_E**	* **A**, o, aa	* **A**, o, aa
ae	* **A**, ae	* **Ā**, a, ae, ai, ay, a_e	ae	ae
ee	* **E**, ee	* e, ea, ee, ey, e_e	ee	ee
* ie	* **I**, ie	* **Ī**, y, ie, i_e, igh	* ie	* ie
* oe	* o, oe	* **O**, oa, oe, ōw, **O_E**	* oe	* oe
ue	* **U**, ue	* w, **OO**, ww	* uu	* oo
au	au	* au, aw, ong	au	au
oo	oo	* uu	oo	* uu
oi	oi	* oi, oy	oi	oi
ou	ou	* **OU**, ow	ou	ou
f	f	* f, ph	f	f
k	k	* c, k, x, q, ck	k	k
r	r	r	r	r
t	* t, **D**	* t, **D**	* t, **D**	* t, **D**
* y	* **Y**	* **Y**	* y	* y
ch	ch	ch	ch	ch
tt	th	* tth	th	* thh
th	* dh	th	* dh	th
nk	nk	* ngk	nk	nk
nx	nx	* ngx	nx	nx
wh	wh	wh	wh	wh

Appendix 6

Table A6-3: Four Diagraphic Proposals on the Internet
Part 1 of 2

- The column heading is the name of the alphabet at www.barnsdle.demon.co.uk/spell
- This table excludes letters used the same in all alphabets.
- Letters used for more than one phoneme are in bold capitals.
- Phonemes spelled with more than one letter are shaded.
- An asterisk precedes letters that are not the *most used* for the sound in English.
- See superscripted notes at the bottom of the next table.

N'wenglish Phoneme	Letters Used to Represent the Phonemes			
	Phonetic English	Simplified Spelling	Fanetiks	Rationalized Spelling[2]
a	a	a	* aa	**A**
i	i	i	u	* e, **I**, y
* o	* o	* o	* o	* **O**, ah
u	u	u	u	* **A**, **U**
ae	ae	ae	ae	* a_e, ay
ee	ee	ee	ee[1]	* a_e, ee
* ie	* ie	* ie	* ie[1]	* **I**
* oe	* oe	* oe	* oe[1]	* **O**
ue	**UE**	ue	ue[1]	* oo
yue[3]	* **UE**	yue	yue	* **U**
au	au	* aw	au	au
oi	* auxee, auxui	oi	oi	oi
oo	oo	* ou	oo	* **W**, **U**
ou	ou	* ow	ou	ou
ch	ch	* q	ch	ch
th	* tz	th	th	* dh
tt	th	* dh	* tth	th
zh	zh	* x	zh	zh
wh[3]	* hw	* **W**	* hw	* **W**, hw
nk, nx or ngk, ngx	?	?	ngk	nk
ng or ngg in *finger*	ng	?	ngg	ngg

279

Table A6-3: Four Diagraphic Proposals on the Internet
Part 2 of 2

- The column heading is the name of the alphabet at www.barnsdle.demon.co.uk/spell
- This table excludes letters used the same in all alphabets.
- Letters used for more than one phoneme are in bold capitals.
- Phonemes spelled with more than one letter are shaded.
- An asterisk precedes letters that are not the *most used* for the sound in English.

N'wenglish Phoneme		Letters or Symbols Used to Represent the Phonemes or Silent Letters			
		Phonetic English	Simplified Spelling	Fanetiks	Rationalized Spelling[2]
unaccented vowel (u in N'wenglish)		* ui	* c	* a	* A
Number of Silent Letters or Symbols		1	2	5	0
Silent Letter Type[4]	1	x			
	2		y	y	
	3		w	w	
	4			- (hyphen)	
	5			q	
	6			x	

1 Use *e, i, o,* or *u* instead of *ee, ie, oe,* or *ue* at the end of words except before a hyphen at the end of a line or to show less-common homonyms.
2 Double a single consonant or the first letter of a consonant digraph at the end of a word to show a preceding short vowel (use *kk* instead of *ck*).
3 *Yue* and *wh* are not phonemes but phoneme blends of *y + ue* and *h + w*, respectively.
4 There are no silent letters in N'wenglish. The silent letter types above are as follows:

Type 1: used to show the accent on words spelled the same but with different meanings and accents.
Type 2: used between *ae, ee,* or *ie* and another vowel to prevent their being taken as a digraph.
Type 3: used between *oe* or *ue* and another vowel to prevent their being taken as a digraph.
Type 4: used between two consonants to prevent their being taken as a digraph.
Type 5: used after a short vowel at the end of a word or after a less-common homonym.
Type 6: used instead of dots in an ellipsis or to show closely related words in a multihyphenated phrase.

Appendix 6

There are also four digraphic spelling reform proposals presently on the Internet. As you can see by comparing table A6-3 with table A6-2, the present proposals are an improvement over those found through research into books available at a large research university and a large city library. The proposals in table A6-3, however, are still more difficult than N'wenglish. Without briefly studying tables A6-2 and A6-3 and the previous paragraphs, it would be easy to conclude that the author is simply advocating his own solution simply because it is his creation. The facts speak for themselves, however. Unlike other proposed spelling systems, each N'wenglish symbol is pronounced (read) in only one way, each sound is spelled (written) only one way, and the maximum (or very nearly the maximum) number of choices of symbols to represent sounds are the most used letters used in English for those sounds (See appendix 2).

Is Precise Pronunciation Representation Necessary?

A few scholars want a more accurate means of recording English pronunciations. Almost everyone wants a means of communicating more easily. From a scholarly viewpoint, the American Spelling rules are not unduly difficult. Long experience in industry, however, decidedly shows that anything new:

1. must be convenient and easy to use, and
2. must show broad and immediate benefits to ensure its adoption.

This is true despite how obvious an improvement it is to supervisors, engineers, or "experts" in the organization.

If people want to learn to speak more precisely, reading books by scholarly persons written in American Spelling or N'wenglish will help. Reading dozens of books written in English, even those written by the best of scholars, will not help in the least unless you consult a dictionary after every word you are not certain about. The following facts show that great precision in pronunciation is not needed for understanding most words that we hear.

1. The ability to understand appendix 4 shows that great precision in recording pronunciations is unnecessary. N'wenglish uses thirty-eight phonemes, the minimum for efficient communication.
2. We can usually understand even the most uneducated speakers.
3. Much of what we hear or read is understood largely by the context.

Must Spelling Be Like English to Be Acceptable?

All variation from a perfect one-sound-to-one-symbol correspondence is counterproductive. It may make the alphabet more like English, but it also makes it harder to learn and defeats the purpose of inventing another alphabet.

Knowledge of people's natural tendency to resist change has caused scholars in the past to advocate spelling systems that are less than ideal—at least partly to improve their chances of acceptance among those who could already read. In the twenty-first century, however, it is important to consider three important facts:

1. Some of the strongest resistance to change comes, not from the masses who will benefit the most from it, but from the scholars' own peers, many of whom will gain from keeping our spelling unchanged. In many cases, the beliefs and desires of the scholars' associates will have more influence upon them than the beliefs and desires of the nameless, faceless masses. Scholars who have spent a lifetime studying language skills, reading difficulties, and teaching methods will understandably be skeptical of a system that will make their previous research and teaching skills unneeded.

2. Many scholars believe a simplified spelling system must have some of the inconsistencies of English to be acceptable to those who already read English. Therefore, scholars have not adequately researched the acceptability of a phonemically perfect system that is very different, yet very easy.

3. With our increasingly complex society, in which one form or another of information processing is rapidly replacing manual labor, the need for a highly literate society is reaching crisis proportions. Our position in the family of nations will continue to slip until we are willing to face this resistance to change head-on and solve our literacy problems.

Is N'wenglish the Logical Ideal or Minimum Alphabet?

N'wenglish is not the ideal digraphic language, logically speaking. Ideally, N'wenglish would be changed as follows: use the *X* and *Q* graphemes for the *AU* and *OO* phonemes and add an *E* or a macron to these for the *OI* and *OU* graphemes. The *C* grapheme would represent the *CH* phoneme, as in the word *cello*. The *KS* and *KW* blends would be spelled out, as are the other phonemes represented by *X* and *Q* in

Appendix 6

N'wenglish. In this way the fourteen vowel phonemes would be represented by seven single letters plus the addition of an *E* or a macron to these letters. This proposal would only reduce the number of letters in typical written material by 1.6 percent or less, because all the phonemes involved are among the least used. This small gain does not justify the additional learning involved.

The alphabet with the minimum number of letters is as follows (the first line is the N'wenglish phoneme, the second is the minimum alphabet):

a	e	i,y	o	u	ā	ē	ī	ō	ū,w	au	oi	ou	oo	ch	sh	th	tt	zh	ng
a	e	i	o	u	ā	ē	ī	ō	w	x	x̄	ū	w̄	c̄	c	q	q̄	ȳ	y

The single consonants (*B, D, F, G, H, J, K, L, M, N, P, R, S, T, V,* and *Z)* are the same. Adding an *E* is an alternative to the use of a macron. This alphabet is 4.1 percent shorter than N'wenglish, but only 50 percent of phonemes use graphemes that are most used English graphemes (instead of 81.6 percent as in N'wenglish), and only 67.6 percent of graphemes represent the same phoneme as in English (instead of 97.4 percent as in N'wenglish). A 4.1 percent improvement does not justify the additional learning required

Summary

Scholars and researchers may profit from endless speculations upon the chance that any given proposed alphabet may prove inadequate in some way "if we test it on enough different combinations of many thousands of words." The following quote by Edward Rondthaler and Edward Lias should resolve the matter:

> Vivian Ducat…puts into words a truism we instinctively know to be correct but do not fully appreciate until it is expressed very simply: "Anything becomes familiar if you see it often enough."[4]

With N'wenglish you very soon become familiar with the thirty-eight phonemes from seeing them over and over, spelled the same way every time. Those who might benefit from more research or who are too cautious about (or resistant to) change will no doubt want to examine other possibilities. Phoneticists might desire an alphabet that includes several more sounds, although, for the practical purpose of understanding what someone is saying, N'wenglish is more than adequate. But the significant points are these:

- N'wenglish is logical, workable, and very easy to use.
- The chance of significantly improving upon N'wenglish, regardless of how much research is done, is very small.
- The need for a workable solution to English illiteracy is very great and growing.
- Hundreds of millions of people will be hurt by our failure to act upon what we already know!

Appendix 7
Is There Really a Literacy Crisis?

The information presented in the text of this book will, in most cases, be sufficient to convince any open-minded reader of the truth of the literacy crisis. This appendix is included because those who have a vested interest in disbelieving a literacy crisis may have seen and believed one or more of the reports and perhaps a recently published book claiming otherwise. There is a large volume of material published by educators which, in effect, defends the practices and beliefs of educators. The groups most likely to disbelieve that there is a literacy crisis are teachers, educational administrators, some of the politicians most closely involved in educational policies, and some of the parents of students who learned to read with little difficulty. Even though persons believing they will benefit from maintaining the status quo may be open-minded, if they have read and believed material published by a profession that they revere, when they see conflicting information, they may tend to discount it as containing errors or omissions that render it untrue, as the author of the book mentioned above apparently does.

The first chapter of this book, published in 1998, disputes the reality of a literacy crisis in the U.S. by supposedly answering seven statements about education in the U.S. which the book classifies as myths. As a safety engineer in a solid propellant rocket missile plant, it was necessary to carefully examine what the engineers advocating as an improvement in the manufacturing procedure, ingredients or equipment offered as proof that the change was safe. Failure to do so could result in an explosion that killed dozens of people and destroyed facilities, products and equipment worth millions of dollars. What was offered as proof was sometimes found to be no more than the engineers' biased evaluation of what they saw as an improvement. The presentation of facts in the first chapter of the above-mentioned book was similar to many of the engineers' presentations of facts. Although the facts presented may appear impressive, when carefully analyzed they do not add up to a proof of what they are supposed to prove.

Unlike this book, the above-mentioned book does not answer opposing views point-by-point. For example, it mentions Dr. McGuinness' book but never mentions any of the facts she presented in her book. The same is true of all of the research findings presented in this book, nearly all of which was available to the author of the above-mentioned book.

The **first statement** dismissed as a myth was the claim that student's reading abilities have declined in the last twenty-five years. The federal government's National Assessment of Educational Progress (NAEP) testing began in the late 1960s. NAEP data are shown for nine of the test results for the 1971 to 1996 period. These data show little if any change in test scores during this period. There are three problems with this, however. The first is that most of the decline in reading ability occurred before 1971. Little change in teaching methods occurred between 1971 and 1996. The decline in reading ability has been continuing to some extent ever since about 1810. The most serious decline occurred since the early 1920s when whole-word or look-and-say methods increasingly came into use. Further declines occurred as a multitude of pleasant and time consuming activities were introduced and as a similar multitude of detriments to learning occurred, as chapter five of this book explains. Student Aptitude Test (SAT) results, which students desiring to attend college often take, showed the most recent decline, beginning in the early 1960s.

A second problem with using only the NAEP data to gage reading ability is that it only compares what individual students are learning about reading in their age group in school as compared to the average student scores for that age group and is not in any way tied to the results they achieve later as adults in functional literacy tests. The educational problems detailed in the NAEP's 1985 report that came to be known as the "Nation At Risk" report (which an April 20, 2003 report shows to still be a serious problem) and the 1993 report titled "Adult Literacy in America," which is summarized in the first two chapters of this book, shows that 48 percent of adult Americans read so poorly they have difficulty holding a job that provides an adequate income. What is important about reading is not so much what is *learned* as what is *retained* and *how useful* what they have learned is in helping them cope with the everyday problems of life.

A third problem, as Dr. McGuinness shows, is that teachers can manipulate reading test scores by telling poor readers and non-readers to stay home on reading test days. Dr. McGuinness does not document how prevalent the practice is, but she *has* found evidence that the practice exists.

The bottom line on this argument, however, is that proving there has been little change in students learning to read in the last twenty-five years obviously does not prove that a literacy crisis does not exist.

The **second statement** dismissed as a myth is that 40 percent of children in the U.S. cannot read at a basic level. The author points out that although the proficiency levels were established by "a broadly representative panel of teachers, education specialists, and members of the general public," there is disagreement between where the proficiency cut-off for each level should be between fourteen of the states and the NAEP. In some cases the states showed their students to be more proficient than the NAEP tests. Other states showed their students to be less proficient than the NAEP tests. This led to charges of "arbitrariness" in the cut-off levels. The author does not prove that the 40 percent claim is wrong, but he claims that it has not changed in twenty-five years and therefore if it *is* true, it has been true for twenty-five years and makes the author wonder "how the nation has managed to survive up to this point."

As with the first myth, even if he had proven that more than 40 percent of U.S. students could read at a basic level, it would not prove that there is no literacy crisis.

The **third statement** dismissed as a myth is the claim that 20 percent of U.S. children are dyslexic. In this case, he is correct. He points out that the number of students judged as dyslexic is dependent entirely upon the cut-off point below which students were labeled as dyslexic—because of poor reading ability—in the study which was most often cited in support of this myth: the Connecticut Longitudinal Study (CLS) of the early 1990s. The CLS was *not* based upon any neurological measurements. Note 5 in this section also correctly points out that choosing the cut-off points for each competency level upon what average students in the group can do is not a reading standard at all—it is just a measure of what average students in the group can do. Some brain disorder specialists in 2004 estimate that no more than 2 or 3 percent of students have neurological reasons for being unable to read. Disproving that fewer than 20 percent of students are dyslexic, however, does not prove that there is not a literacy crisis.

The **fourth statement** that is dismissed as a myth is that students of the baby boomer generation read better than today's students. In this case he may be correct, but proving that today's students read as well as students of the 1940s and 1950s does not in any way prove that the "Adult Literacy in America" study is incorrect. Most of the drop in literacy occurred before 1950.

The **fifth statement** dismissed as a myth is that U.S. students are among the worst readers in the world. He presents data from "the most recent round of testing" by the International Association for the Evaluation of Educational Achievement reported in 1992, which showed that U.S. nine-year-olds ranked second and U.S. fourteen-year-olds ranked ninth in a thirty-one nation study. Without knowing more about the conditions and controls upon the testing, the results are questionable at best. For example, economic conditions in many nations are such that the schools do not have the financial resources to teach every student to read, so only the top students are allowed to stay in school. In any case, even if U.S. students are not "among the worst in the world," this does not prove that there is not a literacy crisis in the U.S. and other English-speaking nations.

The **sixth statement** judged as a myth is that poor readers are increasing while good readers are decreasing in number. He presents NAEP data for 1971 to 1994 showing that this is not true, but once again, the major drop in literacy occurred before 1971.

The **seventh statement** he calls a myth is that test scores dropped dramatically in California because of the whole language teaching method. He correctly points out that none of the data used to make this claim is dated before California began their whole language type of

Appendix 7

teaching and is therefore invalid. He then presents data from fourth grade teachers—by which time every student should have been, but wasn't—a fluent reader and finds a slight disadvantage for teaching by the phonics method. The scores were 220, 221, and 208 of a possible 500 for whole language-emphasis, literature-based, and phonics teaching, respectively. As Dr. McGuinness conclusively proves, however, unless the proper method of teaching phonics is used, the teaching will be ineffective. Perhaps the most important factor in using the phonics method is that it should be the first and only teaching method for beginning readers—anything else is confusing to the beginning student and develops in the student the bad habit of *guessing* at the pronunciation of letters, letter combinations and words. Also, as note 12 of this chapter points out, Fisher and Hiebert's 1990 study "often found *little* correspondence between what teachers called themselves ('whole language,' 'phonics') and the teaching method they actually used."

This is a relative short book: eighty-six pages of text. The first chapter is fourteen pages. Chapters 2 through 7 are basically a defense of California's use of "whole language" and "literature based" teaching methods. The author is an Assistant Professor of Education at a California university. Although he includes an extensive bibliography, he admits that many of the findings in the reports are open to very different interpretations. In any case, it appears that none of the reports he references prove that there is no literacy crisis—if they do, he certainly does not present them.

Notes

Chapter 1

1. Mark Clements, "What's Wrong With Our Schools," *PARADE*, May 16, 1993, p. 4.

2. Knight-Ridder Washington Bureau poll of registered voters by Princeton Survey Research, September 3-15, 1996, "Our Concerns," *The Salt Lake Tribune*, October 6, 1996, p. A14, col. 6.

3. Gannett News Service, "New Hope For Urban Education," *The Salt Lake Tribune*, January 14, 1998, p. A5.

4. Richard Whitmire, for Gannett News Service, "Parents in '90s Desperate About Quality Education," *The Salt Lake Tribune*, April 7, 1996, p. A10, col. 1-2.

5. Taylor Syphus, "He's Learning to Read," *The Salt Lake Tribune*, December 16, 1995, pp. E1, E10.

6. Edward Klein, "Everything Would Be Better If More People Could Read," *PARADE*, May 21, 1989, p. 5.

7. Mary Jordan, writer for The Washington Post, "Nearly Half of Adults in America Lack Necessary Literacy Skills, Study Says," *The Salt Lake Tribune*, September 9, 1993, p. A1, col. 2-3. This quote from Mary Jordan is apparently her assessment of the facts presented in the National Center for Education Statistics' (NCES) report entitled "Adult Literacy in America," which can be found at http://nces.ed.gov/pubs93/93275.pdf. A subsequent report titled "Literacy in the Labor Force," which can be found at http://nces.ed.gov/pubs99/1999470.pdf and which is part of the same study shows that Mary Jordan's assessment is correct. In 1992 the U.S. population was 190.5 million. Sixty-two percent of the population were employed, 7 percent were unemployed, and 31 percent were out of the work force (page 12 of the report). The mean annual earnings of the Level 1 *employed* respondents for the three types of testing was $12,797. Comparable Level 2 and 3 annual salaries were, respectively, $16,073 and $20.963 (p. 122). The annual earnings of those who are unemployed or out of the work force would, on the average, be far less. The federal government's definition of poverty in 1991 for a four-person family was an annual earnings of $12,500 (p. 178). There are obviously many reasons for any one individual being either full-time employed, part-time employed, unemployed, or out of the work force, just as there are many reasons for any one individual making a low annual salary, but these figures are including all of the different categories of people and therefore strongly indicative of the negative effect of poor literacy skills upon earning ability. According to the NCES report, forty-eight percent of American adults were found to have only a Level 1 or Level 2 competency.

"New Math: Money Doesn't Equal School Excellence," *The Salt Lake Tribune*, September 10, 1993, p. A1, col. 5-6.

8. Personal communication to the author from Edward Rondthaler, August 25, 1988. He stated that this was to be added to the next edition of: Edward Rondthaler and Edward J. Lias, *Dictionary of Simplified American Spelling* (New York: The American Language Academy, 1986).

9. Sanford S. Silverman, *Spelling For the 21st Century* (Cleveland, Ohio, self-published), pp. 23, 9 and 11-13. A common spelling rule is "*I* before *E*, EXCEPT after *C*, OR when sounded like *A* as in *neighbor* and *weigh*." There are times when the letters *I* and *E* following *C* or that have the "long" *A* sound do not follow these exceptions—they are exceptions to the exceptions.

10. Kenneth H. Ives, *Written Dialects N Spelling Reforms: History N Alternatives* (Chicago, Ill.: Progresiv Publishr, 1979), p. 30.

11. Frank C. Laubach, *Forty Years With the Silent Billion*, (Old Tappan, N.J.: F. H. Revell Co., division of Baker Book House Company, 1970), p. 478.

12. Ibid., p. 36.

13. Jonathan Kozol, *Illiterate America* (New York: New American Library, 1985), pp. 5, 226, as quoted from the *Washington Post*, November 25, 1982, and Foundation News, January/February 1983.

14. David Broder, for Washington Post Service, "American Education System Still at Risk," *The Salt Lake Tribune*, January 17, 1990, p. A8, col. 3-5.

15. Edgar Guest, *Collected Verse of Edgar A. Guest* (Chicago, Ill.: Contemporary Books, Inc., 1934), p. 285.

Chapter 2

1. Michael Harrington, *The Other America*, rev. ed. (New York: Macmillan, 1969) as quoted by Kozol, pp. 12, 228.

2. Kozol, ibid, pp. 8-10, 227-228.

3. Jordan, ibid.

4. Facts from the 1992 Educational Testing Service report as listed by The American Literacy Council on their Web site on May 5, 2004 (http://www.americanliteracy.com/literacy_figures.htm).

5. Diane McGuinness, Ph.D., *Why Our Children Can't Read* (New York: Simon & Schuster, 1997), pp. 7-8.

6. See note 3.

7. McGuinness, ibid, p. 10.

8. See note 3.

9. See note 4.

10. See note 7.

11. "Comparing Graduation Rates," *The Salt Lake Tribune*, December 13, 1998, p. AA1, col. 1-2.

12. See note 5.

13. McGuinness, ibid, p. 9.

14. Kozol, ibid, p. 65.

15. Richard Harwood, writer for the *Washington Post*, "SAT Scores Bad News for Newspapers," *The Salt Lake Tribune*, September 4, 1991, p. A6, col. 3-5.

16. Cited in Chester E. Finn, Jr., *We Must Take Charge* (New York: Free Press, 1991) as quoted by Dr. William Bennett, *The Index of Leading Cultural Indicators* (New York: Simon & Schuster, 1994), p. 89.

17. A quote of Albert Shanker, President, American Federation of Teachers, cited in Carol Innerst, "Schools 'Really Bad' Says AFT Leader," *Washington Times*, July 5, 1990, as quoted by Dr. William Bennett, ibid.

Notes

18. Kozol, pp. 5, 226, as quoted from the *Washington Post*, November 25, 1982, and *Foundation News*, January/February 1983. A more recent comparison is available by comparing the U.S. adult literacy rate of 48 percent (see the first section of chapter 2) with the international literacy rate of 72 percent ("Numbers," *Time*, July 26, 1999, p. 17). It may well be that the evaluation criteria used in the international study was less rigorous than in the U.S. study, but it should be noted that many of the other nations do not have mandatory elementary school education as does the U.S., and a much smaller percentage of the population in many of the nations have enough education to achieve literacy. Furthermore, many nations do not try to ensure that every student can graduate from elementary school, as the U.S. does. As a result, the "best and brightest" in many other nations receive an education; the others "flunk out."

19. Eugene C. Gluesing, "A Return to Basics, Not More Money, Is Solution to Our Education Woes," Common Carrier, *The Salt Lake Tribune*, January 7, 1990, p. A18.

20. Editorial, "Nakasone 'Mistake' Underlines Sizeable U.S. Literacy Void," *The Salt Lake Tribune*, September 28, 1986, p. A16, col. 1-2.

21. Rick Gladstone, Associated Press writer, "Reading Writing on the Wall? America May Face Literacy Crisis," *The Salt Lake Tribune*, February 21, 1988, p. F4, col. 1.

22. Associated Press, "Competitively Speaking, U.S. Sinking," *The Salt Lake Tribune*, June 22, 1992, p. A1.

23. Gannett News Service, "New High School Grads Can't Write, Say Profs," *The Salt Lake Tribune*, January 9, 1998, p. A12, col. 1-2.

24. U.S. Department of Education, Office of Educational Research and Improvement, *Adult Literacy in America*, September 1993, as quoted by Dr. William Bennett, p. 88.

25. U.S. Department of Education, National Center for Education Statistics, *International Assessment of Educational Progress, A World of Differences*, 1989, as quoted by Dr. William Bennett, p. 85.

26. Kozol, ibid., pp. 37-39.

27. Ibid., pp. 41-43.

28. Anne C. Lewis, special to the *Baltimore Evening Sun*, "Press Misses Scary Story In Failing to Cover Literacy Adequately," *The Salt Lake Tribune*, September 14, 1989, p. A17, col. 2-3.

29. Kozol, ibid., pp. 42, 233-234.

30. "$1.1 billion will be spent on adult literacy projects," *Deseret News*, July 26, 1991, p. A3.

31. Kozol, ibid., p. 42.

32. John McLaughlin, for Newhouse News Service, "Gimmicks Won't Erase Literacy Crisis," *The Salt Lake Tribune*, September 12, 1986, p. A18.

33. See note 25.

34. David Harman, *Illiteracy: A National Dilemma* (New York: Cambridge Book Company, 1987), pp. 38, 39.

35. The Associated Press, "Skills Lacking, So Companies Offer Training," *The Salt Lake Tribune*, April 13, 1990, p. B10.

36. Frank C. Laubach, *Teaching the World to Read* (New York: Friendship Press, 1947), p. 111.

37. Kozol, ibid., p. 105.

38. Laubach, *Teaching the World to Read*, p. 113.

39. Kozol, ibid., p. 43.

40. Ibid., p. 57.

41. Dorothy Shields, *U.S. News & World Report*, May 17, 1982, as quoted by Kozol, ibid., p. 58.

42. Kozol, ibid., p. 123.

Chapter 3

1. Laubach, *Teaching the World to Read*, pp. 13-14.

2. Laubach, *Forty Years With the Silent Billion*, pp. 475-477.

3. Laubach, *Teaching the World to Read*, p. 2.

4. Dr. Mont Follick, *Reform English Spelling* (London: Jason Press, 1946), p. 13, as quoted by Sir James Pitman in a speech February 7, 1964, at Manchester University, published in *Alphabets for English*, ed. W. Haas (Manchester University Press, 1969), p. 39.

5. Laubach, *Teaching the World to Read*, pp. 73, 76-77.

6. From a speech January 28, 1965, by Axel Wijk at Manchester University published in *Alphabets for English*, pp. 56-57.

7. Sir James Pitman, *Alphabets and Reading* (New York: Pitman Publishing Company, 1969), p. 264.

8. Pitman, ibid., p. 263.

9. Laubach, *Teaching the World to Read*, p. 75.

10. See note 8.

11. See note 6.

12. David Crystal, *The Cambridge Encyclopedia of Language* (New York: Cambridge University Press, 1987), p. 358.

13. Richard Lederer, *Crazy English* (New York: Pocket Books, 1990), p. 11.

14. Gwynne Dyer, Freelance Service, "English Poses Little Threat To Many Other Languages," *The Salt Lake Tribune*, October 16, 1997, p. A11.

15. See note 12.

16. See note 14.

17. *Los Angeles Times*, "World's Population to Hit 6 Billion This Weekend," *The Salt Lake Tribune*, July 17, 1999, p. A4, col. 4-6.

18. Crystal, ibid., pp. 357-358.

19. Silverman, ibid, p. 41.

20. Gwynne Dyer, Freelance Service, "The French should wake up and start learning English," *The Salt Lake Tribune*, November 1, 2004, p. A15.

21. See note 14.

22. Haas, ibid., p.57.

23. See note 13.

24. Godfrey Dewey Ed.D., *English spelling: Roadblock to reading* (New York: Teachers College Press, Teachers College, Columbia University, 1971), p. 77.

25. Crystal, ibid., p. 57.

26. Haas, ibid., p. 56.

Chapter 4

1. Kozol, ibid., p. 5.

2. Carman Hunter and David Harman, *Adult Illiteracy in the United States* (New York: McGraw-Hill Book Company, 1985), p. 165.

3. "A Jam: Jail Population Jumps 23% in 3 Years," *The Salt Lake Tribune*, October 26, 1987, p. A4.

4. Aparna Kumar, for the *Los Angeles Times*, "2 Million Inmates in the U.S.," *The Salt Lake Tribune*, April 7, 2003, p. A9, col. 1.

5. Associated Press, "U.S. Crime's Price Tag Runs $450 Billion a Year," *The Salt Lake Tribune*, April 23, 1996, p. A7.

6. Lewis, ibid.

7. *Washington Post*, "Illiteracy 'Crisis' Scares U.S. Executives," *The Salt Lake Tribune*, October 8, 1995, p. F8.

8. Associated Press, "Job Seekers Can't Read Or Do Math," *The Salt Lake Tribune*, May 8, 1996, p. B12, col. 4-5.

9. David Wallechinsky, "Are We Still Number One?" *PARADE*, April 19, 1997, p. 6.

10. Kozol, ibid., pp. 16, 229.

11. See note 9.

12. Kozol, ibid., p. 17.

13. USA TODAY, "Booksellers Feel Sales Bind Despite Economy," *The Salt Lake Tribune*, May 4, 1999, p. C13.

14. Dana Nichols, Gannett News Service, "Words of Warning: Workers Read Poorly," *The Salt Lake Tribune*, October 28, 1992, p. A5, col. 1-2, and Kozol, ibid., pp. 16, 17, 229.

15. See note 12.

16. Kozol, ibid., pp. 13, 18, 230.

17. Kozol, ibid., pp. 13, 228.

18. *Boston Globe*, May 10, 1983, as quoted by Kozol, ibid., pp. 20, 230.

19. *New York Times*, March 29-30, 1979, as quoted by Kozol, ibid., pp. 20, 230.

20. Kozol, ibid., pp. 20-21.

21. See note 5.

22. Jonathan Kozol, *Illiterate America* (Garden City, N.Y.: Anchor Press/Doubleday, 1985) back jacket cover (hardback edition, all other quotes are from the soft cover edition).

23. "Job picture: The past six months," *The Salt Lake Tribune*, February 5, 1991, p. D7.

Chapter 5

1. Kozol, ibid., p. 27.

2. Hunter and Harman, ibid., p. 37.

3. Ibid., pp. 41-43.

4. Edward Klein, ibid.

5. Kozol, ibid., p. 5.

6. Florida Judge Charles Phillips, cited by Laubach Literacy International, Inc., and the *Washington Post*, November 25, 1982, as quoted by Kozol, ibid., pp. 226, 229.

7. Hunter and Harman, ibid., p. 51.

8. Ron Hutcheson, Knight-Ridder News Service, "Lawmakers Cramming for the Next Political Test: Education Reform," *The Salt Lake Tribune*, December 30, 1997, p. A1, and Kozol, ibid., p. 5.

9. Kozol, ibid., p. 5.

10. Hunter and Harman, ibid., p. 43.

11. Kozol, ibid., pp. 24, 25, 28.

12. Ibid., pp. 23-25 and 28.

13. Silverman, ibid, pp. 37-38.

14. Kozol, ibid, pp. 14 and 23-28.

15. Silverman, ibid, p. 30.

Chapter 6

1. T. S. Watt, "Brush Up Your English," *Manchester Guardian*, June 21, 1954, as quoted by Edna L. Furness, *Spelling For the Millions* (Nashville, Tenn.: Thomas Nelson Inc., Publishers, 1977), p. 3.

2. Crystal, ibid., p. 165.

3. Ibid., p. 200.

4. McGuinness, ibid., pp. 46-47.

5. Ives, ibid., pp. 39, 40.

6. Ibid., pp. 25, 80, 81.

7. Edward Rondthaler and Edward J. Lias, *Dictionary*, p. 5.

8. M. M. Dougherty, et. al., *Instant Spelling Dictionary* (Little Falls, N.J.: Career Publishing, Inc., 1967), pp. 4, 258.

9. Personal letter from Edward Rondthaler to the author, August 25, 1988. The quote was from material to be added to the next edition of his book, *Dictionary of Simplified American Spelling*.

10. Ives, ibid., pp. 22-23.

11. Samuel Noory, *Dictionary of Pronunciation* (New York: A. S. Barnes and Co., 1965), pp. IX, X.

12. Ives, ibid., p. 30.

13. McGuinness, ibid., p. 78.

14. Ibid., p. 158.

15. Ibid., pp. 156-169.

16. Pitman, ibid., pp. 47-48.

17. Traugott Rohner, *Fonetic English Spelling* (Evanston, Ill.: Fonetic English Spelling Assoc., 1966), pp. 6-7.

18. Raymond Wilson, *Nine O'Clock Bell* (Harmondsworth, Middlesex, England: Puffin Books, 1987), pp. 36-37.

Chapter 7

1. Arthur W. Heilman, *Phonics in Proper Perspective* (Columbus, Ohio: Charles E. Merrill Publishing Company, 1968), pp. 112-113.

2. Pitman, ibid., pp. 256-257.

3. Jeanne Chall, "New Views on Developing Basic Skills With Adults," paper prepared for National Conference on Adult Literacy, Washington D.C., January 19-20, 1984, as quoted by Kozol, ibid., pp. 11, 227, 228.

4. Harman, ibid., p. 94.

5. Ives, ibid., pp. 59-60.

6. Laubach, *Teaching the World to Read*, pp. 31, 76.

7. Pitman, ibid., pp. 99-100.

8. Harman, ibid., p. 41.

9. Cal Thomas, *Los Angeles Times* syndicate, "Better Public Schooling Idea," *The Salt Lake Tribune*, September 13, 1997, next-to-last page of section A.

10. Rudolph Flesch, *Why Johnny Can't Read—and What You Can Do About It* (New York: Perennial Library, 1983), p. 2, chapter 8.

11. Ives, ibid., pp. 28-29.

12. Silverman, ibid, p. 12.

13. Dewey, ibid., pp. 42-43.

14. Kozol, ibid., pp. 65, 238.

15. See note 10.

16. Flesch, ibid., pp. 76-77.

17. Laubach, *Teaching the World to Read*, pp. 108, 103.

18. Silverman, ibid, p. v.

19. Rudolph Flesch, *Why Johnny Still Can't Read* (New York: Colophon Books, 1981), pp. 167-168.

20. Thomas, ibid.

21. Nina Shokraii Rees, for Knight-Ridder News Service, "Power Shift in Education Could Mean More Accountability in Schools," *The Salt Lake Tribune*, June 20, 1999, p. AA3.

22. "New Math: Money Doesn't Equal School Excellence," ibid.

23. Dr. William Bennett, pp. 82-83, 91-92. The state rankings were quoted from Eric Hanushek, "The Economics of Schooling: Production and Efficiency in Public Schools," *Journal of Economic Literature*, September 1986.

24. Kozol, ibid., pp. 66-69.

25. Cooperative Institutional Research Program, *The American Freshman: National Norms for Fall 1989, 1990* as quoted by Dr. William Bennett, pp. 86-87.

26. Richard Whitmire, Gannett News Service, "With Inflation, Are Students Really Making the Grade?" *The Salt Lake Tribune*, September 7, 1997, p. A11. See also Erin Van Bronkhorst, The Associated Press, "It's Getting Easier to Get Good Grades, Critics Say," *The Salt Lake Tribune*, April 26, 1998, p. A5, col. 1-2.

27. Pitman, ibid., p. 48.

28. Ibid., p. 55.

29. Dewey, p. vii (foreword by Ben D. Wood, Director, Bureau of Collegiate Educational Research, Columbia University).

30. Hunter and Harman, ibid., p. xviii.

31. Pitman, ibid., p. 161.

32. Ibid., p. 49.

33. Rondthaler and Lias, *Dictionary*, p. 8.

34. Axel Wijk, *Regularized English* (Stockholm, Sweden: Alqvist & Wiksell International, 1977), pp. 8-11.

35. Ives, pp. 27, 28, 31.

36. Ives, ibid., p. 31.

37. Pitman, ibid., pp. 38, 54.

38. McGuinness, ibid., p. 169.

Chapter 8

1. It is a relatively simple matter to set computer keyboards so that pressing the alt (or option) key along with A, E, I, O, or U produces a lowercase vowel with a macron and pressing the control (or command) key with A, E, I, O, or U makes an uppercase vowel with a macron, so no more keystrokes than capitalized letters are needed.

2. Charles Kenneth Thomas, *An Introduction to the Phonetics of American English* (New York: The Ronald Press, 1958), pp. 255, 259, 260.

3. Ibid., pp. 147, 175, 187.

4. Frank C. Laubach, *Teaching the World to Read*, p. 233.

5. Dewey, *English spelling: Roadblock to reading*, p. 174.

6. Of the five hundred most commonly used words [from Godfrey Dewey, Ed.D., *Relativ Frequency of English Speech Sounds*, rev. ed. (London: Harvard University Press, 1950) Table 3, pp. 19-23] which comprise 70.98 percent of a typical sample of English prose, 263 words are unchanged in length, 193 words are shorter by one letter, twenty-three words are shorter by two letters, five words are shorter by three letters, one word is shorter by four letters, and only fifteen words are longer, all by one letter.

   The data in appendix 2, table A2-1, are also based upon Dewey's data, pages 8, 9, and table 3, pages 19-29. Table 3 is based upon 100,000 words of connected matter (excluding numerals and proper names) representative of both written and spoken English. It includes words from each of the following:

   15 percent (i.e., 15,000 words) from newspaper editorials and 15 percent from newspaper news (six different newspapers, three each)

   15 percent from modern fiction (5 percent each from two novels, two short stories, and two dramas)

   10 percent from speeches by three U.S. presidents

   5 percent (5,000 words) from each of the following:

   five business manuals

   nineteen advertisements

   three scientific magazines

   five magazine editorials

   1 percent each from the Bible, two sermons, and two religious magazine editorials

   personal correspondence of two individuals

   five "special articles" from four different magazines

   the first one hundred words, top of second column, from fifty consecutive pages of the *Saturday Evening Post*

   the first one hundred words, top of second column, from fifty consecutive pages of *Literary Digest*.

Chapter 9

1. Silverman, ibid, pp. 19-21.

2. McGuinness, p. 235.

3. Ibid., p. 210

4. English Spelling Reform Web site article "Why not Spelling Reform," http://www.barnsdle.demon.co.uk/spell/gyd.html, pages 5 and 6 of 9, accessed on May 1, 2004.

5. Dyslexia Study In *Science* Highlights The Impact of English, French, And Italian Writing Systems Web site http://www.sciencedaily.com/releases/2001/03/010316073551.html pages 1 and 2 of 2 accessed May 3, 2004.

6. Alison Motluk, "Why English is hard on the brain," *New Scientist*, January 20, 1996, p. 14.

7. McGuinness, ibid., pp. 210-211.

8. Ibid., pp. 212, 217-218.

9. Ibid., p. 224.

10. Ibid, p. 212

11. Ibid., p. 213.

12. Ibid, pp. 222, 225.

13. Ibid., p. 227.

14. Ibid., pp. 229-230.

15. Ibid., pp. 230-231.

16. Ibid., pp. 231-232.

17. Ibid, p. 273.

18. Ibid, p. 275

19. Ibid, p. 276.

20. Silverman, ibid, pp. 17-18.

Chapter 10

1. Pitman, p. 274.

2. Ibid., pp. 264-265.

3. Flesch, ibid., pp. 89-99.

4. Noory, ibid., pp. X-XIV.

5. Mario A. Pei, "Language," *The World Book Encyclopedia* (Chicago: The World Book-Childcraft International, Inc., 1979) vol. 12, p. 62.

6. Crystal, ibid., p. 123.

7. I. J. Gelb, *A Study of Writing* (Chicago: University of Chicago Press, 1963), p. 13.

8. William Dwight Whitney as quoted by Dewey, ibid., p. 176.

9. Flesch, *Why Johnny Can't Read* and *Why Johnny Still Can't Read.*

10. Miriam Balmuth, Ph.D., *The Roots of Phonics, 2d ed.* (Timonium, Maryland: York Press, Inc., 1992), pp. 30-31.

11. Rondthaler and Lias, *Dictionary*, p. 13.

12. Dewey, ibid., p. 173.

13. Crystal, ibid., p. 147.

Chapter 11

1. Flesch, *Why Johnny Still Can't Read*, p. 100.

2. Flesch, *Why Johnny Can't Read*, p. 82. These figures were "arrived at scientifically by sampling a large unabridged dictionary and asking children whether they could define the words."

3. Flesch, *Why Johnny Still Can't Read*, p. 101.

4. The author will provide the publisher with a list of twenty-seven suffixes and an alphabetized glossary of 1,131 English words and their N'wenglish equivalents based on Dewey's 100,000-word sample. The computer program will combine the words and suffixes and perform a spell check to be sure valid words have been produced—if not, there will be an audible signal, and the word will be highlighted on the monitor for the typesetter to correct. These words will be added to the database of N'wenglish spellings (the initial 1,131 words. These 1,131 words are all of the root words in the 100,000-word sample that occurred more than ten times and account for 87.4 percent of the 100,000 words. When combined with the twenty-seven suffixes, the resulting database will contain a very large portion of the words that will be seen in most writings.). The program will also highlight heteronyms for the typesetter to choose the correct N'wenglish word for the context. As new books are typeset, any word not in the database will be highlighted for the typesetter to correct and add to the database. After a few months, very few words will need the typesetter's attention.

5. Pitman, ibid., p. 250.

6. Ibid., pp. 159-160.

Chapter 12

1. Harman, ibid., p. 100.

2. Lewis, ibid.

3. Joe Rolando, "Forum Sees Poor U.S. Education As Threat to Competitiveness," *The Salt Lake Tribune*, January 12, 1989, p. D5.

4. This is based upon *Statistical Abstract of the United States 2003*, table 218 showing a total cost of public education, K-12, of $422.1 billion and table 217 showing a projected 2002 fall enrollment of 47.613 million students (33.709 million, K-8, and 13,857 million, 9-12). The latest firm figures were only slightly less: $8,509 per student based upon $401.8 billion with an enrollment of 47.223 million students in 2000 from the same tables.

5. Molly Ivins, "Congress Risks Public Costs of Illiterate Immigrants," *The Salt Lake Tribune*, p. A17, col. 1-4.

6. Mike Bowler, for the *Baltimore Evening Sun*, "Invest in Education to Reduce Crime," *The Salt Lake Tribune*, January 18, 1990, p. A14, col. 3-5.

7. Curt Anderson, for the Associated Press, "Despite a drop in crime, prison population keeps growing," *The Salt Lake Tribune*, p. A3.

8. Kozol, ibid., p. 12.

9. National Committee on Excellence in Education, *A Nation at Risk*, 1983, as quoted by Dr. William Bennett, ibid., p. 89.

10. Kozol, ibid., pp. 6, 21.

11. Ibid., p. 29.

12. Calvin Osburn, "Corporate Training, Education Must Become Standard Policy," Common Carrier, *The Salt Lake Tribune*, May 6, 1990, p. A26.

13. Broder, ibid.

14. Fredreka Schouten, for Gannett News Service, " 'At Risk' Report 20 Years Later," *The Salt Lake Tribune*, April 20, 2003, p. A13.

15. As quoted in Ives, ibid., p. 28.

16. Rondthaler and Lias, *Dictionary*, pp. 5-6.

17. Ibid., p. 4.

18. Heilman, ibid., pp. 112-113.

19. "Reading the Future," *The Salt Lake Tribune*, September 14, 1993, p. A8, col. 1-2.

20. Personal communication to the author from Edward Rondthaler, August 25, 1988.

Appendix 4

1. Adapted from "The Gospel of John," *The New King James Bible, New Testament* (Nashville, Tennessee: Thomas Nelson Inc., Publishers, 1979) pp. 142-182.

Appendix 6

1. Pitman, pp. 188-189.

2. Paula Mitchell Marks, "The Three-Hundred Words," *American History Illustrated*, March 1985, pp. 30-35.

3. Adapted from appendix II of Pitman, pp. 314-315.

4. Rondthaler and Lias, *Dictionary*, p. 292.

Glossary

Allophone: variations of a phoneme which are not different enough to be used to distinguish between words in a given language or dialect. (Sounds that are allophones in one language or dialect might be phonemes in another. For example, the English phonemes *R* and *L* are allophones in Japanese.)

Blend: the sound of two or more letters combined into one syllable. (The term "combination" is sometimes used in the text as a synonym for blend. When two or more consonants are combined, they can also be called a consonant cluster.)

Combination: See blend.

Consonant Cluster: See blend.

Digraph: two letters used together to represent a single phoneme.

Diphthong: a blend of two vowel phonemes. The sound goes so quickly from one vowel to the other that it is perceived as a single phoneme.

Grapheme: a letter or letter combination that represents a single phoneme. In N'wenglish only single letters and digraphs are used as graphemes. There are only ten digraphs (fifteen if macrons are not used) in N'wenglish. (In English, letter blends up to five letters long are used for a single phoneme, and there are at least 268 of them.) See the "Sounds per Symbol: Effect upon Reading" section of chapter 6.

Heteronym: one of two or more words with the same spelling but with different pronunciations and meanings.

Homograph: (1) one of two or more words spelled and pronounced the same with different meanings (such as sound: a condition, a noise, a body of water) and (2) one of two or more words with same spelling but different pronunciations and meanings (same as heteronym).

Homonym: one of two or more words with the same pronunciation but with different spellings and meanings; it is also called homophone.

Homophone: same as homonym.

Macron: a line that is added directly above a vowel to show its pronunciation.

Phoneme: the smallest sound that distinguishes one word or syllable from another in a language or dialect.

Sound: phonemes, allophones, or any combination of phonemes and allophones.

Syllable: A syllable is a single sound composed of: (1) V, (2) CV, (3) VC, or (4) CVC where
1. V = any one* of the fourteen vowel phonemes
2. C = any consonant or consonant cluster

> Note: 1. Vowels and diphthongs can be at the start, middle, or end of a syllable; consonants can only be at the start or end.
> 2. A sound must have a vowel to be a syllable.

Glossary

3. Many consonants can't be said without vowels. (See table 8-2.)

* The diphthongs, as shown in the "Understanding Pronunciation" section of chapter 8, are considered single phonemes. Whether other vowel-vowel combinations are considered diphthongs or two syllables depends upon how quickly they are blended together by the speaker. For example, the word *usual* could be two syllables if the *UE-U* combination is pronounced quickly (i.e., a diphthong)—or with a more careless pronunciation as *yuezhul*. It can also be three syllables: *yue-zhue-u*

Bibliography

"$1.1 billion will be spent on adult literacy projects." *Deseret News*, Salt Lake City, July 26, 1991, p. A3, col. 1.

Associated Press. "Competitively Speaking, U.S. Sinking." *The Salt Lake Tribune*, June 22, 1992, p. A1, col. 1.

———. "Illiteracy a Big Problem at Small Firms." *The Salt Lake Tribune*, June 5, 1992, p. A6, col. 1-2.

———. "Job Seekers Can't Read Or Do Math." *The Salt Lake Tribune*, May 8, 1996, p. B12, col. 4-5.

———. "Schools Add Record Revenue to Three R's." *The Salt Lake Tribune*, August 29, 1991, p. A8, col. 3-5.

———. "Skills Lacking, So Companies Offer Training." *The Salt Lake Tribune*, April 13, 1990, p. B10.

———. "U.S. Crime's Price Tag Runs $450 Billion a Year." *The Salt Lake Tribune*, April 23, 1996, p. A7.

Balmuth, Miriam, Ph.D. *The Roots of Phonics, 2d ed.* Timonium, Maryland: York Press, Inc., 1992.

Bennett, William J., Ph.D. *The De-Valuing of America.* New York: Simon & Schuster, 1992.

———. *The Index of Leading Cultural Indicators.* New York: Simon & Schuster, 1994.

Blumenfeld, Samuel L., Ph.D. *Is Public Education Necessary?* Old Greenwich, Conn.: The Devin-Adair Company, 1981.

———. *The New Illiterates.* New Rochelle, N.Y.: Arlington House, 1973.

Bowler, Mike for the *Baltimore Evening Sun.* "Invest in Education to Reduce Crime." *The Salt Lake Tribune*, January 18, 1990, p. A14, col. 3-5.

Broder, David. for Washington Post Service. "American Education System Still at Risk." *The Salt Lake Tribune*, January 17, 1990, p. A8, col. 3-5.

Bryson, Bill. *The Mother Tongue.* New York: Perennial, an imprint of Harper Collins Publishers, 1990.

Cannon, Angie for Knight-Ridder News Service. "Survey Discovers Positive Change in the Country's Outlook." *The Salt Lake Tribune*, February 4, 1996, p. A11, col. 1-5.

Chall, Jeanne. "New Views on Developing Basic Skills With Adults." paper prepared for National Conference on Adult Literacy. Washington D.C., January 19-20, 1984.

Clements, Mark. "What's Wrong With Our Schools." *PARADE*, May 16, 1993.

"Comparing Graduation Rates," *The Salt Lake Tribune*, December 13, 1998, p. AA1, col. 1-2.

Crystal, David. *The Cambridge Encyclopedia of Language.* New York: Cambridge University Press, 1987.

Dewey, Godfrey Ed.D. *English spelling: Roadblock to reading.* New York: Teachers College Press, Teachers College, Columbia University, 1971.

———. *Relativ Frequency of English Speech Sounds.* rev. ed. London: Harvard University Press, 1950.

Dougherty, M. M., et. al. *Instant Spelling Dictionary.* Little Falls, N.J.: Career Publishing, Inc., 1967.

Dyer, Gwynne. Freelance Service. "English Poses Little Threat To Many Other Languages." *The Salt Lake Tribune*, October 16, 1997, p. A11.

Editorial, "Nakasone 'Mistake' Underlines Sizeable U.S. Literacy Void." *The Salt Lake Tribune*, September 28, 1986, p. A16, col. 1-2.

Flesch, Rudolph. *Why Johnny Can't Read—and What You Can Do About It.* New York: Perennial Library, 1983.

———. *Why Johnny Still Can't Read.* New York: Harper Colophon Books, 1981.

Follick, Mont, Ph.D. *Reform English Spelling.* London: Jason Press, 1946.

Furness, Edna L. *Spelling For the Millions.* Nashville, Tenn.: Thomas Nelson Inc., Publishers, 1977.

Gannett News Service. "New High School Grads Can't Write, Say Profs." *The Salt Lake Tribune*, January 9, 1998, p. A12, col. 1-2.

———. "New Hope For Urban Education." *The Salt Lake Tribune*,

January 14, 1998, p. A5.

Gelb, I. J. *A Study of Writing.* Chicago: University of Chicago Press, 1963.

Gladstone, Rick. Associated Press writer. "Reading Writing on the Wall? America May Face Literacy Crisis." *The Salt Lake Tribune*, February 21, 1988, p. F4, col. 1-2.

Gluesing, Eugene C. for "Common Carrier" column. "A Return to Basics, Not More Money, Is Solution to Our Education Woes." *The Salt Lake Tribune*, January 7, 1990, p. A18.

Haas, W., ed. *Alphabets for English.* Manchester University Press, 1969.

Hanna, Paul R., et. al. *Phoneme-Grapheme Correspondences as Cues to Spelling Improvement.* Department of Health, Education and Welfare, Office of Education, 1966.

Harman, David. *Illiteracy: A National Dilemma.* New York: Cambridge Book Company, 1987.

Harrington, Michael. *The Other America.* rev. ed. New York: Macmillan, 1969.

Harwood, Richard. writer for the *Washington Post*. "SAT Scores Bad News for Newspapers." *The Salt Lake Tribune*, September 4, 1991, p. A6, col. 3-5.

Heilman, Arthur W., Ph.D. *Phonics in Proper Perspective.* Columbus, Ohio: Charles E. Merrill Publishing Company, 1968.

Hunter, Carman and David Harman. *Adult Illiteracy in the United States.* New York: McGraw-Hill Book Company, 1985.

Hutcheson, Ron. Knight-Ridder News Service. "Lawmakers Cramming for the Next Political Test: Education Reform." *The Salt Lake Tribune*, December 30, 1997, p. A1.

Bibliography

"Illiteracy 'Crisis' Scares U.S. Executives." *The Salt Lake Tribune*, October 8, 1995, p. F8, col. 1-2.

Ives, Kenneth H. *Written Dialects N Spelling Reforms: History N Alternatives.* Chicago, Ill.: Progresiv Publishr, 1979.

Ivins, Molly for Creators Syndicate. "Congress Risks Public Costs of Illiterate Immigrants." *The Salt Lake Tribune*, p. A17, col. 1-4.

"A Jam: Jail Population Jumps 23% in 3 Years." *The Salt Lake Tribune*, October 26, 1987, p. A4.

"Job Picture: The past six months." *The Salt Lake Tribune*, February 5, 1991, p. D7.

Jordan, Mary. writer for the *Washington Post*. "Nearly Half of Adults in America Lack Necessary Skills, Study Says." *The Salt Lake Tribune*, September 9, 1993, p. A1, col. 2-3.

Klein, Edward. "Everything Would Be Better If More People Could Read." *PARADE*, May 21, 1989, p. 4-6.

Knight-Ridder News Service. "Inmate Increases Set Record." *The Salt Lake Tribune*, December 4, 1995, p. A10.

Knight-Ridder Washington Bureau poll of registered voters by Princeton Survey Research, September 3-15, 1996, "Our Concerns." *The Salt Lake Tribune*, October 6, 1996, p. A14, col. 6.

Kottmeyer, William. *Except After C.* New York: School Division, McGraw-Hill Book Company, 1988.

Kozol, Jonathan. *Illiterate America.* New York: New American Library, 1985.

Laubach, Frank C. *Forty Years With the Silent Billion.* Old Tappan, N. J.: F. H. Revell Co., 1970.

———. *Teaching the World to Read.* New York: Friendship Press, 1947.

Lederer, Richard. *Crazy English.* New York: Pocket Books, 1990.

Lewis, Anne C. Special to the *Baltimore Evening Sun.* "Press Misses Scary Story In Failing to Cover Literacy Adequately." *The Salt Lake Tribune*, September 14, 1989, p. A17, col. 2-3.

Lounsbury, Thomas R., LL.D, L.H.D. *English Spelling and Spelling Reform.* New York: Harper & Brothers Publishers, 1909.

Marks, Paula Mitchell. "The Three-Hundred Words." *American History Illustrated*, March 1985, pp. 30-35.

McGuinness, Diane, Ph.D. *Why Our Children Can't Read.* New York: Simon & Schuster, 1997.

McLaughlin, John. for Newhouse News Service. "Gimmicks Won't Erase Literacy Crisis." *The Salt Lake Tribune*, September 12, 1986, p. A18.

"Mr. Clinton, Take Note...." *PARADE*, January 18, 1998, p. 19.

"New High School Grads Can't Write, Say Profs." *The Salt Lake Tribune*, January 9, 1998, p. A12, col. 1-3.

"New Hope For Urban Education?" *The Salt Lake Tribune*, January 14, 1998, p. A5.

"New Math: Money Doesn't Equal School Excellence." *The Salt Lake Tribune*, September 10, 1993, p. A1, col. 5-6.

Nichols, Dana. Gannett News Service. "Words of Warning: Workers Read Poorly." *The Salt Lake Tribune*, October 28, 1992, p. A5, col. 1-2.

Bibliography

Noory, Samuel. *Dictionary of Pronunciation.* New York: A. S. Barnes and Co., 1965.

Osburn, Calvin. "Corporate Training, Education Must Become Standard Policy." Common Carrier. *The Salt Lake Tribune*, May 6, 1990, pp. A26, col. 1-3.

Pei, Mario A. "Language." *The World Book Encyclopedia.* Chicago: The World Book-Childcraft International, Inc., 1979, vol. 12, p. 62.

Pitman, Sir James. *Alphabets and Reading.* New York: Pitman Publishing Company, 1969.

Raudsepp, Eugene. "Games That Stimulate." *Machine Design*, July 21, 1977, pp. 88-94.

————, and George P. Hough, Jr. *Creative Growth Games.* New York: Perigree Books, 1977.

"Reading and Writing Skills of Children Are Inadequate, Says Education Czar." *The Salt Lake Tribune*, January 10, 1990, p. A4, col. 1-3.

"Reading the Future." *The Salt Lake Tribune*, September 14, 1993, p. A8, col. 1-2.

Rees, Nina Shokraii, for Knight-Ridder News Service. "Power Shift in Education Could Mean More Accountability in Schools." *The Salt Lake Tribune*, June 20, 1999, p. AA3.

Rohner, Traugott. *Fonetic English Spelling.* Evanston, Ill.: Fonetic English Spelling Association, 1966.

Rolando, Joe. "Forum Sees Poor U.S. Education As Threat to Competitiveness." *The Salt Lake Tribune*, July 12, 1989, p. D5.

Rondthaler, Edward, and Edward J. Lias. *Dictionary of Simplified American Spelling*. New York: The American Language Academy, 1986.

Schouten, Fredreka. Gannett News Service. "'At Risk' Report 20 Years Later." *The Salt Lake Tribune*, April 20, 2003, p. A13.

Silverman, Sanford S. *Spelling For the 21st Century*. Cleveland, Ohio: self-published, 2003.

Syphus, Taylor. "He's Learning to Read." *The Salt Lake Tribune*, December 16, 1995, pp. E1, E10.

Thomas, Cal. *Los Angeles Times* syndicate. "Better Public Schooling Idea." *The Salt Lake Tribune*, September 13, 1997, section A.

Thomas, Charles Kenneth. *An Introduction to the Phonetics of American English*. New York: The Ronald Press, 1958.

Ulmer, Curtis. *Teaching the Culturally Disadvantaged Adult*. Englewood Cliffs, N.J.: Prentice Hall, Inc., 1973.

United Press International. "Most Children Fail U.S. Writing Test." *The Salt Lake Tribune*, December 4, 1986, p. A5.

USA TODAY. "Booksellers Feel Sales Bind Despite Economy." *The Salt Lake Tribune*, May 4, 1999, p. C13.

Van Bronkhorst, Erin. The Associated Press. "It's Getting Easier to Get Good Grades, Critics Say." *The Salt Lake Tribune*, April 26, 1998, p. A5, col. 1-2.

Vedantam, Shankar. Knight-Ridder News Service. "How Smart—or Dumb—Is America?" *The Salt Lake Tribune*, December 21, 1995, p. A10, col. 1-6.

Wallechinsky, David. "Are We Still Number One?" *PARADE*, April 19, 1997, p. 6.

Washington Post. "Illiteracy 'Crisis' Scares U.S. Executives." *The Salt Lake Tribune*, October 8, 1995, p. F8, col. 1-2.

Whitmire, Richard. Gannett News Service. "Parents in '90s Desperate About Quality Education." *The Salt Lake Tribune*, April 7, 1996, p. A10, col. 1-2.

———. Gannett News Service, "With Inflation, Are Students Really Making the Grade?" *The Salt Lake Tribune*, April 26, 1998, p. A5, col. 1-2.

Wijk, Axel. *Regularized English.* Stockholm, Sweden: Almqvist & Wiksell International, 1977.

Wilson, Raymond. *Nine O'Clock Bell.* Harmondsworth, Middlesex, England: Puffin Books, 1987.

Index

A

accent(s), foreign, 136–37, 163
accent(s)/(un)accented, emphasis, 122, 126, 127, 129, 134–36, 137, 161, 162, 189, 216
Adult Basic Education (ABE), 36, 52
adult functional illiterate(s), 17, 23–26
adult illiteracy, 13, 196, 198
adult literacy training costs, 52, 53
age of skepticism, 2
allophone(s), 313
alphabet(s), 87, 90, 101, 104, 114, 115, 120, 121, 141, 147, 149, 151, 155, 205, 208, 219, 274, 275, 276, 277, 278, 279, 280, 282, 283
  minimum, 282
  N'wenglish, 155, 156
  purpose of, 205
  universal, 46
alphabetic language, 2, 6, 8, 9, 12, 15, 17, 18, 19, 77, 177
  ease/difficulty of, 87
  number of phonemes required/used, 73
alphabetical order, 155, 187, 216
alternate/variant spelling(s), 80, 92, 165
American Enterprise Institute, 196
American Language Academy, 88, 292, 324
American Spelling, 7, 275, 276, 281, 292, 302, 324
assimilations, 136
attention deficit disorder, 1, 11, 145

B

Balmuth, Dr. Miriam, 172
Bennett, Dr. William, 111, 209, 212, 318
bilingual, 50, 90, 165
blame, 4

blame(d)/blaming, 14, 15, 72, 81, 162, 196
blend(s)/blending, 10, 77, 78, 106, 122, 125, 130, 131, 134, 137, 138, 139, 151, 152, 156, 164, 191, 216, 274, 282, 313, 315
blending sounds extremely rapidly, 172
Blumenfeld, Samuel, 1, 146, 210, 212, 318
book publishing, 56, 205
boring reading textbooks, 16, 109, 166, 196
brain anomalies/disfunction, 1, 2, 11, 27, 145, 146, 147, 148, 288
Bullock, Sir Alan/Report, 117–18, 195

C

challenge(d), challenging, 7, 11, 19–20, 28, 64, 94, 115, 179, 206, 207, 211, 212
change, resistance to, 7, 9, 11, 23, 80, 104, 141, 149, 170, 171, 177, 179, 193, 207, 209, 282, 283
Chinese picture writing, 16, 76
combination(s), xii, 73, 76, 78, 87, 105, 126, 138, 150, 158, 165, 189, 215, 216, 289, 313, 315
compete/competitor(s)/competitiveness, 8, 13, 19, 29, 30, 35, 52, 56, 59, 144, 165, 167, 173, 180, 185, 192, 196, 202, 203, 205
comprehension, 154
computer program(med)/programming, 15, 88, 127, 165, 184, 309
consonant blends, frequency of use, 138

context, 2, 73, 75, 98, 103, 116, 120, 136, 137, 144, 151, 168, 173, 174, 182, 217, 281, 309
Corporate Literacy Programs, 38–39
cost of illiteracy. *See* chapters 4 and 5
cost of solving illiteracy, 197–98
creative problem solving, 6, 267
crisis of illiteracy, 285–89
Crystal, David, 50, 169, 175
cultural alienation, 44, 165, 207
cure for illiteracy, 5–7, 207

D

danger of not curing illiteracy, 40–42
defensive thinking, 9, 74, 80, 93
destroying the benefits of an alphabet, 87
developmental delays, 145
Dewey, Godfrey Ed.D., 39, 50, 80, 107, 108, 114, 137, 173, 175, 195, 219, 306, 309, 319, 336
dialect(s), xii, 18, 73, 136, 166, 313
dictionary, 7, 74, 75, 76, 81, 87, 92, 93, 114, 125, 133, 138, 161, 162, 163, 165, 205, 221, 222, 223, 224, 281, 309
digraph(s), 76, 81, 91, 92, 124, 125, 126, 127, 130, 137, 140, 151, 152, 153, 155, 156, 189, 215, 216, 219, 274, 275, 281, 313
diphthong(s), 124, 126, 130, 132, 153, 154, 276, 313, 314, 315
discipline, 4, 12, 159, 191, 200
drill, for teaching, 8, 72, 119, 146
dropout, 26, 36, 39, 63, 197, 204

Index

Dutch spelling reform, 104
dyslexia, 1, 145–48

E

economic survival, 13, 29–31, 202
educational
  history, 12
  research, vi, ix, 1, 9, 15, 17, 27, 37, 62, 105, 106, 107, 115, 117, 120, 138, 141, 143, 145, 147, 149, 154, 166, 173, 178, 183, 187, 188, 193, 194, 195, 207, 209, 212, 273, 281, 282, 283, 284, 286, 335
  system costs, 110–12
  system improvement, 110–13
electronic media, 103, 131
embarrassment, 32, 33, 39, 65, 157, 159, 200, 208
employability, 61–62
English language
  characteristics of, 46–50
  for worldwide communication, 121–22, 164, 204
  history of, 74, 229–30
European languages, 17, 117, 118
exercise one, 136
exercise two, 140
expert(s), x, xi, 11, 32, 46, 47, 55, 72, 172, 178, 179, 183, 203, 206, 209, 210, 211, 230, 281

F

fear of the unknown, 9, 68
fighting symptoms or disease?, vii, ix, 12–13, 192, 195, 199, 201, 207, 209
Flesch, Dr. Robert, 39, 107, 109, 110, 166, 172, 178

Follick, Dr. Mont, 46, 104, 319
Fonetic English, 96, 173, 275, 323
foundational cause of illiteracy.
  See root cause of illiteracy
frozen spelling, 77, 80, 93, 169, 205
frustration of failing, 4, 12, 18, 120, 146, 186, 188, 200, 207

G

glossary, 313
grade inflation, 113
grade-level completion, 32–33, 35
grapheme(s), xi, xii, 73, 75, 76, 77, 78, 79, 80, 87, 91, 93, 94, 121, 122, 125, 127, 141, 143, 144, 158, 275, 282, 283, 313, 314
  N'wenglish, choice of, 123, 124, 123–26, 228
  per phoneme, 87, 93, 219
guessing versus reading, 149, 191

H

Hanna, Paul R., 88, 336
Harman, David, 38, 62, 106, 194, 195, 207
Hebrew spelling reform, 104
Heilman, Dr. Arthur W., 100, 206, 209, 211, 212, 320
heteronym(s), 163, 172, 173, 174, 309, 314
history, learning from, 6, 42
history, linguistic/etymological, 74, 168
homograph(s), 175, 314
homonym(s), 76, 126, 163, 170, 172, 173, 174, 175, 314
homophone(s), 98, 173, 175, 314

329

how English phonemes are formed, 132
human-suffering costs of illiteracy. *See* chapter 5
Hunter, Carmen, 62

I

illiteracy, x, 1, 3, 201–4
   and crime, 4, 62
   cause, 71–73, 92, 205
   disadvantages of, 3–5, 102–3, 195–97
   extent, 23–31
   hidden, 31–32
   propagation/growth of, 40–42
   reasons for underestimating, 31–35, 195–97
   solution, 123–27, 180–84
illiteracy solution, 5–7
illiterate parents, effects of, 42
immigrants, 25, 40, 41, 106, 163, 165, 170
impossible for some, x, 4, 115, 119, 120, 149
inaccessible written material, 167
initial teaching alphabet (i.t.a.), 140, 159, 188, 200, 273, 274
Institute for Educational Leadership, 197
intelligence, 6, 16, 52, 114, 115, 146, 147, 192
irregular eye-movements, 116
Ives, Kenneth, 39, 88, 89, 90, 104, 107, 118, 119

K

Kozol, Jonathan, 5, 27, 41, 53, 54, 59, 61, 108, 193, 201, 211, 339

L

LACUS (Linguistic Association of Canada and the United States), 86
Laubach Literacy programs, 18, 36, 108, 110
Laubach, Dr. Robert S., vii, ix
Laubach, Frank C., vi, vii, 18, 39, 40, 43, 44, 46, 48, 104, 108, 110, 136, 230, 274
learning disabilities, 2, 145
learning to read
   difficulty of, 115–20
   ease/difficulty of, 1–2, 15–18, 39–40, 71–73, 75–78, 198
   English versus other languages, 15–18
   logic, 87, 90–92, 96, 117–19
   motivation, 71–72, 158–59, 194
   time required, 12, 15, 37, 109
   versus exposure to, 32
letter names, 155
Lias, Dr. Edward, 117, 174, 206, 208, 283
limits, assumed but nonexistant, 6, 7, 139, 210, 271
linguistic ability, 115, 188
linguistically perfect, 121
Lister, Joseph, 101
literacy
   advantages of, 43–44, 102–3, 194
   crisis, x, 197, 285–89
   desperate worldwide need, 13–15, 46
   functional, 3, 13, 23–26, 31, 40
Literacy Volunteers of America, 36, 38
Lounsbury, Thomas R., LL.D., L.H.D., 74, 119, 170, 212, 322

Index

M

macron(s), 124, 125, 126, 137, 162, 163, 189, 274, 275, 282, 305, 314
McGuinness, Dr. Diane, 1, 2, 11, 16, 24, 26, 27, 72, 90, 91, 107, 120, 143, 144, 146, 154, 157, 172, 191, 192, 286, 287, 289
memory/memorization, 8, 10, 14, 15, 16, 17, 18, 70, 72, 77, 80, 88, 90, 91, 92, 105, 108, 113, 114, 116, 119, 125, 127, 143, 146, 147, 149, 150, 155, 166, 184, 189, 192
Mensa, 111, 114
minimum alphabet, 219, 282, 283
mistakes of illiterates, workplace, 57–58

N

Nation at Risk, A, 201–4
National Assessment Governing Board, 24, 26
National Center for Educational Statistics, 24
National Commission on Excellence in Education, 113, 201
national literacy programs, 36–37
newspaper circulation, 56
Noory, Samuel, 90, 168
note to language scholars, 121
N'wenglish spelling
    advantages, 10–12, 121, 161–66
    characteristics of, 123–28, 137–42
    choice of letters to spell the phonemes, 228, *See*
    choice of phonemes, 122
    defined, 127
    differences from English, 137–38
    disadvantages, 171–75
    implementing, 180 92
    length of words, 137
    logic, 127
    memory aids, 10, 126, 189
    reading textbooks, 183–84
    rules, 126
    upcoming school improvements, 187–90
    versus other proposals, 138–42
Nyikos, Julius, 86

O

ordinary person, 102

P

Pasha, Kemel, 104, 177, 207
passers and passing, 31
Pasteur, Louis, 179
philosophical overtones, 169
phoneme to grapheme correspondence, 73, 74, 75–77, 80, 86, 87, 91, 121, 122, 141, 143, 147, 148, 165, 320
phoneme(s), xi, xii, 10, 16, 18, 73, 75, 76, 79, 80, 81, 87, 91, 94, 120, 121, 122, 123, 124, 125, 127, 129, 130, 131, 133, 137, 138, 139, 141, 143, 144, 147, 149, 151, 152, 153, 154, 155, 156, 157, 205, 274, 275, 281, 282, 283, 313, 314, 315
    frequency of occurrence, 219
    minimum required, 122
Pitman, Isaac, 274, 275, 277

331

Pitman, Sir James, x, 11, 39, 47, 92, 101, 104, 113, 114, 115, 119, 140, 141, 146, 159, 162, 163, 188, 192, 200, 273, 274, 275
plural and past tense, 128, 168
Portuguese spelling reform, 104
poverty, 3, 5, 14, 25, 41, 44, 45, 63, 204, 207, 292
pride, 13, 18, 34, 155, 198
problem solving, 115, 119
pronunciation, 87, 88, 114, 118, 129–37, 143, 161, 162, 163, 165, 167, 168, 205
   change with time, 74
   guidelines, 129–37
   how to pronounce the phonemes, 132
   improving, 129–37, 162, 188
   of N'wenglish letter names, 156
   precision of, 142, 281
   standardization, 132, 137, 162
puns, 172

Q

quality of public education, 3, 190
quick fix for illiteracy, 193

R

reading
   difficulty and reasons for, 73–74, 75–78, 105
   difficulty of teaching, 105–8, 116
   English versus other languages, 109–10, 119
   remedial, 106–7
   research, 107, 193
   speed-reading, 171

rebelliousness over deprivation, 40–42, 44–46
Reformation of the 21st Century, viii, 181
rights, 63–66, 68, 165
Rohner, Traugott, 96, 173, 323
Roman numerals, 212
Rondthaler, Dr. Edward, 7, 88, 117, 174, 206, 208, 283, 292
root cause of illiteracy, vii, 12, 44, 72, 143, 195, 208, 209
Russia(n), 45, 47, 49, 104, 110

S

school board, 185, 186, 208
self-esteem/-image/-reliance/-respect, 4, 12, 33, 39, 43, 64, 65, 158, 159, 194, 200, 273
sensory overload, 35
silent letter(s), 75, 77, 78, 87, 126, 137, 163, 164, 189, 215
silent minority, 33
Simon, Senator Paul, 41
social revolution(s), dangers of, 41
Spain, 88, 104, 107
spelling classes, English, 15, 88, 185
spelling reform, 7, 20, 100
   in other nations, 104–5
   method of implementing, 180–84
   objections to, 166–71
   seldom considered, 7
spelling, English, 82–85
   characteristics/inconsistency of, 15–18, 70, 87–92, 94, 119–20, 127–28
   English versus other languages, 15–18
   forgetting, 16, 162

rules, 16, 88, 108, 114, 127, 128, 170, 274
spelling, N'wenglish. *See* N'wenglish spelling
Standard Broadcast English, 182
standard of living, 56, 59, 63, 210
standardizing effect upon pronunciation, 131
state and local literacy programs, 37–38
summary, 204–6
syllable(s), xii, 48, 73, 76, 91, 116, 122, 126, 127, 129, 130, 131, 133, 134, 137, 138, 143, 153, 154, 158, 162, 163, 164, 189, 216, 276, 313
symptoms versus cure. *See* fighting symptoms or disease?

T

teacher who couldn't read, 32, 200
teaching/teaching method
　adults, 35–40, 52, 198
　English, 107–9
　English versus other languages, 110, 116–19
　guidelines/principles, 148–51
　N'wenglish, 180–84, *See* all of Chapter 9
　psychology of, 158–59
textbooks, 15, 19, 48, 71, 106, 108–9, 144, 148, 173, 183–84, 205, 207
Thatcher, Margaret, 117
theory versus practice, 44, 146, 148, 197, 205
Thomas, Dr. Charles Kenneth, 133, 134
Turkish spelling reform, 104

U

U.S. census report(s), 34, 35, 63
U.S. problems, ranking, 3
unbiased thinking, 179
unbiased thinking needed, 101–3, 177–79
unemployment, 35, 41, 44, 62, 204, 207
uninformed voter, 64
unrealistic views of illiteracy, 102–3
usage frequency of letters for English phonemes, 219

V

vocabulary, 16, 18, 50, 143, 164, 166, 170, 173, 183, 184, 192, 217, 230

W

ways a book can be read, 11
Webster, Noah, 87, 90
Whitney, William Dwight, 171
word list(s), 143, 173, 174
word use frequency, 160, 306
writing, 5, 9, 28, 38, 41, 88, 90, 110, 115, 119, 127, 137, 138, 150, 151, 153, 155, 164, 169, 170, 172, 178, 190

Acknowledgments

Acknowledgment is due first to those who have, thus far, been most affected by this project, which began in 1985 following more than five years of research and writing and thirteen years of typesetting, additional research, and perfecting. My wife, Ruth Ann Cleckler, and daughters, Marilyn and Linda, are due special appreciation for their tolerance of my using irreplaceable time working on this book during most of my "free time" for the past eighteen years.

The assistance of Jack Mleynek and Stephen Walter, Ph.D., is gratefully acknowledged. Jack Mleynek is a retired Delta Airlines pilot who has been an education reform enthusiast for many years. He carefully reviewed the second edition of this book and made many helpful and practical suggestions, most of which were incorporated. When Dr. Walter reviewed this book he was the International Literacy Coordinator for the Summer Institute of Linguistics in Dallas, Texas. He reviewed the first two editions. Many of the differences between the first edition and the second edition are a result of his comments. His review of the second edition resulted in important changes and corrected several errors from a linguistic viewpoint.

A very special "thank you" is due to my editors Norlan De Groot and Seamane Flanagan. Their diligence and attention to detail is amazing and very much appreciated. Any errors that remain are entirely my own.

The assistance of two additional reviewers, Doug Matheson and Lyman Losee, is also greatly appreciated. Doug Matheson is an education reform advocate from Madera, California, and Lyman Losee is a retired Hazards Analysis engineer and engineering supervisor in the Salt Lake City area. Their reviews and suggestions were helpful in making several necessary changes.

The contributions of researchers of Literacy Research Associates, Inc.—Patsy Bond; Ruth Cleckler; Ardy Kritz; Lyman Losee; Doug Matheson; Jack Mleynek; Rose Pye; Robert J. Quigley, Sr.; Cindy Shogren; Stephen Walter, Ph.D.; Brian Woodford; and Paul Young—is gratefully acknowledged.

Much of the data in the tables in this book and in the companion volume, *Let's End Our Literacy Crisis Workbook*, were adapted from two very useful sources: *Phoneme-Grapheme Correspondences as Cues to Spelling Improvement*, by Paul R. Hanna, et al., published in 1966 by the Office of Education of the U.S. Department of Health, Education and Welfare, and *Relativ Frequency of English Speech Sounds*, rev. ed., by Godfrey Dewey, Ed.D., published in London in 1950 by Harvard University Press.

Ordering N'wenglish Versions of Previously Published Books:

You may order one or any number of books of each title. Send for a free catalogue of currently available N'wenglish versions of previously published books. Each book that has not yet been issued in N'wenglish will be available after receipt of a firm order for at least 30,000 books of any one title (50,000 for books not previously published by the publisher of this book). The publisher will make N'wenglish versions available on the following timetable and for the following approximate price. Working in cooperation with a large group of book buyers—whether as individuals or as part of one or more groups or associations—will obviously expedite the publication of any book you may be interested in. The approximate price is $2.00 per 10,000 words. Books with extensive tables and figures will cost extra. When the N'wenglish version is ready for publication, you will be notified of the exact cost, and your book will be shipped approximately two weeks after receipt of payment. See next page for the ordering address.

For books previously published by the publisher of this book (write for a free catalogue):

available date (after receipt of 30,000 orders):
 books of up to 300 pages: five months
 301 to 600 pages: seven months
 601 to 900 pages: nine months
  over 900 pages: eleven months or more

For books whose copyright has expired, previously published by other publishers:

available date (after receipt of 50,000 orders):
 books of up to 300 pages: ten months
 301 to 600 pages: twelve months
 601 to 900 pages: fourteen months
  over 900 pages: sixteen months or more

To order additional copies of this book on the internet, go to

http://pdbookstore.com

To order the workbook, Let's End Our Literacy Crisis Workbook, on the internet, go to

http://www.literacy-research.com/wb

or

send a check for $12 (includes shipping and handling) to

**Literacy Research Associates, Inc.
P.O. Box 57978
Murray, UT 84157**

About the Author

Bob C. Cleckler grew up in Texas where he was an avid reader from early childhood. After studying elementary and secondary education and art at Hardin-Simmons University for two years, he switched to an engineering curriculum. Upon graduation from the University of Texas with a Bachelor of Science degree in Chemical Engineering, he joined Hercules Incorporated, where he worked for twenty-nine years. During this period he conducted many short research programs to solve various types of manufacturing problems and wrote dozens of extensive technical reports on his findings. He also taught numerous adult classes as an officer in the U.S. Army Reserve, Utah National Guard Special Forces, and elsewhere.

In his position of Assistant Secretary of the Plant Process Control Board, in the Safety Department of Hercules Incorporated, Cleckler was responsible for analyzing numerous procedures for susceptibility to unintended explosive initiation at a $400 million, solid propellant rocket motor plant. His failure to consider all possibilities could have resulted in an explosion, killing dozens of people and causing millions of dollars in damage. These scientific and statistical studies of manufacturing problems were an ideal preparation for what has been a consuming interest in our literacy crisis. He became passionately concerned about illiteracy in 1985 after reading about the physical and emotional pain and suffering of illiterates described in Jonathan Kozol's book *Illiterate America—a passion that has extended to the present time.*

Let's End Our Literacy Crisis

In order to learn the publishing business, Cleckler worked for four years as a desktop publisher for a trade paperback publisher. He typeset 144 books of all types during that time and attended the American Booksellers Association conventions for each of the four years, where he discussed an earlier version of this book with several publishers and booksellers. That book, entitled *Instant Literacy for Everyone* and published in 1993, is now out of print but was still listed by Amazon.com when this book was published.

Cleckler read every book on the subject of his research at the University of Utah's Marriott Library and at the Salt Lake City main library. Although he does not have a degree in education, he has spent far more time in private study than would be required to receive a Ph.D. in education. His private study consisted of analyzing and correlating the life's work of several educational and linguistic scholars. His private study enabled him to examine aspects of education and linguistics that Ph.D. programs in education almost never delve into. This is largely because of the peer pressure on linguists and educators to search for traditional or conventional means of improving literacy that will not upset the status quo. Because his scientific training and experience are very different from those of linguists and educators, he is able to explore *all* solutions and then carefully, scientifically evaluate them. Compassion for the suffering of unemployed and "underemployed" illiterates, as well as concern for taxpayer costs and the adverse effect of U.S. illiteracy on international trade made him feel compelled to form Literacy Research Associates, Inc., a nonprofit educational corporation, and to write this book.